Conversations with Dostoevsky

Conversations with Dostoevsky

On God, Russia, Literature, and Life

GEORGE PATTISON

Great Clarendon Street, Oxford, OX2 6DP,
United Kingdom

Oxford University Press is a department of the University of Oxford.
It furthers the University's objective of excellence in research, scholarship,
and education by publishing worldwide. Oxford is a registered trade mark of
Oxford University Press in the UK and in certain other countries

© George Pattison 2024

The moral rights of the author have been asserted

All rights reserved. No part of this publication may be reproduced, stored in
a retrieval system, or transmitted, in any form or by any means, without the
prior permission in writing of Oxford University Press, or as expressly permitted
by law, by licence or under terms agreed with the appropriate reprographics
rights organization. Enquiries concerning reproduction outside the scope of the
above should be sent to the Rights Department, Oxford University Press, at the
address above

You must not circulate this work in any other form
and you must impose this same condition on any acquirer

Published in the United States of America by Oxford University Press
198 Madison Avenue, New York, NY 10016, United States of America

British Library Cataloguing in Publication Data
Data available

Library of Congress Control Number: 2023945416

ISBN 978–0–19–888154–4

DOI: 10.1093/oso/9780198881544.001.0001

Printed and bound by
CPI Group (UK) Ltd, Croydon, CR0 4YY

Links to third party websites are provided by Oxford in good faith and
for information only. Oxford disclaims any responsibility for the materials
contained in any third party website referenced in this work.

Preface

The conversations that follow offer an interpretation of Dostoevsky's Christian view of life. This not only includes his beliefs regarding God, the Bible, and Christ but also extends to his psychology and politics, and to how he understood his own literary work. His 'religion' or even his 'theology' cannot be isolated from the totality of his writings, fictional and non-fictional.

I hope that the conversations speak for themselves and I believe that the views attributed to Dostoevsky have good support in his novels, letters, notes, and in the memoirs of those who knew him—although, clearly, collating and presenting them has necessarily involved selection, interpretation, and occasional invention. It must also be remembered that the Dostoevsky who speaks here is not straightforwardly identical with the Dostoevsky who lived from 1821 to 1881 since he also has some knowledge of how his work has been received subsequent to his death as well as having a new perspective on the totality of his life on earth. From this present perspective he is perhaps better placed than in his earthly lifetime to see his work as others might see it and therefore also to be more aware of what could be seen as its shortcomings. In short, this is an interpretation. The commentary section seeks to support this interpretation by further discussion of the main points addressed in the conversations and references to other relevant primary texts as well as to secondary literature.

If Dostoevsky is not identical with the Dostoevsky who lived from 1821 to 1881, nor is the narrator identical with the author—a point that Dostoevsky readers should be better placed than most to grasp. It must be emphasized that these conversations are about Dostoevsky and not the narrator, but it is nevertheless appropriate and even necessary to make a couple of short observations about the latter. His problems, as I see them, are neither material nor, in the clinical sense, psychological. His life is a moderately comfortable and moderately successful middle-class life. His career doesn't seem to be going anywhere, but he seems to be happily enough married, has friends, and enjoys a range of cultural activities. He is not depressed, though he sometimes speaks as if he might be. What is fundamentally wrong with him is that he lacks perspective on his life or, to speak the language of the early twentieth century, he has no coherent world view. Because of this lack he is not seeing or appreciating the good things that are there in his life and is insufficiently motivated to change the things that need changing. In order to live better (and, for that matter, enjoy his life more), he needs a better moral and spiritual framework than the inconsistently motivated pragmatism that keeps him going from day to day. Although his conversations with

Dostoevsky do not result in anything as dramatic as a conversion, they do help him start the process of building such a framework. Whether he will eventually find faith or discover that he doesn't need it is not fully resolved. That is not exactly 'another story' (as Dostoevsky said of *Crime and Punishment*'s Raskolnikov), but what follows is only part of a longer story of which we get to see neither the beginning nor the end. At least, that's my opinion. You may think differently.

My first guide in studying Dostoevsky was Diane O. Thompson and I remain grateful for the direction she gave. Since then, many students and colleagues have helped deepen and sharpen my approach, especially those who participated in the Dostoevsky classes held in the Oxford Faculty of Theology (2004–11) and the participants in the residential courses at the Danish Church's Pedagogical Centre at Løgumkloster, together with my co-tutor, Iben Damgaard. I am grateful to all who read and commented on the blog in which these conversations were first made public or who helped with references, including Niels Grønkjær, Sarah Hudspith, Kate Kirkpatrick, Marina Ogden, Lewis Owens, Sergei N. Sushkov, and Luke Tarassenko. Your comments helped keep me going, even if there were some sharp disagreements. I am especially grateful to those who have read all or part of the book manuscript and offered important advice, including Sarah Young, Simon May, Caryl Emerson, Irina Kuznetsova-Simpson, and an anonymous reader for Oxford University Press. Hilary Pattison has provided detailed feedback on large and small points, as well as encouragement and enthusiasm. Thank you.

Contents

PART ONE: THE CONVERSATIONS

First Conversation, Part One: Beneath a Dead Sun	3
First Conversation, Part Two: Guilty!	19
Second Conversation: Good Books	37
Third Conversation: At a Dinner Party	61
Fourth Conversation: Christmas Cards	89
Fifth Conversation: Light from the East	115
Sixth Conversation: The Jewish Question	143
Seventh Conversation: We Are All Here	163
Epilogue	185
Postscript	189

PART TWO: COMMENTARY

Introduction	197
Commentary on the First Conversation, Part One	203
Commentary on the First Conversation, Part Two	215
Commentary on the Second Conversation	223
Commentary on the Third Conversation	241
Commentary on the Fourth Conversation	253
Commentary on the Fifth Conversation	261
Commentary on the Sixth Conversation	277
Commentary on the Seventh Conversation	285
Commentary on the Epilogue and Postscript	293
Bibliography	297
Index	305

The conversations recorded here took place between November 2018 and May 2019.

PART ONE
THE CONVERSATIONS

...the causes of human actions are usually immeasurably more complex and varied than our subsequent explanations of them.
The Idiot

First Conversation

Part One: Beneath a Dead Sun

How It All Began

Fyodor Mikhailovich smiled. Diffidently. He leaned forward. I couldn't tell whether it was because he was thinking about how to answer my question or because he was waiting for me to say more. But I couldn't think of anything to add. A minute or more passed. Or so it seemed. Sighing gently, he looked up, not quite meeting my gaze.

'Faith. Why do you ask me about faith?' he asked, in a quiet, self-deprecating voice, as if he was the last person in the world to have anything important to say on the matter. 'You've surely read that when it comes to faith I never escaped the crucible of doubt in which my own faith—such as it was—was formed?'

'But Fyodor Mikhailovich,' I replied, anxious that this extraordinary opportunity might slip away from me, 'you more than anyone have shown what faith could be in a world such as ours. You saw first-hand some of the worst things that human beings do to one another and to their fellow creatures; you explored every permutation of human malice; you looked into the abyss; you were face to face with death; you gave voice to the uttermost desolation of the abandoned heart. And yet you believed. You must have seen something, you must have received some word to bring back to us?'

He smiled again and seemed politely amused by my little speech, though there was nothing obviously amusing in what I had said, still less in the anxious and agitated way in which I'd said it.

'I hope you're remembering that I was only a writer? A teller of tales? As to what I wrote in my novels—I made it all up. I can't put it more simply than that. Surely you know that?' His eyes twinkled teasingly for a moment, as if he was joking, but he sounded serious, even a little sad, as he continued. 'It's all made up. It's fiction. It's not real. You could even say: it's all lies.'

'Surely not, Fyodor Mikhailovich! I mean, I don't agree with everything you wrote (if you don't mind my saying so) but what about the words you gave to Sonia, to Zosima, to Alyosha? Weren't they true? Thousands if not millions have thought so.'

Fyodor Mikhailovich stood up, slowly and uncomfortably, like someone who had become stiff from sitting for too long. His breathing seemed slightly laboured. Going to the window, he looked down at the street below, washed by intermittent gusts of rain. There was little traffic at this late hour and only the occasional pedestrian, hood up, head down, hurried past, going somewhere—or nowhere.

'You know,' he said gravely, 'even now, even in my present state, there are moments when I could wish for a cigarette.' He waved his hand, as if to brush the idea aside. He continued to look out of the window, talking almost to himself.

'It's hard to explain, you see. Perhaps if you yourself were a writer you would understand. The fact is that even with the best will in the world, even when the artist's intentions are entirely pure—and what writer dare say that of himself?—a story remains a story, fiction is fiction, and—a lie. You could even say that the truth, once uttered, is a lie, as one of our poets said.'

'Fyodor Mikhailovich,' I protested, 'Fyodor Mikhailovich, you can't be saying that everything you wrote, everything you taught us, was nothing but lies? That would mean it was not literature but propaganda! Surely you're not saying that words can never speak the truth?'

'Listen,' he said, quietly but seriously, turning back to me. 'You have to think about why you are asking me these things. If the words I wrote in my books were the truth, why shouldn't they be enough for you? What can I add? If I'd lived another five, ten, or twenty years I could probably have said more, but it was not to be. I didn't have Count Tolstoy's constitution—though sometimes it's maybe best to die before you get too old and too angry with the world. What I've learned since then—*here*—I may not reveal. If that's the kind of knowledge you're after, you'll have to ask God and his angels. And even if I could,' he added, almost as an afterthought, 'anyone, anyone at all, from this side could tell you as much or as little. We writers turn out to be fairly peripheral figures in the great synthesis.'

* * *

At this point, I should probably explain the nature of the conversation I am reporting, which, as you will be starting to guess, was of a rather peculiar kind. The most obvious peculiarity was that the man talking to me here in the sitting room of our Glasgow flat had been dead for over a hundred years—since 1881, to be precise. The second—and to my mind hugely more important—peculiarity was that this man I was talking with, just as I could be talking with you, was the Russian writer Fyodor Mikhailovich Dostoevsky. Yes, that Dostoevsky. *Crime and Punishment*, *The Brothers Karamazov*, and all the rest of those big heavy novels. How this was possible I still don't know, though if you accept the reality of some kind of afterlife, then I suppose anything is possible.

Now when I say that it was all 'just as I could be talking to you' this isn't quite accurate. I'm unable (and, believe me, I've tried) to believe that the whole thing was a hallucination or series of hallucinations. I could see him. I could hear him. He walked about the room, picked books off the bookshelves, and drew the curtains. One evening he drank a beer with me. Other people too saw him. He was, then, 'real'—but there was definitely something odd about him. For a start, he didn't always look exactly the same. Even within the space of a single conversation he might change from the magisterial personage of the portrait that you've probably seen on book covers to the traumatized ex-convict newly arrived back in St Petersburg after a ten-year exile or, sometimes, to the youthful idealist, dreaming of a humanist utopia, and then again to the awkward unhappy schoolboy who never had enough money for tea. Yet perhaps he didn't really change any more than any human face changes under the impact of memories and ideas.

We've all seen old people becoming momentarily young again when they remember a happy event from long ago. And some of us have seen how death can wipe away the lines from faces scarred by suffering, restoring a kind of hallucinatory youth. It seems quite plausible, then, that someone now living a more ethereal life might manifest their inner thoughts and feelings still more expressively and spontaneously than we do, bringing about greater physical changes—but that's only my idea.

On the subject of his face, it was recognizable from photographs and paintings, but these—even the best—can only ever give a shadowy reflection of the thing itself. It was, strangely, a beautiful face. There was nothing of the half-criminal, half-lunatic, envious and ambitious face famously described by Georg Brandes in the 1880s, a brilliant but fantastical description that stamped itself on posterity's image of Dostoevsky as an epileptic genius teetering on the brink of madness and criminality.

For the sake of complete accuracy, I should also add that it wasn't just his face that changed but also his size, even his clothes...though 'change' is perhaps too strong a word. Let's just say they were adaptable—even though at any given moment the stuff of his jacket or the leather of his shoes seemed as tangible as my own. I remembered his own description of how the Devil appeared to Ivan Karamazov as a shape-shifting down-at-heel sponger, but this was different. Whereas the Devil was clearly trying to avoid being pinned down, 'dodging away', as a former colleague used to say, Dostoevsky's 'metamorphoses' (I can't think of any other way of describing them) always seemed to bring what he was saying into sharper focus.

A strange interlocutor, then. So, how did it all begin? Where? When? And why?

* * *

I've already said that this first conversation was taking place in my flat, which is on the second floor of a late nineteenth-century tenement block in Glasgow's West End. Like many Glasgow tenements, ours isn't altogether unlike those that Dostoevsky would have known in St Petersburg and, unlike most of our neighbours on the close, we've never got round to modernizing it. I had the impression that Fyodor Mikhailovich felt quite at ease there. But that's not the only thing. His Russian city and my Scottish city had both been fashioned by the contradictions and absurdities of capitalism's hyperactive and misspent nineteenth-century youth. They were cities where you could find the grotesquely rich and the unbelievably poor, old money and nouveaux riches, the insulted and the injured, revolutionary dreamers, swindlers, spongers, drunkards, down-and-outs, sellers of love, gamblers, mystics, and saints—all of them constantly being spewed out and mixed together by the voracious maelstrom generated by the making and losing of money on a grand scale. A cast of characters for any aspiring novelist. And then there are the winters...and the rain...and the shadows beyond the streetlights...the footsteps of a solitary walker crossing an empty bridge...the uncanny feeling of someone following you...or perhaps you yourself are on some shadowy mission? Everywhere there is matter for stories in these 'intentional' cities, as Dostoevsky once described St Petersburg.

Perhaps that's all a bit fanciful. Maybe all of this could have happened in any city, town, or village. Perhaps visitors from *there* feel at ease anywhere in our world. Perhaps I should just keep my thoughts to myself and get on with telling you how it began.

So. There I was, sitting up in my flat on that inevitably damp evening in early November. At that time, I often stayed up for an hour or so after Laura (my wife) had gone to bed. Some people might say I was going through a midlife crisis, though that's rather melodramatic to my way of thinking. It's true that my academic career had never been stellar and it had more or less stalled. There hadn't been a second book after the publication of my PhD thesis (*Deaths in Venice: Literature, Film, and Opera*) and the intervals between articles and conference invitations were getting steadily longer. Even worse from the point of view of my line manager was that I'd never had much success in any of my applications for external funding, just a one-off £3,000 for a workshop I ran a couple of years back. I'd been firmly told that I should be looking for five-figure sums at least and had been reminded in our last meeting of other colleagues who'd secured £1,000,000 plus for their projects. I'd put in a bid for a big grant last year, but the feedback was, to say the least, discouraging—despite the help I'd had from Laura, whose job (which she did very well) was advising applicants for these kinds of things. If universities were nothing but businesses, I'd probably show up somewhere in the debit column. Mostly I could shrug all of this off, telling myself that I still enjoyed teaching...but did I? When the students didn't turn up, hadn't prepared for classes, or inexplicably failed to hand in their work, even teaching seemed pointless, though there were still days when they seemed genuinely interested and the class would be buzzing with ideas. I'd made my own mistakes, of course, not all of them of a strictly academic nature. As they say, I've done some things I'm not proud of, but I don't need to go into that just now. I was a long way yet from throwing in the sponge (or so I told myself), but I needed time alone at the end of the day to unwind, to read, to listen to some music, or just to think. Sometimes with a glass of whisky. Occasionally, two glasses. Three at most. Scapa, when I could get it. I'd often end by switching off the reading light on the side table and letting the darkness gather me in.

On that evening I'd been reading Dostoevsky's short story *A Gentle Spirit*. It's narrated by a man who is standing by the body of his dead wife, stretched out on the kitchen table, ready for burial the next day, and he's trying to work out what went wrong in their life together. Probably not the best thing to read if you want cheering up. We never learn his name but he tells us that he's a pawnbroker and explains how he'd become very taken with a young girl who started coming to his shop. Each time she came she pledged smaller and smaller items and it was easy to see that she was on the brink of falling headlong into Petersburg's lower depths. Taking advantage of her powerlessness, he marries her and thereafter subjects her to a routine of extreme mental cruelty. That's not how he sees it, of course. He doesn't seem to think he's in the wrong at all, but the story is so well written that we're able to see what he doesn't want to tell us. In the end she's driven to suicide, jumping out of the window of their flat, though, in a strange detail, clutching an icon. All through the night he stands over her body and goes over the sequence of events that led to this outcome.

His final words are a statement of despair as powerful as the famous speech in which Ivan Karamazov denounced God for creating a world in which the progress of history allowed for the torture and murder of children—crimes that he illustrated in grim detail. Just like Ivan's 'rebellion' (as Dostoevsky called it), the pawnbroker's words constitute a terrible challenge to Christianity or to any optimistic view of human existence.

> 'Oh, blind force! Oh, nature! Men are alone on earth—that is what is dreadful. "Is there a living man in the country?" cried the Russian hero. I cry the same, though I am not a hero, and no one answers my cry. They say the sun gives life to the universe. The sun is rising and—look at it, is it not dead? Everything is dead and everywhere there are dead. Men are alone—around them is silence—that is the earth! "Men, love one another"—who said that? Whose commandment is that? The pendulum ticks callously, heartlessly. Two o'clock at night. Her little shoes are standing by the little bed, as though waiting for her...No, seriously, when they take her away tomorrow, what will become of me?'

I first read these words when I was going through a fairly standard phase of student nihilism and it was like finding my own voice for the first time, hearing someone saying what I'd been thinking and feeling but couldn't find the words to say. Looking back, it's probably the fact that I heard someone else saying it that stopped me from following the logic of the words themselves all the way to— what? Other Dostoevsky characters who say very similar things kill themselves, or try to, or just give up: what one psychologist labelled 'chronic suicide'—going on living, but without there being any point or joy in it. The despair of meaninglessness, someone called it. Of course, it's unsurprising that words like these speak to 'disillusioned youth' but I wasn't a 'disillusioned youth' any longer. That was thirty years ago. In the meantime, I'd become a fairly normal middle-aged person living a fairly normal middle-class life and even my 'midlife crisis' (if that's what it was) was fairly normal—no great dramas, just grey shading into grey. It's just the way things are in the world we're living in. Get used to it, some would say.

Laura wasn't jumping out of the window but was either reading or sleeping in the next room. So why was it that Dostoevsky's story 'spoke to me'—especially when, as he said, it's only fiction?

It would be ridiculous to try to explain Dostoevsky better than he explains himself and, in any case, every one of us will read these words in their own way. But I ask you: putting aside adolescent and midlife crises, haven't you too had moments when you realized that the world is entirely indifferent to anything you might think, speak, do, or feel; that all the words that you and me and all of us endlessly exchange with one another are, in the end, pointless; that even if you've found someone to love and you have friends with whom you meet, eat, party, and debate—despite all that, there is a point of ultimate isolation from which you can't escape, a point at which you are completely alone? And even if you're happy enough in your life, what difference does your happiness make to the world? It doesn't—and, once you realize that, then even Christ's words of love ring hollow. The sun comes up, the sun goes down, night falls—who cares? Short answer: no one.

As it says further down the page—THE END.

I shut the book, keeping my finger in the page. No thoughts came. Or rather, a thousand thoughts came, but none of them were clear enough to catch hold of. I added a dash of water to my already well-watered whisky and sipped at it, more for something to do than because I needed the alcohol. Or maybe just for the comfort of the residual warmth. I dimmed the light and shut my eyes. Again, thoughts that were no thoughts. There was nothing more to think. Half-past eleven. Time to go to bed. Putting the book down next to the glass, I stood up, stretching my arms above my head, fingers locked. 'So…' I said under my breath.

'So?'

For a split second I wondered if I was repeating myself, but at some level I knew it wasn't me speaking. Like many people I sometimes hear voices, usually when I'm very tired or under some kind of influence. But those 'voices' normally sound as if they're coming from far away, like a distant echo of my own thoughts. This 'So?' was too present, too physical.

And there wasn't just a voice, there was *someone*, a shadowy someone, sitting on the far side of the fireplace.

You may sometimes have wondered what you'd do in this kind of situation. Would you grab a poker and chase the intruder away? Would you maintain an impressive silence before slowly and politely asking for an explanation? Would you faint with shock? Or would you just shake your head in disbelief and conclude that you must have dropped off to sleep? Well, I can tell you that whatever you've imagined, it makes no difference. In real life, you don't think, you just react. And, having had what they call 'good manners' instilled in me from a young age, if someone speaks to me in an averagely polite kind of way, I answer—even when that someone is a shadowy figure who wasn't there a moment ago, shouldn't be there, and maybe wasn't even real.

'So?' There was a challenge there, but the underlying tone was enquiring, perhaps even humorous—though I also sensed a hint of irony.

'So,' I repeated, 'well, the fact is, I just don't know what to make of it... "Men are alone"... "Who said 'Love one another'?"... THE END... Is that really it? Is that all?'

'This is what was in your book?' he asked politely, 'Do you want to say more? I can't answer your questions if I don't know what they're about!'

'No, of course, I'm sorry.' I picked the book off the table, an old second-hand edition in a gold-embossed red cloth cover. 'It's by Dostoevsky. Do you know Dostoevsky?'

I was starting to make out that my mysterious interlocutor was probably about my size or a bit shorter and was wearing a suit made of some heavy wool-like material, not very well-fitting and rather old-fashioned. He seemed neither young nor old and although I could see that he was balding, with wispy strands of hair floating away from the sides of his broad domed forehead, he gave an impression of solidity and energy, not like an old man at all. I couldn't make out his expression, but I could feel his dark eyes fixed on me, as if to hold me in their grip.

'Certainly I know him,' he replied, in an amused voice. 'I am Dostoevsky.'

This was not expected.

(Understatement.)

'You're Dostoevsky?' was all I could think of to say. Then, overwhelmed by the absurdity of the situation, I said it again. 'You're Dostoevsky—*the* Dostoevsky?'

'Yes, of course,' he replied politely, 'Who else would I be?'

'Who else would you be? You could be anyone!'

'Not really. After all, you invited me and I don't see anyone else.' He lifted his hand, gently took the book from me and opening it read out the words on the title page. "Fyodor Dostoevsky, *The Eternal Husband and Other Stories*. Translated from the Russian by CONSTANCE GARNETT. William Heinemann Ltd. Melbourne. London. Toronto." Interesting. Imagine, they even read me in Australia.' He returned the book. 'Here. Why don't you sit down? You'll be more comfortable.'

As I say, I didn't think. I just reacted and, being brought up to answer when spoken to I did what I was told. I sat down. Up to this point I could probably have dismissed my visitor or tried pretending that he was just a product of tiredness and whisky, shaken myself, and gone to bed. Now, however, I'd gone up a level. I was committed. I wasn't just answering his questions, I was doing what he told me to do. From this moment on I was conceding his reality, giving him the right not only to play with my thoughts but to take up space in my life. That's how I see it now, of course. Back then I just did what he said and sat down, still clutching the book.

I was, I admit, lost for words. Who wouldn't be? We sat silently facing each other for—I don't know how long. He looked at me attentively, as if waiting for my question. I looked at him, trying to get him into focus. Not very successfully as yet. He spoke first.

'You had a question, I think?'

'Er...yes...of course...' I fell back into silence, struggling to remember what I'd asked just a few minutes beforehand.

'About the human condition, I think?' he added encouragingly.

'Yes...the human condition...We are alone. Are we really alone? Is that true? Sometimes it feels true. And, if it's true...can love really mean anything? Yes, those were the questions—my questions, *your* questions, that is, what the husband says, after his wife's suicide. But they're powerful words, Mr Dostoevsky...'

'Please—Fyodor Mikhailovich.'

'Yes, thank, you, of course...Fyodor Mikhailovich. They're powerful words—and I don't think you could have written them if you didn't feel them. But, still, you believed, you went on believing, in God, immortality, love...You had faith. What is it, this faith? How is it possible?

What Is Truth?

We are, then, back where we started. As you probably remember, Fyodor Mikhailovich didn't give a direct answer to my question about faith but started saying how everything he wrote in his novels and stories was just fiction, something he'd made up, in short—a lie. Anyway, he'd said, he was only a 'peripheral' inhabitant of the next world—'the great synthesis', as he called it—and that if I really wanted answers, I'd better ask God. Which was quite a conversation stopper. Especially as I wasn't sure whether I believed in God.

'Well, maybe if God had turned up instead of you, I would ask him—but he didn't. I've only got you and since you're the person who wrote these words you must have something to say about them. And even if you did just make them up, even if they're what you call "lies", it seems to me that they're saying something true, something we can't help feeling about ourselves—something we've got to deal with. You can't just say "It's all lies—now go and ask God." If it's that easy to ask God, why did you bother writing this...and all those thousands of other pages? And why did you bother coming here?'

Fyodor Mikhailovich chuckled quietly.

'Fair questions, fair questions—we'll make a "Russian boy" of you yet!' Returning to his chair, he drew it a couple of inches closer and, lowering his voice, continued in a more confidential tone, as if imparting some great secret. 'Well, maybe He is here and you're just not seeing Him—and if you were to see Him then you might be shouting "Hosannah" instead of asking questions.'

I smiled, recognizing the allusion to one of my favourite passages in *The Brothers Karamazov*. People sometimes forget that Dostoevsky didn't just write about crime, punishment, and the eternal questions—he could also be very funny. When the shape-shifting Devil I mentioned earlier appears to Ivan Karamazov, he tells a story about a Russian nihilist who doesn't believe in God or immortality and, when he dies, is deeply shocked to wake up in the afterlife. At first, he refuses to budge and stays on the spot for a billion years before he eventually gets up and walks the quadrillion miles to the pearly gates, still deeply vexed by the fact that he really is immortal. He goes in. Immediately, he's overwhelmed and starts shouting 'Hosannah' even more loudly than many of those already gathered round the divine throne—so much so that some of the other spirits think he's overdoing it.

'Like that Russian nihilist. I see. Yes, probably. But even if *He* is here, I can't see Him: I can only see you. I don't suppose you can open my eyes for me?'

'No, of course, not,' he replied, sounding almost irritable, as if it was something that had already been explained to me umpteen times. 'If it was that easy, atheism would have been vanquished long ago. I can't do what only God can do. I can't even teach you to pray. But I can tell stories.'

'Which, you say, are lies.'

'Yes.'

Impasse.

Fyodor Mikhailovich tapped his finger on the arm of the chair and didn't give the impression of being in a hurry to make the next move. Of course (obviously), it was amazing to have *him* sitting there, speaking to me, almost (I'm tempted to say) 'in the flesh'. Only (obviously), not 'in the flesh'. Even so—amazing. But I too was starting to get irritated.

'Fyodor Mikhailovich,' I said, 'you can't just leave it at that. Please help me out here. I mean, I do understand the difference between fiction and fact, but there's a world of difference between the kind of invention that goes into writing a novel and a straightforward lie. Even if you insist on calling your novels lies, they're not like the lies that some of your characters tell, and an awful lot of them do seem to be compulsive liars. Wait, let me think a moment.'

It seemed an embarrassingly long time before I hit on a very obvious example that I knew perfectly well and should have remembered right away.

'Yes, of course...old man Karamazov. A total liar! He seems to lie for the sake of it or just to rub people up the wrong way. I think he even calls himself "The Father of Lies" at one point—like the Devil, I suppose. Perhaps he's the worst of all?'

'Very good,' he said approvingly, 'that's a good example, maybe the best—though we could easily add to it. We mustn't forget the people who lie to themselves and have a completely misplaced sense of their own importance. And then, just think of all the self-deception there is in love, like Katerina Ivanovna, believing she's in love with Dmitri Karamazov because to think otherwise would mean admitting that she'd been made a fool of.'

'You mean she's not in love with him?'

'Isn't it obvious? If she'd just faced up to the facts as to why he behaved towards her as he did then she'd never have imagined herself to be in love with him. But because she was proud and because her pride led her to prefer an illusion of love to the sordid reality, she followed him to his home town and was as responsible as anyone for what happened next. Of course,' he smiled, 'if she'd been more sensible I wouldn't have had a story to write! And then there are the proud young men who think they're through with love, when really they're just aching to have someone love them. They'd rather be seen as cold and loveless than admit they need somebody else's love.'

I thought of Stavrogin, the anti-hero of *The Possessed*. Many critics see him as seducing the beautiful Liza out of idleness, or malice, or both, but I've always thought he was precisely the kind of person Fyodor Mikhailovich had just described.

'Yes, yes, yes,' he said, noticing my thoughtfulness. 'You'll find some of them in my novels too. And then we come to the husband you've just been reading about. If he hadn't had such false ideas about himself and wasn't so obstinately committed to them, he would never have treated his wife in the way that he did, killing any love she might have had for him. Yes, dig down into any tragedy, and you'll find there's a lie at the root of it all. In fact,' he continued in a measured and deliberate tone, 'it all began with the lie. Every act of inhumanity, from the very beginning of history right through to the end—it all began with the lie.'

'You shall be as gods,' I interjected, eager to show I was following his train of thought. 'Was that where it started?'

'You shall be as gods...Yes, they were ready to hear that lie, though perhaps they had already been lying to themselves and to each other long before the serpent turned up with his smooth-talking trickery. Maybe they even began to lie in the very same moment in which they began to speak. Think of a little child. The moment it learns how to talk, its world turns upside down because everything can now become something else: a piece of wood can be a doll, a farmer, a horse...and all because the child says so. It's all very innocent and entertaining, of course. The child's happy, mama and papa are happy, and all the aunts and uncles are happy too. But before you know where you are, little Ivan has graduated to outright fibs, either to get something he wants or to get himself out of trouble. It's quite a business! They say money is the root of all evil but money itself is just another way of lying. Just like language, money can turn anything into anything: I may be an unprepossessing sort of fellow but, thanks to money, I can become a Don Juan; I may be entirely without intelligence but, thanks to money, I can become a genius; I may be utterly dull but, thanks to money, my dullest witticism is met with gales of laughter. That's why Shakespeare and Goethe both knew that money was the only serious competitor to literature. But believe, me, long before there was money, there was language. "In the beginning was the Word"!'

'Fyodor Mikhailovich,' I exclaimed. 'This is shocking! How can you, a writer, say we'd be better off without language and condemned to silence, like animals? And when the Bible says, "In the beginning was the Word", isn't that meant to be a good thing? Didn't God Himself talk with Adam and Eve in the garden? And all those prophets proclaiming "the word of the Lord". Aren't words what it's all about?'

'In the beginning was the Word.' He repeated the words slowly and softly, as if absorbed in how they sounded. 'This is true, this will always be true, this is the truth. But our words—are they "the Word"? Is everything we say "the Word" just because it is made up of words?'

'I see what you mean. I think. Right. But can't we use language to speak truth as well as to lie? And isn't there a difference between the kinds of lies that people like old man Karamazov tell and what you're saying in your novels? Don't the novels tell us something true about ourselves, something we all need to know? So why insist on calling them lies? Why can't we just call them stories—because if they're nothing but lies then not only me but thousands and thousands of your readers have been complete dupes. And I don't think that's what you wanted, is it? Face it, you did inspire people, you held out a hand to people in despair and they grabbed it... your stories gave them faith, at least enough faith to go on living. That's nothing like old Karamazov and his lies, is it? If it's all just lies, then you must be one of the biggest confidence tricksters of all time.'

* * *

Fyodor Mikhailovich smiled again but looked thoughtful. I could feel him getting ready to say more and waited, slightly anxious that I'd overdone it.

'What is a lie? Well, if you want an answer to that question, you first have to know what you mean by truth,' he said after a while and then paused again before continuing. 'If, like many of my own contemporaries, you believe that truth is the same as facts, then maybe my stories, and maybe Christianity itself are indeed nothing but lies. Some of them would do away with fiction altogether—think of Dickens's Mr Gradgrind. And if that's what truth is, then, as I think you know, I'd always take the side of Christ against truth. Quixotic, you'll say—but I've got a soft spot for that crazy knight errant, maybe the greatest fictional character ever invented. But do we have to accept that truth equals facts? I don't think so. Sometimes facts can even stop us seeing the truth. Living according to the logic of facts *and nothing else* is the law of the anthill, not human beings.'

'Like you say in *Notes from Underground*?'

'Exactly; but let me give you another example—the *Notes* are a bit too complicated, too *ideological*, at least for now.'

Taking a deep breath, he began to speak in the manner of someone reciting a speech that he had learned by heart.

'One day I am out in St Petersburg. It's a Sunday, and people of all classes are also out taking a walk. The smart crowd are promenading on Nevsky Prospect and in the Summer Gardens, showing off their fashionable costumes, seeing and being seen. But even in the back streets, people are taking the air; perhaps they only go a few hundred yards from their door—only those who are really drunk would dare show themselves on Nevsky at such an hour. As for the rest, they stay close to home. Meeting a neighbour, they stop and talk for a few minutes; perhaps this is their one hour of freedom in the entire week. Amongst them I see a young man. He's about thirty years old. He's done his best to dress up well, but his clothes are old and worn, probably third hand. He has a little boy with him, about two years old. He's been cross with the boy, but now he's picked him up and the child is clinging to his neck. Over his daddy's shoulder, he sees me looking and frowns crossly, and holds on all the more tightly to papa. Of course, it's rude of me to stare, but I can't help myself. What do you ever learn about people if you only ever talk to those you meet in polite society? It's the people you don't know you should be learning from. Get out there, look at them. If possible, talk to them. But look, while I've been talking, they've gone, father and son, absorbed into the crowd. Just two in a million. Who are they? I don't know and I'll probably never see them again.'

He stopped and looked at me quizzically.

'I'm not boring you, am I?' he asked.

'No, not at all. I can picture what you're saying very clearly—but I don't see what it's got to do with what we were talking about.'

'Very good. I'll come to the point as quickly as I can. They're gone. I never see them again, but I can't stop thinking about them. Who are they? Where have they been? Why? The man's the kind of worker you see in a locksmith's or a printing office. Solid, reliable work—but not well paid. Where's the mother? I'm thinking that she's dead, probably not long since, maybe about two months ago, almost certainly of consumption. While daddy's at work, he pays some old woman even less than he earns to look after the little boy, perhaps one of the people they share a flat with. By the way,' he said, changing his tone, 'did you know that back then you could have got five or six families into this flat you share with your wife and son? It makes you think, doesn't it?'

I nodded, uncomfortably.

'Back to my story then. On weekdays he leaves the boy with the old woman, but today is Sunday and they've been out on a visit, let's say to the dead wife's sister, over in the Viborg district. The sister and her husband are probably a notch or two up the social ladder and they don't really have much in common with our young widower. They drink tea together, but don't say much. They say their goodbyes awkwardly and the father carries the boy home. It's a long walk from the Viborg side to Liteiny, especially if you have a lad of two to carry most of the way. No wonder the father's quick to snap, and tomorrow he has to get up early for work. What do you think?'

'Yes, it's all possible—though I suppose you could make up quite different stories about them too?'

'Of course—I could. That is—that was—my métier. So: is my story true?'

'Well, I don't know. I've no way of knowing. I mean, I believe you saw a man and a boy, but as for the rest—I just don't know.'

'No more do I. But would it be truer just to stick to the facts and say: "On Sunday afternoon I saw a man and a boy. I don't know anything about their circumstances or where they lived, so I'm not going to say any more. I'm going to keep to the facts"?'

'Well, that would certainly be true—but it wouldn't be as interesting…or as human. The way you speak about them, they become somehow real, three-dimensional personalities.'

'Thank you. Not just facts, then. We're agreed. Keep to the facts and you can hand the man and his boy over to the statisticians who will tell you all about employment rates, wages, rents, the prevalence of consumption, and then produce a logarithm which will tell you how to make them and all the other millions of workers happy and contented. Or that's what they promise. You may even manage to turn society into that anthill, full of happy contented beings—but you won't have human beings, people as alive as you and me,' (he gave a quick grin as he said this) 'people who feel and cry and hope and love as we do. Maybe nothing I made up about my worker and his boy is true, maybe I got every fact wrong, maybe mama is at home getting a good Sunday dinner ready for them all. I don't know. But my story, my fiction, opens your eyes. Next time you pass a poor man out on the street with his little boy you'll remember my story and you'll think to yourself, "There's more to him than meets the eye. That man and his boy have a whole life I know nothing about, a life full of joy, and grief, and love, as rich as anything in Shakespeare or Sophocles—or even Dostoevsky." Isn't that how it will be? And because you think this, you'll respect them more, maybe you'll even love them more. Am I right?'

He watched me steadily.

'Yes, yes, that's true. So, what you're saying is that even if fiction doesn't tell us the truth, even if it's all made up, it shows us something about the world we wouldn't otherwise see?'

'Not just about the world, but about us, us human beings. "The man in man". Each of us, you see, is much, much more than how we seem and much, much more than the whole sum of facts—even the whole sum of true facts—about us. Maybe we all have to become artists to see ourselves and our world as they truly are.'

That made sense. It also made sense of why I'd always loved his novels and stories since I first started reading them in my late teens—because they show us something about each other that we can never see just by looking, a whole other dimension, as it were. And he'd also indirectly explained why his novels were, as I'd said, very different from the kind of fibs told by old man Karamazov, fibs that, in the end, didn't tell you anything about anything and only served to hide what he was really up to. But, once again, the conversation seemed to have gone off at a tangent. What did any of this have to do with those famous eternal questions, with God, immortality, faith?

I needed another whisky.

'Do you mind…?' I asked, reaching toward the bottle.

'Not at all…please, carry on.'

'Sorry, would you like one?'

He smiled ruefully. 'No, no—but thank you. That's not how we do things here.'

'Here?'

'Where I am, now. My "here", your "there". But, please, carry on, don't let me stop you.'

I didn't.

First Conversation

Part Two: Guilty!

Guilty?

I'm not sure that I really wanted the whisky. Maybe I just wanted to be holding onto something. This whole thing was very, very strange but at least the glass in my hand was real.

'Now look,' I said, 'I'm not getting my head round this, so let's go back a step.' (A favourite teaching move, mostly used when I'd lost track of where I was going.) 'I can follow what you were saying about art and reality but what we started talking about was faith: God, immortality, the eternal questions! So, let's say I do learn to look at the world with the eyes of an artist, how is that going to help me find God? Doesn't art sometimes have the opposite effect, like T. S. Eliot said about Webster seeing the skull beneath the skin? Don't rather a lot of artists spend a bit too much time on the dark side? In fact, some people would say that about you—that you're always writing about sickness, violence, and despair—"a cruel talent", someone said.'

Fyodor Mikhailovich looked momentarily vexed and muttered something under his breath that I couldn't hear. I continued.

'I mean, if we're talking about *A Gentle Spirit*, it's a very different scenario from your father and son story. In that case, your artist's eye helped you to see the dignity that the world couldn't—or wouldn't—see. But in this case, you take a grieving husband whose wife has just committed suicide and turn him into a twisted self-hating sadist. You tear him apart and leave him in despair—alone in the universe, beneath a dead sun, unable to believe in love. Maybe he deserves it, but your "artist's eye" has led us away from faith, not towards it—so how are you going to get him from despair to faith? How can he learn to love again—or perhaps learn to love properly for the first time?'

All these months later, as I go back over that first conversation, when we'd known each other for less than an hour, I have to say that I'm rather embarrassed at how I spoke to Fyodor Mikhailovich. I realize that I probably sounded more like a rather irritable teacher dissecting an essay by a not very competent student rather than someone talking to one of the world's greatest writers (the greatest, according to Virginia Woolf), though what I actually said probably wasn't quite as coherent or as confrontational as I've recorded it here. As if there could be any easy answers when talking about one of his most difficult and brilliant stories and about some of the deepest challenges facing any human being! In my defence, I can only say this was a chance that I could never have dreamed of, a chance that would probably never come again. I had to get the answers I wanted now, before it was too late. The devastating finale of Dostoevsky's astonishing monologue had taken me to a place in my own experience from which I'd spent many years trying to escape. This wasn't just an exercise in literary criticism, it was trying to find out if there was any point to being alive at all. And the situation itself was beyond unbelievable. Can you be surprised if I was a wee bit 'hyper'?

Fortunately for me, both now and in our subsequent conversations, Fyodor Mikhailovich showed himself to be a man (and I suppose that even in his supernatural state he was, still, a man) of exceptional patience. I never experienced the irritability or mood swings that many of his contemporaries reported. Or not to any significant degree. I suppose that the world felt very different from how it did when he was literally 'in' it!

'You've finished?' he asked politely.

'Yes…of course…I'm sorry if I'm being too simplistic—but these questions really matter to me. I mean, I do understand that novels are novels and that you, maybe more than any other novelist, hid your own opinions behind those of your characters. Maybe a novelist has to. At the same time, I'm sure you were wanting to tell us something…to open a door…to show us a new way of looking at the world…to help make faith possible. But if it all ends in a paradox and the truth isn't the truth, doesn't it all become just a game? But I don't believe that. I don't believe it for a moment.'

Again he paused and I had the feeling he was rather pleased with what I'd said.

'Yes, yes, yes, you're right. It's certainly not just a game. But the question is a difficult one. From a certain point of view, what he sees *is* the truth. And it's not just because he's a bad character. Even the science in which everyone now believes tells us that, in the end, the universe is entirely indifferent to whether we human beings exist or not. It's blind, purposeless, lifeless. One day our sun will die and then we will be no more—but the stars will continue in their circuits. I'm not saying science is wrong but if you believe that that's all there is to say about the nature of reality, then the failures of your own life are going to seem even more terrible than, maybe, they really are.'

During this last speech he held his hands clasped together, but when he was finished he released them and let them rest on the arms of his chair. Shutting his eyes and slowly nodding his head very slightly, he continued in an almost meditative way, as if talking to himself.

'Yes, he's seen the truth, that is, the truth of a world without love. And it's not just the inexorable laws of nature, it's the truth of his own life, a life without love. But even those who live without love need another human being, another voice, another presence in their lives. That's what she was or what she could have been for him—except he didn't take the chance. He didn't let her be herself and now she's gone, out through the window, and he's all alone. Again. More so than ever. This is the truth, his truth, what his life has come to. But there's another truth—if he'd wanted to learn it. And it's not very far away. He doesn't have to learn any new facts: he just has to look at what he already knows in a different way. The difference is miniscule, no bigger than an onion, but it's also a difference that would change everything for him.'

'An onion?'

'It doesn't matter—I thought you might recognize the allusion. Perhaps we'll come back to it. Yes... it's the smallest of steps—but also the biggest, the matter of a moment, but a moment that affects the whole of a person's life.'

As he spoke, he seemed to become more and more engrossed in his own thoughts. His head sank forward and it was almost as if he had gone into some kind of reverie. Realizing that I probably shouldn't be interrupting him, I nevertheless urged him to carry on. 'Sorry—but, please, just what is this step he has to take?'

Fyodor Mikhailovich shook his head, sat upright, blinked a couple of times, and then looked at me sternly.

'Despair. He must despair. He must plead guilty and ask for forgiveness.'

'But surely he is guilty—and knows it. Isn't the whole point of his confession to tell the whole world how guilty he is?'

'Not exactly,' Fyodor Mikhailovich replied. When, after a brief pause, he continued, I caught something like a flash of glee in his eyes, putting me in mind of a prosecutor closing in on the crucial point in a cross-examination.

'The question is: what is guilt and what is it to be guilty or to confess your guilt? Most people don't understand this at all. They think it's just a matter of fact—did he or didn't he do it? If he did, he's guilty; if he didn't, he's not guilty. Remember what Ivan Karamazov said, that everyone wants to kill their father—but the world knows many of these mental parricides as obedient and loving sons, who aren't guilty of anything at all.' Pause. 'I think you haven't read my *Diary of a Writer*?'

'I've read about it...' I answered, not wanting to risk offending him any more than I might already have done, though sensing that he did in fact know exactly what I had and hadn't read.

'But you haven't actually read it?'

'Er, no,' I had to admit, slightly confused. Perhaps the whisky hadn't been such a good idea.

'It's strange,' he said, almost as if he was talking to himself. 'My English and American readers don't seem to read it very much. Of course, I do say some rude things about England in it and I know what they say in return—that's it's full of Russian jingoism, all very regrettably retrograde and reactionary. In my own view, though, some of the best things I've ever written are in the *Diary*. In fact, that's where you'll find this story we're talking about right now.'

'Really?' I exclaimed, passing over his conflation of England with the rest of the United Kingdom. 'I thought it was just a short story, like in this collection here.'

'*Just* a short story...?'

'Sorry, I didn't mean that in a bad way, but...'

'I know, I know,' he replied consolingly. 'It *is* a short story, but it's also what one of my new friends on this side would call "a thought experiment". We can talk more of that another time, but I'm digressing. You see there's a lot in the *Diary* about guilt and what it means to be guilty. Not fiction, but real life, cases that happened in Russia, in my own time, not unlike quite a lot of cases happening in your country today—alas.'

He sighed.

'These are difficult things to talk about, and I should emphasize that I never wanted anyone to be locked up, or beaten, or put to death for what they'd done. I've seen too much of what that means. Punishment isn't the answer, but acknowledging your guilt is... the first step.'

As I'd had to admit, I hadn't read *The Diary of a Writer* (actually a kind of journal that Dostoevsky published monthly and that consisted entirely of his own thoughts about issues of the day), but I did know that he'd written about several criminal cases and that some of these were about the kind of cruelty to children that Ivan Karamazov cited as evidence against the existence of God. I'd read that in one case he'd even helped get a verdict reversed by pointing out that the woman concerned was suffering from post-natal depression—long before the term itself was known. I couldn't remember any other details, though. I felt rather like one of my students who hasn't done their homework and is hoping that they're not going to be asked the next question. Only there wasn't anyone else to ask. In the event, Fyodor Mikhailovich let me off fairly gently.

'You want me to explain?' he asked.

'Please.'

'I suppose you know that jury trials were still quite an innovation in my time in Russia and it's no surprise that they produced some odd results. A clever lawyer could easily persuade a novice jury one way or the other. Even when all the facts pointed to the guilt of the accused, even when it was admitted that, indeed, such-and-such a woman had attacked her lover's wife with a razor with the intention of killing her; that such-and-such a father had beaten his seven-year-old daughter with birch rods so violently that even the neighbours were terrified by her screams; or that such-and-such parents had treated their children like animals, keeping them in filthy conditions and beating them with leather straps, again and again—each time our poor soft-hearted jurors concluded "Not guilty!" Can you imagine? Of course, there's always an explanation, there are always attenuating circumstances, there can even be provocations, and the letter of the law may tell us this is not torture but simply punishment, the kind of punishment that, in those days, all good middle-class parents thought it right to mete out. The facts. The facts are the facts, but the truth once uttered is a lie, and even the facts can be put together in such a way as to turn even torture into well-meaning parental discipline.'

As Fyodor Mikhailovich spoke, he became quite agitated. His face narrowed and his eyes flashed. At first he had just tapped his fingers intermittently on the arms of his chair but as he went on he started to wave his hands around with increasing energy. Whatever he had seen in the world he now inhabited, it was clear that he was still unreconciled to the outrages that adult human beings inflict on children, who, as he said in *The Brothers Karamazov*, hadn't yet eaten the fatal apple. I didn't know the details of the cases he was talking about, but I couldn't help thinking about a particularly horrifying case that had recently happened here in Scotland. I'll spare you the details.

'I'm sorry,' he said, taking a breath (or what seemed like a breath). 'As I say, even here there are times when I could wish for a cigarette—or even a good whisky,' he added with a smile, nodding reassuringly at me.

'But I repeat,' he continued after a moment, raising his hands dramatically, 'I am not demanding the maximum penalty of the law, not even for these torturers. I do not want them imprisoned, beaten, or executed, though I understand the outrage of people who do. Remember, when Ivan asked Alyosha what to do about the general who'd had the little boy torn to pieces by his dogs, even mild, sweet-tempered Alyosha said "Shoot him". But that doesn't help either. Just because I wrote a novel called *Crime and Punishment*, people imagine I'm obsessed with punishing. Not at all. All I want is that the guilty are not acquitted. That their guilt is clearly stated. And that they accept it—that's the most important of all. Let them be found guilty—and let them go free.'

'Just like that?' I interjected, quite shocked.

'Not "just" like that. No. If you'd read my *Diary*' (said matter-of-factly, not reproachfully) 'you'd have read how I imagined a judge speaking to such a person. He makes it clear that it's not a matter of going home and forgetting about it, going back to "just" the way things were before. No. There has to be change. In my time, the father was the authority figure in the family, but, as I—or my imaginary judge—pointed out, even fathers sometimes need to be re-educated by their children and to listen to their children's needs. I know that families are very different in your time, but, yes, parents, whoever they are, must learn to be parents to their children. I disagree with much that the prosecutor said about the Karamazov family, but he was right on one point: being a parent isn't—or isn't just—a biological fact. Parents have to become parents. And when they abuse their position and their power, they cannot hide behind their rights as parents—they have to own up. The guilty have to know that they are guilty.'

By this time he was shaking his right index finger, not unlike a judge scolding the prisoner in the dock. Slowly, he lowered his hand, till it came to rest again on the chair.

'Well then. Now you see.'

'Yes.'

I'd been quite carried away watching (as well as listening to) his peroration. Fyodor Mikhailovich had been gradually raising his voice as well as his hands and I wondered vaguely whether Laura might have heard and if she'd come through to see what was happening. But all of this seemed to be at a tangent to what we had been talking about and the devastating climax of *A Gentle Spirit*.

'But our widower—what does any of this have to do with him?' I asked. 'I mean, surely he *does* acknowledge his guilt. The whole story is in a way his confession, isn't it?'

Fyodor Mikhailovich thought for a few seconds, gently nodding his head.

'In a way, yes. But only in a way. It seems to me that he's still not acknowledged what he did to her, only how their relationship has affected him. From start to finish he makes himself sound like a victim, incapable of behaving in any other way. A creature governed by "blind force" you could say. He even blames her for not understanding him better and not responding as he wanted her to! Why, if only she'd been more attentive, he wouldn't have had to treat her the way he did: that's what he thinks. It's all her fault and, in the end, it's not her misery but his own solitude that bothers him: how he can go on living without her.'

'Isn't that rather harsh? After all, he himself has set out the charge sheet. He tells us just what he's done, how he's behaved. He provides all the evidence we need to find him guilty—morally, if not legally.'

'Yes, yes, yes—but why? Why's he doing this? Let me give you another example, a better known one, I think. You remember that in *The Possessed* (which, by the way, isn't quite what my title means, though it's quite good in its own way), I had Stavrogin go to Bishop Tikhon to confess how he'd raped a twelve-year-old girl and then waited in the next room, doing nothing, while she hung herself?'

'I remember. It's unforgettable. Horrific. In a way I'm not surprised they didn't let you publish it.'

'Nor was I, though it was very frustrating. But you'll also remember that he didn't go to confess his sin in the way that a normal penitent does: he'd already arranged for a full copy to be printed and ready to be published for the whole world to read.'

'Yes, I remember.'

'Now some people might think that was a sign of how deeply he'd repented, letting the whole world see what he'd done. But, as I hope you also remember, Bishop Tikhon could see that a gesture like that wasn't the same as really accepting it inwardly. Wanting to be seen—and maybe even admired—as a great sinner isn't quite the same as actually repenting. For many people there's a kind of glamour in sin, even the worst of sins. And perhaps that's how it is here too. Of course, if you want to be fussy, you could say that our pawnbroker's just talking to himself. He's not produced a written, let alone a printed, confession. And yet, it's as if he's rehearsing his story for the benefit of the world, for the imaginary audience we each of us have inside our heads.'

'You mean like in one of Shakespeare's monologues, like Richard III or Hamlet.'

Fyodor Mikhailovich seemed pleased at my remark, shaking his whole upper body in approval.

'Exactly! It's a performance. It's not the heart speaking. The heart would say something very different. In fact, the heart wouldn't need to say very much at all: it's only got one thing to say, to love and to ask for love, to forgive and to ask forgiveness.

'We've been talking about people who commit crimes but won't own up to what they've done, people who want to say to anyone who'll listen: "Not guilty! My conscience is clear! Don't blame me!" But the real problem is not the evidence of the facts—did he or didn't he do this or say that. The real problem is that this is completely back to front. People who love, even if they haven't committed any crimes, want to be guilty, they don't just want to forgive but to be forgiven; and they don't just think of themselves as guilty but infinitely guilty, guilty of everything, before everyone; in fact, the guiltiest one of all.'

* * *

I recognized these last words from *The Brothers Karamazov*, where Dostoevsky introduces a character called Markel, a teenager who's dying of consumption and has a kind of mystical experience that culminates in asking the birds to forgive him and declaring that we could all be in paradise today if we really wanted to be. He tells his family that the way to experience this is to realize that we each have to acknowledge our guilt to everyone, to accept that we are guilty for everything, and even to see ourselves as more guilty than anyone else. After Markel's death his younger brother grows up, joins the army, has a conversion experience, and becomes a monk; as the saintly Elder Zosima, he emerges as the spokesman for Dostoevsky's own spiritual vision (at least, that's what most commentators think). Zosima repeats Markel's words many times in his teaching and Alyosha Karamazov, Zosima's favourite disciple, hears them ringing in his ears when he too has some kind of mystical vision.

Still, there was something about it that didn't quite feel right. When my friend Peter was training as a psychotherapist he kept telling me that the main aim of therapy was to help people let go of guilt because guilt tied us to the past, making it impossible to move on from the bad scenarios of the past and stopping us from committing to real-time relationships in the present—and to some extent I could recognize that in my own life, even without having had counselling (Laura had suggested it several times, but I'd never felt things had got that bad: whether I was right or not, I'm not now sure). I'd been able to follow what Fyodor Mikhailovich had been saying about the need for people who really had done bad things, the torturers and murderers, to accept the reality of what they'd done. But this seemed to be something else. As Markel's mother said to him, he hadn't done anything really bad in his life, so how could he be the guiltiest of all? None of us is perfect, but how does thinking of ourselves as 'guilty' help?

'That's always puzzled me, Fyodor Mikhailovich,' I had to say. 'Why "guilty"? Isn't guilt something we need less of? Isn't it guilt that's to blame for most of our neuroses?'

'I suppose that's what your modern psychologists tell you, is it?'

'Well, yes. Aren't they right? Isn't guilt what stops us living life to the full? Isn't guilt the enemy of love?'

'Do you think it is?'

'I'm not sure. I think it can be…I've read about…I've known neurotic types who've been almost literally crippled by guilt to the point at which you want to shout at them and say "Snap out of it! Just get out there and live! Sin a bit!"'

'Sinning would do them good, would it?' Fyodor Mikhailovich asked quizzically.

'Well, you know what I mean…'

'I think I do,' he answered, sadly. 'You mean that if you don't like the way you're feeling about yourself, just go and take it out on somebody else and don't worry too much about who you hurt along the way. Is that it?'

'I don't quite mean that…in fact I didn't mean that at all. I just mean something more like: accept who you are and get on with being yourself.'

'Even when the rest of the world is suffering?'

'Well, no, of course not, but don't you have to get yourself sorted out before you try sorting out anyone else?'

I don't know whether Fyodor Mikhailovich actually shook his head at this point or if it just felt like it.

'Your Western individualism really is incorrigible,' he said. 'You've had war after war, you've had famines and mass unemployment, you're destroying the beautiful and mysterious planet you inherited, the rich grow richer and the poor poorer and all you can think of is being yourself! You seem to think it's a crime to do what somebody else tells you to do or needs you to do if it means not doing what you want to do yourself!'

I felt he was misinterpreting what I had meant.

'No. Not at all. Of course, we have to care about others and do what we can to help, but surely we can only do this when we're able to see for ourselves that it's the right thing to do and not because somebody else is telling us. Why does guilt have to come into it?'

'Because you are guilty!'

'But why should I feel guilty? I've never killed, robbed, or raped, or anything like that. I mean, I don't think I'm perfect, but on the whole I haven't intentionally done anything to harm anybody else.' (OK. I know others have ended up being hurt by things I've done but, as the song says, 'I didn't mean to hurt you…I'm not that kind of guy'—to which the cynic within me always whispers 'That's what they all say…')

'I didn't say "feel guilty", I said you *are* guilty—there's a difference. I don't want you to feel guilty, just acknowledge that you are.'

'I don't see how I could be guilty without feeling guilty, but I don't want to play with words. So, please, tell me what exactly I am guilty of?'

'I can't tell you that, but you tell me: is everyone in your world happy? Are they all enjoying life to the full? Do they all have enough to eat, even in your own country? Can they live without being afraid that a stranger or neighbour will strike them down? Are children free from the cruelties and predations of adults?'

'I know, I know. All sorts of terrible things are happening in the world, but I don't see what I can do about them; I mean, I try to do my bit, to be responsible, to help a neighbour when asked, support charities, do my recycling, but I can't deal with all of the problems out there, nobody can, no government can. We just have to accept that there's very little that individuals can do—or else we'd go mad!'

'Go mad? I wonder. But let's assume that what you say is true; tell me, are you happy? Have you always been happy? Does your presence bring happiness and joy to others?'

Fyodor Mikhailovich's questions hurt. As I've explained, my life wasn't too great right now, but, trying to be objective about it, I wasn't a bad person, not too bad, anyway, and no worse than most. As to happiness... well, my life was mostly happening in shades of grey, but there were still things I enjoyed: work wasn't all bad and there were what my CV calls my 'interests'. Family. Friends. Books. Music. Food. The hills. Not necessarily in that order. I could go on. The whole range of middle-aged middle-class interests. You could probably write the rest yourself. But had I ever really escaped—do any of us ever really escape—that residual solitude that Dostoevsky had described at the end of *A Gentle Spirit*? Could I honestly say I was *happy*, happy at the very core of my being, or was my happiness only ever a momentary respite, a distraction from something else, from the vision of isolated souls wandering aimlessly in an empty world beneath a dead sun, as Fyodor Mikhailovich had described the human condition? OK, that's a bit melodramatic—but isn't that what fiction does: *dramatize*?

'Not always, I have to admit, but I don't go out of my way to be quarrelsome or unpleasant. I'm just ordinary, a mix, you could say. But what are you trying to say?'

'Don't you see? Don't you remember Markel—we could be in paradise today if we opened our eyes and saw the world as it really is! That's what you—what most of us—are guilty of: closing our eyes to all the beauty, all the wonder, all the happiness that could be ours, that God wants to be ours; guilty of living in the world as if it was a prison house or a gambling hall or even as if it was just "ordinary" and not the paradise that it is. We're all guilty of making the world less than it is and, even worse, stopping others from seeing it too. And, please, observe that it's not a matter of trying to love the unlovable, which always fails, but of seeing that all people, if you see them as they really are, *are* lovable—and, once you see that, loving is not so hard, the heart does it on its own.'

I had to think this through. It sounded wonderful, but it also sounded a bit too much like looking at the world through rose-coloured spectacles.

'Well, I'm sure it would be nice to live like that but surely it's not enough to stop someone living just a couple of blocks away from abusing their child, let alone prevent wars, famines, or global warming—I'm supposing you know about that?—is it?'

Fyodor Mikhailovich's tone was gentle, but he was unrelenting.

'It's not about "nice". It's not what your age calls a lifestyle choice. It's about acknowledging the truth, which, as we've established, means being able to see more than just the facts. Of course, if what you mean is that you have to start where you are and not with some impossible utopian ideal, I entirely agree. But you don't start with yourself. You start with others. With the world you see and the people you see around you. And it's not up to you where that leads. I know you don't like the word guilt, but just think of the many times you've passed someone in the street without particularly bothering about them, when you've not returned a smile, a child's smile perhaps—let alone the times when someone looked to you for help and you brushed them aside or turned your back on them, pretending you just didn't see. How can you know where that momentary refusal to show love led? How can you know all the consequences flowing from even the smallest act of omission? Wouldn't you be justified in spending a lifetime trying to track down just one of those you've failed to love as you might and making amends? Just one. And how many are there that you might have helped and didn't? And remember, "In as much as you did it to one of the least of these…" We are each other's keepers: that's who we are, and if we aren't that—who or what could we possibly be?'

'Being guilty is taking responsibility for each other, then?'

'Aren't you listening! Who are you to take responsibility for someone else when you've failed to listen to love's call—again and again and again! It's not about you becoming a moral hero, it's not about how you'd like to be or how you'd like the world to be, it's about seeing the truth—that you owe a debt you'll never be able to repay because you owe everything you have and are to the world, to your brothers and sisters, you belong to them and they to you. "We are members one of another."'

I was both puzzled and, I have to say, a bit hurt. I didn't see how what I was saying involved turning my back on others, though I did start to feel that there was something missing in the way I'd put my side of the argument.

Pro et Contra

Over the course of our last few exchanges, Fyodor Mikhailovich was starting to look tired; the folds of his clothes seemed to be flattening out, almost as if he was becoming two-dimensional; even his face seemed to be fading, looking more and more like an old photograph rather than a living person. Now, suddenly, he snapped back into focus and, rubbing his hand together, smiled broadly, even mischievously, and looked me in the eye. Meeting his gaze was like looking down into an immeasurably deep well, the kind that goes so far down that you can hardly see if there's any water there—until you catch a faint glitter reflecting the sky above.

'That's it, then,' he said firmly. 'Now you see what our hero has to do.'

'I...I think so.' To be honest, I wasn't quite sure, but I assumed it was something along the lines of pleading guilty. Whatever that meant.

'And remember that only he can do it,' Fyodor Mikhailovich continued, ignoring my hesitation. 'There's no historical necessity that's going to ensure a happy ending. The philosophers told us that thesis and antithesis would necessarily lead to a final synthesis, but it doesn't always happen...'

'That sounds like Hegel!' I interrupted. I hadn't read much Hegel, I admit, but you can't teach in the humanities for twenty years without coming across some of the great man's ideas.

'I suppose it is like Hegel,' he acknowledged.

'But did you read Hegel?' I asked, realizing as I spoke that this too could have sounded rather rude. He didn't seem to notice.

'I read Hegel in Siberia,' he said, 'It made me want to weep.'

'Weep? Really? I've never heard of Hegel making people weep!'

'I don't suppose he does have that effect on many, but my circumstances were quite peculiar. I'd been in prison for four years, four years of hard labour, my fingers cracking with frost in the winter and my entire skin itching with midge bites in the summer; I'd seen men beaten to death, dying in wretched conditions in the hospital, scenes of brutality and savagery beyond belief. And just think of the men I'd lived with: men who'd committed the most bestial acts imaginable—and acts you couldn't even imagine—men who'd murdered their own families locked up alongside idealists and dreamers whose only crime was to imagine a better world. And what did Hegel have to say about those four years of terrible intense reality? Nothing. Nothing at all. Or, more precisely, he said—he actually said!— that Siberia is not and cannot be a part of world history. So there you are—all that experience, all those suffering, all those poor wretches, not only exiled from Russia but exiled from history itself.'

He stopped, sighed, and looked mournfully down at the rug, shaking his head very gently.

'A man who knew so much and thought so much—and yet he could say that! Could he really have thought about what he was saying? I don't know. I haven't yet had a chance to talk with him *here*, though I'm told he's not so very far away from where I myself am—but, of course, I'm not in charge of how these things are organized. Anyway, that's all beside the point. But he was right to see that the way to truth is not a simple and direct way, as ordinary logicians and Euclidean geometers like to think. It's a jagged and oscillating line, making its way from one extreme to the next and contradicting itself at every turn.'

'Right—the famous dialectic!'

'Exactly. Or, as I prefer to think of it: pro et contra.'

'The title you gave to one of the parts of *The Brothers Karamazov*!'

'Just so. Well remembered.' (He really did seem quite pleased with this. Perhaps I was on the way to redeeming my ignorance about the onion.) 'The difference of course is that I leave both my characters and my readers with the pro and contra—and then it's up to them to decide. There's no necessary happy ending: it's all down to freedom. But there's also something else.'

'What's that?'

'It follows that the moment immediately before the final revelation of truth is the extreme opposite of truth. As Hegel might say, it's the negation or antithesis that prepares the way for the final affirmation or synthesis. Or as the rest of us might put it, the darkest hour is the hour before dawn.'

'Which means that the husband…'

'Yes, the husband… the truth is exactly the opposite of what he says: we are not alone, the sun does shine on all and gives life to all, and Christ's commandment is the one true law of the human heart, as it always was.'

'So why did you say he'd seen the truth?'

'Because he has embraced the negation and therefore seen one side of the truth; but he hasn't yet seen the whole truth, the positive truth, the synthesis. He's nearer the truth than when he began because he's learned what the life he used to live has led to and what the world really is like if you don't have love. Now he has to turn around and see what it's like when you do love! But—Nota Bene!—he had to learn this through experience, he had to be shaken out of his ignorance and indifference and it took everything he'd experienced to get him to this point—just one step away from the whole truth, the step he hasn't yet taken; just one step—but if he doesn't take it, then he's as far away from the truth as it's possible for a man to be. Still, perhaps he will take it—in the very next second! Or perhaps he never will! Who knows what happens next?'

'Who knows? Fyodor Mikhailovich, surely you know—as you said at the beginning, you made it all up!'

'Me? How could I know? Who knows the mystery of another person's heart?'

'But he's your creation, can't you make him think and do whatever you like?'

Probably it was the whisky or the late hour talking, but I was in danger of forgetting myself—again. Here I was, telling Dostoevsky—Dostoevsky!—what he could or couldn't write! Perhaps there was a limit to his patience, since I felt a slight chill in the silence that followed. Then again, maybe it was just the temperature dropping after the heating had gone off and the last log in the wood burner had burnt itself out.

'It's not that straightforward,' Fyodor Mikhailovich resumed, looking at me, with almost visible forbearance. 'If only it were. We writers look at reality with an artist's eyes, but we don't invent it, we don't "make it up", to use your expression.'

Actually, I thought it was his expression, but refrained from commenting.

'And, if he does take this step, what then? What difference will it make—I mean she's dead, isn't she, and nothing he can say will bring her back or change the past?'

'That's what the positivists would say, I agree. But don't underestimate the power of memory. Just remembering things otherwise might start to change the world, no matter how little—remember the onion! As we said about Richard III and Hamlet: they talk in monologues because they're both locked into their own worlds. But if the pawnbroker knew he was guilty, if he really knew how guilty he was, he'd stop talking in monologues and talk to *her*, asking her forgiveness, asking everyone's forgiveness—like Alyosha in the garden—and if he did that, then he wouldn't be alone any more and the world wouldn't be so cold. To acknowledge your guilt is to let others into your world. It's to let yourself love. To see others with the eyes of love.' He stopped, folded his hands, and nodded in satisfaction.

The way he said it was touching, I admit—but I couldn't help blurting out yet another unconsidered reply.

'You say that, Fyodor Mikhailovich, but your novels are full of people who are utterly unlovable. In fact, I don't think even you loved all of them very much—I don't think you loved old man Karamazov very much and it doesn't seem like you loved poor little Smerdyakov at all. At least, you don't seem to have given him any redeeming features.'

Fyodor Mikhailovich sighed. 'And what sort of novels would I have written if I'd filled them with loveable people? Would they be the sort of novels you'd want to read?'

I shrugged. 'Perhaps not.'

'I'm sure not. I was a novelist, and that means presenting people in the way that they actually appear in their world. It's not what I think of them that matters, but how they appear to each other—and none of them ever has a final view on any of the others. None of them is God and even the author isn't God. Literature isn't the last judgement. The most I could do was to show the possibility of redemption. Remember Fedya the convict: a thug who killed for money—but I reminded the reader how he'd been sold by his master to pay a gambling debt, a man reduced to the status of a thing; yet even though he's violent, unlettered, guilty of murder and sacrilege, he goes on hoping for forgiveness; somewhere, deep in his heart, he knows that the Mother of God will remember him with mercy, just as she remembered the sinners who had sunk so deep in hell that even God had forgotten them.'

'Yes, I understand that,' I said, remembering that Fyodor Mikhailovich always had a soft spot for the peasants, even the peasant who prayed for forgiveness in the act of murdering someone for a silver watch. 'But', I continued, 'that doesn't seem to be true of all your characters, like the ones you describe as arrivistes and lackeys.'

'Arrivistes and lackeys!' he chuckled. 'I like that. But listen: I say again, these are novels and because they are novels they show the world as it appears in all its degradation to real human beings with all their prejudices. I'm not passing judgement on any real actual people. None of us ever knows enough about anyone else to do that. I knew prisoners in Siberia who'd committed the most hideous of crimes and never showed any sign of repentance or contrition—but who knows what was going on in the inscrutable depths of their hearts?'

'Yes, but that still doesn't tell us how to find any redeeming feature in the kind of despair that *A Gentle Spirit* ends with.'

'Really not? You surprise me.'

'Really not. Can you explain?'

'I can try. For a start, I've already explained that although he still has one more step to take (a colossal and paradoxical step, admittedly), he is now in a position to take it, if he dares to do so—and if he does take that step, he will re-enter the world and become capable of love. But there's another, very important point. A couple of minutes ago, I called him the hero. But is that correct?'

'Well, I can't see who else is. The whole story is his story, as he told it—like one of Shakespeare's monologues, as we said.'

'Very well. But we writers think very carefully about our titles, you know. Now tell me, if *Richard III* is about Richard III and *Hamlet* is about Hamlet, who is *A Gentle Spirit* is about?'

'About a gentle spirit.'

'Exactly. And is he "a gentle spirit"?'

'Not at all. Quite the opposite—I'd say he's more like a soul in torment.'

'So who is the "gentle spirit"?'

'That's his wife, of course.'

'Very good.'

'You mean the story is really about her, then?'

I thought for a moment.

'But, Fyodor Mikhailovich, if that's the case, then it still doesn't help very much since she too is in despair—more so, even, since she kills herself. All you seem to leave us with is the alternative—ultimate solitude or suicide. Not much of a choice!'

It had become very quiet outside. I could hear someone singing drunkenly. I wondered whether he imagined himself happy. He didn't sound like he was in paradise.

Fyodor Mikhailovich straightened himself, sitting forward and putting his hands on his knees.

'I have to be going soon,' he announced abruptly, 'So I'll be as brief as possible. Let me ask you: do you really think that just because someone commits suicide, we can assume they're in despair?'

'Why not? Isn't she in despair?'

'Yet she was clutching an icon.'

'Doesn't that make it worse?'

'What it means is that there is something in what she did that we cannot understand. Yes, I know that the Church regards suicide as a sin and will refuse to bury her, but perhaps she herself still hoped the Mother of God would have mercy on her, the kind of mercy she could not show to herself. Isn't what she does a way of saying "Yes, I know I'm guilty, but I know that there is someone who can love me, someone who will love me, someone who does love me despite my guilt"? And who are we to deny her? I know I can't, because I can imagine movements of the heart that are so deep and yet so subtle that we can never see them with the outer eye. We cannot say this was simply self-will. We cannot condemn. We can only hope, for others as well as for ourselves. *He* had given up all hope, in this moment there was nothing in his world except self-will and perhaps his next step too would have been to end his life—that also happens—or perhaps it would have been to faith. We do not know. But she—maybe she was still hoping, giving herself into the hands of God's own Mother.'

I found myself nodding. Although the 'God's Mother' bit didn't speak to me (I don't have that sort of religious background), there was a lot there to think about. Inevitably, I thought back to the people I'd known who'd killed themselves, each of their deaths a terrible enigma. Their faces seemed to pass before me, one after the other, almost as if they were pleading to me and I could almost imagine hearing their distant voices—but too far away to hear their words; too far away—on the far side of death. Even after many years, the question remained: Why? Why? Why? And what had each thought or felt in that final instant? Had there been any hope? Had any of them died clutching a metaphorical icon?

I looked up. He was gone. I was alone.

Had I been asleep? It goes almost without saying that I asked myself that question straightaway, but even on that first night I knew that this wasn't a dream or hallucination. I was awake and the conversation had been as real as any conversation I'd ever had with a 'living' friend—I put scare quotes round 'living' because I was left with some uncertainty as to whether life and the limits of life were quite what I'd previously imagined.

I didn't pinch myself. I didn't need to, but my head was humming, bursting even, as I replayed everything that had happened in the last hour at 16× speed. I couldn't go to bed straightaway. I picked the book up. I put it down. I went to the bookcase. I went to the window. I could still hear the drunk guy singing, but it was very faint by now, several blocks away. Happy or unhappy. A night bus drew up at the stop opposite our flat, its engine throbbing. Suddenly, I was very tired. This could wait till morning. This had to wait till morning.

Laura stirred enough to make room for me when I got to bed, but only half woke. I didn't sleep much, replaying the images, the words, the thoughts, over and over. I slept a little, eventually, but my mind was filled with wild, chaotic images. The alarm went, as usual, at seven o'clock. Laura got up almost straight away. I turned over and pretended to be asleep.

Second Conversation

Good Books

Dickens & Co.

By the time I'd showered and dressed, Laura had nearly finished her breakfast. On the radio, a bishop was saying something about the Church and climate change.

'Sorry. I couldn't wait,' she said, looking up. 'I need to be in for half-past eight.' It was now ten to.

'That's fine,' I replied. 'Coffee. That's the main thing.'

'I seem to have made it rather strong this morning.'

'That's good. Good for me.'

'Ah-ha. You were late last night. Too much whisky?'

'Not really.'

The bishop had been replaced by a tetchy exchange between an interviewer and a junior government minister.

'Is there any more yoghurt?'

'In the fridge. Where it always is. If you weren't drinking whisky, what were you doing?'

'I didn't say I didn't have any whisky. Just some. I was reading.'

'More Dostoevsky, I suppose?'

'Of course.'

'You're reading a lot of Dostoevsky. Work? Fun?'

'A bit of both, maybe. I'm trying to fill in some of the gaps—what I haven't read or what I've forgotten.'

'Fair enough. I haven't read Dostoevsky for years. I loved it when I was a student. I was your Grushenka and you were my Dmitri and, yes, I would have followed you to the salt mines! But I don't know if I'd still like it—all his women seem to be suffering or mad or just ridiculous. And have you noticed that the men never give up their lives to follow them to the salt mines!'

'They do in Tolstoy.'

'Really?'

'Yes. In *Resurrection*. But he was definitely a worse misogynist than Dostoevsky.'

'Well, I didn't know. But all that talk about God is a bit much. I mean, I believe in something, but I just don't think that people get so worked up about whether God exists anymore, do they?'

'Maybe Russians do.'

'Maybe—only I'm not Russian. Still, perhaps I should have another go.'

The voice of the newsreader cut across what she was saying. 'For a second night in a row, rockets have been fired...'

'Oh God. They're all so bloody stupid! But I have to go...What time are you back?'

'About seven—the students will probably expect me to buy a round of drinks after the seminar. Noblesse oblige and all that.'

Conversations with Dostoevsky: On God, Russia, Literature, and Life. George Pattison, Oxford University Press.
© George Pattison 2024. DOI: 10.1093/oso/9780198881544.003.0003

'Fine. Will you get the salmon out of the freezer before you go? I must dash.'

'Will do. No, don't bother. I'll clear your things. What have you got on today?'

'Meetings, meetings, meetings. Nothing unusual. Just a lot of it.' She cradled my head momentarily and pressed a kiss on it. 'Love you. Don't forget the salmon.'

'I won't.'

I did. That is to say, I forgot—but remembered just as I was shutting the door.

Once Laura had gone, I had about an hour before I needed to leave. We both worked at the university. I taught comparative literature; Laura, as I've said, was in admin. It was only a quarter of an hour's quick walk to my office, but although I wasn't lecturing till eleven there were a few emails that needed answering first. Which left me an hour or so to think through what had happened the night before. I took my second cup of coffee with me to the sitting room and looked down at where Fyodor Mikhailovich had been sitting. The only evidence for his visit was a crumpled cushion, but since Laura had been sitting there earlier in the evening that didn't prove anything.

What had really happened? Had I been visited by Dostoevsky—or, at least, his ghost? And if it was his ghost, was 'ghost' the right word?

Dostoevsky. 'Fyodor Mikhailovich' as I was starting to think of him.

Let's say it had been a hallucination or that I'd just been dreaming, a kind of waking dream, perhaps? Did that matter? Even if it had all been in my mind, things had been said that I needed to think about. Seriously, though, I knew it hadn't all been 'only in my mind' but I've never been interested in spiritualism or the occult and I wasn't tempted to start wondering about how—if it was 'real'—it could have happened. The main thing was what we'd been talking about.

Going over (and over) what he'd said, I didn't feel I'd got the answers I'd been looking for. The question as to how one could go on living if, like Dostoevsky's fictional pawnbroker, one believed that the world was dead, empty, and loveless remained unresolved. At least I wasn't yet persuaded. There's a Bergman film in which someone asks that same question about how to go on living and the only answer they get is 'Because we must'—but that doesn't really help. Even more difficult was how one might believe in God in a world like that—but we hadn't even got on to God. Fyodor Mikhailovich had given a kind of answer, speaking about how the pawnbroker needed to become guilty, as in the Elder Zosima's teaching that we should each think of ourselves as being guilty of everything and confess our guilt to everyone. But that hadn't led very far.

There seemed to me to be two problems with what he'd said. The first was that the kind of guilt Zosima talked about wasn't what we mostly think of when we hear the word 'guilt'. It wasn't—or wasn't quite—like being guilty of some specific crime and it wasn't—or wasn't quite—like the kind of guilt that therapists help you get rid of, the dark residue of unresolved childhood conflicts. It was something more general or perhaps more basic. A guilt everyone had, a guilt we should accept. But how?

From what Fyodor Mikhailovich had said, thinking of yourself as guilty in that way would motivate you to being more actively loving towards others. I still didn't get that, but allowing it to be true, just how far should you go? He didn't seem to think there was a limit, which might work for moral heroes, the sort of people who dedicate their lives to working for refugees, the homeless, trafficking victims, whatever, but it seemed too much to ask from people living ordinary everyday lives. I mean, me. Of course, I could probably give more to charity, I could probably volunteer in the community, there's probably a lot more I could do, but on this principle, I'd never have done enough. And even if, like Zosima, I gave everything up to become a wandering penitent, it would mean letting a great many people down. Like leaving Laura with a big chunk of mortgage to pay off. That wasn't an option. Running away from my real responsibilities in the real world didn't seem the right way to assume responsibility for my existence.

In any case, a Dostoevskian saint who went around believing they were guilty of everything also reminded me of all that harping on about 'unworthy servants' that I remembered from my childhood churchgoing. Dostoevsky portrayed Zosima as a joyful kind of saint but it was hard to see the connection between guilt and joy. It all sounded dreadfully serious. Worse still, depressing. Which, I suppose, is what most people would expect from a conversation with Dostoevsky. I've known people who say that reading Kierkegaard can drive you mad, and maybe it's the same with Dostoevsky.

These questions, and variations on them, niggled away at the back (and sometimes at the front) of my mind over the next few weeks and there was also the nagging question: was I ever going to see him again? Had this been a once-off visitation from the other world (or wherever he'd come from), or, if he was going to come again, was there anything I could do to make it happen? I remembered a scene from a movie in which Andy Warhol said he'd tried to call God on the telephone but hadn't been able to get an answer. How do you 'call' the other world? I certainly wasn't going to go to a séance or get out the tarot cards.

Perhaps it would help if I knew why he'd come in the first place. Had something about the way I was reading his story tuned me in to some sort of cosmic wavelength that enabled us to communicate? Could I find that wavelength again? Was there some sort of technique, some sort of spiritual mindfulness that I could practise, to put myself in touch with him? The problem, of course, was the familiar paradox about not being able to do something once you become self-conscious about doing it. In any case, if I had somehow tuned in to his supernatural mind, why was I finding it so difficult to process what he'd said? If it was mind meeting mind, where was the flash of understanding? But perhaps *I* had nothing to do with it. Perhaps it was all his initiative, for reasons that I was unable even to guess at. In which case there was nothing I could do.

Despite my scepticism about being able to invoke his presence, I made a point of staying up over the next few nights. I tried to pretend that I didn't have any special aim in view, but I didn't really fool myself for one minute. And even though it felt a bit artificial, as if I was practising some kind of sympathetic magic, I made a point of reading more Dostoevsky. Fairly randomly. It was hard to focus, though, wondering whether 'he' was going to reappear at any moment.

He didn't. After a couple of weeks, I decided that I couldn't expect to see him again. At least, I told myself that that's what I'd decided. Goodbye, Fyodor Mikhailovich. It was nice knowing you. I'll reread *The Brothers Karamazov* now, I promise. And I really will start on *The Diary of a Writer*, just as soon as the semester's over. Maybe they'll have the answers I'm looking for. What was it he'd said? 'If the words I wrote in my books were the truth, why shouldn't they be enough for you? What can I add?' Perhaps I just had to become a better reader.

First up then, *The Brothers Karamazov*. And—wonders untold!—I solved the riddle of the onion straightaway. Looking through the contents pages, I noticed there was a chapter entitled 'An Onion'. I immediately looked it up to see whether it was relevant, and it was. It describes how Grushenka, the object of Dmitri Karamazov's passion, is tempted to seduce his innocent brother, the novice monk Alyosha Karamazov. But she stops herself just in time and later explains what made her change her mind by telling a story about a malicious old woman who'd spent her entire life being mean to people. When the old woman dies, she's thrown into the lake of fire where the wicked are punished for all eternity. She's obviously not very happy about this, but an angel tells her that if she can think of one good deed she's done, this might help. She eventually remembers that she once gave an onion to a beggar. The angel promptly holds out an onion to her, telling her to grab hold of it so that he (are angels he's or she's?) can pull her out. Things are going well, until some of the other souls see what's going on and try to grab on to her legs so that they can be hauled out too. But she won't have any of it and kicks them away. At that moment the angel lets go of the onion and she falls back into the fiery lake. The point being that her selfish obsession with her own salvation made it impossible for her to be saved.

An onion, then. Which seemed to suggest that what Fyodor Mikhailovich had meant was simply that all the pawnbroker had to do was to stop thinking about how he could go on living after his wife's death and start thinking of others instead. This didn't seem too difficult. In principle.

Meanwhile, the semester was continuing and my list of things to do was piling up, as it always did. Although work didn't exactly drive my mysterious visitor to the back of my mind, it did give me other things to think about. Laura's department workload was relentless. We both needed some space and a couple of weeks after Fyodor Mikhailovich had been and gone we drove out and walked round the Conic Hill by Loch Lomond, letting the great vista that opened out over the loch and towards the snow-capped Arrochar Alps take the stress away. For a couple of hours only. But at least it was a couple of hours and life felt better. What was there to be guilty about? Maybe I didn't need to beat myself up about those eternal questions. Maybe they were really only nineteenth-century questions. Maybe life was its own answer. And yet... something was missing. Or that's how it felt.

* * *

It was now late November and already starting to get dark when I left the office shortly before four. I'd just been sent what one of my students hoped was the penultimate draft of his thesis to read through (I was more doubtful) and I was less likely to be disturbed at home—especially now our son James was away at university.

As I approached our block, I could see from the street that the sitting-room light was on. Probably, then, it had been left on all day, unless Laura had come home early, which was unlikely, given her seemingly endless series of over-extended meetings. Deep down, I knew just who it was going to be, though I didn't allow myself even to form his name in my mind. As I opened the inner door to the hallway the flat was completely still—and yet I sensed someone there.

'Laura?' I called out, knowing it wasn't her.

There was no reply.

The door to the sitting room was ajar and the light coming from it lit up the hall in an interesting way.

'Hello?' I called.

Again no reply.

Pretending to myself that I wasn't even aware of *his* presence, I put down my briefcase, took off my jacket and hung it on the coat stand. Just like normal. Only then did I go into the sitting room.

You won't be surprised to hear and, to be honest, I wasn't surprised to find that Fyodor Mikhailovich was there, although I'd vaguely assumed that if he did appear again it would have been late at night and not in the middle of the afternoon. This didn't really seem the right time of day for visitors from *there*. Be that as it may, he was standing by the bookcase and examining a thick paperback he'd taken down from the shelves. I couldn't straightaway see what it was.

Looking up he gave me a welcoming smile, almost as if *I* was the visitor. Very matter-of-factly, he remarked that it was always interesting to see what books people had and that he was very pleased to see Mrs Radcliffe there (some years back Laura had bought a lot of early women's fiction) as well as Charlotte Brontë. 'But you don't seem to have any Walter Scott?' he concluded, with a hint of disappointment.

'Er... no,' I mumbled, 'I'm afraid we don't. Actually, I have to admit that I've never read Scott.' I immediately regretted this confession and attempted to make amends. 'I mean, I've tried several times, but I just can't get into it.'

That probably made it worse.

Fyodor Mikhailovich shook his head.

'I'm astonished. I'd imagined that everyone in Scotland would know their great national writer like everyone in Russia knows their Pushkin, their Tolstoy, and, if I may say so, their Dostoevsky.' I sensed he was teasing and even that there was an element of play-acting in his disappointment. 'You know—you probably do know—that when I was a boy my brother Mikhail and I devoured Scott's Waverley novels. You could say that it was reading Scott that made me want to be a writer—and one of the first things I wrote was a play about your Queen, Maria Stuart, though I probably got that idea from Schiller.'

'Really?' I said, not quite sure where this was going. I did have a distant memory of having read about the MQS play that, like most juvenilia, had never seen the light of day.

He didn't respond directly but, lifting the book in his hands, smiled again—he seemed to be in a very cheerful mood—and said that despite the lack of Scott he was glad to see we had some Dickens. I looked closer and saw that the book he'd picked out was *The Old Curiosity Shop*.

'*The Old Curiosity Shop*,' I said mechanically.

'Yes,' Fyodor Mikhailovich replied. 'I'm sure you know that Dickens was one of my favourite authors. I even managed to read *The Pickwick Papers* and *David Copperfield* in prison—unofficially, of course.'

'Really?' I seemed to be repeating myself. I needed to up my game. 'I've often read that Pickwick was the inspiration for your Prince Myshkin.'

'That's not entirely wrong—though Don Quixote was probably more important. Still, I loved Dickens, even though I could only read him in translation.'

'So what language did you speak when you met him—I'm sure he didn't speak Russian?'

Fyodor Mikhailovich chuckled.

'Well, of course, I never met him, though I suppose it was possible. No, I don't know where you got that idea from.'

'I'm sure I read it somewhere,' as, indeed, I had.

'No. I'd definitely have remembered that!'

That was that, then. It was probably one of those internet things—a nice idea getting turned into a fact because a million people believe it. But this non-existent meeting reminded me of something that I'd thought about several times since our first conversation—that it had all been in English. But how did that happen? Especially if Dostoevsky didn't speak it. Perhaps it wasn't the most important thing we could be talking about, but it was interesting. Why not ask him?

'And yet, Fyodor Mikhailovich, you're speaking English now—very fluently, I may say, with only a very slight accent. Does that mean you can now speak any language you like?'

He gave a quiet laugh.

'It's complicated. I wouldn't say that I'm speaking English, but you're hearing me in English and, for my part, I understand what you're saying perfectly well.'

'You mean it's a kind of mind-reading or telepathy? That you can kind of bypass language over there?'

'No. We don't bypass language, as you put it. As we talked about last time: "In the beginning was the Word." But...how can I say...our relation to language is...different. Yes, we too need words just as you do—we're not angels—but it's all somehow...freer.'

'Language—but not as we know it,' I joked, not expecting him to get the allusion. He didn't.

'Not as *you* know it,' he replied rather seriously. 'Besides, you shouldn't be surprised. Virgil spoke to Dante in Italian, a language that didn't even exist when he was on earth.'

He paused.

'I cannot—I may not—explain this other life to you, but I will say that the words we're speaking now are a bit like prisms or, better still, a series of prisms through which what we are trying to say gets refracted. It's the same light, but it comes out looking different on the other side. And that would still be true if you learned Russian or I spoke English.'

I found that vaguely comforting. I always encouraged my students to read European writers in the original even though I could only read Dostoevsky in English, meaning that I must be missing out on a lot of the nuances. But perhaps it didn't make such a big difference. Even if the translations were imperfect, maybe they were still transmitting some of that original light, to use his analogy. And if Dostoevsky could only read Dickens in Russian, it somehow didn't seem so important that I could only read Dostoevsky's novels in English.

'So it doesn't matter that I can only read you in translation?' I asked.

'Of course, you should learn Russian if you can—you're still young enough to do so. They say it takes seven years before a foreigner can read me in the original and, God willing, you have more than seven years ahead of you. But even if you were a native Russian speaker, today's Russian is no longer my Russian or Count Tolstoy's Russian. It can't be, because the world in which Russians live today is different from the world I knew. Just think of everything the Soviet Union did to our language!'

'Does that mean that it's really only your contemporaries who could understand what you were saying or get any benefit from your books?'

'Of course not. But what I wrote grew out of and belonged to that Russia, my Russia. It couldn't have come from anywhere else or been written in any other language. And I also needed Russian soil, Russian cities, Russian people, and even Russian weather in order to write. At the end of the four years I spent abroad, I was nearly washed up as a writer. I don't know if I could have gone on. It was worse than after the four years in prison, which, in a way, gave me everything.'

'But what you wrote wasn't just for Russia, surely? I mean, I've known people from South America, Africa, Asia, from everywhere really, who've said that you're the only European writer who writes about the kinds of people they know in their lives and the kinds of questions that matter to them.'

Fyodor Mikhailovich looked pleased. He may even have flushed slightly. I'd noticed before that he was still appreciative of praise. His face appeared rounder and brighter than the last time.

'Thank you, that's good to know. It confirms my view about the distinctive universality of Russian literature, even though most of your contemporaries, I think, regard this as slightly ridiculous. But, of course, I couldn't have written anything that would speak to your friends if I hadn't written in Russian as a Russian. Perhaps the easiest way of putting it is to say that, like our Russian verbs, every word has two aspects. One aspect faces towards its own time and place, the other is more... universal.'

'The word in the word, like the man in man?'

'Yes—if you understand it in the right way. Because you mustn't forget that the man in man is not the philosopher's principle of universal humanity, he's this man, this Russian, this Scottish, this English man. He's real and he can only be universal if he's real or, at the very least, striving for reality. In other words, putting "Dostoevsky" to one side for a moment, Scott and Dickens would never have meant what they did to me if they hadn't spoken out of the truth of their own time and place and their own language.'

That was fairly easy to understand, though it did seem to mean that there were parts of what Dostoevsky wrote that I would never quite 'get'. But, applying what he'd said about twenty-first-century Russians and nineteenth-century Russians, perhaps it wasn't any different from how there were parts of any English writer from one hundred and fifty or more years ago that I would never quite 'get'. And what he'd said also implied that these weren't the really important parts.

* * *

It felt a bit awkward standing there, so I suggested we sit down. Fyodor Mikhailovich didn't object, and we took the same seats that we'd occupied on the first evening. 'This is a very comfortable chair,' he remarked, smiling appreciatively. Our manoeuvring had interrupted the flow of conversation, though, and there was a short but awkward silence before Fyodor Mikhailovich spoke again.

'This is very interesting. You're a teacher of literature, but you've never read Scott... how can you teach modern literature if you haven't read Scott?'

'Well, it's not really my period... I mostly work on the twentieth century,' I said, rather flustered, feeling that this was a typical academic answer that didn't throw an especially good light on the academy and its compartmentalizing habits. Trying to recover some lost ground, I added that I'd read Dickens—*A Christmas Carol* (of course), *Great Expectations*, *Hard Times*, and a couple of others. I didn't mention that I probably knew several of them better from film and television adaptations than from the books themselves.

'But not *The Old Curiosity Shop*?' he asked.

'No. It's not one that people read so much now. I think it's probably too sentimental for our postmodern taste.'

Dostoevsky was still holding the book, marking a page near the end with his finger. He looked at me, not exactly questioningly but as if waiting for me to say more. I was aware of feeling rather embarrassed. What I had just said was, I think, undeniably true, but at the same time I knew instinctively that there was something not quite right about it—starting with the fact that I'd never actually read it.

After leaving me in a state of discomfort for what seemed like an interminable length of time (though it was probably no more than half a minute), he spoke again.

'Postmodern? That's interesting. You postmodern people don't like sentimentality, then—and yet, if I'm correct, your contemporaries are always talking about their feelings. That doesn't seem to make sense.'

'That's not quite what we mean by sentimental,' I said defensively. 'When we say that a book or a picture is "sentimental" we mean that it plays on our feelings without regard to truth.'

'And your postmodern generation would say that the death of Little Nell isn't true?'

'I suppose that's right…'

'And do you agree with your generation?'

Although I hadn't read *The Old Curiosity Shop*, we'd been given the chapter with the death of Little Nell for a seminar on mourning in literature back when I was a student, as I now explained to Fyodor Mikhailovich. I added that I remembered it as being fairly sickly and that our tutor told us that people shed more tears over it than over all the rest of nineteenth-century literature combined.

'It all seemed a bit…well…too much,' I concluded.

'You haven't read *The Old Curiosity Shop* but you've read the death of Little Nell. It's a strange way of reading to read just a small extract like that, if you don't mind my saying so?'

'I suppose it is, but it happens all the time. Especially in teaching. You have to select. To focus. Otherwise it's just all too overwhelming, too amorphous for the students.'

'Hmmm.'

Fyodor Mikhailovich sighed and appeared to read in the book.

'The death of Little Nell. Too sentimental, you said. "Sickly".'

'Yes…though, OK, maybe that's a bit strong.'

'Let's see.'

He began to read, slowly, intensely, enunciating each word very carefully. It was compelling and I could begin to see why his own readings were so popular.

'She was dead. No sleep so beautiful and calm, so free from trace of pain, so fair to look upon. She seemed a creature fresh from the hand of God, and waiting for the breath of life; not one who had lived and suffered death. Her couch was dressed with here and there some winter berries and green leaves, gathered in a spot she had been used to favour. "When I die, put near me something that has loved the light, and had the sky above it always." Those were her words. She was dead. Dear, gentle, patient, noble Nell was dead. Her little bird—a poor slight thing the pressure of a finger would have crushed—was stirring nimbly in its cage; and the strong heart of its child mistress was mute and motionless for ever. Where were the traces of her early cares, her sufferings, and fatigues? All gone. Sorrow was dead indeed in her, but peace and perfect happiness were born; imaged in her tranquil beauty and profound repose.'

He stopped and, after a pause, looked up as if to see my response. I still had the impression that he was amusing himself at my expense but, at the same time, there was a deep sadness, especially around the set of his mouth.

I have to admit that, against all expectations, I did find it quite moving. In its way. It was, certainly, extraordinary writing. But I still felt there was something not quite right about it.

'Yes, it's quite something,' I conceded. 'But there's nothing really beautiful about the death of children, is there? And doesn't that make it...false? Dishonest, even? I mean you could never have written that, could you?'

His expression was, I'd say, solemn. And, suddenly, I remembered that he too had lost a child, his three-year-old son Alexei, who'd died of an epileptic fit. And perhaps he'd been crushed by his little boy's death, like the father of the little boy Ilyusha whose death he described in *The Brothers Karamazov*. And yet he too had, in his own way, beautified the boy's death, writing about how he looked in the coffin, 'as though chiselled in marble' (I checked this out later). Which was, certainly, verging on what I'd called sentimentality. But I'd never experienced the death of a child. I don't think any of my friends had either. So how could we know what it would be like? What would be the 'right' feeling?

'Fyodor Mikhailovich,' I blurted out, 'I'm so sorry if...'

He held his hand up.

'Please, I understand. We're talking about literature and it's all too easy to forget the reality from which it comes. As regards myself and my loss...you know it's said that Christ still bears the scars of crucifixion in His heavenly body and it's the same for all of us here who've suffered in so many different ways: the scars remain, though we see them in a different light and feel them—differently.

'But Little Nell,' he continued, more cheerfully. 'You know I was so impressed by her that I borrowed her for one of my own novels. I even called my Little Nell "Nellie" and gave her an English grandfather—just in case my readers didn't make the connection for themselves.'

'Really? And does she die?'

'She does. About the same age as Dickens's Little Nell. Thirteen or so. You haven't read it?'

'No.' He seemed determined to show up my ignorance today. 'Which novel is it?'

'*The Insulted and the Injured.*'

'And what happens?'

'Think of everything that can go wrong in a child's life. Nellie's mother was abandoned by her lover and after being rejected by her own father was left to die in a strange land. The grandfather wouldn't care for Nellie and even sent her out to beg. When he too dies, she only just escapes being pimped. Aged thirteen, remember. Luckily, she's rescued by those who become her friends and, as her suffering brings them together, they learn to forgive each other.'

'But she dies—so no happy ending?'

'No happy ending. No sentimentality, as you put it, though I'd be disappointed if the last few pages didn't bring a tear to the reader's eye. It was one of the passages people most wanted to hear at my public readings. Russians aren't afraid of tears, nor should you be. It's not that her death was terrible, though. She died surrounded by friends, she laughed, she joked, as was her way... but death isn't the worst of it. The worst of it was that she died unforgiving, still unable to forgive her father for ruining her mother's life. That's where the tragedy lies. Like Russians, but unlike what you called your postmodern generation, Dickens's readers weren't afraid of tears. Even the strongest wept at the death of Little Nell. But they needed there to be some consolation. If not a happy ending, then peace at the last. Reconciliation all round—because even the beauty of death, the beauty there can be in death, is no good unless there is also reconciliation. Unfortunately, your Victorians had forgotten their own Shakespeare. They couldn't really believe in tragedy, even though (perhaps because) so many tragedies were happening all around them in their own society. That's the reality of life—your life. It can't be denied or avoided. I think Dickens knew that, but his readers didn't—or didn't want to. On this point, if nothing else, we Russians knew better. We knew that suffering can be inconsolable. And we don't expect our writers to cheat us. I'm not forgetting that suffering too can be a lie, but when it's the truth, we mustn't pretend otherwise.'

'So, in a way, you changed Dickens's story completely.'

'In a way. At the same time, I'm very happy to admit that I couldn't have written anything if it hadn't been for Dickens, for Sand, for Balzac, for Hugo, for Schiller, for Goethe, for Cervantes, for Shakespeare and, of course, for Pushkin, Gogol, and Lermontov and many, many others. You can even find inspiration in what critics would call second-rate literature, not to mention the sayings, songs, and tales that ordinary people repeat from generation to generation. Only God creates out of nothing. The rest of us have to make do with what we receive. Spinning, weaving, patching, dyeing, reusing, like so many old clothes, you could say.'

I liked that idea. It fitted with the kind of literary theory that made every text into a collage of other texts. I once had an artist friend who said that his only method was to keep on recycling failure until it became a success. But could you apply that idea to literature as a whole? Was Fyodor Mikhailovich saying there was nothing original about his own work? I felt that I had to protest.

'That's a nice picture, Fyodor Mikhailovich, and I can see that it allows scope for brilliant new arrangements and wonderful variations on old themes: but what about the "new word" that you and some of your characters talked about? Wasn't your vocation—Russia's vocation—to speak a "new word" to the world? Which surely means more than just recycling whatever your predecessors wrote, doesn't it?'

Fyodor Mikhailovich looked round, as if searching for something. It again struck me that he seemed exceptionally good-humoured today and quite undeterred by what could have seemed like rudeness on my part.

But before he could speak, I jumped in with a further point.

'I mean, quite honestly—without getting too theoretical about it, just as a matter of fact—no one had written novels like yours ever before; some of your commentators even said you'd surpassed the whole idea of the novel.'

Lifting his hands in self-deprecation, Fyodor Mikhailovich spoke slowly and deliberately.

'I'm only a writer, not a logician, so please don't expect me to present you with a seamless argument. Yes, Pushkin spoke a "new word" in literature. He put up the signposts for the rest of us to follow and he discovered the types that we were then able to expand and fill out—Onegin first and then and only then Rudin, Bezukhov, Valkovsky; Tatiana first and then and only then Natasha, Sonia... and, yes, this whole event, what people would call "The Russian Novel", was a new word. We weren't the only ones to believe it: those Europeans who read us could also see that it was a new word. But this doesn't mean that we could have spoken it without your Dickens, your Cervantes, or your Shakespeare.'

Pausing briefly for breath, and shaking his index finger in admonition, he continued in almost lecturing style.

'You must also take into account that it was a new word and could only be a new word because it spoke from our knowledge of a reality that, until that time, hadn't existed: the Russian people.'

'But,' I quickly interjected, 'the Russian people had existed for hundreds of years, all the way back to medieval Rus'—hadn't they? And, surely, there'd been a lot of Russian history happening between Rus' and Pushkin?'

'Yes, yes, yes,' he responded, shaking his head as if bemused by my slowness. 'But the point is that the Russian people had not yet entered world history as a people, as Hegel might have said—though, as we talked about last time, he didn't think that Siberia ever would or ever could do that. And, yes, Russia had from time to time intervened in European affairs, but these were always interventions around dynastic struggles, the affairs of monarchs, generals, and diplomats. It was not yet a matter of the Russian people and it was their reality, their experience, their spirit, their suffering, their Christianity that made our new word possible. Yes, Russia existed, the Russian people existed, but they only entered into history when Bonaparte, unaware of their existence or their strength, thought to impose his will on them and become the arbiter of their destiny. Yet, in the end, it was Russia that showed him the limits of his power.'

I'm not especially nationalistic, neither on behalf of England nor my adoptive Scotland, but I was tempted to remark that maybe Nelson, Wellington, and some others had also played a part in checking Napoleon, but I wanted to get back to literature, where I felt on safer ground than talking about a history I didn't know very much about.

'So. What you're saying is that literature is set in motion by historical events or, at least, real events… that it reflects a reality that pre-exists it… so that if there's to be a new word then something new has to happen in the outside world? But if that's true, then it's no longer a matter of art being the product of individual genius à la romanticism but a kind of collective event? The writer isn't just expressing his own personal vision but bringing into language all that is important in his contemporary reality and using all the resources of literature as a whole to do so?'

'Exactly,' Fyodor Mikhailovich almost chuckled. 'But please, I'm not one of your students. I'm only a writer, not a theorist; a writer doesn't write to answer theoretical questions about the nature of literature, he writes because he reads and it's because he reads that he's able to read "the signs of the times" and give them voice in his writing. If you want to write—read. Read everything.'

'But some books are more important than others, surely?'

'Yes, of course.'

'And the most important?'

He answered without hesitation.

'The Bible.'

The Bible

Perhaps I should have expected that answer, but I didn't.

'The Bible?' I echoed.

'Yes, yes, yes. And, by the way, not only do you not have any Walter Scott, I couldn't see a Bible on your shelves, either.'

'Really? I'm sure I've got one… I've certainly got one in my office… Luther's translation, anyway… there must be one at home.' This was definitely more embarrassing than not having any Scott. But I really was sure that I did have a copy somewhere. Of course, I might have anticipated his answer. I knew that several of his novels quoted the Bible, as in the scene from *Crime and Punishment* in which Sonia reads the story of the raising of Lazarus aloud to Raskolnikov or when the passage about Christ turning water into wine is read over Zosima's dead body in *The Brothers Karamazov*. But apart from dithering over whether I actually had a copy or not, I couldn't immediately think of anything to add. It wasn't something I'd thought a lot about. Fortunately, Fyodor Mikhailovich came to my rescue.

Leaning forward, one leg folded over the other and with his hands clasped over his knee, he seemed almost to be talking to himself. 'Could I have written any of my novels without having the Bible in my heart? I don't think so. And not just because of those passages that my characters quote. It's the pattern from which the whole is cut. It is, to borrow what you were saying before, the word in the word, and that word is the power that can make our endlessly recycled words truly "new".'

He nodded to himself, thoughtfully.

'But you,' he asked, 'Do you know your Bible?'

I was a bit taken aback but also rather relieved to be able to give a positive answer—at last!

'Actually, I do, quite well. I can't give you chapter and verse, but I went to a Church primary school where we had Bible stories every day; we also had several different collections of Bible stories for children at home. So, yes, Adam and Eve, Cain and Abel, Noah's flood, the Tower of Babel, Abraham, Jacob, Joseph and his brothers, Moses, David...and, of course, the New Testament as well. I suppose I forgot a lot of it later, but it's all there, somewhere, so at least I can recognize when it's being alluded to.'

He gave a quiet laugh. 'And don't forget the women—Sarah, Miriam, Rahab, Esther, the Lord's mother, the Magdalene. They're important too, you know!'

'Of course, of course,' I replied, slightly put out. 'In any case,' I added (not that he would necessarily be interested) 'it's a very different situation with my students. I recently taught a literature and philosophy class and not one of them knew who Job was. Only two or three knew anything about Abraham apart from the fact that he was in the Bible—even though some of them, I'm sure, thought of themselves as Christians.'

'That's good,' he nodded encouragingly; 'not what you say about your students, but about hearing and reading the stories as a child. I had a book of "A Hundred and Four Stories from the Old and New Testament"—in fact it's the book that I learned to read from. Scarcely anything since has made a deeper impression on me. Those stories already taught me—in a childlike way, of course, not in the way I understand them now—about our human desires, our weaknesses, our lies, and our longing for salvation. And those stories you just mentioned—think what they contain! They teach us about the power of the lie and, looking many centuries into the future, spell out the lie of our own time, the lie that knowledge is more valuable than life; they teach us how envy engenders murderous intentions, making us forget our duty to be each other's keepers; it was from these same stories that I not only learned about the titanic pride that claims power over others but also about the wanderer who left his father's house to follow the call of God and whose struggles with God sanctified the land where he finally made his home; they tell us about the boy who was sold into slavery by his brothers but, as God had planned, became rich and powerful and was able to rescue them from famine; about a people who cried out for freedom from slavery and about the prostitute who helped them gain the promised land; not to mention the king who wasn't ashamed to dance through the streets in honour of God and who wept humbly and without shame for the death of his treacherous son…all of that and much, much more. Who could have invented such things? Such words unmask the lies with which we are wont to console ourselves but, more than that, they show the world of truth to which we should aspire. Everything is there. But is that true about your students not knowing Job?'

'Yes, I'm afraid so.'

'They don't know Job! What a pity for them. What will they do when they too lose everything—as he did, as most human beings, sooner or later, lose the best that they have? What words will they have to express their pain? What words will there be to give them hope? Will they be able to bless God and to bless the life God has given them in the depths of their suffering as Job did? Will they be able to endure and to delight in happiness when it returns?'

I couldn't really answer these questions and perhaps he wasn't expecting me to. But I wanted to hear more about what he'd said about the Bible being the pattern from which the whole of his writing was cut and 'everything is there'.

'What you're saying reminds me of the argument that the Bible is what one critic called the Great Code, an archetypal collection of stories out of which the entirety of Western literature has grown, a kind of collective imaginary?'

'Maybe…but that all sounds rather theoretical. I'd prefer to say quite simply that these stories matter because of the reality they show us. The Bible is not just a collection of stories that the Hebrews told around the campfire to keep each other entertained or a history of what happened once upon a time: it's a revelation of who we are. It's not ancient history: it's about powers at work in our lives now, powers that we can never contain or manage. It's an "irregular comet", not fitting into any system, and it portends the disturbance of everything comfortable, everything that reeks of self-satisfaction, everything that makes us think we are above reproach. In the end, it's a judgement on us, on us all, and on our literature.'

'Judgement, Fyodor Mikhailovich? Really? You're starting to sound like those fundamentalist American preachers who say we'll be damned if we don't believe in every last word of the Bible. I don't know—last time it was guilt, this time it's judgement. Have I completely misunderstood everything you wrote?'

He sighed and looked at me with an expression of tolerant frustration.

'Please. Listen to what I'm saying. It's not the Scriptures that judge us. It's the reality they reveal. And what is that reality?' He paused momentarily for dramatic effect. 'Love. I never said or wrote anything else. Love, the love that reaches out and embraces even the most wretched—especially the most wretched—of all the insulted and injured on earth. I've heard of the kind of preachers you're thinking about and our Church had them too, preachers for whom belief in Satan is even more important than belief in God. Think of Ferapont in *The Brothers Karamazov*. But does Scripture itself ever speak of judgement without also speaking of infinite compassion and tenderness for every "unfortunate"? Yes, the voice of judgement is terrifying, especially to those who know just what they deserve, but, as I had that drunkard Marmeladov say, "He" will surely forgive, and He will forgive even those who know themselves to be swine, "made in the image of the Beast and with his mark". When the arms of love reach out in welcome, what could make us feel our unworthiness more intensely, what judgement could be more unendurable—if those same arms did not also embrace us?'

This was reassuring—though I couldn't help recalling the passage from *A Gentle Spirit* that had been the starting point of our conversations and that spoke so despairingly about the impossibility of love in a world like ours. What could make us—make me—believe that the kind of love Fyodor Mikhailovich was talking about was a reality and not just wishful thinking? I wasn't ready—at four in the afternoon—to push that question further. It may have been evasion on my part, but I was quite happy keeping the conversation on a more literary level—for now, anyway.

'Thank you,' I said. 'That's helpful. But what do you mean when you say that the Bible is a judgement on literature? That's not exactly an idea I've come across before.'

'No? It's not so very difficult. Think of the words I took as a motto for *The Brothers Karamazov*: "unless a grain of wheat falls into the earth and dies, it remains alone; but if it dies, it bears much fruit".'

'I'm sorry. I don't see the connection.'

'How can I explain? You see, it's not a matter of holding up a big black book and saying: "Believe in this book!" You need to open the book and shake it so that its words scatter in all directions, like a sower scattering seed. What happens then? The words, you could say, disappear, they go underground: they break up and dissolve in the processes of life, but then, when they re-emerge, maybe unrecognizably, they do so in a way that is fruitful and nourishing for those who hear them and make them their own, who love them, no matter what form they take.'

'But how is that a judgement on literature?'

'Look at all these books on your shelves, in your university and public libraries, all your newspapers, all the words written, printed, and distributed you've ever read. What are they all about? Do they bear fruit? What are they good for? Do they increase love? Do they help the writer's fellow human beings? Are they even meant to? Or are they exercises in egoism and will to power? Let me be clear, it's not a matter of quoting the Scriptures, but of expressing the life they express.

Grand Inquisitors and devils know how to quote the Scriptures, but although Dmitri Karamazov only ever quotes Goethe and Schiller—badly—his misquoted literary words nevertheless lead him towards salvation. The reality about which the Scriptures speak is alive and active in him, as it was alive in Shakespeare, Goethe, and Schiller. Wherever our words become words of life it's a sign that they've sprung from that original seed.'

This was strong stuff and I needed a moment to take it all in.

'So. Right. OK. Let me make sure I'm getting this right: what you're saying is that even if a literary text never ever mentions or quotes from the Bible, it can still express the spirit of the Bible—and the other way round: that even a text that quotes the Bible may be quite opposed to its spirit?'

'Exactly. But if a person is moved by the spirit of love that inspired the Scriptures, then they will recognize that spirit in the words they hear, whoever speaks them. And they will also recognize that those words are speaking about them, as Sonia loved the story of Lazarus—because she could see that it was her story.'

'Because she saw it as a promise that she too could be rescued from the dreadful life she was living?' I interrupted. Like many readers of Dostoevsky, the scene in which the prostitute Sonia reads aloud the story of the raising of Lazarus to the murderer Raskolnikov as he goes mad in a hell of his own making had made an indelible impression on me when I first read it. More recently, I'd been wondering whether it was maybe a bit too melodramatic, but I wasn't going to start that discussion now.

'No. She loved it because it showed her how the love of Lazarus's sisters was so strong that it could move the Saviour to do what was impossible for men and bring their brother, his friend, back from death. How you read shows who you are—and Sonia was probably thinking of her own salvation least of all.'

After a brief pause, Fyodor Mikhailovich continued.

'Don't think you can keep the Scriptures in the past; once you open them, you will—you must—see the present in a new way, and you will begin to understand just what's at stake in your questions. That's why it was so important for me to have my characters read the Scriptures aloud and quote from it in their conversations. The Bible isn't a set of proof texts for convincing doubters, the way your Western Protestants use it. They are the words of a living voice, speaking out of and speaking to the continuing unfolding of life.' He smiled a little shamefacedly. 'I should, of course, say "some" Protestants—you see I'm developing a rather more tolerant view of these things from my present point of view, though even here nothing happens in a flash. Learning still takes time, even though it's a different kind of time. "Quadrillions of years" in an instant, you could say. And remember, I'm not for a moment denying what you would call the Bible's "literary" value, but what's really miraculous about it is that these words and all they show us about life are written in ways that can arouse the imagination of a child, just as my imagination was aroused by the mention of camels in the story of Job. A child won't understand if you start talking about divine infinity, but if you talk of nomads and their camels wandering in an empty desert and seeking a land to call their own, it will understand—and it will remember until the time is right when you can start talking about infinity. You don't need to make every story into a "lesson" and maybe that's the worst thing you can do.'

'Fyodor Mikhailovich, I can see how all of this makes sense if we're speaking about the Old Testament stories. But how does it work for the New Testament? I grant you that the parables of the prodigal son, the good Samaritan, the lost sheep, and so on, and all the stories about Jesus offering forgiveness to sinners or healing the blind and the lepers have that same story-like quality that you get in the stories about Joseph and his brothers…'

'Yes, these are essential,' he interjected.

'Yes,' I insisted, 'I can see that but when we get on to Paul and some of the other parts of the New Testament, doesn't it all become, how can I say, too "theological", doesn't it turn the stories into dogmas?'

'Really?' He looked genuinely surprised.

'It's probably what most people today think, if they think about it at all. And they'd add that Paul is largely responsible for Christianity's hatred of the body and, especially, sexuality.'

'Sexuality? I'm not quite sure what that means. I've been told that the man who started all this talk about sexuality, Sigmund Freud, read me (rather irresponsibly, from what I hear), although (of course) I never read Freud. But I can't see how you can be talking about the same Paul who wrote that great hymn to love, explaining how love is greater than knowledge, greater even than faith or hope; the same Paul who wept with those who wept and rejoiced with those who rejoiced, who was happy to be poor if he could make others rich, content to be weak and to find strength in weakness; the same Paul who endured beating, stoning, shipwreck, cold, and nakedness for Christ's sake; Paul, who warned fathers not to provoke their children and urged us to see that we are all members of one another? Is all of this "theological" as you put it? "Every creature of God is good and nothing is to be rejected, if it is received with thanksgiving." What did Plato, or Kant, or Hegel ever say that was more human, more life-affirming than that? How does that lead to hating the body?'

I have to admit that I'd been playing devil's advocate to some extent. I was aware of the passages to which Fyodor Mikhailovich referred, at least in a general sort of way, and I was aware that even some philosophers were starting to find Paul a rather interesting figure again, despite the popular view that he was to blame for everything that was wrong with Christianity.

'Nevertheless,' I persisted, 'wasn't it Paul who made Christianity into a matter of obedience to authority rather than relying on the spontaneity of love?'

'Authority? Yes: but what kind of authority? The only authority Paul ever speaks of is the authority of one who emptied himself of all his divine glory and was content to be found in the form of a servant. And a servant's authority, I think you'll agree, is very different from an emperor's. Christ, Christ in his humility, in the form of a servant—did Paul ever speak or write of anything else? In fact, Christ is what the Scriptures are all about, from start to finish, or so it seems to me. If you can show me anything in Scripture that is *not* pointing to Christ, then I'm happy to let it go. We're judged by Scripture, but Scripture is judged by Christ. You could even say that he is the Word in the word in the word.'

'Like a Russian doll...' I blurted out. Fyodor Mikhailovich just smiled.

'Seriously, though,' I continued, 'I'm not sure where this is getting us. I mean, I've read what the Bible says about Christ, sure, but it's all long ago and far away. I'm sure He was a wonderful and inspiring person, but the problem is seeing how any of that can make sense in our world today, when people don't believe in miracles and aren't expecting any Messiah.'

I paused, struggling for my thought.

'Let me put it like this... I mean, if Christ turned up in our world today, would anybody even listen to him? Wouldn't they just dismiss him as a religious maniac and send him off for psychiatric treatment?'

Fyodor Mikhailovich continued to listen, smiling softly.

And then, suddenly, I realized something that I'd probably read about and probably even said to my students but now saw with complete clarity, as if I was seeing it for the first time.

'Ah!' I exclaimed, 'isn't that just what you were trying to do?'

He looked puzzled.

'How do you mean?'

'Trying to show what it would be like if Christ were to reappear in our world today. Isn't that what *The Idiot* is about? Isn't your Prince Myshkin a kind of Christ figure, what Christ would be like if he were to be reincarnated in nineteenth-century St Petersburg?'

'Say more,' he replied.

'Well, I read somewhere that the way you describe him at the beginning is just like the icon of Christ, and he arrives in Russia as a mysterious stranger, just like Christ coming to earth. Then he says that he's come to teach, he sees into people's motives, forgives fallen women, turns the other cheek, and has ecstasies in which he is transported to heaven... even the fact that people regard him as an "idiot" and treat him as mad is a bit like what happens in the gospels—"He came to His own people, and His own people received Him not." You know,' (a sudden memory came back to me) 'I was once at a seminar in which a famous philosopher said that the only form in which God could appear in our world today would be like Shakespeare's "Poor Tom" or Dostoevsky's "Idiot". In other words, he'd be someone who couldn't make himself understood. Like a madman or an idiot. And it wouldn't end any better than last time, despite the fact that we're meant to be a Christian society—or so people used to say.'

'And do you agree with the famous philosopher?'

I hesitated. I really was fascinated by 'the idiot', but—as most of the other characters in the novel also think—he was definitely a bit strange.

'I think he only half fits the bill. He offers unconditional love, granted, but he doesn't seem capable of action. He just stands there while everything around him falls apart. No one gets saved and, if anything, his behaviour just makes it worse. Don't get me wrong. I think he's an amazing character. He's always appealed to me in a special way. I think you also spoke of him as a "beautiful" personality and I get that—but it's a rather ethereal beauty. He's not the same as the Christ we read about in the gospels. I can't imagine him taking a whip and driving out the money changers. I suppose you'll tell me to go back to the gospels, then—to which I'd say that this is precisely the problem: they don't belong to our world, they don't tell me what it would mean to encounter Christ today, in the world as it really is. Now. Today.'

As Fyodor Mikhailovich listened he continued smiling quietly to himself, but I felt there was something sad about that smile.

'I have to say that I don't entirely agree,' he began. 'As regards my "idiot" he was never meant to *be* Christ nor is he an allegory. I know that people often say that he was my attempt to create a "Christ figure", as you call it, and that I failed for the kind of reasons you spell out very clearly—not to say brutally. But I do wish people would stick to the books I actually did write rather than criticize me for not having written the books they think I wanted to write. Yes, there are sentences in my notebooks that suggest that Myshkin was to be a Christ figure—that he *was* Christ—but you have to be very careful how you use a writer's notebooks. The reality is that Myshkin was doomed to fail from the outset—and precisely because he was never sufficiently grounded in our Russian reality. Doesn't Christianity say that Christ had to become fully man if He was to save us? But what does that mean if not to belong fully and identify fully with a particular time and place? In that regard Sonia Marmeladova is more Christlike, but perhaps we'll speak more of her another time. In any case, neither she nor Myshkin are meant to "be" Christ, but they each reveal a single ray of His light. No character in a novel could ever be all that Christ is. It's Scripture that shows us Christ as He truly is and if a novelist wants to bear witness to Christ then the most he can do is to point the reader back to Scripture. Or, better, arouse a memory of Scripture, which may be indirect, allusive, or just enough to raise a question. That, I think is what happens in Myshkin.'

'But Fyodor Mikhailovich, you actually do introduce Christ as a character into one of your novels?'

'I do?'

His surprise was surely affected.

'Yes—and I'm sure you know what I'm talking about. The Grand Inquisitor.'

In *The Brothers Karamazov* Dostoevsky has Ivan Karamazov tell a story (he calls it 'a poem') about Christ returning to earth during the Spanish Inquisition. He arrives in Seville, where the Grand Inquisitor is in the middle of an auto-da-fé, burning hundreds of heretics alive at the stake. The Inquisitor immediately recognizes him and has him arrested. Later, he visits Him in His cell and harangues Him for making life too difficult for ordinary human beings. In particular, he says that Christ should have yielded to the Devil's three temptations in the wilderness which, according to the Inquisitor, were not temptations at all but incomparably sublime ideas for winning the adherence of the masses by the power of 'miracle, mystery and authority'. Christ's problem was that He valued human freedom too highly and only wanted disciples who would follow Him out of love—not out of the desire for earthly bread or political or religious power. All the while Christ says nothing and, when the Inquisitor is finished, simply kisses him on the lips. The Inquisitor lets Him go.

'Ah. Not *my* story—Ivan Karamazov's story.'

'Very well. Ivan Karamazov's story, but, either way, the Christ who appears in that story seems very weak, almost bloodless. More so than Prince Myshkin, even! Jesus denounced the Pharisees and tax collectors and drove the profiteers out of the Temple with a whip, but your Christ—Ivan Karamazov's Christ—just stands silently in front of the Inquisitor and listens to his long, rambling, self-justifying speech without doing or saying anything.'

'Yet we are told that Christ Himself remained silent before His accusers.'

'But He did break His silence in the end. He told Pilate that his kingdom wasn't of this world.'

'And mine kisses the Inquisitor on the lips. Isn't that "doing" something?'

'I suppose it shows that He loves and accepts the Inquisitor despite the fact that he's busy destroying everything that Christ stood for. But that's part of the problem: shouldn't He be confronting him with his betrayal, speaking truth to power, rather than just standing there, silently? That's why your critics say He's too weak: a suffering Christ who loves—but doesn't save. Maybe even can't save. And what use is a Christ who can't save?'

Fyodor Mikhailovich shook his head.

'You really are in a muddle,' he said. 'As I've just explained, there's a limit to what any novelist can do and this story is a story within a story, told by a young man who's even more muddled than you are. Nevertheless, even he has glimpsed one ray of truth. Christ is love. But the only way you can communicate love is: love. I don't see any other way. Yes, He could have turned stones into bread and made Himself universally popular; He could have performed spectacular miracles and made Himself an object of worship; and He could have called upon His legions of angels and taken control of the nations of the world. But if He'd done those things, if He'd compelled people's love or tricked them into loving Him, then it wouldn't have been love. The Roman emperors used bread and circuses to keep the loyalty of the crowd, but they never even pretended to rule through love—let alone freedom. And, just to be clear, although I shocked you by saying that love was even more important and even more basic than freedom, it has to be freely given and freely received. There can't be any compulsion or deceit.'

I thought for a moment.

'I like all this,' I said, '...and I'm drawn to the kind of Christ you're talking about, but I don't see anything supernatural about Him. In other words, I don't see why we should regard Him as essentially different from any of the other great reformers or teachers of humanity. Perhaps the way in which His life embodied His teaching and the fact that love is ultimately more attractive than knowledge or duty might make us rank Him above some of the others, Plato or Kant, but that doesn't make Him God. Yet that's the point, isn't it?'

'Yes, yes, yes, that's the point. That's why Renan and none of the others who've tried to portray Him simply as a historical figure ever got even close to understanding Him. And that's why novelists too can never show more than a very small part of the whole.'

'But what does it mean to say that he's God?'

At that moment we were interrupted by the sound of the outer door being unlocked. Laura was home. What would happen next? Would Fyodor Mikhailovich stay? What would I say? 'Laura, I'd like you to meet...Fyodor Mikhailovich, this is my wife Laura...' What on earth would she think? Or was he, after all, a hallucination? What would happen when these two realities met?

'Hi,' Laura called out, opening the inner door. 'It's only me.'

I looked back to Fyodor Mikhailovich. But he wasn't there. It wasn't that he'd vanished with the kind 'whoosh' you get in a film when a ghost vanishes. He just wasn't there. I was alone. The only sign of his having been there was *The Old Curiosity Shop* lying on the table. I definitely hadn't got that out. I felt stunned. There was nothing to be done, though. I just had to act normally. As normally as I could.

'Hi,' I answered, going into the hall to meet her. 'How was your day?'

Third Conversation

At a Dinner Party

Talking about Dostoevsky

About ten days after Dostoevsky's second visit, we had a couple of friends round for dinner. We'd known Martin and his wife Tamsin since he and I were graduate students and we'd overlapped for a couple of years at Cambridge before I got my job at Glasgow. Martin had followed a few years later, though in his case this was to take up a full professorship (I've never got further than senior lecturer). He'd changed more than most of my contemporaries, almost beyond recognition. As a student he'd cultivated a distinctive retro image: think beatnik verging on Goth. He always dressed in black, with thick black-rimmed glasses, and straggly, unwashed hair. He more or less chain-smoked noxious French cigarettes and ostentatiously spurned anything Anglo-American. His thesis had been on the existentialist film director Robert Bresson, which fitted his image rather well—but which came first, I'm not sure. We both had an interest in existentialism, though I'd never let it influence how I dressed. By the time we met up again in Glasgow he was, as I just said, almost unrecognizable. He still smoked, though not as much. He had also converted to Catholicism. I don't really have any inside knowledge on Catholic Church politics, but I suspected he was probably what the media would call 'conservative', maybe even very conservative. His invariably rather grubby and sometimes torn rollneck jumpers had been replaced by neatly pressed shirts and even, occasionally, a tie—though his ties always had quite unusual hand-designed abstract patterns. This was, probably, down to Tamsin, whom people always described as 'artistic'. Under Tamsin's careful management their four children all seemed to have incredibly active social, cultural, and sporting lives. When we first met, she was very New-Agey and at one point had an aromatherapy practice and maybe still did, though she too now attended church with Martin and they both went off together on retreats in a monastery somewhere in the Highlands (they always spoke about these retreats in mysterious voices, as if they were some kind of espionage operation).

Our third guest was Carl, a new colleague who'd only been in Glasgow about a year. Carl was in his early forties, a bit younger than the rest of us. He was a philosopher, which I always found challenging. I'd met him at a seminar at which he gave a paper on Derrida and postmodern politics and though I hadn't really followed what he'd said, he was clearly keen to get to know people outside his department and we had a good talk afterwards in the pub. I'd thought it would be good for him and Martin to meet, as Martin ran a course on film and philosophy and they both had a French connection. My hunch was that Carl was a fairly secular leftist and he and Martin might have some serious intellectual differences, but that could be interesting too. I also thought it would be good for him to meet Laura, since he was working on a big grant application that would have to pass through her office at some point.

The conversation had ranged fairly haphazardly over the normal kind of professional issues we had in common, including the marketization of higher education, the exponential growth of bureaucracy, the eccentricities of our predecessors, a new exhibition at the Edinburgh modern art museum, and a hilarious discussion (or so it seemed at the time) of bad religious films, during which I commented (as I always did) that *The Life of Brian* was completely unnecessary since the kind of Hollywood Jesus films it spoofed were so bad that they sent themselves up. We'd touched on the issue of Scottish independence. I could see both sides, but Laura was very keen, as were Martin and Tamsin. In Martin's case it seemed to have something to do with Catholicism and I couldn't help wondering whether he might have some quixotic ideas about restoring the Stuart dynasty, though even he probably wasn't that crazy. We picked up that Carl was rather vehemently opposed, so we quickly skirted away from that one. It's a subject on which passions can get a bit out of hand.

We were starting dessert (a rather extravagant fruit tart that we'd brought in from a patisserie on Byers Road) and as I was cutting into my first slice Martin asked what I was reading.

'Apart from student essays?'

'Naturally.'

I didn't hesitate.

'Dostoevsky, mostly.'

'Dostoevsky, Dostoevsky, Dostoevsky,' intervened Laura from the far end of the table. 'I even think he talks to him when I've gone to bed.' I stiffened. Did she know something?

'Still, he's got me reading him again,' she added. I'd noticed (of course) that she'd rather quickly worked through *Crime and Punishment* for her bedtime reading and had just started on *The Idiot*, though, strange as it may seem, we hadn't really discussed them much, apart from the kind of brief exchanges that can be summed up in words like 'interesting', 'OK', 'amazing', 'aaargh', and occasional queries as to how to pronounce Russian names (not that I knew much more than she did).

'Really,' said Martin, stretching out the first syllable to unnatural length. It sounded like he was going to say more, but he paused and rather ceremoniously took a bit of tart, followed by an ostentatious sip of the dessert wine.

'This is quite delicious,' he said. 'Congratulations.'

'No congratulations needed,' laughed Laura, 'I've had so many desserts go wrong that we decided to rely on the professionals.'

'Very French,' commented Martin. 'But...Dostoevsky, that's interesting. You know a chapter of my thesis was about Dostoevsky.'

I'd read his thesis years ago, after he'd turned it into his first book. I had to admit that I'd forgotten the Dostoevsky chapter, though I vaguely recalled something about one of Bresson's films having been an adaptation of *The Idiot*. But I couldn't remember which one.

'Yes you do,' said Laura, 'It's *Au hasard Balthasar*, we watched it last year...you remember, the one about the donkey.'

'The donkey? Oh, right...it gets beaten...stolen...abused...and shot...is that it?'

Martin smiled magnanimously.

'A perfect plot summary,' he commented.

'But I can't see a connection to Dostoevsky.'

'Well, it's not exactly an adaptation,' said Martin. 'More of a variation on a theme. Patient endurance of suffering.'

'Like Christ,' said Tamsin, quietly. We all looked.

'Yes,' she explained, 'the oldest known picture of Christ shows him on the cross—with the head of a donkey. We saw it in the catacombs last year, didn't we, Martin?'

Martin nodded.

Well, yes, I thought to myself, that fits. As I'd said to Fyodor Mikhailovich, I'd always felt there was something Christ-like about Prince Myshkin and had a momentary image of him as the 'man of sorrows' of Christian art. Dylan's 'I am a man of constant sorrow' also flashed through my mind, as did Eliot's line about an 'infinitely gentle, infinitely suffering thing'.

'Actually,' Martin said, 'he adapted several other Dostoevsky novels as well—*Crime and Punishment*, *A Gentle Spirit*, *Four Nights of a Dreamer*—updating them all to 1960s Paris. Very existentialist. *Une femme douce* even features Les Deux Magots!' Sensing all-round incomprehension, he explained. 'You know, the place where Sartre and de Beauvoir used to sit and write. In any case, he's probably the only director to have really understood the religious side of Dostoevsky.'

I didn't immediately remember seeing any of the films he'd mentioned, though I'd long ago been impressed by *The Diary of a Country Priest*, which, like the donkey film, was decidedly miserabilist—only it's not about a donkey but a priest who's alienated from his parish, loses his faith, and dies. It ends with the words 'All is grace', though the priest's 'God' seems indistinguishable from the absence of God. Well, if experiencing the absence of God was more or less identical with a state of grace, perhaps I wasn't so far from having faith. Which didn't seem a very cheerful prospect.

Carl laughed.

'The only Dostoevsky film I've ever seen was the Hollywood version of *The Brothers Karamazov*...'

'With Yul Brynner!' said Tamsin eagerly.

'And William Shatner,' added Laura. 'In case you were a *Star Wars* fan?'

Carl grinned. 'Well, actually...when I was about fourteen...I don't remember Shatner in it, though—but it's a while since I saw it and probably wasn't paying much attention.'

'He was Alyosha, the monk, the good brother.'

'Ha ha! I don't remember a good brother. In fact, I can't remember anything especially religious about it. A lot of drinking and brawling…but it's all a bit vague.'

'No,' said Martin authoritatively, 'like most films it leaves out the religious side entirely. I think the version you're talking about had a few monks with long beards for local colour, but there's a pre-war German version that went even further and cut out Alyosha and Zosima altogether.'

'What!' I exclaimed. 'How can you have *The Brothers Karamazov* without two of the most important characters! Maybe the most important!'

'Check it out' said Martin, raising his eyebrows, 'It's called *The Murderer Dmitri Karamazov*—though, of course, Dmitri wasn't even the murderer.'

'The last time I saw *Crime and Punishment* on television,' Tamsin began, 'they even cut the amazing speech by the old drunkard…what was his name…?'

'Marmeladov,' I added.

'Yes, probably. Anyway, him. You know where he says that even though he's completely bad and wretched and a useless drunkard Christ will come and save him too. It's one of my favourite bits.'

'Yes, it's a great speech,' I nodded.

'Even the Soviet version kept it in,' said Martin. 'And did it rather well! I suppose some BBC middle manager decided that a modern secular audience wouldn't like it. "We don't do God" kind of thing—though as I remember they added a lot of sex in back alleys. It's like Woody Allen changed the ending of *Crime and Punishment* so the Raskolnikov character gets away with it. Crime without punishment. Very ironic, maybe, but I'd prefer to say nihilistic. A sign of the times.'

I was puzzled. I hadn't remembered a Woody Allen version of *Crime and Punishment*, though I knew that he mentioned Dostoevsky in several of his films.

'*Match Point*,' said Martin, dismissively. 'Raskolnikov as tennis coach in millennium London. And it's much too long.'

'Going back to Bresson,' said Laura, 'all the films I've seen…well, there's *Joan of Arc*—that doesn't end well…the country priest loses his faith and dies…and we've already mentioned poor little Balthasar…it's all pretty dismal.'

'What do you expect?' Martin replied. 'He's a Catholic director who understands that self-sacrifice is the highest expression of faith. Yes, the priest loses his faith and dies but he also learns that it's not his will or what happens to him that matters, but God's will. That's why he can say "All is grace". It's triumphant—not "dismal", as you put it. You see' (I could sense him gathering himself for a speech), 'I'm not saying *you're* guilty of thinking this, but Catholicism isn't the kind of how-to-make-friends-and-influence-people feelgood religion that everyone seems to want nowadays—even though Pope Francis seems a bit that way inclined. But Catholicism is a religion of suffering and that's why it can speak for sufferers and to sufferers; that's why the priest prays over the chalice that he might have the grace to be immolated together with Christ. And Bresson is great because he's the one who comes closest to showing that in film. Tarkovsky, perhaps—but it's all a bit too overdone and sententious, don't you think? Bresson keeps to the bareness of reality. And Dostoevsky? I think he too understands this inner connection between faith and suffering. So—the "idiot" suffers and dies. Like Christ.'

Of course, he was misremembering, since Myshkin doesn't die at the end of the novel but relapses into a comatose state. And it sounded like Martin was making suffering an end in itself, which I didn't think was what Fyodor Mikhailovich was saying. As I read him, suffering was an unavoidable part of the human condition, but it was something we had to be rescued from through love. The characters in the novels who go in for extreme religious suffering, like wearing chains or feats of prodigious fasting, aren't always—are hardly ever—models of love. Some seem to be downright evil: like the nihilists, they seem more interested in demonstrating their own willpower than love.

'I'm not sure that's right...about Dostoevsky...' I began, but Carl had already jumped in. I'd noticed that he'd had a long and quite involved talk with Laura earlier on, but hadn't taken much part in the general conversation, apart from a brief comment about nationalism being the curse of contemporary Europe when we were talking Scottish politics—and, of course, he had chipped in about the Hollywood Karamazov film.

'But this is exactly the problem with existentialism as a whole,' he announced. 'I don't know Bresson's work, so I can't comment on that and I dare say that from a literary point of view Dostoevsky is a very important writer, but this ideology of self-sacrifice and this obsession with negative emotions is not the answer to anything. It's no surprise that the existentialists picked up on Dostoevsky because, like him, they offer a very clear depiction of the self-contradictions of modern bourgeois society. That's fine as far as it goes, but because they rejected rationality they couldn't offer any constructive solution to those contradictions. Communism also failed but at least communism was in principle committed to applying reason to the problems of society. Whatever you think of him, Lukács was right to label existentialism "parasitic subjectivism", even if he ended up as an apologist for Stalin. OK, I don't go that far, but there's all the difference between a cry for help and actually trying to find a solution.'

I suppose that I had myself been inclined to associate Dostoevsky with existentialism and our conversations had started with my own existentialist-style questions about the meaninglessness of life, but I was beginning to see that Dostoevsky didn't quite fit the existentialist frame. Whatever Carl said, he *had* been concerned with finding a way out of the crisis of his time—the crisis of capitalism, if you want to call it that—but (and I was increasingly thinking he was right) you couldn't find a reliable way out if you didn't start with the human heart itself. I don't know if Dostoevsky had ever read Pascal, but he'd have understood Pascal's line that the heart has its reasons.

Carl, I suspected, had been unaware of Martin's Catholicism, though he knew now—and (obviously) had other views. In any case, both of them seemed to be falling into a rather unnuanced view of Dostoevsky that I didn't want to let pass.

* * *

'Existentialism...I do half get what you're saying, and I suppose it could all get a bit too self-indulgent along the lines of "my life is meaningless therefore life is meaningless"' (was I talking about myself?) '...but Dostoevsky wasn't really an existentialist...not in the sense you're talking about, was he?'

Carl began to answer, but Martin cut in.

'You misunderstand me,' he said, addressing himself to Carl. 'Catholicism culminates in the will to self-sacrifice. But it does *not* reject reason. On the contrary, the Church has a very high view of reason. Reason enables us to understand the necessity of God's existence, it enables us to live moral and socially useful lives. It affirms the principles of social order, the family, the economy, the state. It's not irrationalism, as you seem to be thinking.'

Carl smiled.

'Dostoevsky? Catholicism? Where should I begin. Look, I don't know a lot about religion, but it does seem to me that in our secular society the development and articulation of moral norms doesn't require any kind of religious underpinning, whether that's institutional, as in Catholicism, or individual and emotional, as in existentialism and Dostoevsky. I mean, art's always going to be emotional and expressive, so I don't criticize a writer for that. But it's like going to the theatre: you enjoy the play, but then you come out into the real world.'

'Surely it's more complex than that,' I began. 'Isn't literature a part—a crucial part—of society's attempt to work out the kind of world we live in and the kind of world we want to live in? Just look at the whole history of the relationship between literature and social reform in the nineteenth century or literature and political action in the twentieth.'

'Yes, to a degree. But as for literature and political action, I don't think that's an entirely happy story. Just think of the writers who endorsed fascism or Stalinism. Social reason is something very different from literature.'

'The needs of the soul,' declared Martin.

Carl and I both looked at him in some surprise, as he'd doubtless hoped.

'The needs of the soul—I fail to see how you are ever going to develop a programme for improving society unless you understand the needs of the soul. Human beings cannot be reduced to algorithms and, surely, social reason (as you call it) has to take that into account?'

'Look, don't get me wrong. I'm fine with writers and artists expressing what you call the needs of the soul but you can't base collective norms on how we feel about things. These are different kinds of discourse and we need to be able to keep them apart.' Carl took a deep breath before adding (rather provocatively) 'And the same goes for religion.'

'I'm intrigued...' said Martin, but didn't immediately continue. Carl clearly thought this was an invitation to develop his point further.

'Religion, any religion, is always social and therefore has to have some scope for managing relations between individuals and the larger community. To that extent it has a positive relation to reason, like you say about Catholicism. Even when religious norms don't really bear any relation to the real world, believers invariably try to give reasons for them, which is a kind of admission of the real power of reason. Art and literature, though, don't have to do that. Where's the "reason" in an abstract painting? Literature is more complex, I admit, but a writer like Dostoevsky is perfectly justified in exploring emotional crises without ever having to explain them. There's nothing wrong with that, as long as we remember it's just art.'

Again, I didn't think this was right. Apart from the fact that he clearly didn't know about the importance of Dostoevsky's views about Russian society, I was—I am—sure that literature (and Dostoevsky in particular) had real things to say about the real world. In any case, Fyodor Mikhailovich had said as much in our last conversation. When hadn't literature been 'engaged'? But before I could say anything, Martin had taken up the challenge.

'I don't have a view on what you call "literature" in general,' he said, 'but even though Dostoevsky was wrong about many things—including, as far as I can see, Catholicism—he was a very social thinker. In fact, he hardly ever stopped talking about Russia and the malign effects of Western influences, so he'd have been very disappointed if someone restricted him to writing about emotional crises and nothing more.'

I could see that Carl was trying to formulate a response but before he could do so Martin cut across him.

'Of course, I suspect you wouldn't like his nationalism very much and I don't either, though his social teaching was part of what attracted some of the Catholic thinkers of the interwar years, I believe.'

He was starting to sound rather irritable and I could see that Laura was a bit worried that he was about to go off on one. Martin's speeches could last a long time but I was relieved to notice Tamsin giving him a familiar warning look. He immediately checked himself and restarted in a much more conciliatory tone.

'Still, you might like the marvellous 1932 Russian version of *The House of the Dead*—you can easily find it on YouTube.'

Everyone looked blank, waiting for Martin to continue, as he was obviously going to.

'No one's seen it? Right. Here's the thing. It starts with Dostoevsky giving a tremendously successful lecture to crowds of middle-class admirers—lots of elegant ladies—and then, afterwards, a government minister takes him aside and praises his powers of persuasion. "You should work for us," he says, "we need you to help prevent Revolution." But, while he's talking, Dostoevsky starts to look ill. Finally, he gasps out, "You remind me of the Grand Inquisitor" and goes into a fit—then we get *The House of the Dead* as a kind of flashback to his own early days of revolutionary purity. It's rather clever.'

Carl nodded, slightly mollified.

'Interesting. Yes, I see that. And that would make it palatable for the Soviet authorities.'

'Something like that,' agreed Martin. 'But it's really rather paradoxical, because it tries to whitewash Dostoevsky's adoration of the tsar and makes him an exponent of Socialist Realism *avant la lettre*. But there you are, you can't get round the fact that all art has a social context and a social… what can we say?… "impact" to use that hideous word.'

We all groaned. It was a favourite word with academic bureaucracies.

'OK,' resumed Carl. 'But this just underlines my point, really. Things like Dostoevsky's nationalism and the way the Soviets distorted art to serve their ideological aims just shows that we need a separation of powers. It might have been better if Dostoevsky had stuck to psychological dramas and the Soviets had let artists do what they liked instead of forcing them to toe the party line. It's a simple category mistake.'

Martin was toying with the final crumbs of his tart, and I could see that he was planning a further response, but before he could say anything, Laura jumped in. As I said before, we hadn't really discussed Dostoevsky all that much, despite both being rather immersed in reading him (though we hadn't been reading the same novels at the same time). She'd liked him a lot when we first read him as students, especially *The Idiot*, but I'd been getting the impression she wasn't quite so carried away this time.

'It's not his politics I object to,' she said. 'It's how he treats women.'

We all looked at her.

'How so?' asked Martin.

'I'll tell you in a minute,' she replied, 'but first my lovely husband is going to make the teas and coffees, aren't you?'

'Of course,' I said, 'but don't start before I get back—I want to hear it!'

In the Pantry

I took orders and went through to the kitchen, a rather small affair for the size of the flat, more like what my grandmother would have called a scullery (the estate agent called it 'the butler's pantry'). There was only really room for two people and it was therefore quite a shock when, having put the kettle on and turning round to set the tray, I realized that someone else was there. It was *him*.

'Fyodor Mikhailovich!' I gasped in a half-whisper. 'What are you doing here?'

He raised his hands in a gesture of helplessness.

'Why shouldn't I be here?'

This seemed oddly assertive, almost as if he regarded himself as a kind of permanent fixture.

'Of course you can be here...that's not what I meant, but I can't talk now...we've got guests...and I have to get back to them as soon as I've made the teas and coffees...'

'Yes, yes, yes—I know. But I'm interested to hear what your guests—and your wife—have to say about me. And, of course, what you say to them!'

I don't know quite how to put this, but there was something odd about him. Obviously, the whole business of his being there was odd from start to finish, but after two meetings I was starting to feel that talking to him was—almost—like talking to anyone else. But now, in such an enclosed space, in such close physical proximity, his presence was disturbing. He was definitely *there* and I was sure that if I put out my hand I would touch him. Yet, at the same time, he didn't seem to take up any space. I mean, if he'd been anyone else, he'd have had to keep getting out of my way but as it was he just seemed to adapt to my movements without doing anything—almost like a three-dimensional shadow. But he wasn't a shadow, he was there, definitely there. Present. Perhaps more so than I was. A real presence, you could say.

'What do you want me to say to them?'

He looked at me reproachfully.

'Come, come, you've learned nothing from my novels if you're still thinking that what *I* have to say is what matters. Keep my ugly mug out of it! What *you* have to say—that is the question.'

'But all this discussion about existentialism—are you interested in all that? I mean it all happened a long time after...' (this was delicate) '...after you were alive' (which sounded better than 'after you died').

He smiled broadly.

'It's true that I have other things to think about than what people in your world are saying about me, but I also have to admit that I've not yet reached the stage of being totally disinterested. And I've made some interesting new acquaintances here in the last hundred and fifty years, kindred spirits you could say, not to mention admirers. And some of them have also been described as existentialists. Well then, what do you think? Was I an existentialist?'

'What do I think? Well, I'm not a philosopher...but if existentialism means everything being focussed on the individual, on the "I", then I think you weren't an existentialist. Your novels are full of real, passionate individuals but they are who they are only because of how they interact and speak with each other. Not one brother Karamazov, but three!'

'Excellent. I grant that if you have to choose between abstract systems—like Hegel's—and the individual then you must choose the individual. The passionate young Dane made that very clear. But individuals too are only abstract until you see them in the whole of their relations to others, their families, their world, their history. I think he too is starting to see that now.'

Laughter could be heard from the dining room.

'I'm sorry, I must let you get back to your guests, but let me add one thing. Your existentialists got many things wrong, but the best of them —like our nihilists— had a kind of honesty and courage that deserves respect. If history is meaningless or tragic, let's face up to it and not pretend otherwise, as the bourgeois do— keeping up the outward forms, such as religion, but not really observing them. Nevertheless, many of them—again like many of our nihilists—were ultimately cynics, using specious arguments to hide from their own contradictions and to avoid showing themselves to be the fragile trembling beings that they—all of us— really are. And then, as always, it was others who had to pay the price. Some people complained that, like the existentialists, I always overdid things, that I took my characters and my stories too far, that it was all too *intense*. But how can you go too far, how can you be too intense when it's a matter of truth? The problem is that the existentialists—some of them—insisted that they were the only ones who had a right to decide what was true and what wasn't. They weren't prepared to allow any other voices into the conversation. That's where they went wrong. But you have your guests to see to, and I'm very interested to hear what your wife—and you—will have to say about women! We'll speak more later.'

He watched me prepare the tray and eased aside to let me pass. We almost touched and, if he had been anyone else, any 'living' person, then it would have been unavoidable. But we didn't. It was weird.

Colours

When I got back to the others, the atmosphere had become much more relaxed. I passed the cups around, trying to appear as normal as I could despite being thrown by Fyodor Mikhailovich's uncanny reappearance. I might even have been shaking a little.

It seemed that while I was out of the room Tamsin had explained a new way of talking about novels that she'd picked up in one of her book groups, a kind of game, really. It involved assigning colours to particular characters or novels (for a whole novel, you were allowed up to three) and it had been decided that we were all going to have to do this with Dostoevsky.

'Your idea, Tam,' said Martin. 'You start. Show them how it's done.'

'Right,' she said, rolling the 'r' in a rather exaggerated way. 'Where shall I begin?'

'*The Brothers Karamazov*,' I suggested.

'I've only read *Crime and Punishment*,' said Carl.

'Well, then,' said Tamsin, looking questioningly at him, 'what colour is *Crime and Punishment*?'

He thought for half a minute or so.

'Grey—and red.'

'Explain,' said Martin.

'Well, it's set in St Petersburg, so it's grey. Foggy, damp, dark, and dingey—at least, that's what it was like when I visited and how I always imagine it. And red, well, red is his "bloody project".'

'That's a bit grim,' said Laura.

'It is grim,' Carl replied, 'A mad axe man—horrible. At best it's the logic of terrorism, inventing a pseudo-political cause to justify your rage against the world. If Raskolnikov was alive today, he'd probably join ISIS. I just can't see why so many people seem to identify with him or want him to get away with it.'

'Do they?' asked Laura.

'He's got a point,' chipped in Martin. 'Tarkovsky says something like that somewhere. Though not the ISIS bit, obviously.'

'Must be true then, if Tarkovsky says it,' teased Laura.

'I always loved Raskolnikov,' said Tamsin, sadly.

'How about you?' said Martin, turning to me and ignoring Tamsin's plaintive confession. 'Was Raskolnikov your youthful alter ego?'

I remembered Martin as I first knew him.

'I think that was a bit more your style,' I answered. 'But hang on, there's something wrong here. Calling it grey makes it sound like Glasgow in November, but doesn't it all happen in the summer, in the heat and dust? Isn't there a scene' (I knew there was) 'where Raskolnikov looks out over the city from the other side and there's a cloudless sky, the water is bright blue, and the cathedral all gold? There's nothing dark and dingey about it at all. In fact, I think Dostoevsky says at the very beginning that it's an exceptionally hot July so that you could read the whole thing as a kind of overheated summer fever?'

Carl shrugged. 'He's not a very bright and sunny character, though, is he?'

'Fair enough, but I wouldn't say he's "grey" either.'

'So what colour is he?'

'You started all this, Tam,' declared Martin. 'Are you going to adjudicate? Is Raskolnikov grey, blue, black, or star-spangled? What are your colours?'

'Mine? Green and purple.'

'Green and purple?' I asked, amused. 'Tamsin, I know you're the artistic one, but how do you get that?'

'You're meant to be the literary critic,' she said, 'aren't they in the book?'

I thought about it for a moment.

'Green...yes—Sonia wraps herself in a green shawl the first time she comes back from walking the streets and...and .... in Raskolnikov's dream of the peasants beating a horse to death there's a church with a green cupola in the background...and at the very end, when he looks out over the steppe, I picture him standing in a green wood...'

'I think that's only in a film,' Laura said drily. She had, after all, read it just a couple of weeks ago, so she was probably right.

'Hmmm. Perhaps it is.'

'And Sonia?' hinted Tamsin.

'Sonia? The green shawl and...' I thought furiously. 'No, I'm stuck. What else?'

'The house where she lives, the Kapernaumovs', it's green, isn't it?' asked Laura.

'Full marks,' said Tamsin. gleefully.

'So what?' asked Carl, drily. 'What's that got to do with anything? The house has to be some colour, doesn't it, so why not green? It all seems a bit random.'

'First you have to get the purple,' said Tamsin. 'Colours are only meaningful when you see them in combination.'

'Porfiry!' I suddenly remembered. The police investigator—his name, Porfiry, that means "purple", doesn't it, just like Raskolnikov means "split personality", and Sonia "wisdom"?'

'Wonderful,' exclaimed Tamsin.

'So how does this work?' asked Carl. 'I'm still trying to get how this tells us anything about the novel.'

Tamsin looked at him as if to say he was being very foolish but might be indulged just this once.

'Green is the colour of the new life, as in spring, and it's also the colour of the Holy Spirit, like in Rublev's Holy Trinity icon, so green is Sonia's colour because she's the source of life and divine wisdom.'

'And purple?'

'It's the colour of authority, like the emperor's toga, the colour of order, earthly power, human justice—in Porfiry.'

'Right,' I cut in. 'So you see Raskolnikov as split between Sonia's spiritual wisdom and Porfiry's human justice, between love and law?'

Tamsin smiled, shaking her head slowly in mock reprobation.

'You do always sound like you're giving a lecture. But, if you want to put it that way, why not.'

'Very interesting,' I said thoughtfully. 'Actually, this is a great method for discussing literature, Tamsin. I might try it in class!'

'Please do. No acknowledgement needed. No fees payable.'

I had sensed Laura getting a bit tense during the last few exchanges. Nevertheless, she smiled fondly at Tamsin as she came back into the discussion.

'Dear Tamsin. You're so nice. But this thing about Sonia—Saint Sonia—is just what I can't stand.'

'What's "this thing", Laura?' asked Martin.

'Sonia. I mean, the way she gets talked about as if she's the Virgin Mary or maybe even Christ, but her whole character is a male fantasy about passive and suffering women sorting their lives out for them.'

'Wow,' said Martin enthusiastically, clearly looking forward to a challenge. This was territory where they'd often clashed before, though not with reference to Dostoevsky.

'Yes, what do you mean, Laura?' asked Carl.

I was a bit taken aback. Laura had hinted a couple of times that she wasn't very happy with the way Dostoevsky portrayed women but I hadn't realized she felt quite so strongly.

'Spell it out,' demanded Martin.

'Very well. Sorry to upset the fans' (she looked at me, with a mixture of amusement and something else I couldn't quite identify—reproach or pity perhaps), 'but this is how I see it.'

'The Woman Question'

'Right. *Crime and Punishment*. Sonia. It's pretty obvious we're meant to see her as some sort of saint, but, basically, she's a cliché—the good-hearted prostitute, an innocent who sacrifices herself to save the family from her drunken father and crazy stepmother, degrading herself to help others. Everyone comments on her name being Sophia and how that's meant to connect her to divine wisdom and I didn't miss the clue about the thirty silver pieces she brings back after her first night on the streets. What Tamsin was saying about her being associated with the colour green was new to me, but I can easily accept that maybe that was deliberate on Dostoevsky's part…'

'I'm sure it was,' I interrupted, though quietly. Laura carried on regardless.

'And, of course, she reads the raising of Lazarus story…but that whole scene…what can I say? It's too much, too intense, too melodramatic, almost a kind of peepshow: prostitute reads Bible to murderer—Oooh! Shock! Thrill! He confesses. She understands (of course) and accepts (of course) and even has to follow him to Siberia (of course). Well, that's a great outcome for her, especially when she flips from being sacrificial victim into the Virgin Mary, a "little mother" to all the prisoners. She's perfect, of course—a perfect embodiment of male fantasy, sexual *and* pure, both at the same time, asking no questions, just waiting and serving.'

'Quite a charge sheet!' declared Martin.

'Seems about right,' added Carl drily.

'Who's going to defend Dostoevsky?' asked Martin, looking from me to Tamsin.

'Surely you are, Martin,' Laura answered. 'You're the one who's keen on self-sacrifice.'

'I am, I don't deny it. And I suppose I'd be happy to see her as some kind of Saviour figure, a co-redemptrix, if you like—OK, you probably don't,' he said quickly, seeing the expression on Laura's face. 'But without getting too Catholic about it' (a nod towards Carl), 'isn't it important...isn't it necessary sometimes to surrender our own goals, our own good for the sake of others, for our families, for the people we're in love with...?'

'Of course. Every parent knows that,' said Laura. 'The problem—my problem—is that it's one-way traffic. She gives everything up for him. What does he do for her? Apart from having killed her friend, he torments her and drags her off to Siberia...And she's only able to get back on her feet because of the money left by Svidrigailov, nothing to do with Raskolnikov. Without that money—guilt money—she and her family would just have gone to the wall.'

'Yes, but...' I started. Laura looked at me warningly but I carried on. 'Yes, but he did one thing, one very important thing: leaving out the fact that he gave money for her father's funeral, he saw her as a person, as his equal, and defended her against being set up as a thief. Surely that counts for something.'

Laura gave a kind of sideways nod as if thinking about it.

'Maybe. That's all true. But leaving Raskolnikov out of it, the best Dostoevsky could let her do was to give everything up and follow him so that, through her, he could be saved.'

'But that is Christ!' interjected Martin.

'I don't doubt it—but how is it that, since Christ, it's only ever been women who've had to do the sacrificing?'

Tamsin had been listening closely.

'Laura,' she said, very deliberately, 'two things. Firstly, she loves him. And,' she smiled, 'remember he's described as being exceptionally good-looking, even if he's completely dirty—rather like Martin was when I first met him.'

'Love seeks not its own.'

'Thank you, Martin, don't distract us with your pious quotations' (Martin pretended to look offended: this was clearly an ongoing theme). 'And, second, she becomes someone in Siberia. Instead of being despised, she's looked up to and respected. And, finally, she gets him to love her. She gets what she wants!'

'I suppose that's one way of looking at it,' said Laura, clearly unconvinced. 'But what about the other women in the novel, Sonia's mother or Raskolnikov's mother, not to mention the grisly old pawnbroker? Sonia's mother is completely crazy, totally obsessed with fantasies about how she once belonged to high society, shrieking and losing her rag, and generally behaving in all the ways that so-called "hysterical" women were meant to behave.'

'Yes, but' (me again) 'isn't Dostoevsky asking us to pity her, isn't he saying this is how it is for people in this society, that someone like Katerina Ivanovna gets dragged down by poverty, the kind of poverty we can't imagine, by her husband's alcoholism, by consumption; she's crazy, yes, but Dostoevsky shows us why she's crazy and confronts us with the question as to how anyone could endure a life like that?' Turning to Carl, I added that even the Soviet critics approved of Dostoevsky's social realism. 'So he's not attacking her as an individual, he's attacking the system that made her like that.'

'What about Raskolnikov's mother?' asked Martin. 'She seems fairly harmless.'

'I'm not saying she's an evil person, but she behaves pretty unfairly to both her children. She pushes Dounia into getting engaged to Luzhin, who's a complete jerk, and puts Raskolnikov in an unendurable double bind. "We all look up to you, Rodion, we'll sacrifice everything for you, Rodion, we don't expect you to do anything for us, Rodion, and, by the way, if you don't do anything your sister is going to have to marry a complete jerk just for the money." Bad motherhood or what? But my point isn't that she's a bad mother. It's that Dostoevsky doesn't seem capable of portraying a good, strong, self-assured woman with her own agenda, holding her own in the world.'

'Dounia, though,' I said, 'doesn't she do just that? OK, she goes along with the plan to marry Luzhin for a while—but she takes the first opportunity to ditch him and she stands up to Svidrigailov: she's even ready to shoot him when he tries to blackmail her into sex.'

Laura smiled, holding up her hands.

'Very well, I give you Dounia. But she's the exception who proves the rule.'

'But even if Laura's right, I don't see that it's Dostoevsky's fault,' said Tamsin, 'it's just how it was for women in the nineteenth century. Either get married for money or...poverty, prostitution, becoming an old maid...pretty bad, whether you're rich or poor. I think he's just telling it like it is. True love really was the only way out—if you could find it.'

'I'm not sure of that,' said Carl, who'd been following the exchange quite closely. 'Maybe that's how novelists portrayed it, but the woman who interested me most was Raskolnikov's sister, the one you were talking about just now—what's her name?'

'Dounia.'

'Right, Dounia. Dounia and his friend, you remember...'

'Razumihin.'

'Right, Razumihin...isn't what brings them together the idea of a shared project, the work they're going to do together? Why their relationship works is because it's not just about looking into each other's eyes but doing something for the good of society. You get that same idea in Chekhov too, and the characters who fail are the ones who can't find work. That's where the women's problem is too. Especially the idle rich and the very poor. Back then, that is.'

'But work needs self-sacrifice too,' added Martin. 'You can't work without giving up your immediate self-interest.'

'Enough,' said Tamsin, perhaps sensing (as I did) that Martin was in danger of getting on his high horse. Or perhaps she was just watching the time. It suddenly struck me that it was quite a relief that none of them had read *The Possessed*, since this contained even more extreme images of women's abjection than anything that even the most critical reader could find in *Crime and Punishment*.

* * *

Of all the abject women in *The Possessed*, the most wretched was, surely, Maria Lebyadkina. Some people have seen her as a holy fool, but I imagine that most readers today would find her more foolish than holy. She's described as a strange, crippled woman, her face powdered and rouged, with an artificial rose in her hair. She spends her days telling fortunes from playing cards, looking at herself in a mirror (which I imagine to be broken), and nibbling pieces of dry bread. She has a fantasy about her lost prince, perhaps inspired by the children's books of chivalric tales lying on her table. On the one occasion when she appears in public she behaves erratically and what she says doesn't make any sense. Yet, as it turns out, she is the unacknowledged wife of the incredibly handsome and wealthy Stavrogin, the arch-demon of the novel, regarded by a group of mostly fairly mad would-be revolutionaries as a kind of Messiah-in-waiting. In true Byronic fashion, the aristocratic Stavrogin seems to be capable of just about any crime or outrage, including the rape of a twelve-year-old girl, Matryona. Afterwards, he sits silently in the next room while she hangs herself. He even gives his consent to the murder of the wretched Maria. Although many of the details remain hazy, it emerges that Stavrogin had probably only married this sad, mentally unbalanced woman as a kind of provocation to society—and then abandoned her. It's typical of his twisted personality that despite being irresistibly attractive to women, he chooses to marry someone whose only qualification is her abjection. You could say that poor, sad Maria is a kind of anti-icon of female abjectness, subjected to a progressive social, physical, and psychological degradation that she is incapable of resisting.

And yet (isn't there always an 'and yet' with Dostoevsky?)—and yet, despite all this, she is the one person in the novel who really sees through Stavrogin, who's not only lionized by most of the other characters but seems to have exerted a similar spell over several generations of critics. She says that she'd expected a falcon but saw only an owl and a shopkeeper; he is, as she now sees him, not her prince at all—just a bad actor.

Maria is an extreme, but none of the other women (most of whom seem also to be infatuated with Stavrogin) comes out very well either. All in all, then, not a very proto-feminist text. I have to admit I didn't really know what to make of it myself—and even started to wonder whether Laura might not be right. In a way, it wouldn't be surprising. You still get novels and films—even academic studies— that have an extraordinary blind spot with regard to the representation of women. What can we expect from a man—a Russian man—of the nineteenth century? Perhaps we just have to leave that aspect to one side. But if what he has to say about half the human race isn't worth taking seriously, why should we bother with the rest?

Meanwhile, Laura had been encouraged by the others to carry on and do a similar hatchet job on *The Idiot*. Listening to her, I suspected that she was maybe less scandalized by this but was now in role and enjoying herself. I wasn't sure. Even when you've lived with someone for thirty years, you're not always sure of why they do what they do or say what they say.

As she explained it, the central figure of the novel is a woman, Nastasia Phillipovna, who has been sexually exploited since early adolescence by her guardian and is about to be conveniently married off (with a generous fee to the prospective husband) to enable her guardian to make a respectable society match. A kind of *La Traviata* situation. She is, we're told, exceptionally beautiful and Prince Myshkin himself goes into raptures when he accidentally sees a photograph of her. It's this beauty that arouses the uncontrolled passion of the violent Rogozhin and makes her an object of pity to the prince himself, who (perhaps) imagines that his pure love will save her, like Christ saved the fallen woman 'who loved much'. He is even ready to marry her and it is as she arrives at the church that she changes her mind and goes off with his rival.

'Obviously,' Laura was saying, 'she's murdered and, obviously, it's her own fault because she throws herself into the arms of Rogozhin, despite knowing exactly the kind of man he is—just like victims of domestic abuse still get blamed for not leaving their abusers. You know, "whatever they say, it's what they want". I'd even say that, for Dostoevsky, the only good woman is a dead woman.'

As she was speaking, I pictured the final, unforgettable scene in which Rogozhin and Myshkin keep vigil over Nastasia's body. Rogozhin has stabbed her in the heart in such a way that very little blood flowed onto the wedding dress that she is still wearing and that has now become her shroud. It's a kind of perverse Pietà: the dead woman as object of veneration. We're told that she'd been reading *Madame Bovary*, hinting that even if Rogozhin wielded the knife, it was really a kind of suicide—like Madame Bovary herself, like Ophelia, like Cleopatra, like so many passionate and, in men's eyes, dangerous women. And not only in literature.

'Now, now,' chided Martin, 'she's not the only woman in the novel and, as far as I can remember, quite a lot of the others are really quite normal. Aren't the Epanchin girls nice, solid, bright young middle-class women? I seem to remember something about them having good appetites. I see them as ready to live life on their own terms, not as victims at all. Much as I approve of victims.'

'Their mother's a sweetie,' contributed Tamsin. 'I mean, she's touchy about social etiquette and a bit whacky, but she's a really good woman, and kind, very kind.'

'OK, there are some "normal" women in it, whatever "normal" is,' retorted Laura, thinking it over. 'But Aglaya, who's meant to be everybody's darling, is just a conceited airhead, as everybody's darling often is.'

'Emma,' volunteered Martin.

'Emma?'

'Jane Austen's Emma.'

'Oh, that Emma. Maybe—and, yes, Aglaya too thinks she can twist everybody round her little finger. But, when you come down to it, I just don't see what she's got going for her apart from youthful charm.'

As I say, I felt that Laura was starting to play to the gallery, even if there was a serious point behind what she was saying. Anyway, I felt it was time to lighten the mood.

'And there's me thinking she reminded me of you,' I said, probably rather ineptly.

'You mean I'm a manipulative airhead?' she replied archly, but with a twinkle in her eye.

'It's the charm he meant,' said Martin.

'The charm—and, in any case, I'm not accepting that she is an airhead. I see her as very intelligent, prepared to challenge the social conventions governing how a young woman should behave, and really quite brave in confronting the difficult situations and extremely difficult personalities she gets involved with.'

'Only "quite" brave?'

'Really brave, then. She takes big chances. With Myshkin. With Nastasia. It ends badly, but, as we're always telling our kids, "it's not about winning or losing"…'

'Doesn't she become a Catholic?' asked Martin. 'I suppose that for Dostoevsky that's about the worst thing that could happen to her!'

'She does,' said Laura, 'and not just a Catholic but a Polish nationalist who turns her against her family, against Russia… You see, that's her punishment for trying to live life on her own terms.'

'Well, maybe that's how it is at the end of the novel,' I suggested, 'but we don't know what happens to her in the end. I imagine that she'll pick herself up, find a way through, and "make it", whatever making it means.'

'But on that basis,' said Carl rather sarcastically, 'just about any character in just about any novel could end up "making" it.'

'Maybe,' I acknowledged, 'but I think Dostoevsky gives us the clues.'

'I suppose you were in love with Myshkin?' Martin said, turning fondly to Tamsin.

She laughed.

'Oh no! Rogozhin every time. Those saturnine good looks. The danger. Much more my type.'

We all laughed. It was hard to see how Rogozhin could be Tamsin's type!

'Come on, Martin,' she added, 'we must let these people get to bed.'

'Just when it was getting interesting,' he complained.

'He means, "Thank you for an interesting evening from start to finish,"' Tamsin explained.

'Yes, it really was,' added Carl, also starting to get up.

Of course, it took another quarter of an hour before everyone had left.

'So,' I said to Laura as we began clearing the table, having brushed away the ritual offers of help. 'I'd no idea you disliked Dostoevsky that much.'

She shrugged.

'I didn't say I dislike him. I just think he bought in to some of the worst myths about women there are. As most male writers did back then. As they still do, more often than not. If he's "worse" it's only because he's more consistent. He goes all the way.'

We could agree on that.

'But,' I said, gathering the wine glasses onto a tray, 'I thought you yourself identified with Aglaya when we both first read *The Idiot* twenty or whenever years ago?'

She smiled. One could say enigmatically, but it was late, we were tired, and maybe she just smiled.

'Probably I did—but luckily for me you're neither Myshkin nor Rogozhin.'

I laughed, almost losing the balance of the tray.

'Definitely not.'

* * *

It was one of our relatively few house rules that the person who'd done the cooking left the other to do the washing up. Normally that just meant loading the dishwasher, but there was quite a lot more than that tonight. Laura suggested leaving it till the morning and offered to help, but I insisted. I obviously couldn't say to her that I was expecting a second visit from Fyodor Mikhailovich, though what she'd said earlier about me talking to him made me wonder whether she had her suspicions. But she was probably only joking.

I could still hear Laura moving about when I became aware that I was not alone. Having filled the dishwasher, I was starting to wash the glasses when I sensed his presence. He was standing just inside the doorway, though, as I said before, there was something weird about the way he was that evening. It was almost like being in a confined space with a Picasso portrait, where the body seems to be occupying several different planes at once or even shifting between them. Though quite what that would be like, I don't really know. In any case, I didn't watch him all the time, as he told me to carry on with what I was doing, which I dutifully did, although it meant mostly having my back to him and then having to look over my shoulder to speak, which was awkward. But even though I didn't get a good long look at him, I had the impression that his face (or should I say his 'aura') changed several times while we were talking; sometimes he seemed young and passionate, sometimes older and calmer, as if oscillating between two very different views on the subject—women—that were, nevertheless, the views of one and the same person.

'I'm sorry to say that I wasn't very impressed by how you defended me,' he remarked, after our opening pleasantries. 'I think I preferred your wife's attack. We authors like our readers to be passionate, even when they disagree with us. It shows that something has happened!'

'Well, yes, I realized I wasn't doing very well. But it's quite difficult when you're the host and I thought Martin and Carl were going to come to blows at a couple of moments.'

'Oh no. Compared with the scandal scenes I witnessed, this was all very polite, very English, if I may say so. You should have spent an evening with Belinsky and his crowd!'

I was rather disappointed to hear that. Clearly, I had a way to go before counting as one of Fyodor Mikhailovich's 'Russian boys'. I was, after all, not a character in one of his novels, only a reader.

'Still, what you said about Aglaya was interesting. People often make the mistake of assuming that the end of a novel is the end of the characters' lives and, of course, they go on developing, like Raskolnikov, like the raw youth, like Alyosha and, yes, very probably Aglaya might return to Russia. She must have something of her mother's deep love of Russianness in her, I suppose. I didn't have plans for her myself, but why not? In fact, all of you said some good things—self-sacrifice, work: these are essential to life. And colours! That was wonderful. People talk about character, plot, dialogue, and all the rest, but imagine a novel without colour!'

'But Laura,' I said, 'she was very harsh on you. I'm sorry about that.'

'No, don't be. As I just said, I relish my more passionate readers. It shows they're paying attention. Remember what we said about dialectics—truth only progresses through *pro et contra*. And what question is more difficult than the woman question (as we called it in my time) or, to put it more accurately, the question as to how men and women are to live together in love, with understanding and respect? Or, even more precisely, the question as to how we are to be human together?'

'Are you saying that you yourself were a kind of feminist?'

I could see him smile and, in fact, he did look rather pleased with himself.

'I think so, but—of course—in my own rather peculiar way. You know, I didn't like the custom of kissing women's hands, a superficial and false kind of chivalry. I preferred a straightforward handshake. Men should always talk to women as equals—though usually the women are their superiors. Some people probably thought that made me a democrat. And it's true, I did believe women should have full civic rights, should enter higher education, should be able to earn their own living, and, of course, choose whom they loved.'

'So if that's how you felt, what about all these beaten, mad, pitiable, and murdered women in your novels? I mean, what Laura said about the only good woman being a dead woman was wrong, but I can see why she said it.'

There was a pause. I'd turned back to the sink, but sensed him coming closer—though when I looked round he didn't seem to have moved.

'Look,' he said, 'you could make a similar list with the men, though I'm not denying that I was particularly preoccupied with violence against women. And that doesn't just mean the moment when a man swings the axe or wields the knife, and it doesn't just mean the beatings and the neglect. For the most part, if I can borrow a phrase from Ivan Karamazov, women, like men, have eaten the apple. They are not children. Few are entirely innocent. They are often complicit in the crimes committed by the men. All the same (and this is as deep a sickness in our Russian society as in the West), the earth continues to cry out against all the wrong done day after day to women, to those who have borne our bodies in theirs and nurtured us at the breast, those to whom we owe our entire respect and love. How was this possible? Why does it continue?'

'But I think that what Laura was saying was that you give so much time to describing this violence (and doing it so well), that your novels actually encourage it, even if that wasn't your intention.'

Again a pause. If his last little speech was something of a passionate outburst, he now shifted to the mode of patient explanation with which I was becoming familiar. At least, that's how it started off until it began to gather pace.

'A novelist isn't a photographer. He's free to make things up. In a sense, everything he writes is made up. We discussed that before. But even if he sees things that the photographer's eye can't see, he has to remain faithful to reality. In fact, when it comes to the cruelties inflicted on women, even though they're as plain as day, "they have eyes and see not, ears and hear not". You didn't need to look behind closed doors to see the prostitution of children in St Petersburg or London. It was there on the streets. But the bourgeois chose to walk by on the other side—except, of course, for those who found their pleasure in such vileness. And they were not few. Everybody knew that the Russian peasant beat his wife, even the saintly Makar in my story thinks he probably should have whipped his young wife into order. We all knew it and yet we treated it as a fact of life, like the sun rising and setting, unless it ended in murder or suicide—but that, everyone thought, was just the order of things. A man merely suspects a woman of unfaithfulness, and that, he thinks, is reason to kill her. The jury will quite probably let him off anyway. What can a novelist do, then, to open people's eyes? Is he to say "peace, peace" where there is no peace? No. Once he has seen how things are, he must bear witness. Of course, he cannot dictate laws, he cannot administer the medicine that society needs, but he can bear witness.'

These last few words were spoken almost in rapture. I'd stopped washing the glasses and was listening intently, though I didn't turn round until he had finished. When I did, I found myself being looked at with an unblinking stare that was both stern and sad, immeasurably sad. For some reason, I felt uncomfortable, as if I too was being accused.

'Knowing what to do is difficult, though…' I muttered rather feebly.

'Knowing what not to do isn't that hard,' he replied. 'Where is it written that we should beat or rape or kill? Where is it written that we should treat with contempt beings who are every bit as good as we are and often better? Just stopping all of that would be a start.'

He paused again.

'Of course,' he continued, relaxing a little, 'being a novelist means you have to expect people to write and say all manner of foolishness about you. I accept that. If one of my characters says that women need a despot to rule over them, there are readers who then say "Dostoevsky thinks women need a despot to rule over them"—even when the character in question is a raw youth who admits that he has no experience of women and doesn't understand them! This, I'm afraid, is what you must expect. There is only one out of all the negative reviews and damning remarks that has ever really hurt me and that I still cannot entirely let go.' He stopped, as if waiting for me to ask him to continue, which of course I did.

'It's the story put out by Strakhov—my friend!—that I myself had committed the crime of Stavrogin, that I'd molested a child—how could he, how could *he*, our friend, say that? It's as if being a witness to a crime makes you a criminal. Your crime? Forcing the people who want to look the other way to see what they're refusing to see. I did it by revealing Svidrigailov's obscene fantasies about children in *Crime and Punishment*, I did it in the story of Nellie—I went as far as I could, though when it came to Stavrogin it was too much for them. I doubt if Svidrigailov's fantasies or the story of Nellie would have been published at all in England in those days, even though people could see the same kind of thing any Saturday night on the streets of London. But what Stavrogin did to poor little Matryona was too much even for Russian readers. Was I wallowing in it, did I relish such things? Not at all! I was repelled—as everyone should be—and for that very reason I refused to keep quiet. Perhaps it was my experience as a prisoner, learning to see life from the other side, the side that everyone else ignored or just forgot about, that made me go to such extremes. But there are some things you can't forget about and can't keep quiet about. Russia had to be made to see what was happening in its midst. Only then could there be justice, healing, change.'

'But how can it be changed? And I mean *be* changed: the same is happening now, perhaps even on a greater scale thanks to the internet—if you know about that?'

'Yes, I've heard something,' he muttered dismissively. Gesturing me to carry on with the washing up, which, reluctantly, I did, he continued, once more slipping into schoolmasterly mode.

* * *

'How can it be changed?' he began, repeating my question. 'Like much else, it goes back to the lie, the first lie, "You shall be as gods." Perhaps it was the woman who took the fruit, but it was the man who thought he could become a god. Of course, he wasn't a god and still isn't, but he goes on believing it. The major in our prison camp used to tell us "I am your tsar and your god" but it's not only the obvious examples like him. Every man appears to think he's some kind of lord. An indelible impression from my childhood was the royal postman beating the driver of the droshky with his fist to make him go faster, while the driver whipped the horse. That's how it goes. One man is knocked down to the bottom of the social pyramid and so he beats his wife. Another, perhaps a very gifted and even a wealthy and powerful man, is not respected as he thinks he should be and so he too beats his wife or finds other more sophisticated ways to degrade her.'

'Like the pawnbroker in *A Gentle Spirit*?'

'Exactly.'

'Or Raskolnikov, wanting to dominate every trembling creature?'

'Like him too. But it doesn't always end in murder. A boy at my school used to boast of how he and a friend would come up behind a young lady in the street and then walk either side of her telling crude stories, naming the unnameable parts of the body and their actions, all just to torment her—until one of them got a well-deserved slap round the face. Who did they think they were? They didn't yet know they wanted to be gods, but they knew they wanted to be masters and they thought that was how to do it—not realizing they were just drowning themselves in filth. Not to mention the men who procured pornographic photographs of women—a phenomenon I was amongst the first to expose. Of course, this is all obvious. What is even more effective is the power that money gives a man. Once he's got money he doesn't need the whip or swearing. Once he has enough in the bank his will is done and everyone is glad to do it—but he knows who's lord.'

'Not every peasant became a wife-beater though?'

'Very few didn't. His wife, his children, and his animals—they were the only creatures over whom he had any power. But it needed a truly great power to break the habit. It needed Christ's power, the only power strong enough to bring about the kind of repentance that made some of them take to the roads and wander as beggars through all of Russia and even as far as Jerusalem. They had to leave their whole world behind because in that world they couldn't do otherwise. Or that's how it seemed to them.'

'And yet not every woman submitted. Aren't there women in your novels who stand up for themselves?'

He seemed amused by my question.

'Of course—though it depends what you mean by stand up for themselves. You see, I'd say Sonia stands up for herself. I don't deny that she was physically degraded by being prostituted, but that doesn't make her a lesser person. No matter what happened to her, she kept her inner integrity. But in the sense that you mean, yes. Think of Grushenka in *The Brothers Karamazov*. She's not a "good" person in a conventional bourgeois sense and, yes, she too is a woman who was seduced and abandoned at a very young age and she too has her romantic fantasies. But look at how I describe her. She's someone with her feet on the ground, a smart businesswoman, very sane and very strong. She sees through her fantasies and puts her past behind her. She's like Russia itself: broad; she can bear much suffering (perhaps more than Dmitri) and, at the same time, she can give herself over to great joy. She's sensual, but she's also sensitive to holiness. When she's about to seduce Alyosha, she hears how his beloved spiritual master has just died and it changes her. That onion again! However,' he checked himself, 'you probably don't want me to run through a list of all the women in my novels. We'd be here till dawn! Let me just say that you'd find as varied a cast as you would with the men. At least. And, like human beings everywhere and at every level of society, men and women are both flawed, imperfect, deceived, deceiving, and self-deceiving in various degrees. If there's a difference it's only that in our society then, as in most societies throughout history, women have been the most insulted and the most injured and, just for that reason, their faults are all the more magnified. As in any society, those who have the power are usually better at concealing their faults and even making those faults seem like virtues. But the truth is that making yourself into your own god isn't just an offence against God, it's an offence against other human beings—even if there will always be some who believe you when you say you're a god and worship you for it. The Stavrogins and Ivans will always find followers.'

'But sometimes it's the women who are adored and idolized and hold sway over the men. Where do they fit in?'

If it's possible for someone in his condition to look shamefaced, I'd say that, at that moment, he did. Ever so slightly, ever so fleetingly. He smiled again, but his lips were pursed.

'That too happens. And, as you probably know, I have nothing to boast about in that respect. I knew only too well what it is like to be under the spell of an overwhelming passion, to lose one's grip on oneself, to forget one's responsibilities to others, to reality—to become terribly, terribly guilty.'

'Apollonaria Suslova?' I asked.

He sighed.

'The shame takes a long time to disappear, even when you know and have experienced that there is forgiveness and even though our time "here" is not your time. It's true that I behaved disgracefully, and the worst of it is not just that I made myself contemptible in my own eyes but that I could run around Europe chasing this young person and abandon Masha, sick and, as I knew, dying. And, yes, Polina was a remarkable person, a brilliant person, but that doesn't make my behaviour any better.'

There was a pause. I couldn't help thinking, painfully, that I understood what he was saying rather better than he might have thought. I had half looked round to speak to him but sensing that he didn't yet want to continue I turned back and started quietly drying the glasses. I felt that he'd come a step or two closer as he resumed talking.

'I think your questions are making it all seem much too simple, as if, on the one side, you have the slaves and on the other the masters or, if you like, mistresses. As I pointed out before, those who set themselves up as gods, the Raskolnikovs and Stavrogins, are not what they think they are. What is seen as their strength is often—mostly—a way of concealing their weakness, from the world and from themselves. Equally, those who seem like slaves may have depths of inner strength that makes them able to endure all things. Like Sonia, like our peasants—don't forget them—like Christ. The last shall be first—though I don't deny, indeed, I was determined to show, that the innocent can be broken and their lives devastated by the cruelty of their tormentors. At least in this world. If you look for justice under the sun, you'll be disappointed. Tragedy is always possible, as we've discussed before.'

'So the relationship between men and women is tragic?'

'It can be, of course. But love is also possible and, as your friend pointed out, genuine love is likely to find some way of working together for the universal good. Like so many of those wonderful young people who went out to the remotest corners of Russia to help bring education and health to the people. It is possible for human beings to bring out the best in each other, you know,' he ended, gently and almost consolingly.

'I think I do know that,' I said, 'even if I don't always live up to what it demands.'

'None of us does,' he replied. 'Love is much harder than atheism, whatever that opinionated French existentialist thought.'

I guess he meant Sartre, who said something about how atheism was a hard road and he'd followed it to the end.

We seemed to have reached a point of understanding. But I had one more question.

'What am I going to say to Laura, then?'

'Your wife? About how I describe women in my novels?'

I nodded.

'Why do you have to say anything?'

'Well, she's wrong, isn't she? I mean, she insists on seeing only the negative side of it and makes you out to be some kind of misogynist, which I don't think you are. In fact, I'm sure you're not. How can I persuade her otherwise?'

He shook his head.

'What happens between me and my readers,' he said, 'is between me and my readers. Let me say again, there is nothing wrong in disagreeing and even disagreeing passionately. You don't need to be quite so English. *Pro et contra*, remember?'

'Yes, but it's not just that we disagree—I think she's wrong.'

He laughed.

'Isn't that what disagreement is?'

'But she's not seeing the other side—like you've just explained to me.'

'Listen,' he said, 'if it's your wife you're concerned about, you need to finish the washing up and get yourself to bed. As far as I'm concerned, if my characters have got under her skin, then she won't be rid of them till they've had their say. The novels speak for themselves or they don't speak at all. I can't give you a set of footnotes to explain what's really going on. That's a different kind of exercise and, in any case, it can only ever help you find your way to the novel: it can't tell you what's going on in it. No. Leave her be. Disagree. See where it ends. Now, you need to finish off your chores, don't you?'

What could I say? Even though it no longer seemed quite so astonishing to be visited by Dostoevsky, I couldn't say I was used to it and, obviously, I wanted to get the most out of every meeting. And quite apart from what he thought about women, we hadn't really finished talking about Christ. But, of course, what he said about his novels speaking for themselves was right—and I was very tired. It was getting on for half past one.

'I suppose you're right,' I said. 'I'm nearly finished, anyway.'

'Good, then I'll just slip away. But don't worry. I know there are unresolved questions. We will talk again. Until we meet.'

'Yes...thank you...' But even as I mumbled a few farewell words, he had gone, turning as if to go out of the door, as he did last time, but it didn't seem to me that he went out. It was more like he'd just disappeared through the door into another dimension. Which I suppose he had. I was left with a wine glass in one hand and a tea towel in the other, feeling faintly silly. I put the glass down and rested my hands on the edge of the work surface before shaking my head and, as he'd suggested, finishing off the few remaining glasses.

When I got to bed, Laura seemed to be asleep but, as I got in, she half-turned.

'You're late. Talking to Dostoevsky again?'

Was she joking? Just what did she know?

'Of course,' I replied, 'who else?'

Fourth Conversation

Christmas Cards

A Madonna

Christmas came and went. After everything that had been happening, I thought that I should probably go to church, which I did, to midnight Mass. James surprised me by saying that he would like to come too, but at the last minute he went off to the pub with his friends. Laura stayed at home, saying she needed some quiet and that it was a good opportunity to call her brother in America.

Church wasn't a great success. As I arrived, I was given a small pile of leaflets and books and although the priest kept telling us what page to turn to it seemed that there'd been a problem with the printing and one chunk of the service was missing entirely while another had been duplicated. It wasn't how I imagined the deep solemnity of the Orthodox ritual that Dostoevsky would have known. But I shouldn't quibble. It was well meant. The sermon was about the shepherds and how it was the poor who first heard the gospel, which I guessed Fyodor Mikhailovich would have liked. And there was something rather moving, quite profound even, about this very mixed congregation shuffling out of their seats and standing in line, heads bowed, waiting to receive communion. I didn't go up myself. You might think that having now been visited (three times) by someone—a spirit?—from the other world (or, as he put it, 'the great synthesis'), I would be ready to make this act of faith. But the fact is that I was very unsure as to what these conversations really meant. And although I was prepared, if pushed, to own up to some kind of mid-life crisis, there were moments when I wondered whether these visits weren't a sign of some more radical mental breakdown. I mean, it's not normal, is it? But even if Dostoevsky's visits were real, they hadn't yet answered the questions about God or some ultimate meaning in life with which we started. Maybe that 'great synthesis' that Dostoevsky talked about was just more of the same, literally ad infinitum. He'd talked about still learning, even 'there'. And sometimes still wanting a cigarette. But was that something worth hoping for?

New Year too had come and gone. We'd stayed home, but you can't entirely escape the sound of a Glasgow Hogmanay. Now the holiday was coming to an end, too soon—as always. The Christmas decorations were looking a bit tired and it was probably time to be taking them down. Laura was out for drinks with members of her team and I wasn't expecting her back till late. I still had a paper to finish writing for a conference that was happening later in the month plus a short review to write (deadline yesterday). There were times when I might have worked on these in the evening, but, quite frankly, I just didn't feel like it. I could take a night off. Thinking about nothing. Or nothing much. I *hadn't* been thinking about Dostoevsky. The nearest thing to a prompt was a piece about Russian policy in the Middle East in the early evening news. Once again, it seemed, Russia had become our official enemy. So much for the end of history. After the news I channel-hopped, checked my streaming channels, and skimmed our DVDs, but nothing appealed. Maybe I should just listen to some music. These days, I rarely had the mental space to listen to anything serious in a sustained way unless we actually went out to a concert. But what? Bach? Shostakovich? Pärt? Jazz? Jazz, maybe.

With such deep questions on my mind I went through to the kitchen to get a beer. When I came back, *he* was there.

He was standing in front of the mantelpiece, hands clasped behind his back, bending forward and shaking his head appreciatively. The cause of his enthusiasm seemed to be one of the Christmas cards, but I couldn't immediately see which one.

Without turning towards me and almost as if speaking to himself, he said, very quietly, 'I like this card. It's good to see it here.'

'Er…yes…which one?' I replied lamely.

He took the card and opened it.

'It says "From Fran and Jack. Maybe next year! Lots of love." Old friends?'

'Er…yes…' (I wasn't doing very well.) 'Laura's friends really…though I know them too, of course. But what's the picture?'

He handed it to me. Rather clumsily, I put down my bottle and took a closer look. It was one of those Italian Renaissance Madonna-and-Childs that come in endless variations on the sort of Christmas cards sold by big national charities. I have to admit I never look at them all that closely. A bit bland for my taste. I still didn't see anything special about it.

'Raphael. "Madonna della Seggiola",' I read out from the back of the card.

'Yes,' he said. 'Do you like it?'

I had to be honest.

'Er…not especially. I mean, I can see that it's very well done, but, honestly, I'd say that it was probably just an excuse for painting a pretty young mother and child. I certainly don't see anything particularly religious about it, even if she does have a halo.'

'Now, let me get this clear. You're not sure if you believe in God, you haven't really read the Bible since childhood, but you like your Christmas cards to be religious?'

'Point taken. But I did go to church at Christmas. Midnight Mass—even if I didn't take communion. Sometimes I do, if I'm moved.' (It must have been at least half a dozen years since I had.) 'Just occasionally you get that sense of wonder you had as a child. It's a world away from what they now call "the holiday season". I mean, just look at these cards.' I gestured towards the array of winter landscapes, Christmas trees, blazing log fires, choirboys, tables laden with rich foods, and just a few nativity scenes that Laura had grouped together on the mantelpiece. A couple of cards even had images of the senders with their smiling children rather than the traditional 'holy family'—welcome to the age of the selfie!

Fyodor Mikhailovich nodded sympathetically. 'Of course, your Christmas is nearly over—and ours only begins tomorrow. But coming back to this picture: you don't think it's religious—just a pretty mother and child, as you put it?'

'Well, I can see that it's meant to be Mary and Jesus with John the Baptist, but there's nothing to tell you that the baby has come to save the world. He's just a rather big baby. Or maybe even a toddler. As I say, it's hard to see anything more than a nice young mother and child. Not that there's anything wrong with that. It's a beautiful thing to see. An archetypal human image, you could say. But it doesn't speak to me of God.'

'But I don't imagine you want an old man in the sky either?'

'No, of course not.'

'Your God can't be an old man or a young woman, then. He (if you still want him to be a "he") has to be outside the world altogether, quite out of sight—in another world, perhaps?'

Fyodor Mikhailovich had been sounding almost jokey, but there was a serious undertone and, not for the first time, I had the uncomfortable feeling that he could read my thoughts.

I realized that his question was not intended to catch me out, but I felt like I was caught in a double bind. The problem—my problem—was precisely that I couldn't see any place for God in a world like ours. It wasn't that I was some kind of misanthrope or fancied myself as a latter-day Schopenhauer. I could see that there was a lot of good in the world, but it wasn't at all evident to me that the goodness was stronger than... well, to use a word I don't really like using very much: evil. I couldn't see any law of love directing the course of things and, that being so, there was very little to protect us—to protect *me*—from the kind of bleak vision with which Dostoevsky had concluded his story *A Gentle Spirit*. That, you'll remember, was where this all started, and a bleak vision it was—a world without meaning or love, motionless beneath a dead sun. And yet, and yet, and yet! Didn't there have to be something more? But what? Old-fashioned religiosity with all its talk of miracles and prophecies just seemed naïve, and even if someone could prove that there must be some kind of creator, that wasn't really enough. I could imagine a beautiful divine mind creating a perfect mathematical universe that would be intellectually satisfying for those who could do the equations, but why would such a God care about human beings and their suffering? Probably even bacteria or viruses have a mathematical beauty—but that doesn't mean anything to those they kill. And that, I suppose, is why I still had a lingering affection for the Christmas story of a God who could appear on earth in human form, 'born as one of us' as a hymn we used to sing at school had it; a God you could see and touch but who was still, in some sense, 'God'. Not that I believed this—but I liked the idea. All the same, this picture was just too ordinary. Why had he singled it out? Why not the Fra Angelico *Annunciation* that was next to it and which, to my mind, was much more 'spiritual' (whatever that means)?

I looked again. The painting was in roundel form. The Madonna was shown sitting in a chair, with a green embroidered shawl draped over her shoulders and a loose striped turban round her head. I remembered the detail of the green shawl in *Crime and Punishment* and wondered whether that was why Fyodor Mikhailovich liked it so much. She had the kind of soft regular features you see in a lot of Renaissance paintings and can still see today in Italy. It wasn't the camera-conscious face of the smartphone generation. Like the faces you see in early photographs, it was a face that wasn't used to being looked at, a reticent face that didn't give everything away at first glance. The woman's large observant eyes gazed steadily back at me as if to say, 'You may look, but keep your distance; no one comes near my baby unless I want them to.' The baby itself (as I said) looked more like a two-year-old than a newborn infant and did in fact appear rather apprehensive, as if seeking assurance from his mother as to whether I was to be trusted. An infant John the Baptist was leaning against the mother's knee, looking up at what legend supposed to be his cousin. The whole thing was beautifully balanced, very tender, winsome, you could say, but was it anything more? Was this God's mother and her divine child?

* * *

Fyodor Mikhailovich was watching me closely and, after a full half a minute, remarked that the picture had been very important to him when he was living in Florence. 'Indeed,' he went on, 'I spent many hours in front of it. It needs a lot of time to take in and, fortunately, Anna Grigorievna and I were living only a few minutes from where it was on show.'

'Where was that?'

'The Pitti Palace,' Fyodor Mikhailovich replied.

I'd been to the Pitti Palace myself but couldn't remember seeing this particular painting amongst the many hundreds of religious paintings that covered its walls, mostly in the mannerist style that I don't like much. I didn't mention this, however. And something else was puzzling me.

'But, Fyodor Mikhailovich,' I began, 'I'd have thought this was just the sort of religious art you wouldn't like—isn't it too Western, too humanistic, and, dare I say, too Catholic?' (I was hesitant about bringing Catholicism into it as I knew he'd been strongly, even violently, anti-Catholic in his lifetime.)

'That's all true,' he said, smiling thoughtfully and nodding. 'It is very Western, very humanist, very Catholic—but why should that mean I can't like it? Remember when we talked about Dickens? Dickens was very Western, very humanist, and very Protestant—and, as you can imagine, I didn't have a very high opinion of Protestantism either. But if I can enjoy Dickens and even borrow a little from him in my own writing, why not Raphael? Didn't I even say that I thought Raphael and Shakespeare were worth more than the entire output of the modern industrial world—even if I did put the words in the mouth of that feeble and inveterate liar Stepan Trofimovich Verkhovensky?'

'Yes, of course I remember what we were saying about Dickens. But isn't there a difference? Dickens wrote about human situations, even if he is sometimes a bit pious. But this is meant to be a religious picture, a picture of the Saviour, and yet it turns the mystery of salvation into something all too human. In fact, I'd see it as a prime example of art serving a secular agenda, art for Renaissance popes in all their worldly splendour—a long way from the stable at Bethlehem.'

Fyodor Mikhailovich sighed, rather like a parent who's been asked to read a story for the hundredth time.

'May I...?' he asked, indicating that he'd quite like to sit.

'Of course, of course.'

I followed his example, and so we were back, face to face, in the same seats as on that first night. The next thing he said really surprised me, perhaps more than just about anything else he'd said up to this point in our meetings. Yet it was really the most ordinary remark in the world—which is why, in the circumstances, it was so astonishing.

'That beer looks good—please, carry on. In fact, I wouldn't mind a glass myself!'

On the evening of his first visit he'd declined a drink and I'd assumed that whatever kind of body he now possessed couldn't deal with actual food or drink, that it was, perhaps, only a 'body' for my benefit, a kind of appearance and he'd definitely seemed less than substantial on his last visit. But perhaps that was wrong. After all, he'd just taken a Christmas card off the mantelpiece. Pure spirits don't do that kind of thing. I jumped up and quickly got him a glass and poured his drink. He held it to the light and smiled appreciatively.

'That looks very good,' he said, taking a sip and putting the glass down. He settled himself into the chair, pressed his hands down on his thighs and launched into a short speech.

'You see,' he began, 'people have always misunderstood me on this subject. As I thought about it then (and I don't think I was entirely wrong: just look at what a good Catholic like Dante had to say about the Church of his time)...as I thought about it then, yes, the pope had turned the seat of Peter into an earthly throne and was even prepared to use the sword against his enemies, fighting for territory like any earthly monarch. And the Jesuits...the Inquisition...I didn't make those things up. But I never thought that every Catholic was wicked. I saw for myself the same kindness and the same faith amongst the common people in Italy that I'd seen in our own peasants. I've never believed that any Church, any institution, can entirely obscure Christ's call to love. As I just said, I never had any great esteem for Protestantism, but I admired those pious Protestant doctors who worked amongst the poor in Russia, living on next to nothing and taking nothing except what the peasants could freely afford—I think anyone would say that was true Christianity, wouldn't they?'

'You mean like that old doctor who gave a bag of nuts to Dmitri Karamazov when he was a little boy?'

'Exactly. Dr Herzenstube I called him, because his faith was from the heart and he could find happiness in a small act of kindness to a young lad who'd been abandoned by his father—and who can ever calculate what goodness comes from such small acts?' He paused and, picking the card up from the table where I'd put it down, looked at it thoughtfully.

'Yes—yes, she is very human. A beautiful young mother and child. There is nothing more human—and there is nothing closer to the mystery of Christ.'

Can spirits be emotional? Even if this too was a performance for my benefit, his voice seemed almost to tremble.

'You know we went to Florence soon after we lost our dear little Sonia; I suppose that this picture had a special meaning at such a time—if only I could have seen my Anna like that, nestling our beloved child on her knee.' He paused and sighed. 'As I would see her the next year with Liuba. This is life's most beautiful moment, don't you think? Perhaps the smile a mother gives to her child contains the whole secret of faith.'

When Fyodor Mikhailovich spoke of Sonia, he seemed suddenly to become strangely insubstantial, as if he was almost about to fade away, but then, at the mention of the mother's smile, it was as if the blood rushed back into his face. Only, of course, it didn't and couldn't (I suppose), as he didn't have any blood. All the same, I wasn't sure that I agreed. If that was all there was to faith, then maybe all my questions were much ado about nothing. But I nodded, anyway, not saying anything.

The silence was intense. My parents would have said it was an angel flying overhead.

'I may add,' he continued, almost defiantly, 'that I even asked a Catholic priest to say Mass for Sonia when we were in Florence. We are all human beings, after all.' He grimaced. 'I could see that he was very kind, but, of course, he had to refuse. We didn't have anything like an ecumenical movement then.' Waving towards the other cards, he continued, 'But these pictures, where you see the little mother dressed like a queen, adored by processions of kings in velvets, satins, and pearls, with their chests of gold, jewels, and spices, accompanied by their magnificent retinues—what did the gospels say about all that? Forget the gold, the jewels, the velvets, the satins—even the camels (though, as I said before, they might be just what's needed to stir the imagination of a child). That's what Raphael did. He left the gold and showed us a human beauty, the kind of beauty you could probably see in any town or village. Indeed, they say his model was just an ordinary village girl he saw one day and realized that she was exactly the "Madonna" he was looking for.'

I have to admit, to my shame, that, as Fyodor Mikhailovich was speaking, I remembered something I'd read about Raphael's amorous liaisons with his models and wondered whether this young woman too had been the object of his extra-curricular attentions. Not very Madonna-like, if so.

'I have to admit that I've never even really looked at the painting very closely.'

'That much I guessed,' he smiled, sympathetically. 'You see, what Raphael understood was that if you want to find God don't try to look outside the world. That pretty girl, as you called her, was well known for her kindness to the beggar folk and, long before Raphael spotted her, one of those she'd helped prophesied that she'd be remembered for all time as the Queen of Heaven. Which didn't make much sense to her at the time, but—there you see her. That's maybe just a story, but what it's saying is true: that it's in the world, amongst the peasants, the poor folk, the beggars, the sick, the outcast, and those who care for them out of simple kindness—that's where you have to start looking. Christ didn't take an earthly throne, but, as it says in one of our legends, he wandered through the Russian land in the guise of a peasant...'

I thought again of the Christmas sermon I'd heard about the shepherds.

'Yes,' I interrupted, 'there are legends like that in England too: "And did those feet, in ancient times, walk upon England's pleasant mountains green?"'

Immediately I regretted jumping in again, but Fyodor Mikhailovich didn't seem to mind. He just nodded away, looking thoughtful.

'Yes, yes, yes...perhaps in every country. Remember the onion! You have to look in the right places and not be surprised if the Mother of God looks just like a pretty Italian peasant girl. That's much more likely than her looking like some pale lady in waiting. Humility. No great choruses of angels, no fireworks or spectacles, just the most basic human reality—that's where we have to start. Birth. In fact, it's also where we have to finish. Death.'

Humility

Birth and death. The parameters of human existence. Binding us to the earth, irrespective of our wants and wishes. Fyodor Mikhailovich was right: if you held onto that, you'd probably have no difficulty in practising humility. But humility was a bit of a problem.

'Humility,' I said, 'that isn't a very fashionable virtue. In fact, you could say that most people today actually regard it as a failing. Those of us who work in universities today are actively encouraged, you could even say compelled, to be the opposite of humble. It's no longer enough to teach and keep up with developments in your field, you have to keep telling the world how world-beating and world-changing your teaching and research are. It's not good enough to be good enough—it has to be better than anything else that's going on, which it obviously isn't because everybody else is having to say the same about their work.' I saw him looking at me rather quizzically. 'No, really, I'm not exaggerating. And it's not just universities, it's the same in business, sport, politics...everywhere. I suppose politics always has been about ambition and self-promotion, but these days it often looks more like a celebrity gameshow.' I was getting a bit carried away and realized that he might not have a clue as to what I was talking about—especially the celebrity gameshow part.

'Sorry,' I broke off, 'that was probably all a bit irrelevant. I don't suppose you want to waste your time here listening to me complaining about my work!'

'Not at all, not all,' he replied, polite as ever. 'But, I assure you, it was much the same in my time, even if we didn't have "celebrity gameshows", whatever they are. And, of course, I have to admit that there was a lot of self-promotion and vanity in the world of literature—and I can't claim that I was immune. When you're desperate for recognition, even a little success can make you lose your head, like I did after *Poor Folk*. Later, much later, at the end of my life, I suppose I really did become what you might call a celebrity.' He shook his head and smiled wryly. He took another small sip of beer. 'But that's as may be. What is certainly true is that humility is and always has been the basis of any truly Christian life—just look at the teaching of any of the Church Fathers or the lives of any of the saints. Some people have thought my portrait of Zosima was exaggerated, but it wasn't at all. There are many Zosimas amongst the saints and I myself encountered that kind of humility many times—and not only amongst the Elders and monks. Of course, there have always been Church leaders and spiritual teachers who like to dress in fine robes and find pleasure in honorific titles; Princes of the Church, as they say. You can hear them talking down to their flock as if they were God himself on His heavenly throne when, really, they're no better than lackeys—have you noticed how they like you to know how familiar they are with the great men of this world, all the princes, generals, and millionaires they know or claim to know? But none of the true teachers of the Church has ever been like that. The true Elder makes no distinction between great and small. All he ever sees before him is a child of God, a suffering being crying out for fulness of life—in other words, someone who is no different from himself. What, then, can he do for them if he is in the same predicament, you might ask? What can he do? He can pray with them, pray for them, and ask them to pray for him. Perhaps the only difference, if difference there is, is that he believes God hears, though he doesn't know any more than they know what God will do. But the prayers themselves have already sown a little seed of love.'

'I see all that,' I said, 'and your Zosima is a beautiful model of humility. But could he have existed anywhere outside Russia before the Revolution?' (And, I wanted to add, in the pages of a novel.) 'The fact is that, today, most charismatic religious leaders seem to end up being like those Princes of the Church you described. And even if a Zosima-like saint were to appear in our time, how would that work out in everyday life? I mean, we're not likely to start going around prostrating to each other, like he did to Dmitri. That sort of thing doesn't mean anything in our society. It just doesn't happen. People would say it was religious mania—and even in your novel many of those who encountered him saw pride rather than holiness.'

'Yes, yes, yes—of course, you're correct, entirely correct. But remember, Zosima himself insisted that his disciple Alyosha was going to have to leave the monastery and live in the world. He knew that we can't just copy how things were in the past. Even spiritual life has to evolve, which is where I disagreed with the Slavophiles when they insisted on looking back to the Middle Ages. Everyone has to find their own path. In every generation. This beer is good by the way, I like it. It reminds me of a beer I had in Copenhagen...'

'Well, it is a Danish beer,' I said, amazed at how easily one slipped into small talk, even with a dead writer. 'In Copenhagen they say it's probably the best lager in town,' I couldn't help adding.

'Maybe the very same, then,' he said, nodding thoughtfully. Then, standing up, he stretched himself. Was he about to go?

'Now...I think I'd be more comfortable standing. Do you mind?'

'Of course not.' I made to stand too, but he waved me back.

'No, no, do carry on sitting, I just need to move about a little.'

He took a couple of steps, turned, and bending forward looked at me full on, leaning his hands against the edge of the sofa that stood at a right angle to our chairs.

'You see, humility doesn't come from the head but from the heart. It's not an idea that you have to put into practice: it's a whole way of life. Think of the Frenchman's *liberté*, *égalité*, and *fraternité*. Leaving *liberté* and *égalité* to one side (though we may come back to them), it always seemed to me that their vaunted *fraternité* was for the most part an empty word. Do you really think the rich bourgeois sipping his Château Lafitte actually feels any *fraternité* with the street cleaner out there in the rain and snow or with the old woman in the poorhouse—let alone with his African "brother"? Of course, you'll say that it's different now, that is, in your time. Now you have democracy. Everybody is on first name terms, everyone's as good as anyone else. Well, I don't—I can't—follow every detail of how the world has changed since my lifetime, but it seems to me that those who are rich in this world's goods are no more fraternal in their dealings with the underpaid, the unemployed, the homeless, the blacks, and all the rest who can't afford Château Lafitte and cigars than they were in my lifetime.'

'You don't have to persuade me,' I replied. 'I'm sure you're right. Even in this country, this wealthy country, they're talking about the new slavery and the poor are having to use food banks, which certainly don't stock Château Lafitte! But "what is to be done?" Socialism? That wasn't a good word in your vocabulary, was it?'

Fyodor Mikhailovich looked sharply at me and grunted something that came out like a 'Huh'.

'What is to be done? Very good,' he said, obviously recognizing my reference to the novel by Chernyshevsky that envisaged a utopian egalitarian future. I wondered if he knew that Lenin had used the same title. He nodded thoughtfully and then, stepping over to the bookcase, tapped the spine of a well-worn and rather thick paperback. I recognized it straight away as Marx's *Capital* (though I should admit that its being well-worn was more down to the fact that it was a second-hand copy rather than intensive study on my part).

'Socialism,' he said solemnly. 'No, that's not a bad word. Bad things have been done in its name, of course. As I just said, I don't follow what's been happening in your world in any detail, but I know what my country, my Russia, suffered for seventy years. Alas, that was how it had to be because the socialists had forgotten or denied that before you can have socialism you have to have brotherhood and brotherhood is not an ideal: it's an immediate conviction of the heart. You don't have to worry about whether your brother really is your brother or not, he just is your brother. And you don't first have to persuade yourself that every other human being is your brother or sister before you start treating them that way. You just have to see that that's how it is and that you owe everyone everything you owe to a brother. It's who we are. The moment you start asking yourself "Am I my brother's keeper?" you've already forgotten what the words mean. Instead of "I'm just as good as the next man", which was what people were saying in my time and which, to my mind is, what the French *égalité* mostly comes down to, it should be "every man is as good as me".'

He breathed deeply and smiled what seemed to me to be a rather melancholy smile.

'And this,' he continued, 'is what our coarse uneducated peasants knew by instinct, even the convicts, and it's what we educated men and city-dwellers forgot, corrupted as we were by…' he paused again and tapped the spine of *Capital* again. Rather meaningfully.

'Capitalism,' I suggested.

'Capitalism. Money. The most universal and insidious form of the lie, especially the lie that money can make you free. That's what the convicts in the camp believed, and every time it let them down. If they got money, they spent it on vodka and then—extra punishment followed as sure as night follows day. Money doesn't make you free, it just binds you even more surely to a world of lies and then it's no wonder if you find yourself having to shout louder than the others and make all sorts of ridiculous claims about your work if you want to sell your wares. That's the market and, to put it frankly, capitalism and humility are quite simply incompatible.'

'So socialism without fraternity isn't socialism and Christianity without humility isn't Christianity. But if humility is incompatible with capitalism, that also implies that capitalism and Christianity are incompatible, doesn't it?'

He raised his eyebrows and pressed his lips together but said nothing.

'And yet,' I continued, talking to myself as much as to him, 'many of our politicians today still spout the rational egoism you already denounced so long ago, always telling us that economic self-interest is the real motive power of social change and improvement. They say that society improves by calculating what makes each of us individually better off. It's all economics. By the way, do you know that it's now well known that public policy is decided by the application of algorithms—just like you predicted in *Notes from Underground*?'

'I'm delighted you noticed—I actually said logarithms, but it's close enough. And, indeed, brothers don't need logarithms or algorithms to tell them that they belong together.'

'And where does this leave Christmas,' I wondered aloud. 'Where's the humility, where's the Christianity, in a month-long fest of capitalist values?'

Man-God and God-Man

Fyodor Mikhailovich didn't answer my last question, but ran his finger slowly along the shelf, as if checking the titles, stopping at a book that was rather popular at that time, *Homo Deus*. Picking it out, he scrutinized the back cover, emitting a kind of 'Hrrumph'. Returning it to its place, he began pacing slowly up and down, several times pausing rather jerkily, as if to try to catch a wayward thought.

'Homo Deus. They still believe that, do they? Well, they can't say I didn't warn them! Oh yes, it would be wonderful if we were indeed brothers, if we had true solidarity—then perhaps we could become as gods and do so in the way that God wants for us. But that's not how the world is, is it? There are always some people who imagine that they're closer to being gods than the rest or even that they already are gods or, at least, demi-gods. As for the others, they don't know what's best for them, and so it happens as it has to happen. Either the superior ones have to leave them behind or else they try to drag them along. So far so good. The problem is that because the inferior ones don't know what's best for them (or so the superior ones think) they will either have to be compelled or lied to. Usually, there's bloodshed. It's not a new story, of course, but the funny thing is that every generation since the tower of Babel thinks it's new.'

'But don't you think it really is different now? Even compared to your time, science can do things that seemed impossible. We've gone into space, we've split the atom, we've even discovered the basic structures of life. There are so many new powers at our fingertips that perhaps we will at least be able to become supermen, if not gods. All things really are possible now.'

Fyodor Mikhailovich looked at me with some surprise. Very probably, he hadn't expected me to be quite such a scientific utopian. I'm not—but it really does seem that science is in the process of changing everything in a way that no one in the nineteenth century could have anticipated: not just helping us to do more, go faster, and live longer, but even changing our biology. Anyway, I wanted to hear what he had to say.

Turning his back, Fyodor Mikhailovich lifted the curtain aside and peered out of the window into the city night. After about a minute he let it drop back into place, and resumed his speech, only gradually turning to face me.

'If you really believe that,' he began, 'I won't be able to persuade you otherwise. And, please, don't think that I was ever against science. I was, after all, an engineer. As to all the new powers science may have to offer, everything depends on how we—or you—want to use them. You've maybe never heard of Nikolai Fedorov's idea that science would one day be able to raise the ancestors from the dead. Of course, it was a crazy idea, but it seemed to me that there was real humanity in it, the feeling that history's victims and the ancestors to whom we owe so much should not be left behind. Whatever progress is, it's only human progress if it embraces all. All. Just wanting to conquer new planets in the same way that you conquered America, Africa, India, and the Pacific islands or extending your lifespan until you rival the patriarchs, excluding new generations from coming forth and living their lives of passion and joy—that's not progress, it's just refining a machine, and a rather lethal machine, if I may say so, even if the people operating it don't look like evil dictators but—but how can I put it—like "cool guys". Is that what you say now? In any case, it's the machine that gives you bread today and war tomorrow. It's power for power's sake, not for the sake of living, not for the sake of life. And that's before we even begin to look at how human beings have been dealing with the living world around them, the forests, the rivers, the oceans, the teeming creatures given to be our companions in life. You race into the future and all the while the creatures around you are dying. Just think of the birdsong...how could we ever be happy without that wonderful music to accompany us through our lives?'

Stopping, he tapped the spine of *Homo Deus* a couple of times, before turning to address me again.

'Well then. Let's go back to your question: what is Christmas?' Not waiting for my answer, he continued: 'It's certainly not about Homo Deus, the Man-God, but the God-Man, the one who was equal to God but emptied Himself and appeared in the form of a servant, ready to give up all that divine knowledge, all that divine power, and all that divine glory so as to be with the sufferers in their suffering, to humble Himself and be obedient unto death, "even death on the cross". I think we touched on that before. But I ask you: has the world ever seen such an extraordinary act of renunciation? If you really want to be as gods, that's the kind of god you have to be—the self-renouncing god, suffering and dying with all the wretched of the earth. Not a god born in a palace but a god born in a cave.'

I suppose that this referred to the Orthodox Church's icon of the Nativity that shows Mary and her infant in a cave rather than the thatched annex typical of

Western art. I didn't really know much about icons, but a couple of the cards we'd received that year had used this particular image. A curious idea, though.

In any case, as I've said, I had gone to church at Christmas. This year, I'd been prompted by Fyodor Mikhailovich's visits, but there was something that touched me in this story of an infinite, almighty, all-knowing God coming down (so to say) and giving all that God-ness up so as to become the most helpless thing in the world, a newborn baby. With or without the cave. Whether or not it was true. Whatever truth meant in a case like this. But over and above the question of truth, there was also the 'obedient unto death on the cross' part, which I'd always baulked at.

'I understand that, Fyodor Mikhailovich...' I began, but was immediately interrupted.

'You understand it! Congratulations! I wish I did! I don't understand it, but I rejoice in it!'

He was right, of course. I didn't 'understand' it, if you want to be strict about the meaning of 'understand'.

'I stand corrected. What can I say? I'm moved by it, it speaks to me the way a poem speaks to me. Or something like that.'

He nodded. Placated. I continued.

'You see, it's not Christmas that bothers me. It's Good Friday. Why does he have to be obedient unto death, why the death on the cross? A few years ago, a friend of mine got very involved in the Alpha Course and even persuaded me to go along with him a couple of times and...'

Fyodor Mikhailovich looked puzzled.

'Sorry. It was a kind of evangelical course aimed at converting middle-class people like me' (that was probably a bit harsh, but it's how I'd come to think of it). 'It was OK at first, I mean, everyone was very friendly and it was all more approachable than the kind of evangelical preaching that I'd heard as a teenager. But when it came to the crunch, they had the same complicated and frankly unbelievable theory about how Jesus had to die on the cross. They tried to say that God had been so offended by human sin and the devil had to be paid some kind of ransom to let us go that Jesus had to die so as to placate God and pay off the devil. I mean, I'm probably not putting it quite correctly, but it was along those lines. A weird God, too much sin, too much devil, and too much suffering. It just didn't make sense. It almost made me want to be a Muslim: "Allah says" and it's done and that's it. And if God is Almighty—why not? It's a lot simpler, anyway.'

Apart from a gruff 'Hmmm', Fyodor Mikhailovich seemed almost to ignore this tirade, confession, call it what you will. Once more he looked out of the window, perhaps for even longer than before. When he did speak, there was a tenderness in his voice but, at the same time, a kind of rigour, you could almost say severity, that I hadn't noticed before.

'Yes, yes, yes. I agree. That is, I agree about placating God and paying the devil a ransom. These are the kinds of theories that some of the clergy like to invent so as to keep the flock in their place. But God doesn't need to be placated. God is love. And the devil has no power over human souls that cannot be broken by love. Do you remember how Zosima defined hell?'

'The inability to love.' (This was one line from *The Brothers Karamazov* that had remained with me since the first time I read it.)

'Exactly! The moment we begin to love—even when your love is no bigger than an onion—in that same moment the devil has lost all his power over you. But' (he began to sound almost schoolmasterly) 'I can't entirely agree with you about suffering. Of course, He has to suffer: not because He had to placate God or pay off the devil but because the people He came to, the people He accepted and loved as his brothers (and, of course, sisters) were sufferers. Even the ones who thought they were superior, the supermen who wanted to lead humanity into a new era, even they, behind all their big words, were sufferers, afraid to love life as it was and trying to hide their fears by dreaming up imaginary utopias. No: the cross certainly involved suffering—but it was suffering for love's sake. Even on the cross He was love. Remember what He said: "Father, forgive them" for those who crucified Him, and, to the thief who hung there with Him: "Tonight you will be with me in paradise." And if the other thief had just for a moment stopped shouting and swearing maybe he too would have joined them in paradise.'

'You mean that all that stuff about paying the price of sin is just superfluous to requirements?'

'You could put it like that, I suppose. Yes.'

'And the cross isn't there to make us feel like guilty sinners but simply a sign of God's love?'

'In a way, yes—but...' He shook his head solemnly.

'But?'

'But: the point is simply that if you truly love Christ, then seeing him nailed to the cross will teach you what it means to be guilty. It's been said that grief is the price we pay for love, but so too is guilt—it's the debt we owe to all the victims of all the world's injustice. And that's what the cross makes us see.'

'OK. But that's an odd way of putting it. I mean, much as I disagree with the evangelicals, at least they see the cross as getting rid of guilt and not making it worse! And, I have to be honest, I still can't get round seeing guilt as a positive. Like the therapists say, it's a large part of what stops us loving as effectively as we might. Guilt and love just aren't on the same page.'

'I don't suppose you want me to repeat everything I said before,' he replied, and I couldn't help wondering if there wasn't a slight note of irritation in his voice. I shook my head, though I wasn't sure if he was really looking for a response. 'Good! All I'll say, then, is that of course there may be cases where people have the most fantastic and mistaken views about being guilty for all manner of things,

call it. Unearned emotional gratification. But writers can't tell you anything about the next life and they shouldn't try to make us forget that for many, many, far too many people life means suffering without end. What the writers can and should do is to show another possibility, to show that there's more to life than the sum of facts about the world. There are also dreams and—who knows?—maybe dreams really can connect us to other worlds? But the writer can't say that is so. He can only suggest, only sow a seed of hope—and then it's up to you, the reader, to do with it as you will.'

'It still sounds tragic to me.'

'Really? But don't you remember what He said of the hungry, the naked, and the prisoners: "in as much as you do it to the least of these, you do it to me". This means that it's not the lovely well-fed children dancing round the Christmas tree who are the image of Christ, angelic as they are, but the children abandoned by the world, they and their "sinful mothers". If you want to see Christ in the world, that's where you have to look. On the streets—and behind the woodpile.'

Christ

We seemed to be back to what we'd been talking about during Fyodor Mikhailovich's second Glasgow visit. Let's say I believed that Jesus of Nazareth was a beautiful human individual who taught and practised peace and love, I was still left with the question as to how this was going to save people who were living in the kind of desperate situations that Dostoevsky himself had so painstakingly laid bare in his writings and that seemed to be repeated again and again in every generation.

'Fyodor Mikhailovich,' I began, 'that's powerful stuff, but if Christ himself is just another sufferer, then how can he help us? You're making it sound more like he's the one who needs us to help him—just to stay alive. He's become too weak, which, as we were talking about before, is what some people see as the problem with your own Christ figures—and, yes, I do remember that you said that a novelist can only do so much.'

Fyodor Mikhailovich let the curtain fall back into place and turned round towards the room.

'Come,' he said, 'let's sit down and finish that beer. This needs careful consideration.'

We sat down as he suggested and I was relieved to take another mouthful of beer, snatching a moment's respite from all these big issues that were starting to overwhelm me.

'Now, remember what we agreed when we were talking about this before. Christ is love and can only be communicated in and by means of love.'

I nodded, though, to be completely accurate, *he'd* said this and I'd only listened.

'Have you ever met, have you ever read about, anyone who could really unconditionally love another person?'

'I don't know. I've certainly met people who were capable of loving deeply.'

'But unconditionally?'

'I'm not sure that I even know what that would mean.'

'I'm not surprised. It's impossible.'

'Impossible? But why?'

'Because everyone of us is an "I" and being an "I" necessarily limits us in relation to others. Overcoming that limitation is more than the work of a lifetime and it is only in the perspective of eternity that we really see ourselves for what we are in our infinite connection to the whole and, in the whole, to all those other "I"s. Only at that point can we give up our identification with just this little "I" and rejoice equally in every possible manifestation of the whole. Only at that point does egoism cease.'

'And Christ?'

'Precisely because He is Christ from all eternity means that even in the limitations of human flesh He is not limited by his own "I" and can be equally loving to all. The rest of us can only shed this "I" through a long, slow, process... perhaps even an eternal process lasting until the end of time or even beyond time. This life is only a beginning, but Christ opened the way and showed us the end, the goal that is set before us. And, again, that's why historians can never grasp Him because they are always bound to think of Him as some kind of ego-centred personality, whether that's Strauss's mythical Christ, Renan's noble sentimentalist, Lev Nikolaevich's moral teacher, or the revolutionary insurgent who became so popular in the twentieth century. All of these maybe grasped part of the truth—that Christ put the good of humanity before His own individual ego—but none of them shows how He was able to do this. There's the miracle.'

'But why's it a miracle? Isn't it possible to become enlightened through meditation, without any miracles, like the Buddha?'

'That's a comfortable modern Western view of the Buddha, to be sure,' smiled Fyodor Mikhailovich, 'but don't the Buddhists themselves say that he could only achieve that because of all he'd learned and what he'd become through his previous incarnations? He didn't start his last incarnation as a tabula rasa. But this is not a competition between religions. This is about how you find love, how you become capable of love, and you become capable of love through experiencing it—and if you're to become capable of unconditional love then it's only by experiencing unconditional love.'

'I see.' I saw (I think). But I wasn't yet fully persuaded. As if sensing my doubts, Fyodor Mikhailovich held up an admonitory finger.

'Do you? I wonder. In any case, let me just say that although you described "my" Christ as weak and powerless, He is neither weak nor powerless in the eyes of those who recognize Him for who He is. Even in the story of "The Grand

Inquisitor", the common people immediately recognize and love Him when He first appears in Seville—and because they recognize and love Him He is able to heal them and raise their dead. The Inquisitor himself recognizes Him but he doesn't love Him. For him, therefore, Christ becomes just one more helpless prisoner to feed the flames of his magnificent auto-da-fé.'

'So I must love Him before I can know Him and see Him for who He is?'

'Exactly.' Fyodor Mikhailovich smiled and folded his hands together in his lap, as if he had finished saying what he had to say and was waiting for me to make the next move. As if he was expecting something from me. Surely not a confession of faith? If that was what he wanted, the most I'd manage would be like the person in the gospels who called out, 'I believe. Help my unbelief.' But my unbelief needed a lot more help before I could even begin to talk about belief.

* * *

'Sorry,' I said, 'can we go back a step?' (Fyodor Mikhailovich nodded: perhaps he was noticing this was a regular tactic on my part.) 'Right. I kind of half get this. I mean, I do realize that you sometimes have to approach a person or a subject with a certain sympathy or even love before you can fully understand them. No one's ever going to tell their secrets to someone who's consistently hostile or indifferent. A good counsellor is going to get more out of you than a torturer. So, if I'm completely closed to the idea of Christ, that's it, end of story. I have to be open and willing to learn, I accept that, but—and it's a big "but"—I must have some idea of who he is before I can even begin to think about whether I love him or not. Where am I going to get this idea from?'

'There are the gospels—if you actually had a copy of the Bible on your shelves.'

Ouch.

'Point taken—and I should say that I did actually pick up a copy of the Bible to keep at home after we talked about it!' (I'd 'picked it up' from a charity bookshop round the corner but had only leafed through it fairly casually a couple of times.) He smiled. 'But will that be enough?' I continued. 'As I said before, I've known the gospel stories, the parables, the Sermon on the Mount, the Passion nearly all of my life. All the same, as of now, that doesn't change anything. I mean, it's just a book and, who knows, maybe it's all just a collection of myths and legends built around someone who maybe wasn't really like that at all. I don't know if any of it is even true. What I need is something more immediate, something that would show me the kind of difference it would make if someone like that had really existed: if someone like that really did exist, now. Do you understand what I'm saying?'

'You mean—perhaps—meeting someone who was Christlike in actual life?'

'Exactly!'

'I understand. For me too, Christ was also just an idea in a book, a dream of a better world, a utopia, until I saw the living quality of Christian love amongst the poor, oppressed slaves with whom I lived in prison. Of course, many of them were not good men, I've never pretended otherwise. But they reminded me of the gentleness, the readiness to forgive, the truly Christian love, that could be encountered in some of our people, no matter how materially impoverished or brutally treated by their masters. And then, as one of the venerable Church Fathers said, a king is never without his army, meaning that Christ's love continues to be manifest in the saints in all the very different circumstances in which the saints found themselves living. Perhaps, then, that's the first thing to do: to think about those people who have shown you what self-giving love really is like—and their love will point you to Christ.'

I thought for a moment. Again, I 'half' got it, but the problem was that although I'd probably met many people in my life who you could describe as 'loving', I'm not sure that any of them really showed anything you could call Christlike. Nicer than average, perhaps—but scarcely divine. As for the saints, I don't think I'd met any of them and the ones I'd read about all seemed too long ago and faraway to connect with my middle-class early twenty-first-century life.

'Saints,' I said vaguely, 'but who are the saints? How do you get to meet them?'

'Christ is never without his witnesses,' Fyodor Mikhailovich said calmly, 'but you may have to make an effort to find them. Perhaps you need to become a pilgrim?'

I had, of course, already thought about that. And dismissed it.

'That's a nice idea,' I said, 'but my job doesn't give me time for that kind of luxury! In any case, it's not just about me. I'm just one example, me and thousands—millions—of others. We just don't live in a world of saints—and most of those who do set themselves up as gurus or teachers turn out to be fake, like we said earlier! Where can I even start looking?'

'I'm not sure that you're right,' Fyodor Mikhailovich said gently, 'but let's assume that you are. Where, then do you get your ideas of good and evil from? How have you learned what it means to love? If you have any ideals at all over and above earning your salary and enjoying "oysters and champagne", where did you get them from?'

'From my parents and family, in the first instance, I suppose—my teachers and, yes, maybe what I learned at church as a child. But I'm not sure that what I learned amounted to much more than trying to be a reasonably good citizen and neighbour and fit in with what was expected from me. Nothing saint-like—that would be much too extreme for middle England!'

'It might still be worth more than you think,' he said.

'But it's not enough,' I insisted.

'Are you sure?' he asked.

'You mean I'd be better off just getting on with my life somewhere in middle England or, as it's turned out, middle Scotland, instead of worrying over the eternal questions like a nineteenth-century Russian boy?'

He smiled.

'I didn't quite say that,' he said. 'But let me ask you another question. Why are we having this conversation at all?'

'Because you turned up, here in my flat—and without even being asked!'

He chuckled.

'I suppose I did. But I wouldn't have turned up (as you put it) if you hadn't wanted me to. The question is, why did you want me to?'

Had I really wanted him to turn up? I wondered. His being here certainly wasn't making anything easier. But, then again, what reader of Dostoevsky wouldn't want the chance to speak with the man himself? Dickens, I'm sure, would be very entertaining and Thomas Mann would give you a good education, but Dostoevsky, you might imagine, could show you something different again.

I shrugged.

'Because I'd read your books... because they stirred something in me that I wouldn't otherwise have had words for...'

'Which was? What you call your existential despair?'

'Yes, that... but not just that. Also...' I was struggling to find the right words here. 'also that there's a way through that to something else... something more than just settling down and conforming to what society expects... the idea that life could be better, that *we* could be better... a way of living, well, OK, a way of loving that isn't just looking for self-gratification... or being successful... In terms of what we've been talking about, I suppose you could just say it's Christ. Yes, Christ—though if you'd asked me whether I was looking for Christ, I don't think I'd have said I was.'

Fyodor Mikhailovich sighed, though sympathetically.

Did I want to find Christ? Perhaps not in the way that I'd heard very religious people talking about 'finding Christ' but, going back to our first conversation, I suppose I did want to believe that there was someone who could prove to me that love really was worthwhile, that it really was love and not 'blind force' that made the world go round. And perhaps that's who Christ is.

'Well... finding Christ, why not?'

Fyodor Mikhailovich raised an eyebrow at this somewhat evasive answer.

'Of course,' he continued, 'you know that if you want to find Christ, you must find Him for yourself—though I've made some suggestions,' he added gently.

'I know, I know!' I exclaimed. 'But how would I even recognize him! The people of Seville in the time of the Grand Inquisitor and your Russian peasants were all brought up in religious societies so they knew what they were looking for. I mean, how would you even begin to recognize Christ if He came again in this urban, industrial, capitalist, modern—postmodern—world?'

'Again, I can't answer that question,' Fyodor Mikhailovich said, nodding. 'What Christ means in your time is up to you who live in it to work out. But I understand the question. In a way, it was the same question I tried to address in my time, as you yourself guessed. And for all the differences between my time and yours, I see a lot of similarities, some of which we've already spoken about: the mad pursuit of wealth and the ruthless competition it engenders, the constant shaking up of social relations that follows, and the desperate attempt to make ourselves into our own gods and believing that science can tell us how to be better human beings—not to mention destroying the natural world for financial gain. How one can recognize Christ when one is under the spell of all this—that's a difficult question. Perhaps He would be unrecognizable, absurd, or even pathetic—at least in the eyes of those who are wedded to the values of the present age.'

I again recalled the philosopher who'd said that if God appeared in our world today he'd have to be like Shakespeare's 'Poor Tom' or Dostoevsky's 'Idiot'.

'Like your idiot, then?'

He half-smiled.

'But then,' I continued, 'we're back with the problem as to how such a weak Christ can save anyone. We need more than an example.' I stopped and, as I did, became aware of a whining tone in my voice that I didn't really like. I needed to pull myself together.

'I'm sorry—I'm not complaining about your novels, Fyodor Mikhailovich. They help, they really do. And I'm not saying there are any other novels that do better. Most of the twentieth-century novelists who tried to produce Christ figures also ended up with "Christs" who were too weak, sick, or mad to save anyone else. Kazantzakis, Greene, Bulgakov. Probably others. Novelists can reimagine or reinvent old stories—like we were saying last time—but perhaps there's a limit to what any novelist—even you—can do.'

He laughed and even seemed rather pleased by my little speech.

'Of course,' he said, 'yes, yes, yes—of course, there's a limit to what any novelist can do. That's what I've been saying all along. And, as we also said before, the novelist can only confront you with the truth when the story he's telling or, if you like, retelling—no matter how fantastical it might seem—is itself the truth.'

'But there we are again! The truth! I suppose the Grand Inquisitor and your "idiot" make us think about what it might be like if Christ were to come again and that's an amazing idea to play with. But what I want is someone who can really persuade me that Christ's "love" isn't just a nice ideal: it's a universal law; that there is someone who really can say "Love one another" and say it convincingly.'

'You're thinking about the ending of *A Gentle Spirit* again?'

'Exactly. It seems to me that if the world is to be more than an infinite succession of cause and effect—"beneath a dead sun"—then we need more than a fragment of ancient history, more than what the Church has been repeating for generation after generation, and even more than anything a novel can tell us. Where do we find it? Where am I going to hear that voice? When—how—do I get to see the truth?'

Inquisitor", the common people immediately recognize and love Him when He first appears in Seville—and because they recognize and love Him He is able to heal them and raise their dead. The Inquisitor himself recognizes Him but he doesn't love Him. For him, therefore, Christ becomes just one more helpless prisoner to feed the flames of his magnificent auto-da-fé.'

'So I must love Him before I can know Him and see Him for who He is?'

'Exactly.' Fyodor Mikhailovich smiled and folded his hands together in his lap, as if he had finished saying what he had to say and was waiting for me to make the next move. As if he was expecting something from me. Surely not a confession of faith? If that was what he wanted, the most I'd manage would be like the person in the gospels who called out, 'I believe. Help my unbelief.' But my unbelief needed a lot more help before I could even begin to talk about belief.

* * *

'Sorry,' I said, 'can we go back a step?' (Fyodor Mikhailovich nodded: perhaps he was noticing this was a regular tactic on my part.) 'Right. I kind of half get this. I mean, I do realize that you sometimes have to approach a person or a subject with a certain sympathy or even love before you can fully understand them. No one's ever going to tell their secrets to someone who's consistently hostile or indifferent. A good counsellor is going to get more out of you than a torturer. So, if I'm completely closed to the idea of Christ, that's it, end of story. I have to be open and willing to learn, I accept that, but—and it's a big "but"—I must have some idea of who he is before I can even begin to think about whether I love him or not. Where am I going to get this idea from?'

'There are the gospels—if you actually had a copy of the Bible on your shelves.'

Ouch.

'Point taken—and I should say that I did actually pick up a copy of the Bible to keep at home after we talked about it!' (I'd 'picked it up' from a charity bookshop round the corner but had only leafed through it fairly casually a couple of times.) He smiled. 'But will that be enough?' I continued. 'As I said before, I've known the gospel stories, the parables, the Sermon on the Mount, the Passion nearly all of my life. All the same, as of now, that doesn't change anything. I mean, it's just a book and, who knows, maybe it's all just a collection of myths and legends built around someone who maybe wasn't really like that at all. I don't know if any of it is even true. What I need is something more immediate, something that would show me the kind of difference it would make if someone like that had really existed: if someone like that really did exist, now. Do you understand what I'm saying?'

'You mean—perhaps—meeting someone who was Christlike in actual life?'

'Exactly!'

'I understand. For me too, Christ was also just an idea in a book, a dream of a better world, a utopia, until I saw the living quality of Christian love amongst the poor, oppressed slaves with whom I lived in prison. Of course, many of them were not good men, I've never pretended otherwise. But they reminded me of the gentleness, the readiness to forgive, the truly Christian love, that could be encountered in some of our people, no matter how materially impoverished or brutally treated by their masters. And then, as one of the venerable Church Fathers said, a king is never without his army, meaning that Christ's love continues to be manifest in the saints in all the very different circumstances in which the saints found themselves living. Perhaps, then, that's the first thing to do: to think about those people who have shown you what self-giving love really is like—and their love will point you to Christ.'

I thought for a moment. Again, I 'half' got it, but the problem was that although I'd probably met many people in my life who you could describe as 'loving', I'm not sure that any of them really showed anything you could call Christlike. Nicer than average, perhaps—but scarcely divine. As for the saints, I don't think I'd met any of them and the ones I'd read about all seemed too long ago and faraway to connect with my middle-class early twenty-first-century life.

'Saints,' I said vaguely, 'but who are the saints? How do you get to meet them?'

'Christ is never without his witnesses,' Fyodor Mikhailovich said calmly, 'but you may have to make an effort to find them. Perhaps you need to become a pilgrim?'

I had, of course, already thought about that. And dismissed it.

'That's a nice idea,' I said, 'but my job doesn't give me time for that kind of luxury! In any case, it's not just about me. I'm just one example, me and thousands—millions—of others. We just don't live in a world of saints—and most of those who do set themselves up as gurus or teachers turn out to be fake, like we said earlier! Where can I even start looking?'

'I'm not sure that you're right,' Fyodor Mikhailovich said gently, 'but let's assume that you are. Where, then do you get your ideas of good and evil from? How have you learned what it means to love? If you have any ideals at all over and above earning your salary and enjoying "oysters and champagne", where did you get them from?'

'From my parents and family, in the first instance, I suppose—my teachers and, yes, maybe what I learned at church as a child. But I'm not sure that what I learned amounted to much more than trying to be a reasonably good citizen and neighbour and fit in with what was expected from me. Nothing saint-like—that would be much too extreme for middle England!'

'It might still be worth more than you think,' he said.

'But it's not enough,' I insisted.

'Are you sure?' he asked.

'You mean I'd be better off just getting on with my life somewhere in middle England or, as it's turned out, middle Scotland, instead of worrying over the eternal questions like a nineteenth-century Russian boy?'

Our conversation was at a crux. From time to time it had been in danger of slipping into a question-and-answer session with a great writer. The stuff of book festivals. Or perhaps an academic seminar. And sometimes I'd been in danger of forgetting that this wasn't just a matter of finding out what Fyodor Mikhailovich really thought but of getting an answer to my original question as to how to go on living if the world really was a moral desert or, to be a little less melodramatic, how to live with purpose, strength, and joy in a world that was essentially indifferent. Was that how the world really was or was there someone capable of commanding us to love one another? Someone like Christ? No, not 'like Christ'— Christ. So why beat about the bush? There was an obvious shortcut that was staring me in the face or, at least, sitting opposite and waiting for me to speak. The question seemed impertinent, even to me. But I had to ask.

'Fyodor Mikhailovich... excuse me, this may seem a completely stupid question but you—*now*—do you see Him?'

Dostoevsky pressed his lips together and breathed deeply. He was not angry, as I'd feared he might be. The light that I'd once glimpsed deep in his eyes seemed suddenly to shine out in with almost tangible brightness and his face became somehow radiant, even though his expression had scarcely changed. It was as if his whole energy was becoming manifest in his face, which seemed to grow larger in relation to his body. It was almost frightening and I scarcely dared look at him. Some seconds passed and the phenomenon grew even more intense. Abashed, I looked down.

And then, suddenly, the atmosphere eased. Raising my head, I almost expected him to have gone, but he was still there, looking more like he normally did (if 'normally' is the right word to describe a visitor from another world), but, as it were, refreshed.

'What can I say?' he said gently. Taking a deep breath, he added, 'I think it's time to go.'

I wanted to shout out 'Stay!' We were so near, and I needed to make sense both of what he'd been saying and what I'd seen. At the same time, I knew that arguing would be pointless. There was a firmness in his voice that would not be contradicted.

'You must?'

'It's best.'

'Will I see you again?'

'When the time is right.'

I wanted to press him as to when that would be—all the while knowing that such a question would remain unanswered. I remained silent.

I didn't really know what to expect next. Would he dematerialize in some kind of way, like someone in a science-fiction movie being teleported? Would he gradually fade, leaving only an outline that would slowly disappear? None of the above.

'Now I'll go,' he said, standing up. 'Thank you for the beer. I enjoyed our conversation. Really. I hope you have.'

Politely, I stood up. 'Thank you,' I said, not quite sure just what I was thanking him for.

'No, stay,' he said, 'I'll let myself out.'

I watched him walk to the door and go out into the hall. He was gone.

I sat back down and breathed out, long and slow. Something extraordinary had happened. But what?

Fifth Conversation

Light from the East

In the Park

My last conversation with Dostoevsky had raised more questions than it had answered. As I mentioned, Christmas worship at our local church hadn't really inspired me but what he'd said and, especially, the uncanny aura that I'd seen at the end of our conversation made me think that whatever the truth was, it was … what? Supernatural? Maybe. Christianity? Or, at least, whatever it was that Christianity was pointing to—but what about the church? I suppose Dostoevsky would have said that there was only one true Church: Orthodoxy. But I couldn't see myself becoming Orthodox. Martin's Catholicism was weird enough. Anyway, I didn't even know if there was an Orthodox church in Glasgow (as I later discovered, it's only a few blocks away from our flat and I'd walked past it many times).

Don't imagine I thought about these things all the time. Once the semester started most of my energies were quickly absorbed in the usual round of teaching, meetings, grant applications, project reviews, etc., etc. By the time evenings came I wasn't good for much except watching nature documentaries or crime dramas for a couple of hours. And then perhaps sitting, thinking, dreaming. I'm not complaining. As I said before, teaching still had its good days and this semester I was pioneering a new course on the devil in modern literature and had chosen texts from Marlowe, Milton, Goethe, Byron, Poe, Dostoevsky (of course), Mark Twain, and, obviously, Thomas—and Klaus—Mann. I hadn't imagined any of the students had read any of them before and was doubtful as to whether more than half of them would even read the quite short excerpts I'd posted online. Probably they'd just settle for whatever they could pick up from Wikipedia or dubiously reliable study guides they'd found on the internet. In the event, I was proved wrong. There was a lot of sympathy for the devil in the class and discussions were lively.

If I had time in the middle of the day and the weather wasn't too bad (which it often was), I liked to take a walk round Kelvingrove Park to clear my head. Sometimes I'd sit on one of the benches at the top level and look back over the park and out towards the Clyde estuary. Down below, people were doing all the things they do in parks: mothers (mostly) and fathers (sometimes) at the playground with their children or watching over the wee one's first bike ride; students in random bunches talking loudly and excitedly; runners who looked like they were enjoying themselves and runners who looked like the Grim Reaper was close behind; people going briskly towards the city centre in a businesslike way and people coming back again, exhausted. The wind stirred the trees lining the Kelvin valley. It was an unusually mild February day with a high cover of silver-grey clouds and though you couldn't really call it spring, there were scattered bunches of crocuses and snowdrops; daffodil shoots were pushing up through the ground in large clumps and new buds were forming on the trees.

I often found myself thinking about the big Victorian exhibitions that were held here in the park, when Glasgow was at the height of its wealth and prestige. Like London's Great Exhibition they celebrated science, industry, and the British Empire—right below where I was sitting there had once been medieval castles, Indian palaces, and a Russian village. The Mughal turrets on the Kelvingrove museum were a last reminder of those days, the last outpost of an empire on which, they said, the sun never sets. Well, it has set now.

My thoughts about this 'glorious' past were interrupted by a Scottish National Party supporter handing me a leaflet that was covered with the blue and white saltires that had become a symbol of the independence cause. The leaflet was calling me to a big pro-independence rally on the upcoming Saturday. I wasn't likely to go. As I've said, I wasn't unsympathetic, but I didn't like the flags and crowds. And demonstrations don't change anything anyway.

Empire. Nationhood. What was that all about? Apart from anything else, they both seemed a bit irrelevant to the multicultural reality of university life. Perhaps academics were by definition citizens of everywhere (even if that meant they ended up being citizens of nowhere). And whatever its merits, nationalism always seemed to involve some kind of violence. I hadn't been following what was going on between Russia and Ukraine very closely, but I knew that after the Russian annexation of Crimea there was some kind of civil war going on in eastern Ukraine, which I imagined to be rather like the Troubles in Northern Ireland only on a larger scale and, like in Northern Ireland, there were probably at least two and possibly more sides to whatever was happening. And, to be honest, no one—politicians, business people, academics—seemed to be exceptionally exercised by the fighting. There still seemed to be a lot of Russian billionaires in London mixing it with the great and good of the British establishment. Business as usual, then. I mean, they'd even had the World Cup in Russia last summer. Closer to home, a colleague had gone to a conference in Moscow back in the autumn and came back enthusing about the Georgian restaurant where he'd been taken for dinner. He hadn't mentioned Ukraine.

I wondered what Fyodor Mikhailovich's take on all of this might be—I'd been reading *The Diary of a Writer* and, like most Western readers and maybe even some Russians, I'd found some of it a bit too nationalistic; even jingoistic—as, to be fair, he'd warned me. In one article he'd claimed that, as he put it, 'Constantinople will be ours', predicting that it was Russia's God-given destiny to seize Constantinople from Turkey and make it the capital of Orthodoxy, like Rome is for Catholics. Apart from the fact that this was proved wrong by events, it seemed almost delusional. It all reminded me of how, in 1914, clergy across Europe blessed the departing soldiers, assuring them that God was on their side. But surely we'd said goodbye to all that? Like most people of my age, I'd always thought that the worst kind of religion was the kind that cosied up to militarism and imperialism. If Dostoevsky had faced the challenges of suffering and meaninglessness more unflinchingly than any other writer of his time (or since), he seemed to have been blind to the effects of religion being co-opted by imperialism. 'God on our side' might make some people feel good, but didn't it reduce God to a pawn in the politicians' game? And, as far as I was concerned, that wasn't really a God worth believing in. 'When Britain first at heaven's command' and all that? Surely not. Still, I had a lingering suspicion that, if he were alive today (in the normal sense of 'alive'), Fyodor Mikhailovich might be writing 'Crimea will be ours'. But, then again, so what? Did that devalue everything else he wrote?

These were troubling questions, but there were things that I needed to do back at the office and before that I had to go to the library. Later, I had a tutorial meeting with a student. Time to move.

I was just standing up to go when I became aware that there was someone else on the bench. I suppose he must have been sitting there for quite a few minutes, even though I hadn't noticed him. He was middle-aged and wearing a rather featureless overcoat in some sort of close check design. Even though it wasn't that cold, his collar was turned up and the brim of his rather antique-looking fedora hat was pulled down quite far, so that I couldn't immediately make out his features. He was wearing woollen mittens and slowly rubbing his hands as if to keep warm. He was also muttering to himself, though I couldn't make out what he was saying. The kind of odd character you get in the park in the middle of the day, I suppose. I adjusted my jacket, ready to go, and, as I did, he looked round. I immediately sat down again.

'Fyodor Mikhailovich,' I exclaimed. 'It's you!'

'As you see.'

'But...but....?'

'You mean: How can you be here, in public, where people might notice, maybe one of your colleagues? Perhaps they might start asking questions?'

'Well...yes...something like that...I mean...well, they might...if they could see you...or am I the only one who can see you?' It was very confusing, and I was confused.

'Anyone can see me, I suppose.' He glanced round, screwing up his eyes, but there was no one nearby. 'The truth is, though, they're probably not that interested. After all, who am I to them? Just an old man on a park bench.'

He looked up and scanned the view, nodding thoughtfully to himself. I wondered what he made of it and whether he had a particular reason for coming here, just now. Had he been, as it were, 'listening' to what I was thinking? Did he have something to say about what was happening in Russia today? If there was, he didn't seem to be in a hurry to say it. Perhaps he was waiting for me to begin. But how? After some of my previous gaffes, I felt uncomfortable at the thought of launching into a direct interrogation.

War and Peace

'It's a fine view,' I said.

'Mmmm' (non-committally).

'You know they had a Great Exhibition here; two actually—a bit like the one you saw in London, only without a Crystal Palace. But I suppose it was the same idea. Great Britain, land of industry and empire. And this is where it happened. And just down there, beyond that giant crane, is where the shipyards began, making the ships that kept the empire going.'

'Mm' (abruptly).

This wasn't very encouraging. Of course, I knew that he'd seen the Crystal Palace as a symbol of everything he didn't like about the industrialism that was ripping up forest and earth and covering the world with a network of railway tracks, rending the fabric of ancient traditions, and setting class against class. All in the name of prosperity and science. I suppose he also had reasons for disliking the British Empire in particular, since it was basically Britain that had thwarted Russia's move on Constantinople.

Trying to retrieve the situation, I added that in 1901 they'd even had a Russian village built, complete with church, which got only another 'Hmmm'—though this time it could have been interpreted as mildly curious.

'It was all a long time ago,' I said awkwardly, realizing as I said it that for him, perhaps, it wasn't. I had no idea how time worked in his world. 'The Age of Empire, I mean,' I added by way of clarification.

'Hmmm' (inscrutably).

There was a pause. I couldn't think of anything else to say, but then, shuffling along the bench, he pointed at the pamphlet I was still holding.

'What's that?' he asked.

'It's a political pamphlet,' I replied, 'about Scottish independence. It's a big thing here right now.'

'May I look?' he asked and, without waiting for a reply, took it from me. He scrutinized it intently.

'The flag of St Andrew,' he said. 'That's good. St Andrew is the patron saint of Russia too. Did you know that?'

'No. I thought that was St Nicholas?'

'Yes, him too—it's a big country with a lot of enemies. It needs its saints. But you're right—Nicholas is probably more popular. This is good,' he continued, waving the pamphlet at me. 'It's good for a people to be aware of who they are and to come together under the protection of their saint.'

Despite the ubiquitous saltires I didn't really think that Scottish nationalism today was much interested in the protection of St Andrew. But I let it pass.

'It's like I said to you before,' he resumed. 'You have to have brotherhood before you can have liberty and equality. This is what the French and the rest of Europe forgot. And that's why their pursuit of liberty and equality led to war, revolution, and war again. An ocean of blood. And your exhibitions,' he added, holding the pamphlet in one hand and extending his arm to take in the panorama of the park as a whole, 'all that industry and science will never free people if they don't already know each other as brothers. You've had several centuries of it, and it hasn't freed you yet. But this is good,' he concluded, tapping the pamphlet.

I've already explained my rather non-committal position on Scottish independence but this seemed to be a good cue to raise the issues I'd been thinking about.

'Maybe. Maybe,' I said, 'but isn't nationalism really rather dangerous? Doesn't it lead to xenophobia and even war?'

He looked at me with mild surprise.

'Is war such a great evil?'

'Isn't it? Didn't you yourself just say that the way in which the West pursued its goals of freedom and equality led to war? I assumed you meant that was a bad thing?'

'Of course, war is terrible. Nobody would deny that. But perhaps it isn't the worst of all evils.'

'I suppose that might be true if it was simply a matter of warriors facing each other on the battlefield, like Hector and Achilles. But that's not what really happens. You had Ivan Karamazov speaking about the atrocities committed in Bulgaria and he was surely right: it's not just the warriors who get slaughtered, but the innocents, the women, the children, the old people, the sick... and, in modern times at least, most of the "warriors" are only there because they've been conscripted or pressured into it. And, to be honest, I don't expect that the Greeks and Trojans really liked having to kill each other in order to survive.'

'What you say may be true in many cases,' he said, moving closer and wagging an admonitory finger. 'But it's not always true. Surely it's worse to stand by and do nothing when your brothers are being tortured and massacred—as in Bulgaria. Isn't it a Christian duty to lose your life in order to help others?'

'Yes, but...'

Yes, but—Fyodor Mikhailovich was having no interruption.

'And our young Russians... men and women who volunteered to fight or to go as nurses, risking their lives... they didn't need to go, they didn't wait to be conscripted, and they didn't go to conquer but to help. I too volunteered for active service—though they still thought I was too politically unreliable. And, in any case,' he added, looking at me with an almost inquisitorial eye, 'were those who stayed at home, who carried on with their champagne and oysters, their affairs, and their stock market speculations—were they *better*? No. Clearly not. Sometimes war is needed to purify a nation that has fallen prey to mammon and sensuality and forgotten who it is. War is not the worst.'

I could see his argument. But he made it sound too simple.

'Look,' I said, becoming aware that I, in turn, was starting to wave my hands around rather wildly. 'I'm sure—I'd like to think—that if I'd been a young man in 1939 then I'd have joined up to fight Nazism, like my father did. But things aren't often that clear-cut and, most of the time, behind all the fine phrases about resisting aggression and standing up for right there's usually some realpolitik driving the whole thing. And once the cheering has died down, it's usually the innocent who bear the brunt of it.'

I could sense him watching me attentively, as if he could see that I was struggling with a difficult thought. Several times before, I'd had the feeling that he knew what I was thinking—and if that was so, then I'd no reason to hold back.

'I mean, Fyodor Mikhailovich, I'm quite prepared to accept that your young Russian volunteers were motivated by selfless humanitarian sentiments, but, let's be candid, when you wrote "Constantinople will be ours", wasn't that just a straightforward piece of imperial adventurism, just like what Britain, France, Germany, and the other European powers were doing at the time?'

As I was speaking, I became aware of the parallels that could be drawn to what was happening between Russia and Ukraine today, though I hadn't been thinking of that at that moment. Fyodor Mikhailovich listened carefully to my barrage of questions, but his response wasn't at all what I'd expected. He laughed, with an open and unaffected laugh.

'Aha! You really have got round to reading my *Diary of a Writer*! I'm delighted. Congratulations.' At this point he even gave my knee a cheery slap. He was clearly no ghost, as I could feel the pressure of his hand quite distinctly.

'But,' he continued in a more serious tone, 'I think that like most of my Western readers and, yes, some of the Russians, you haven't been reading it very carefully. I never wrote that Russia should simply seize Constantinople for itself. Not at all. My point was that once Constantinople had been taken, Russia would protect it as a place of pilgrimage for all Orthodox peoples, giving a Christian people spread over half the world their own Christian capital, like the Jews had their Jerusalem and the Muslims their Mecca. The shrine of Holy Wisdom. And only Russia had the power to do that. And' (looking at me reproachfully) 'if it hadn't been for your Lord Beaconsfield—Disraeli—it would have happened. No. It wasn't about empire. It was what you now call a humanitarian intervention. Don't you think that's a good thing?'

I wasn't too sure. I'd thought of the humanitarian intervention parallel myself, but it didn't help that I had only the vaguest ideas about the historical background to the events he was talking about. I accepted the idea of humanitarian intervention in principle, of course, but I suspected that there wasn't always too much connection between principle and practice. We intervened when our enemies broke the rules but looked the other way when our friends broke the same rules. And even the worst aggressors usually claimed they were acting in the name of some lofty principle. As I say, I didn't know much about the historical background, but even if there had been a humanitarian element in what Dostoevsky had been writing about it ended up looking more like a straightforward imperial power struggle between Russia and Turkey, using Christianity as a rallying cry. 'In this sign conquer' or something like that.

'Of course, I accept that the Bulgarians and Serbs were suffering under the Ottomans and had every right to try to gain their freedom. But that's my point—it's one thing to free people from oppression: it's another to start redrawing the map on the basis of rather vague ideas about national identity and religion.'

'Not just vague ideas and not just religion—but brotherhood.'

'Yes, but aren't we all brothers? When I was a child we used to sing a song at school about "the brotherhood of man keeps growing". Isn't that the only brotherhood that matters? Christ's fellowship has to be universal, surely? It can't just be Russians or Orthodox who count as "brothers"?'

Brotherhood

Fyodor Mikhailovich looked down and, holding the edge of the bench, shifted his body uncomfortably from side to side.

'You misunderstand me. I know that all men are brothers. Yes, of course. Remember what I wrote about the Chechen prisoner Ali who was with me in the camp and whom I taught to read, using my New Testament. We loved each other and he, like me, loved Christ's teaching about forgiveness. Christ is no stranger to any man. Brotherhood is for all, but there are degrees of brotherhood and a people like the Russian people, bound together in a common faith, under the protection of a common father, their tsar, are brothers in a very special way—just like your brothers are special to you in a way that's different from the brothers next door.'

I didn't actually have any brothers, but that didn't seem worth mentioning.

'So how does that work out today, when Russians no longer have a common faith or a tsar? I know Putin uses talk about Russian brotherhood to justify what he's been doing in Crimea, but to the rest of the world it just looks like a power grab.'

Fyodor Mikhailovich sighed, raised his eyes and muttered something I couldn't make out. He looked troubled, perhaps more so than at any point in our conversations so far, but when he spoke he was very, very firm.

'Let's be very clear,' he said. 'One thing I cannot do—*cannot* do, *may not* do—is to comment on what's going on in your world, in your "today". Your time is your time, not mine, and dealing with it is your duty, not mine. I will say just one thing, though—or, to be precise, repeat what I wrote in the *Diary*. As we've been saying, without Russia the Slavs would never have become free of the Ottomans but it would have been absurd to think that they would thereafter be for ever grateful to

Russia and it was always more than probable that they'd turn towards the West—as happened. It would be tempting in that situation for Russia to use its power to bring them back—but that is the one thing Russia must not, could not do. Violence has no place between brothers. That's what I wrote then. Otherwise, keep me out of it. Whatever my own opinions I may not share them with you. Anyway,' he smiled, 'why would you ever expect a nineteenth-century novelist to solve your world's problems? Even if the human heart hasn't changed that much in the last two hundred years, everything else has. Not least in Russia. I'm sure what you might call "my Russia" still exists and I will be Russian till the end of time, but whatever emerged after the seventy years of communism wasn't the same as the Russia I knew. Similarities, yes—not least in the shamelessness of the rich. But not the same. A president isn't a tsar.'

'So are you saying that everything you wrote about Russia and the West, and about politics and society—that it's all irrelevant? Are you just disowning everything that people have taken—are taking—from your writings?'

He gave a half-smile and shook his head.

'As I just said, the human heart hasn't changed that much but you can't just take what was written in the past and apply it to your own time without interpreting it. That was the Slavophiles' mistake: they wanted to recreate their ideal of the old Russian commune as it existed before Peter. I agreed with them about many things, but what I could see very clearly was that we were living in a very different world and, despite everything that was wrong with it, we had to start with the reality we had.'

'So are you saying that what you wrote—perhaps literature in general—speaks to the individual, emotional side of life but politics and society are always changing?' As I spoke, I remembered what Carl had been saying about keeping a firm line of distinction between art and literature on the one side and political and ethical discourse on the other. But how did that work if, like Dostoevsky, you believed in a Christian society and also believed that literature can bear witness to such a society?

Fyodor Mikhailovich was looking at me sympathetically, as if aware that I was struggling with something I couldn't quite articulate.

'Yes, yes, yes—but what you call politics, isn't that part of the problem?'

'How do you mean?'

'I mean that before you have politics, you have to have brotherhood: that is the rock on which we must build. And' (he smiled) 'I've not forgotten what your wife said: brotherhood *and sisterhood*, men *and women*, brothers *and sisters*, one family!'

His words were, in a way (and I'm sure were meant to be), reassuring. Nevertheless, I suddenly felt very alone. I was, I suppose, the epitome of an uprooted, classless intellectual. I'd never been part of an old-fashioned working-class community (if such a thing still existed) or any other 'community'. Equally, I'd not gone to the kind of school that qualifies you to be 'one of us'. In fact, I'd never really been part of any 'us', except for the small nuclear family I'd grown up in, seeing our relatives once or twice a year for uncomfortable family gatherings and moving house every few years as my father went up the promotion ladder of his company. Just the sort of deracinated liberal—the 'superfluous men'!—that Dostoevsky saw as having such a negative effect on the national brotherhood of all true Russians who still loved their soil and their traditions. Again, I felt bound to voice my objections or, at least, reservations.

'But what about those on the outside, Fyodor Mikhailovich? What about those who aren't members of that family? What about those of us who aren't Russians? How do we get to join the club?'

Fyodor Mikhailovich hesitated, his head bobbing almost imperceptibly in a way I'd become used to. Unexpectedly, he gave a gentle and fond laugh.

'My daughter Liubov, you know' (I didn't) 'had some strange ideas. She always said that I was really a Lithuanian and chose to become a Russian. That was quite wrong, of course, even if our family came from what became Lithuania. But maybe I did have to learn what it meant to be Russian and to reconnect to my Russian roots, something that was only possible because of what I experienced in prison.'

'Yes, but I don't even have any Russian roots to reconnect to,' I complained. 'How does this help me?'

Even as I was talking, I became aware of a rather odd-looking young man walking towards us. I say 'young', but he could have been anything between twenty-five and forty. He had an extraordinary mane of wavy brown hair that framed his thin bearded face, making him look almost like a picture of Jesus in a child's Bible—only with wilder hair. Perhaps John the Baptist rather than Jesus. Even at a distance his face was exceptionally animated. He looked constantly from side to side but without really focussing on anything, giving the impression that he was somehow detached from the world around him. Perhaps he was high on something. He was wearing a dark-grey reefer-type jacket cut in an unusual way, almost military-style and rather old-fashioned. Maybe a survivor of the 1980s New Romantics. Or even the 60s. Clearly not someone entirely at home in the present.

Just as I noticed him, he too noticed us and I was astonished when he immediately raised his hand in greeting. 'Fyodor Mikhailovich! I found you at last!' he called out.

Fyodor Mikhailovich looked round and jumped up—quite energetically—to greet the new arrival. 'Vladimir Sergeyevich,' he said warmly as they embraced and kissed. Still with one arm round Vladimir Sergeyevich (whoever he was), Dostoevsky gestured towards me. 'Here, sit down, join us. I'm sure my friend here will appreciate your help. We're not quite seeing eye to eye today. He might find some of your ideas a bit more congenial.'

Vladimir Sergeyevich reached out a hand towards me but, stopping short of taking my hand, finished the gesture with a small wave. 'Vladimir Sergeyevich Solovyov,' he said and sat down.

A New Arrival

I was, I have to admit, unnerved. I had never read any of Solovyov's works, but I knew who he was—a brilliant young philosopher whose lectures had been attended by Dostoevsky, Tolstoy, and many others and who was widely regarded as the founder of modern Russian philosophy. I also knew that in the last years of Fyodor Mikhailovich's life the two of them had become friends and travelled together to visit a holy Elder (a bit like a real-life Elder Zosima) who had counselled Fyodor Mikhailovich about the death of his son. But what unnerved me most was, to put it bluntly, the fact of another dead person turning up in my life! I remembered a movie in which a woman is visited by her dead husband and they rekindle their love. So far, so good. But then he starts bringing his friends from the other side, until her house is full of dead people. Was that going to happen to me? Was I really losing it? Yet, here we were, in the middle of the park, in broad daylight, with people coming and going. And although both of them certainly looked a bit odd, it all seemed strangely normal—apart from the fact that they were dead.

Fyodor Mikhailovich turned to Solovyov with a broad smile.

'You've come at just the right time. You see, my friend is wanting to know how to become a Russian and I'm trying to explain that that's not the point, but maybe you can explain it better.'

'You don't really think that Fyodor Mikhailovich's message is really just for Russians, do you?' asked Solovyov, looking at me intently. I'd heard the expression 'with eyes blazing'. Now I knew what it meant.

'Well, not exactly that,' I managed to stammer in response, 'but he seems to be saying that there's a certain kind of brotherhood that's unique to Russians.'

'No, no, you're missing the point,' said Solovyov, pressing his hands together and leaning forward. 'Of course, he believed that the Russian people—like every people—had a distinct essence or spirit, one that, until our time, had been kept hidden: hidden until the time was right for its word to be spoken to the world. It was, of course, Christ's own word, spoken 1800 years before but now destined to be spoken anew in our time, spoken in our language but spoken to the world and, I emphasize, *for* the world. The light comes from the East, but it comes to illuminate the whole world.'

'So what was—is—this essence?'

'What was it? Why, what could it be except for the Christian idea of a universal human brotherhood in Christ's name?'

'But hadn't that been proclaimed many times before, maybe even in every generation since Christ's own time?'

'Yes, it had been proclaimed many times—but also forgotten just as many times! And in our time, in our nineteenth century, our age of reason, industry, and empire, our age of unbelief, it was in danger of being forgotten once and for all. That's why it was never more urgent for it to be spoken anew. Russia was a chosen people, but she was chosen to serve the world through her new word, not to rule over it.'

Solovyov spoke quietly, but there was an ecstatic quality in the way he spoke, almost like an orator who had arrived at the key moment of his speech. It was impressive, certainly, but I wasn't sure how to respond. I shouldn't have worried, because before I could say anything Fyodor Mikhailovich intervened.

'You see, the Russian genius is not a genius for ruling, it's a genius for sympathy, for entering into every culture and every human experience. Our literature is not just for ourselves, but draws on every literature—English, French, Italian, German, all literatures—to show every people their own portrait.'

We'd spoken before about how Dostoevsky had been influenced by a whole constellation of major Western writers and had in turn become a part of world literature, but there was something here that niggled.

'I don't doubt that your books help readers around the world to re-evaluate their own lives. Maybe that's what's happening to me now. But I have to say—and forgive me for saying this—that the way you depict foreigners in your novels isn't always very sympathetic. In fact, just about every Frenchman, Pole, or German you introduce is made to seem pretty repellent.'

He smiled at me as one smiles at a child who keeps on getting the simplest of sums wrong.

'Look. The people in my novels are nineteenth-century Russians and that's how they think and talk. How else could it be? Don't you remember what we discussed before about lies, truth, literature, and reality? The point is not what this nineteenth-century Russian thought or felt about that nineteenth-century Polak. The point is what their encounter—and all the human misunderstanding and error it involved—points to in our universal human experience, as Vladimir Sergeyevich just explained.'

I still wasn't entirely convinced, but Solovyov was now speaking again.

'Let me put it like this. Before Fyodor Mikhailovich began writing, who was there to speak for those he called the insulted and the injured, the unfortunates, those rejected by society or just simply ignored and left to one side, the slaves, all of those bypassed by history? Where were their voices? Even when they cried out, they weren't heard. Their reality was, of course, often ugly, chaotic, and even terrifying. But didn't they too deserve a place in history, some part in the development of the great synthesis? And this was the man who gave them their voice, who showed the world all the freedom, all the love, all the humanity of those who had been deprived of freedom, love, and humanity. The man in man!' As he said this, he placed his hand on Fyodor Mikhailovich's rather rounded shoulder and smiled at him, eyes flashing, almost like a lover or devotee. Fyodor Mikhailovich smiled back, with a broad, simple, and somehow humble smile.

'Does that make you a revolutionary, then, Fyodor Mikhailovich?' I asked, suddenly feeling strangely cheerful, as if caught up in the spirit of Solovyov's declamation. 'Were you the spokesman for the wretched of the earth?'

'Not in that way.' He shook his head. 'Of course, I understood them, the best of them, the revolutionaries. What person possessed of any degree of moral sensibility could fail to be aroused to anger by what the people suffered? Except that our human idea of righteous anger isn't always the same as Christ's. Not anger, you see, but love. Brotherhood.'

'Yes,' added Solovyov, 'not a classless society of equal rights but a real community of love—a Church, the true Church of universal humanity.'

'A Church?' I asked. 'You mean the Russian Church?'

'The universal Church,' replied Solovyov.

'The Orthodox heart,' added Dostoevsky. I wasn't quite sure whether this was said by way of correction or explanation.

'But a Church,' I said, 'a Church with buildings, priests, hierarchies, and dogmas? How does that help universal humanity? I mean, I'm not against the Church, but it seems very difficult for human beings to have any kind of religious fellowship without it immediately becoming exclusive and dividing people from one another instead of bringing them together in this universal human brotherhood Vladimir Sergeyevich spoke of.'

The Church

Fyodor Mikhailovich looked at Solovyov, as if inviting him to speak—which he did.

'Of course, you need a Church. I know that many people in your time say that you don't need to go to church to be a Christian and they were saying it in our time too. To be sure, the Orthodox Church has never operated or wanted to operate like a military unit demanding compulsory mass attendance every week and perhaps few of us were as regular in outward observance as some in the West might have imagined.'

He looked across at Fyodor Mikhailovich with what I read as an almost teasing expression. Perhaps Fyodor Mikhailovich himself hadn't been so regular in his worshipping habits?

'But think what happens if you don't have a Church,' he continued, 'if you just have vague ideas of love, freedom, and fellowship. Maybe someone here and someone there will be inspired to live by those ideas, but let's be realistic: where are they going to get those ideas from if there's no one to teach them about Christ and the saints and to show them how to apply their example in practice? Even more importantly, don't imagine for a moment that if you give up having a Church then the state will give up being a state. On the contrary, without a Church the state itself will take over the Church's tasks and take it upon itself to teach people the values they should live by and to punish them if they fail. When they fail. Once you've reached that point, it's then only a small step to complete tyranny. If there isn't a living community to witness to the truth that God alone is God, then you can be sure that Caesar will seize the opportunity and make himself god—as happened in Rome and innumerable times since.'

'So how do we know what belongs to Caesar and what belongs to God? Christ asked the question, but I don't think he answered it and I don't think anyone else has either.'

Solovyov's eyes flashed, ominously, but an amused smile suggested he'd been expecting just this question.

'It's not easy. Ultimately, of course, there can be no division. All life is one and all is moved by the one divine spirit; but here and now, in the middle of history, there's still a long way to go before this is universally acknowledged. For now, there must be Church and state, until the time when the Church has infused the state with Christ's spirit, which is to say that there's no immediate or simple answer to your question. Both the Church and the state relate to the whole of life but they do so in different ways, meaning that they cannot ultimately be separated in the way your Western theorists tried to separate them by saying "This belongs to the Church" and "That belongs to the state", the so-called "division of powers". That just invites endless conflict. But, no: the Church relates to the whole of life and, in the end, it will become the whole of life but only by using its proper means of freedom and love. Without freedom and love, it ceases to be a Church.'

As he was talking, I remembered one of the first scenes in *The Brothers Karamazov* in which there is a heated discussion between Ivan Karamazov and some monks about an article Ivan has written. In this article he had argued that the state should be transformed into a kind of Church, making itself a moral and spiritual organism as well as a means of preserving and ordering human beings' material life in the world. He had also argued that whereas now the fact that a person has committed a crime doesn't exclude him from the Church (even if he also knows that the Church requires him to repent), to be caught committing a crime in the state that has become a Church would result in being completely excluded from every form of society. It would be a kind of terror that no one could endure. The kind of pressure that people experienced in the Soviet Union or Nazi Germany. Even without the threat of torture. Then, suddenly, I also remembered reading somewhere that Solovyov had in fact been a model for Ivan and, without thinking, blurted out that what Vladimir Sergeyevich had just said was surely the argument of Ivan's article.

Dostoevsky and Solovyov looked at each other. Fyodor Mikhailovich raised his eyebrows questioningly. I was afraid I'd put my foot in it—after all, Ivan is eventually revealed as a kind of nihilist and, after being visited by the devil, has a complete mental breakdown. Had I perhaps offended Solovyov by associating him with this strange schizoid character? Much to my relief, he burst out laughing. There seemed to be a lot of laughter today.

'Ha! You're thinking that I'm Ivan?' he asked, as if delighted at the idea. 'Well, you're not the first and some of his ideas aren't entirely bad—if he really means them. The question is: does he?'

He glanced at Fyodor Mikhailovich, who gave an almost imperceptible smile, as if to acknowledge the question, but said nothing.

'You mean,' I said, 'that maybe he's just playing with ideas for the sake of it?'

'Exactly. But the question is a real one. Wars and revolutions have been fought over it—just look at what happened in Europe between the sixteenth and eighteenth centuries. But I'm not talking about the Church taking over the state or the state taking over the Church in a political way. I say again: the Church can only progress by using its own proper means of freedom, love, and brotherhood. If it uses any other means, then it's no longer the Church.'

'Like the Grand Inquisitor!' I said.

'Exactly—although we've been talking about the state turning itself into a Church and the Grand Inquisitor is an example of the Church turning itself into a state. But in the wrong way.'

'The Catholic idea,' muttered Fyodor Mikhailovich, though I seemed to detect a teasing or perhaps self-deprecating tone in the way he said it.

'Not at all the Catholic idea!' declared Solovyov. 'A perversion of the Catholic idea, maybe. I grant you that it was a perversion that did appear on earth, in history. And maybe it lasted many hundreds of years. The Inquisition happened. People tortured and burned their fellow Christians in the name of Christ. There can be no excuse. But that is not the Catholic idea, as you can see from the fact that since our time the Catholic Church herself has learned a greater humility and no longer promotes wars in the so-called defence of the Church. Its authority is and can only be a spiritual authority, not the authority of the sword.'

'Nevertheless,' said Fyodor Mikhailovich, as if reluctant to concede the point, 'nevertheless, what happened remains a warning. Nor were the Protestants any better. They too tortured and burned their enemies. In the end, whether the Church makes itself into a state or the state makes itself into a Church, it's no different from communism. Trying to rule over men's material and spiritual needs at the same time will inevitably end up by destroying the difference between them. It's the politics of the ant heap.'

'We're agreed on that,' interjected Solovyov. 'But I still say that, for now, at the present stage of history—and that may yet last a long, long time—we cannot leave the state to itself. It's not enough just to appeal to the vague spiritual longing of the masses, the "Russian soul", if you like.'

Fyodor Mikhailovich shifted uncomfortably as Solovyov said this, but his friend carried on without seeming to notice.

'Christ's new word needs someone to speak it, someone who can speak it in Christ's name, someone with authority. That is why He appointed Peter to be the foundation of His Church: because without a real living person to be its spiritual father, the Church can never really be the Church, just some kind of religious organization.'

'Yes, yes, yes,' Fyodor Mikhailovich interrupted, 'this is all very fine as an argument, but you must remember that Peter isn't the same as Rome. Yes, every Church needs to be grounded in the life of a human being who is willing to give himself or herself in love and to take responsibility for their flock, but that doesn't automatically justify the argument that the pope must always and forever be the primary authority in the Church. The pope may be Peter's successor, but just because he sits on Peter's throne doesn't mean he has Peter's spirit as well. The spirit blows where it will, does it not?'

'Of course, the pope should not rule alone, which the Catholic Church itself now understands. Peter needs Paul and both need John.'

'Sorry?' I asked, puzzled at these rather obscure references.

'The pope,' Solovyov explained, 'is the successor of Peter' (Fyodor Mikhailovich shrugged), 'while the Protestant churches have taken the mantle of Paul, and we, in the East, are the heirs of John. Only the witness of all three is the true Christian witness, but one must have authority—until the time when God is indeed all in all. And,' he continued, looking sideways at Fyodor Mikhailovich, 'before that happens, the Christian witness must also rejoin the witness of the Jews.'

I wasn't really used to this kind of theological argument and many of its terms were strange to me. Although Solovyov was still looking intently at me, I turned away and scanned the view across the city towards the river. The clouds were darkening and it was starting to look as if it might rain. I turned back to Vladimir Sergeyevich.

'I'm not at all sure where this is going,' I began, 'but I'm inclined to agree—at least, I think I agree—with Fyodor Mikhailovich. I mean, how can you have authority without some sort of compulsion being involved? Isn't the whole point of exercising authority down to the fact that people don't spontaneously do the right thing? So don't you then have to end up forcing them to do it?'

Solovyov shook his head.

'Not at all. If you see someone walking towards a cliff edge, don't you warn them about the danger ahead? Why shouldn't it be the same in the moral universe, when you see someone behaving in ways that are likely to cause harm to themselves or others? Don't you warn, rebuke, persuade? Don't you do all you can to bring them back onto the right way?'

'Yes, but that's different from telling someone what to believe, isn't it?'

'Not at all. Telling someone the truth isn't forcing them to accept it.'

'Not when their own hearts already know that truth,' added Fyodor Mikhailovich.

'Fyodor Mikhailovich,' said Solovyov, taking his friend's hand and speaking in a softer voice. 'You know what I think: that you, more than anyone, have shown how even the most abused heart can still nurture a flame of love for God and even those who imagine themselves made in the image of the Beast are, nevertheless, loved by their creator and are fellow creatures with saints and angels. But if the truth of the heart is to become a universal truth it needs to become manifest, it needs a social form. We believed, didn't we, that such a form existed in Russia and that the love of tsar and people connected the whole of society, but I think we were disappointed.'

Dostoevsky shrugged again. Solovyov turned to me and explained. 'You see, I, like Fyodor Mikhailovich, looked on the tsar as his people's father and when Alexander the Second was assassinated, just weeks after Fyodor Mikhailovich had finished his life in the world, I appealed to his successor to spare the murderers as a father might spare his miscreant sons. But, of course, he didn't. In fact, I lost my post and became what you might call a vagabond, relying on the protection of friends just to stay alive. And all for a letter in which I didn't ask for anything more than simple Christian compassion.' He sighed. 'Alas, in the end, the tsar too was an earthly ruler, like any other earthly ruler—and that is why we need a Church capable of speaking with an independent voice, which our beloved Orthodox Church could not do because it had allowed itself to become little more than a servant of the state, hiding behind the monastery walls and not engaging with the reality of society.'

He paused before continuing. I sensed rather than saw that Fyodor Mikhailovich was shaking his head.

'Let me tell you a story,' Solovyov began. 'Once upon a time St Nicholas and St Cassian had been sent back from paradise to visit earth, for a reason we are not told. On their way through Russia they came across a peasant whose cart had got stuck in the mud. "Come on," said St Nicholas, "we must help this poor fellow out." "But if we do that," replied St Cassian, "my heavenly robe will be stained with mud." "Well, you carry on," said St Nicholas, "and I'll catch up with you later." And so St Nicholas went down and helped the peasant get the cart moving and, of course, his heavenly robe was indeed stained with mud. When they got back to paradise, St Peter was surprised and asked what had happened. St Nicholas explained. "Very well," said St Peter, "because you cared more about the peasant than about your beautiful shining robes, you, Nicholas, will become the most venerated of all the saints in Russia and your feast will be celebrated twice a year. But you," he said, turning to Cassian, "because you worried more about soiling your own robe, your feast will be celebrated only once every four years only." And this is how it is with the Church. The Western Church has taken the risk and gone out into the world and, of course, its robes have been soiled as a result. I do not dispute that. Our Orthodoxy believed that it could keep itself pure behind the monastery walls, but although that too is a way of serving God it is not the better way.'

Fyodor Mikhailovich lifted his hands weakly in what might have been a gesture of protest, before letting them fall back on his knees while emitting a noise that sounded like a cross between a grunt and a laugh.

'I like your story, Vladimir Sergeyevich,' he said, 'but it says the opposite of what you think it says. Of course, St Nicholas is the most beloved saint of the Russian people, precisely because, as you say, he was willing to get down in the mud beside them and be alongside them in their suffering and that is what the Russian Church too has done. The true Russian Church is not found on Mount Athos, it's found in every Russian village and its rites accompany every poor forgotten earthly soul, no matter how humble and downtrodden. The Russian monk was not cutting himself off from the people, he was keeping their treasure secure, so as to give it back to them when they needed it most.'

'But it's not enough to be religious,' insisted Solovyov. 'The Church that prays must also be the Church that acts in the world!'

'That's all very well and good,' said Fyodor Mikhailovich, 'but this so-called independent Church: doesn't its independence mean becoming independent of the people? As long as the people know that the Church is with them, that its teachers are praying for them and caring for them, they will accept it. But the moment when the Church cares more for the Church than for the people—and this must happen as soon as the Church constitutes itself as a separate and distinct organization within society, insisting on itself and its own laws as the condition of salvation—in that moment, the Church is no longer a part of the common life; it has made itself a power over the people. It acts, you say, but its action is for itself and no longer for the people.'

I don't quite know when it began but at about this point I suddenly became aware that the two of them were speaking what I assumed was Russian, as if they were carrying on a conversation they'd been having for a long time and had forgotten about my presence. Maybe this had been going on for several minutes and I had somehow been able to understand it by virtue of the strange alterations of language that were involved in communication between our world and theirs, but after this point I lost track. Fyodor Mikhailovich said something to which Solovyov gave a long reply, delivered in an exultant oratorical style, while Fyodor Mikhailovich was almost literally bouncing up and down as he tried to get a word in. They were causing quite a commotion and I was aware that people passing by were looking rather oddly at them—at us. A couple of young men kept looking back and smirking. A woman I recognized as working in Laura's office nodded at me, with a quizzical raise of her eyebrows. I nodded back, rather uncomfortably.

This continued for a minute or more, until I coughed rather loudly to remind them that I was still there. They both stopped immediately and looked round at me. More or less at the same time they apologized and burst into laughter, simple, joyous laughter, like a child's—and I couldn't help joining in. Laughing with dead people. What next?

* * *

There I was, laughing with dead people in Kelvingrove Park. And I wasn't even embarrassed. Later, I remembered that Dostoevsky's Elder Zosima told his followers that faith can only be communicated through joy. Perhaps there was no answer to my questions—only laughter? But I wasn't prepared to let go just yet.

'Excuse us, please,' chuckled Fyodor Mikhailovich, 'we never could agree about the Church!'

'But aren't you both now in a situation where you know which is the true Church... I mean from your new vantage point, as it were... *there*?'

Fyodor Mikhailovich raised his hands towards his forehead, as if searching for the right words.

'You see, I told you before that we cannot comment on what is happening in your world now and when you say "Church" I think you mean the visible historical institutions that people call churches. But we are still limited in other ways too. We cannot stand in judgement on history. As Vladimir Sergeyevich said, it is only when God will be all in all that we too will know the whole truth. But we do agree—and I think everyone here, where we are, has the same opinion—that, whatever else it does, the Church must act in the world. That was the point of my making Alyosha Karamazov leave the monastery to go out into the world and, once he's in the world, he doesn't set himself up as his disciples' leader, like a new Peter; he is simply their friend, helping them go out into their lives, each in their own way. And remember, it was Zosima himself who sent him out and wouldn't let him remain—as he wanted—in the monastery.'

I remembered from *The Brothers Karamazov* how Alyosha had come across a group of boys throwing stones at another boy, Ilyusha, whose father, it turned out, had been publicly humiliated by Alyosha's brother, Dmitri. Alyosha befriends the boys and helps them to be reconciled to Ilyusha who, in good Victorian fashion, is dying from consumption and whose family are too poor to get help. After Ilyusha's death (which we'd talked about in our second Conversation), Alyosha gathers the boys at a large stone on the edge of the town (presumably a reference to Peter, whose name means the Rock) and urges them to keep Ilyusha's memory alive and to remember how they had become friends with him. This, he says, will be a consolation and a guide to them in the time that lies ahead, a reminder of how they ought to be and how they can be, no matter how wicked the world around them. Keeping Ilyusha's memory alive will be an 'eternal memory' (he said) of what goodness really is.

'So you both agree that the Church must get down into the mud, like St Nicholas, that it must reconnect with the people?'

'The Church—our Church—never left the people; it was always there, alongside them, sharing their suffering and their hope. Christ was always with them, and their hearts understood him. Always.'

This time it was Solovyov who shook his head, but Fyodor Mikhailovich's words brought me back to the problem with which we'd started—the people. Who is this 'people'? Is it only the Russian people? Both Fyodor Mikhailovich and Vladimir Sergeyevich had said not, but that still left me with the question as to just who they were and how I could get to be one of them!

'So, this people, Fyodor Mikhailovich, who are they? How do I find them? How do I become one of them? You say—Vladimir Sergeyevich says—that it's not just about Russians, it's the man in man that matters, universal humanity, sympathy. But where would someone like me begin?'

'Someone like you?'

'Not just me, but someone of my time; someone who's living over two hundred years after the Industrial Revolution began and after all the wars and revolutions and technological transformations of the twentieth century; someone living in a post-industrial, pluralistic, secular age. I mean, there is no "people" anymore; everything has become fragmented and individualized and the "people", such as they are, are probably more preoccupied with building their conservatories or their loft extensions, planning their pensions or just their next holiday in the sun. Does being with the people mean driving to the retail park at the weekend or joining the queue for the next flight to Malaga? Just what does it mean these days?'

They both looked at me intently, perhaps wondering whether I was going to continue, but I'd run out of steam. Fyodor Mikhailovich nodded sympathetically, while Solovyov seemed more doubtful.

Fyodor Mikhailovich spoke first.

'Well, of course, all these tendencies were true in our day already. People were more and more taken up with their own affairs and when it came to their neighbours it was a matter of "What's that got to do with me?" Or, which is the same thing, "Why's it any business of yours?" Of course, this was especially true in the cities and amongst the middle classes, the people who'd been exposed to all those Western ideas about everybody being a law to themselves. As I said—as you know—I felt, I *knew*, that the common people still had a different kind of reality and that the Russian heart was still an Orthodox heart. But you're right, even in Russia that heart has been broken many, many times and it's as true of nations as of individuals that heartbreak can lead to despair—and a heart that's been broken too many times inevitably becomes hardened. Even in Russia—and, yes, even in our time, you could see this already in the West, where spiritual life had become almost extinguished...'

'Come, come,' said Solovyov, a little impatiently, but sympathetically, as one would rebuke a child.

'Very well, but, please note, I didn't say it was extinct and I concede that London, Paris, Geneva, and the spa towns, the places I knew best, weren't the whole of the West. Perhaps the worst of it. Maybe I was unlucky in what I saw and experienced. Florence wasn't as bad and I'm quite happy to think that something of a genuine Christian solidarity still lived on, in hiding, as it were.'

'You yourself said you thought that maybe there was an affinity between the Italian and Russian peasants,' I added, remembering something he'd said in one of our previous conversations.

'Yes, maybe, maybe. But the truth is that even in the cities, even where the life of the community has become most fragmented and individualized, even in the rootless and despairing crowd there remains a certain sympathy, a certain possibility of sympathy.'

'Like the story you told me about the young father you saw out for his Sunday afternoon walk?'

'Exactly.'

Solovyov leant forward and shook a schoolteacherly finger at me.

'You see, this is what Fyodor Mikhailovich can do; it's what he did more than anyone before him ever did. He takes the people who have been uprooted and find themselves adrift in a world of catastrophic forces they cannot control and shows that their hearts too have the same needs as any other human being. I was a philosopher and I spoke about universal humanity—but he shows you the universal in the individual, in any individual, in each individual.'

I couldn't help noticing that Fyodor Mikhailovich looked rather self-conscious and even that he was blushing—just a little.

Still feeling the after-effects of our moment of shared laughter, I almost joked as I asked whether that meant I really could reconnect to the people and rediscover the common human heart at the retail park or the airport.

'Why not? Perhaps those people are building their house extension to care for their ageing parents and perhaps they spend half the night, every night, sitting up by their old father's bedside, helping him to the bathroom, dressing his wounds; perhaps they are travelling to be reunited with a child they haven't seen for half a lifetime or to consummate a love affair that's as deep and as passionate as anything that Romeo and Juliet experienced. And maybe as tragic. And those people down there' (he gestured towards the network of paths below where we were sitting), 'what do we really know of why they're here or what troubles await them when they go home? I could only write about my Russian reality, as it was then, and perhaps I was too hasty to deny that humanity in other nations. In any case, the point is that each of us has to look for that humanity wherever we are, in whoever we meet. There are stories to be told about those people who you say aren't a people. And not only about their crimes and miseries. Love your neighbour, even if he's really rather repellent and someone you wouldn't like to mix with socially. You're no better than him and—more importantly—both of you are probably better than you know.'

'Yes, but it's so hard... there are so many layers to get through, so many masks, so many roles to negotiate. How do I know when I've got to the real person, the one behind the mask?'

'You don't *know*, of course, you feel and trust your feeling. It's like your feeling for life itself.' I guess that I looked blank because he stopped and put a forefinger to his lips as if trying to think. After a few moments he asked what seemed like a complete non sequitur. 'Tell me, are you warm?'

'I'm OK. It's quite mild for February and I'm well wrapped up so, yes, I'm warm enough.'

'How do you know that?'

'I just feel it!'

I began to see what he was getting at, but he wasn't finished.

'And do you see those flowers beneath that tree over there or the buds forming on the ends of the branches?'

'Yes, of course.'

'And what do they mean?'

'Well, they don't really *mean* anything, but I suppose they're a sign that spring will be here in a few weeks.'

'And how do you know that?'

'I don't know. I've always known it. Everyone knows it.'

'Exactly.'

'Exactly?'

'Yes, exactly.'

'But surely there's a difference between knowing whether you're hot or cold or being able to recognize the signs of spring and being able to read the human heart? Isn't there a world of difference between the world of nature and the human world? Yes, I know about Wordsworth and the Romantics... and I know about the Neo-Pagans... and our friend Tamsin is always telling us that we have to tune in to the rhythms of the cosmos. But even if I did, how would that help me be more in tune with my fellow human beings? In fact, it's often struck me that the people who talk most about being at one with the universe tend to be even more self-absorbed than the rest of us, as if dealing with some of the really bad stuff that's going on all around us would ruin their cosmic harmonies.'

Fyodor Mikhailovich and Solovyov looked at each other questioningly, as if asking which of them should reply. Fyodor Mikhailovich spoke first.

Life

'Let's begin very simply,' said Fyodor Mikhailovich. 'Do you like the spring? Do you like to see the flowers and the new growth? Do you enjoy the birdsong?'

'Yes, of course—everybody does.'

'Do you love these things?'

'I suppose so, but...'

'But?'

'Not in the way I love Laura. Of course, in a general sort of way I could say that I love nature and I love going out to walk in the hills, but that's different from loving someone. And if it's Christian love we're talking about, isn't that about loving people? "Love your neighbour as yourself"?'

'It is. Of course it is. But can you really separate the two?'

'Surely you have to? I suppose that the landowner that Ivan Karamazov talked about, the one who had a boy killed for startling his horse with a stone, I suppose he loved his horses and dogs well enough. And Ivan Karamazov himself, didn't he say he loved the sticky buds, that he loved life—but it didn't help him believe in God, did it?'

Fyodor Mikhailovich nodded.

'Yes, yes, yes. But just what did he love? Or should I say, how did he love? As he himself put it, he loved life even though he couldn't see any meaning in it. But that was a very different kind of love from Markel's, wasn't it?'

I nodded, once again recalling the description of Zosima's brother Markel, a teenager dying of consumption who, in his last days, found delight in the birds, trees, meadows, and skies he could see through his window.

'Yes, I can see that—but I'm not sure why?'

'For Ivan... it's a feeling for the life force flowing in his own veins that he sees mirrored in the sticky buds and it's his own will-to-life that he experiences in nature. Markel, of course, is dying, his life force is fading, but he delights in nature for its own sake—perhaps that's why he asks the birds to forgive him, for not having loved them for their own sakes before. But I think I'm not explaining this very well. Vladimir Sergeyevich, you're the philosopher. Can you explain?'

'Of course.' He looked at me enquiringly. 'May I?'

'Please.'

'I think this is best approached in a philosophical way—but don't worry, the sort of philosophy I mean is not for specialists. You don't have to follow long and complex logical arguments. It's more a way of looking at the world as a whole, a "world view" as they used to call it.

'Now you'll remember that Ivan Karamazov himself insisted that he was only prepared to look at the world in the perspective of Euclidean geometry. Although he wrote that notorious article about Church affairs (which we discussed before), he was trained as a natural scientist and that means being trained in the way that a natural scientist was trained in his time, our time. I think science in your time has become somewhat less Euclidean and more alert to the manifold dimensions that encompass our life in the world, but for Ivan and his contemporaries science was limited to the facts of sense experience, to whatever could be measured and numbered and classified. It was materialism, in a very narrow and limited sense, abstracting matter from the whole organic and dynamic movement of which it was a part. So when Ivan says he loves life, it's only this materialistic love of life that he is talking about, the will-to-life as Schopenhauer put it, a blind, purposeless, material urge. As he says to Alyosha, there's no meaning in it. But that isn't life: it's only a half or even less than half of life. Don't mistake me. Materialism too had its justification, its rightful place in the overall development of history. You could even say it was a fruit of Christianity, because Christianity taught men to turn to the earth and not lose themselves in contemplating otherworldly ideas, as the Greek philosophers had done. All things are growing together into a divine unity and that includes matter. But just as it was a mistake to see truth only in ideas, it is equally erroneous to see truth only in matter. The truth is the whole.'

He stopped and looked at me searchingly, as if trying to see whether I'd understood. He clearly decided that I hadn't and set off on a less abstract line of approach.

'Let me put this another way. What Ivan sees when he sees—or rather *feels*—the sticky buds of spring is the power of life, the animal vitality of the Karamazov blood that all three brothers feel coursing within them, especially in the sex drive and the will-to-power. But what Zosima's brother Markel sees when he looks out from his window is the beauty of life, a beauty that's quite independent of him, a beauty one can only marvel at without regard to whether it's any use to us. That's "Platonic" you might say, and, in a way, you'd be right. Plotinus saw it, certainly, but he still thought that, in the end, we had to turn away from the world to see it as it truly is. You see, he didn't know of God as the creator who made and loved all material things for the sake of the wisdom that pervades and orders the world as a whole.

'You and Fyodor Mikhailovich have talked about Christ's Incarnation and everything Fyodor Mikhailovich said was true. I would only add that Incarnation is the supreme moment of a movement that runs from the beginning of creation to the end. It's a process that we too are part of, not only bringing humanity together in universal fellowship but bringing the whole of creation, the whole cosmos, back to God in praise.

'All of this is to say that you cannot love human beings unless you also love the world that has brought them forth in the material dimension of their lives and, equally, that, unlike those friends you talked about, you cannot really love the world of nature if this does not lead you to love your fellow human beings. The sympathy that brings us close to each other is a universal sympathy, it's the divine love that moves all things.'

He stopped again to see whether I was still following him and this time seemed more satisfied with what he saw.

It was a lot to take in. Fyodor Mikhailovich was looking up, smiling, his eyes twitching. I looked down, nodding gently. I think I'd followed it all.

'You see,' began Fyodor Mikhailovich, turning to look at me, 'you see why Markel asks the birds to forgive him and why Zosima tells his disciples to kiss the earth, to kiss it and water it with their tears—remember what he said: "Love all God's creation, the whole and every grain of sand in it. Love every leaf, every ray of God's light. Love the animals, love the plants, love everything and you will see the divine mystery in all things." We are not lords of creation any more than we are lords over each other. On the contrary, we are all too often busy destroying all that God has made well and is constantly striving to make even better. Yes, we must ask the earth and all that lives on earth for forgiveness.'

'Our friend, Tamsin, then... she's right to say we should be tuning in to the vibrations of the cosmos...?

'If she means it with love, if "tuning in" increases love and enlarges your sympathy—of course!'

'That poor crazy woman Maria Lebyatkina—she too talked of watering the earth with her tears: so was she right when she said that the earth was the mother of God?'

'Not quite,' replied Fyodor Mikhailovich and paused, momentarily absorbed in a melancholy thought. 'She too—like, but also very unlike Ivan Fyodorovich—she too had only half the truth, she too loved the earth but without seeing its truth, its truth in God. Not that she was a materialist like Ivan. She wasn't an intellectual at all but lived entirely in her feelings. She was, you could say, lost in her feelings. Literally, lost. And yet she also realized in her strange intuitive way that she needed something more, which is why she dreamed of a prince who would come to her like a falcon and take her with him high up into the sky, so that she could for the first time see the earth in its true perspective. But, of course, it was a fantasy, a feeling that could never find true expression—and, as she said, her prince turned out to be only an owl. Perhaps you like owls, but the peasants used to think that when an owl visits your house it's a sign of death.'

'Whereas Alyosha experiences heaven—the Milky Way—sinking down into the earth that he kisses and waters with his tears. He experiences the unity of both.' This was half a statement and half a question.

'And that's why his experience is inseparable from the need to forgive, to be forgiven, and the realization that others are praying for him.' Fyodor Mikhailovich finished my thought for me.

'Maria sees only the earth, only tears, only death; she cannot see beyond the part to the whole of which it is a part and into which it is constantly growing,' added Vladimir Sergeyevich. 'And yet it is true that the earth and all that is in it manifests the divine wisdom, God's beloved daughter and mother of all things; but it's not the earth that brings forth wisdom nor is the earth itself wisdom: it is wisdom, divine wisdom, that brings forth the earth. This is the wisdom that God loves, cherishes, and makes infinitely fruitful in all the infinite variety of life. In nature and in humanity, both.'

Not for the first time it was as if a flash of light lit up what Solovyov was saying, but the exact sense was elusive and I couldn't really get a clear grip on just what he was saying. I vaguely remembered a passage in the Bible that talks about wisdom as God's beloved daughter, and wondered whether Solovyov actually believed that wisdom was, so to speak, a fourth person of the Trinity. I also wondered how far Fyodor Mikhailovich agreed. We'd discussed his veneration for the Madonna, but this seemed to be taking things to a whole new level.

Probably Fyodor Mikhailovich could see my uncertainty, as he patted me consolingly on the knee.

'Vladimir Sergeyevich thinks about these things as a philosopher thinks. I was only a novelist, a teller of stories. But what Zosima said was true, that "all is like an ocean, all is flowing and blending", and what we think or feel or do may have effects in worlds we never know and what is done in those other worlds may have effects on us, a passing thought, a glance of recognition, a moment of love. Naturally, the materialists, whether they are scientists, philosophers, or just lovers of champagne and oysters, think that both philosophers and novelists are foolish and maybe even just a bit mad. And maybe they're right. But if there is no such unity, if there is no such higher world for our world to aspire to, then, indeed, it is as we discussed in our first conversation and we are no more than insects crawling over the face of an empty and meaningless earth that has no light other than the light of a dead sun. But it is not so!'

He spoke these last words with unusual force. Then, quite suddenly, he became almost jovial.

'By deuce, look at the time! Shouldn't you be getting back to work?'

I don't think I'd ever heard a real person say 'By deuce' and smiled secretly to myself. Probably a trick of the translation service connecting our two worlds. But he was right. It was nearly three o'clock. I had a student coming at three and a class at four. I could forget about a quick trip to the library. Still, if I left now I'd be back in my room by five past and, probably, the student wouldn't turn up until ten past. In any case, she'd wait for at least ten minutes. But it seemed a waste of an opportunity to leave them both just as I was starting to feel—however uncertainly and confusedly—that our conversations were starting to connect up.

'Um...er...I do have a student coming to see me,' I said, in a tone suggesting I'd be happy to be contradicted.

'Then you must go,' said Fyodor Mikhailovich, slapping his hands on his thighs and starting to get up. As he did so, he touched Vladimir Sergeyevich on the arm. 'Come on, my friend, we too have others to see in this city, many others.'

We were all three standing now.

'I go this way,' I said, gesturing towards the university.

'And we go that way,' replied Fyodor Mikhailovich. They each gave a slight bow in my direction, turned, and walked off. Again, I had the impression that they'd slipped into talking in Russian as, I suppose, they would, no longer having to make themselves intelligible to me. After I'd walked a couple of hundred metres, my head full of everything we'd been talking about, I turned to see if they'd vanished. At first I thought they had, but then I saw that they'd gone down to the lower level and were standing looking at the Stewart Memorial Fountain. Fyodor Mikhailovich pointed up at it and, remembering his admiration for Sir Walter Scott, I wondered whether he was telling Vladimir Sergeyevich about Scott's poem of the Lady of the Lake whose statue topped the fountain's Gothic pinnacle. It was a story he could have done interesting things with!

What a conversation. It was, quite frankly, too much to take in. We seemed to have covered the whole history of the world, from creation to apocalypse—though I hadn't gained much more insight into what was going on in Russia today and Fyodor Mikhailovich had steadfastly refused to give an opinion. I'd enjoyed meeting Vladimir Sergeyevich and was keen to read some of his writings—though it was clear that he and Fyodor Mikhailovich didn't agree about everything. At the same time, it didn't seem like the philosopher had any clearer answers to what was happening in my world than the novelist. What he said about cosmic wisdom was very beautiful and, as I say, I felt that his vision had pulled many things together. But, as one of my colleagues always rather brutally asked PhD students after they'd explained their projects, 'So what?'

So what? Well, there was the park...trees...people...and, yes, 'life' (why have I put quotation marks round it, I wonder?). Maybe, in the end, this really was it...just to know, just to feel ourselves part of the great flow of living life—whether or not (as Vladimir Sergeyevich thought) life was divine. Looked at like that, the kinds of successes and failures I spent so much time worrying about didn't seem to matter so much.

I felt a drop of rain and, plunging my hands into my pockets, resumed my way back to the university. As I crossed the bridge, I looked down at the Kelvin, running high from the weekend rains. There was a sudden, brief flash of intense blue-gold-green light skimming the surging brown waters and I recognized the kingfisher that, from time to time, we glimpsed on his daily hunt. Catching fire, as the poet said. Sheer life.

Sixth Conversation

The Jewish Question

An Anti-Semite?

My next conversation with Dostoevsky, the sixth, was both unexpected and painful. I'm still uncomfortable about having to write it up, although it perhaps ended better than at one point I'd feared. The simplest thing is to just tell it like it happened.

There was much to think about after our last conversation! Starting with the politics, I reminded myself that Fyodor Mikhailovich had said quite emphatically that you couldn't apply his writings directly to our time and that his focus was not on social organization but on what he called 'the man in man'. In those terms, what mattered wasn't what he wrote about Russia in the late nineteenth century but about how being Russian in the late nineteenth century revealed universal human experiences of suffering, love, and faith. We, his readers, then had to make sense of that for ourselves. Which, of course, left the question: how? As to the Church, I wasn't much wiser, though I did keep thinking about Solovyov's insistence that our spiritual needs required some kind of community that has a critical distance from the state and doesn't get submerged in the generality of social opinion. That's my gloss on what he said, of course. It's clear that, for him, this had to be the Church. I wasn't quite so sure. Our circumstances were now so different and the Church had become such a small part of life. Meanwhile—and perhaps, in the end, the most important thing of all—there was life to be lived.

A couple of days after the conversation in the park Laura mentioned that her colleague Sally had seen me with a couple of eccentric-looking characters who were having a heated argument in some incomprehensible language that she thought might have been Hungarian.

'I wondered if it was Russian?' she laughed.

'Yes, maybe it was,' I said as vaguely as I could.

'Dostoevsky?' she asked.

'Naturally,' I answered, guessing that the best way of deflecting her question was to tell the truth, while sounding as light-hearted as possible.

'Naturally,' she said, thoughtfully. 'So what were you and Dostoevsky arguing about?'

'Well, I wasn't actually arguing,' I said, which, as far as it went, was true. 'I just happened to be sitting there and they came along...I don't know what they were talking about really...' Again, it was true that when they had slipped into Russian, I had stopped being able to follow them. I was obviously not telling the whole truth—but how could I do that without sounding crazy?

'Well, you never know who you're going to meet in the park, do you?' she remarked, giving me a long steady look that could have been interpreted as inquisitorial, but which I chose to ignore.

'That's right...so, about lunch...'

And that was that.

A few days later I ran into Carl in the cafeteria where I'd gone for a mid-morning espresso. He was on the way out as I was on the way in.

'Hi, I was just thinking of you,' he said warmly.

'Me? Why's that?'

'Dostoevsky…perhaps you've noticed there's going to be a seminar in the religious studies department on Friday next week about Dostoevsky. I thought perhaps I'd go—I imagine you'll be there.'

'No, I hadn't heard of it. What's it about?'

'Dostoevsky and anti-Semitism. It sounds interesting.'

'Dostoevsky and anti-Semitism. Wow!' I gulped. 'That's not something I've ever thought much about.'

Carl looked at me quizzically.

'I mean, I've read somewhere that he was anti-Semitic, but I don't really know what it amounts to. I suppose I'd better come and find out.'

'Great, see you there,' he said. 'I've met the speaker at a couple of events—he's very smart. Oh, and by the way, Laura was really helpful about the grant application. Fantastic.'

'Thanks, I'll pass that on. See you there.'

Later I checked the details on the website. The actual title of the seminar was 'Dostoevsky, Anti-Semitism, and the Third Reich' and was being given by someone called Peter Greenhill-Jones, a senior lecturer in politics and literature at one of the London universities. It didn't sound very much like the sort of topic you'd get in a religious studies seminar but as I'd never gone to one before I suppose I wouldn't know.

It had never struck me that there could be any connection between Dostoevsky and the Third Reich. Like I said, I'd heard about the anti-Semitism and, of course, I knew that many Germans read him in the 1920s and 30s, Thomas Mann for one—but he was definitely not a Nazi. I looked up Greenhill-Jones's webpage, but there was nothing that related specifically to Dostoevsky. I could see why Carl might be interested, since, like Carl, Greenhill-Jones flagged critical theory as one of his areas of research—Adorno and Benjamin were mentioned, amongst others. It seemed he was also interested in the representation of Jews in German culture in the early twentieth century and there was a long list of people and topics he'd written about or given papers on: Wittgenstein, Kraus, Buber, Kafka, Brod, Feuchtwanger, Hamsun, the Nazi ideologist Rosenberg, the movie *Nosferatu*—oh, and Thomas Mann. Obviously, there was quite an overlap with my own interests and I wondered why I hadn't come across him before. Academic compartmentalization, I suppose. In any case, the list didn't offer many clues as to what he might say about Dostoevsky.

I remembered that there was something about 'the Jewish question' in *The Diary of a Writer* and thought that might be a good place to start. Given the usual end of term accumulation of work it was fortunate that the relevant section was only about twenty pages long and wouldn't take too long to read.

I wished I hadn't.

It didn't start out too badly. Dostoevsky writes that some of his Jewish readers have been complaining about his hatred for the Jews and he wants to defend himself. They've misunderstood me, he says. He even gives a long quotation from one of them. So far, so good—though he also mentions something about how Disraeli directed British policy in the service of the Jews, which he'd touched on in our last conversation (from Dostoevsky's point of view, of course, Britain was 'the enemy'). At the time, I hadn't really dwelt on it, but it suddenly seemed more significant.

What was Dostoevsky's response? He starts off by saying that there's no people on earth who complain about their lot as much as the Jews and then goes on to say that the sufferings of the Jews in Russia are really no worse than those of the Russian peasants before the emancipation. Really?

Dostoevsky clearly didn't share my doubts. Instead, he doubled down, adding that one of the unforeseen consequences of the emancipation of the serfs was that the peasants were now at the mercy of the Jews, who were exploiting them mercilessly, just as they exploited the America negroes (his word) after the Civil War. The same thing also happened in Lithuania where the Catholic clergy were the only ones to defend the peasants against a flood of cheap vodka sold to them by the Jews (I'm just repeating what he wrote). Well, at least he finally has a good word for the Catholic clergy, I thought. But, coming back to the Jews, not only do the Russians have *no* preconceived hatred of the Jews (he says), but it's the Jews who hold themselves apart from Russians. Imagine, he says, that instead of eighty million Russians and three million Jews, there were three million Russians and eighty million Jews, 'Would they permit them to worship freely in their midst? Wouldn't they convert them into slaves? Worse than that: wouldn't they skin them altogether? Wouldn't they slaughter them to the last man, to the point of complete extermination, as they used to do with alien people in ancient times, during their ancient history?'

I almost stopped reading at this point. I'm not sure that anyone would be allowed to publish anything like that today. Not even on Facebook. And, apart from the unpleasant content, I was finding it hard to reconcile these words with the Dostoevsky I'd been coming to know, a diffident, humorous, generous, and attentive person who seemed quite incapable of this sort of outburst. But I did carry on. I felt I ought to. I'm sorry to say it was mostly more of the same, insinuating that the Jews maintained some kind of 'state within the state' and pursued their own interests at the expense of the gentiles amongst whom they lived. He acknowledges there are some Jews looking for more humane relationships with their neighbours, but this seemed like a pretty small concession in the wake of everything that had gone before.

Again, I was tempted to give up, though the title of the next section, 'But Long Live Brotherhood', suggested there might be something a bit more encouraging. There was—a bit, and he does come out in support of full civil rights for Jews, which, I guess, wasn't the general opinion back then.

Finally, he tells a story about a Christian doctor, Dr Hindenburg, who reminded me of Dr Herzenstube in *The Brothers Karamazov*. This doctor too was a member of the pious German community in Russia and, like his fictional counterpart, served a mixed community of Jews and Christians, caring for both with self-sacrificing love and humility, even when some of the most impoverished Jews were unable to pay him. At his funeral, both the Protestant minister and the rabbi gave eulogies and Jews and Christians together prayed for his soul. An isolated case, Dostoevsky acknowledges, but it's only such isolated cases that can provide the building blocks for future reconciliation. An isolated case, indeed, that didn't do much to outweigh the charge sheet he'd drawn up against the Jews.

The Paper

After reading this, I have to say I felt fairly disillusioned with Dostoevsky for a couple of days. On the one hand I wished he'd turn up and explain himself. On the other hand, I was quite glad he didn't. It might be the end of a beautiful relationship. I even wondered about giving the seminar a miss, but felt that would be rather shameful. Even if my hero had feet of clay, it was better to know the truth. Anyway, for all I knew the speaker was going to show that there was some more positive side to the picture, though the mention of the Third Reich wasn't very promising. Just what was I about to learn?

The room where the seminar was being held looked out over Professor's Square, a range of grey Victorian buildings in the Scottish baronial style. Splashes of yellow from the first daffodils were appearing in the raised grass plot in the middle of the square and a couple of trees were coming into flower. Spring really was in the air. Almost.

There were about a dozen people there, sitting round a long table that filled most of the room. Carl was the only one I knew. We arrived at more or less the same time and sat together. Only about half of those attending looked like students; the rest were middle-aged and I couldn't tell whether they were academics or mature students. It was a bit different from the mix in our own department. The speaker sat at the end of the table and was concentrating on his laptop while exchanging small talk with the chairperson, a pleasant-looking young man in a Fair Isle jumper. I guessed that he must have been about forty, perhaps younger. He had a shaven head and large black-rimmed glasses and wore a blouson leather jacket. He looked very serious.

The chair told us that Greenhill-Jones had just been awarded a major grant on Literature and the Conservative Revolution 1919–1939, which, again, didn't obviously connect with Dostoevsky. Unfortunately, he didn't make a lot of effort to engage with the audience but read from his laptop with very little variation in tone or inflection, only occasionally looking up to scan the room, perhaps to make sure we were still paying attention. Well, this was the way people were doing things now. I didn't like it a lot, but I suppose I was used to it. And it saved paper.

I made fairly extensive notes, but I'm not going to try to reproduce everything he said here. In any case, you can look it up online if you want to read more, though even in summary it's probably too academic for most, but then it is just that—academic!

The speaker started out by explaining that he was going to set out three ways in which Dostoevsky had made an important contribution to the rise of National Socialist ideology: firstly, by developing a forceful anti-bourgeois and anti-Western rhetoric; secondly, by undermining the ethical credentials of democratic politics; and, thirdly, by portraying the Jews as the main cause of the ills afflicting modern society. He would illustrate this from both Dostoevsky's publicist writings (he meant *The Diary of a Writer*) and his novels.

You can't say we weren't warned.

The paper began with a discussion of the German translations of Dostoevsky's works. Unlike in the English-speaking world, what the translators called his 'political writings' were translated fairly early on, in 1917, and had a big impact on right-wing thinkers. The Nazi philosopher Martin Heidegger was only one of those who praised them. One of the editors actually wrote a book called *The Third Reich* that did a lot to inspire the Nazis. At that time (Greenhill-Jones explained) many Germans were fascinated by what they saw as the extremism of Russian society, as it swung from tsarist autocracy to Bolshevism and from the complete submission of the people to one man to the complete submission of the people to one party—and Dostoevsky was seen as the spokesman par excellence for this Russian extremism.

Like Karl Marx, Dostoevsky accused capitalism of bringing about an endless struggle for the survival of the economically fittest, a struggle that undermined social cohesion and left individuals to sink or swim for themselves. A kind of war of all against all. It's true that this was something he and I had touched on several times, but (which he hadn't mentioned to me) Dostoevsky apparently believed that this capitalist revolution was, essentially, a Jewish revolution. In his view, Jews had no loyalties to the wider society to hold them back from single-mindedly pursuing profit, whatever the social cost. When they saw the peasants socially uprooted after emancipation, they didn't pity them but set about ruthlessly exploiting them. (I'd read this myself, of course.)

From there, Greenhill-Jones went on to argue that Dostoevsky's idea of the unity between tsar and people provided a model for the totalitarian state, which also seemed to involve the idea that his writings showed a strange symbiosis between religious mysticism and terrorism. Alyosha Karamazov was an example of this. Although the novel shows him as a saintly young man trying to reconcile his brothers and make peace amongst some squabbling schoolboys, Dostoevsky's notes show that he would later become a terrorist and be executed. He thought this development was entirely logical.

I didn't really agree with that, not least since Fyodor Mikhailovich and I had touched on how his characters are always evolving in ways that makes it nearly impossible to predict what's going to happen next. The truth is we just don't know what Dostoevsky would have done with Alyosha if he'd lived to write the next chapter. What we do know is that nearly all his novels changed radically in the course of being written, so whatever he ended up writing might have been quite the opposite of what he mentioned to his friends. Who knows? But if I didn't agree with that point, I had difficulty even following the next one.

The argument was along the lines that the Nazis took the idea of the exceptional or superior man from Dostoevsky. This superior man was someone who was not bound by legal or moral codes, an idea developed by Raskolnikov in *Crime and Punishment*. Such a man was entitled to transgress every social boundary for the sake of his higher idea, like (Raskolnikov thought) Napoleon, Caesar, or Mohammed. He would even have the right to shed blood for his idea. Given Dostoevsky's analysis of the effects of capitalism, the emergence of such characters in the modern age was actually quite predictable. From here, Greenhill-Jones said, there was a more or less straight line to the dictator idea that Mussolini and Hitler would seek to embody, though he also mentioned Nietzsche's idea of the *Übermensch* as pointing in the same direction. But here was the twist: such a dictatorship (it seemed) would bring us back to the kind of relation between tsar and people that Dostoevsky so admired. Unlike in bourgeois democracies, with their endless disagreements and debates, leader and people would be one—only this time their unity would be based solely on the will of the leader and not on culture or tradition.

This seemed rather peculiar to me. I could understand the tsar-and-his-people idea and I could understand the Raskolnikov-as-prototype-of-the-dictator idea but they seemed to me to be two completely different things—quite apart from the fact that Dostoevsky never endorsed Raskolnikov's ideas. In fact, the whole point was to show that they were essentially wrong-headed—or so I'd always thought.

Finally—and I suppose I've been putting off getting round to this bit—there was how he depicted the Jews. Of course, he went through the passages from *The Diary of a Writer* I've already mentioned, which left me feeling rather weak, but then he turned to the novels.

'A lot of commentators,' he said, 'especially Christian commentators' (he looked round the room at the assembled theologians who, presumably, were mostly Christian) 'like to draw a line between Dostoevsky the publicist and Dostoevsky the novelist. There is no such line when it comes to the Jews. Dostoevsky's anti-Semitism is just as obvious on the pages of his novels as it is in *The Diary of a Writer*. We don't have time to go through every example and I shall limit myself today to some of the most egregious and characteristic.'

So, which were they going to be? I couldn't immediately think of any examples, but my ignorance was soon vanquished.

He brushed aside the passages where one or other character makes an anti-Semitic remark. That, he conceded, could be down to the novelist portraying people as they actually were, with their real-life prejudices. But that was only the tip of the iceberg.

He began with the character of Isay Fomich Bumstein, a Jewish prisoner—the sole Jewish prisoner—in the prison novel-memoir *The House of the Dead*. This, he said, was the epitome of an anti-Semitic caricature of the Jew. Isay Fomich was described as physically scrawny (Dostoevsky said he looked like a chicken), he was a coward, a money-lender, and his prayers were said to involve bizarre and almost inhuman screeching and wailing. The narrator says that he's vain and boastful and, because of being Jewish, gets special privileges, being allowed to attend the synagogue in town and paying to get himself whipped with birch rods, Russian-style, in the steam bath—which Dostoevsky's narrator incidentally says was a picture of hell itself. The obvious inference was that Isay Fomitch was the most hellish apparition in all of hell. (I didn't remember the narrator quite saying that and made a mental note to look it up later.)

From there on, it seemed that there was at least one anti-Semitic passage in just about every one of the major novels—*Crime and Punishment*, *The Idiot*, *The Possessed*, and *A Raw Youth* all got a mention. Whenever a Jew appeared, he was either a coward or a capitalist.

Finally, he came to *The Brothers Karamazov*. Admittedly, there are no Jewish characters here, but, he pointed out, Dostoevsky makes a point of saying how, at a crucial moment in old man Karamazov's life, he'd gone away to Odessa, where he associated with many Jews. 'It may be presumed that at this period he developed a peculiar faculty for making and hoarding money,' comments the narrator. But, as Greenhill-Jones added, it wasn't just making money that he learned from the Jews. When he came back from Odessa, the narrator says, 'He behaved not exactly with more dignity but with more effrontery'—again a supposedly Jewish trait that Dostoevsky mentions in *The Diary of a Writer*. We are told that 'his depravity with women was not simply what it used to be, but even more revolting', probably alluding to the supposed sexual voraciousness of the Jew. Along with his love of money, this habitual insolence and unrestrained sexual desire also contribute to the tragedy to come. In these ways, and despite being technically a gentile,

Fyodor Pavlovich Karamazov's 'Jewish' characteristics are what cause the disaster that unfolds in the eight hundred pages that follow. If not Jews themselves, Jewishness is at the root of the whole catastrophe.

In a final twist he added that one character, Liza, a highly neurotic adolescent, actually replays myths about Jews crucifying Christian children. It couldn't really get worse—except that when she asks saintly Alyosha if it's true he merely says he doesn't know rather than telling her to stop.

Going back to his starting point, Greenhill-Jones concluded that, for Dostoevsky, the catastrophe of the Karamazov family is a microcosm of Russia itself, corrupted by Judaism, and Dostoevsky's solution is that Russia must find its own superior man, a leader whose mystical sense of union with God empowers him to recreate a modern version of the 'synthetic' state in which all barriers between leader and people have been dissolved and who is ready to tear up all existing laws and conventions in order to attain this goal.

'The conclusion then is unavoidable,' he finished up. 'Dostoevsky was not only an anti-Semite but one of the thinkers who provided the essential materials for the emergence of the Hitlerian state.'

I was fairly sure that this wasn't really a fair representation of Dostoevsky's thinking and it was hard to imagine Alyosha becoming the kind of totalitarian leader Greenhill-Jones had described. In any case, as I said, all the 'superior man' type characters turn out to be flawed and, as he'd explained to me, their apparent 'superiority' is more likely than not the manifestation of an inferiority complex. But what were other people—what were these theologians—going to make of all this?

Discussion

When the speaker had finished, the chair (who declared at the outset that he'd never read any Dostoevsky) asked for questions or comments. There was the customary silence. I was even starting to wonder whether anyone else was going to say anything—I had several things I wanted to ask but this wasn't my home turf and it seemed polite to let the people from the department go first.

The first to speak was an older colleague, maybe retired, who'd been sitting at the far end of the room from the speaker. He'd spent a lot of the time looking out of the window and occasionally checking his phone, and I'd wondered whether he'd been listening at all or whether, perhaps, he was only there out of duty.

He lifted his hand in a rather languid way.

'Professor Allan,' said the chair, clearly relieved that someone was breaking the silence.

'Thank you,' Professor Allan said, 'and thank you to the speaker for a very thorough if somewhat depressing paper.' He spoke with the kind of slightly supercilious drawl that I associated with the more self-consciously superior suburbs of Edinburgh. 'I'm sure a lot of what you say is correct, but surely the point is that at that time nearly everyone in Europe was anti-Semitic. You make a lot of Dostoevsky characterizing Jews in terms of their being ruthlessly acquisitive, cultivating a state within the state, and so on and so forth. But these are all standard tropes that Dostoevsky shared with all his contemporaries. What makes him worse than any of the rest?'

Almost without pausing to think, the speaker answered in a slightly irritable tone, as if this was the sort of question only a fool would ask. Perhaps he also felt he was being talked down to by the older man.

'Well, that's obvious,' he said. 'But I don't see that it makes it any better and the fact is that there were a great many writers, philosophers, and social reformers who were developing a much more positive approach to Jews and Judaism. George Eliot for one. And, as I tried to emphasize, my paper wasn't just about Dostoevsky but about the impact—the deleterious impact—that his ideas had on the first generation of his German readers.'

'But an author can't be responsible for his readers,' replied Professor Allan dismissively. 'And if we're talking about the Nazis, then they were exceptionally unscrupulous readers who tried to enlist all the important figures of Western culture into their cause—Shakespeare, Bach, even Jesus. They claimed them all. So the fact that some Nazis also liked Dostoevsky doesn't really prove anything.'

Prof. Greenhill-Jones shrugged.

'Maybe not,' he smiled, rather grimly, 'but he gave it to them on a plate.'

Professor Allan didn't respond, other than to sniff and resume his contemplation of whatever it was that he was looking at outside the window.

Uncomfortable silence.

'Next question?'

I was working hard on formulating my thoughts, when, slightly to my surprise, Carl (who'd acknowledged not being very knowledgeable about Dostoevsky) chipped in.

'Hi, Peter,' he began. 'I don't have any objections to the main thrust of your paper,' he continued, 'but perhaps relating to the last comment about how Dostoevsky was being so badly misread in the 1920s, I do think many of these readers were projecting back into Dostoevsky ideas that were, basically, everywhere in the radical right at the time—but also the left. If I'm not mistaken, I think the connection between mysticism and terrorism is from George Lukács, although this is the kind of political extremism that moves very quickly from left to right or vice versa.'

'Yes. That's what I was saying.'

'But my point is that it's not necessarily Dostoevsky himself. And when it comes to the dictator theory he is surely only one of many sources—de Maistre, Kierkegaard, Nietzsche, Schmitt, Cortès. And the same goes for anti-Semitism, which was endemic in German culture long before they started reading Dostoevsky. Think of Wagner and what Nietzsche's sister did with her brother's writings, even though he was openly contemptuous of anti-Semites.'

'Maybe. I did mention Nietzsche. But that doesn't absolve Dostoevsky.'

'I don't say it does, but you gave the impression that he was somehow uniquely responsible, whereas I'm arguing that, actually, he was only a very small piece of a much larger mosaic.'

He shrugged again and didn't seem inclined to follow this up.

'Anyone else?' came plaintively from the chair.

But Carl persisted. 'Sorry,' he said, 'maybe I didn't put my point very clearly. The issue seems to me to be really about how important any literary text, including Dostoevsky, was to the development of the radical right. I don't deny that writers and artists had a role on the left and on the right, but it was a secondary role. Any ideas they contributed had to be processed through political debate and were ultimately evaluated on their political, not their literary, merits. OK, so there was an expressionist fringe that saw art itself as revolutionary but they were fairly quickly brushed aside.'

'But that's just my objection to Dostoevsky,' Greenhill-Jones retorted. 'That he's a political theorist who dresses his views up as literature and it's the political effect of his work we should be most worried about.'

'That doesn't make any sense,' said a youngish man in a T-shirt with a geometric design that reminded me of something by one of the Russian constructivists. He seemed fairly self-assured in any case. The speaker understandably stiffened.

'Yes, Greg,' said the chair, who looked worried that things might be starting to get out of control.

'Yeah, it doesn't make any sense,' continued Greg, 'because once you stop reading Dostoevsky as literature, there's no point really. He was a novelist, that's it. In fact, I doubt whether there's a consistent political philosophy in his work at all. But that's not what anyone reads it for, anyway. In any case, you could turn the whole argument upside down. I mean, if you took Bakhtin's view that none of his characters can be identified with Dostoevsky's own voice, then why not see *The Diary of a Writer* as a kind of fiction, a thought experiment, if you like? Putting it out there to see how people react.'

This seemed to me to be not taking Dostoevsky seriously enough. I was sure he did mean a lot of what he wrote in the *Diary* and at least some of it resonated with the fiction.

'If you take that approach, then any writer could mean just about anything,' Greenhill-Jones said severely. 'It reduces writing to play.'

'Isn't that what writing—literature—is?' asked the young man.

'Not at all. For Dostoevsky and the other leading modernist writers writing was a means of trying to change society. That's why what they say about society is the key to understanding them.'

Another pause. I raised my hand.

'Yes?'

'Thanks for the paper. What you say about the articles on "the Jewish question" is obviously correct, and I don't think we can entirely write the articles off as thought experiments, though it's an intriguing idea.'

As I began speaking, a man who'd come in shortly after the start of the paper suddenly leaned forward as if to listen more attentively. He was in his early to mid-thirties, rather pale, with blondish hair and a wispy moustache. I couldn't see him properly as he was sitting to one side and slightly behind where I was, but I'd sensed him fidgeting rather nervously at several points during the paper and generally giving off a sense of anxiety. Some strange people do turn up at university seminars. He seemed vaguely familiar, but I couldn't place him.

I continued. 'But, to be fair to Dostoevsky, although you mentioned that he ended by calling for reconciliation between Christian and Jews, I didn't feel that you gave it sufficient emphasis. I mean, talking about a rabbi and a pastor jointly presiding at the funeral of the German doctor isn't the sort of thing you usually get from anti-Semites, is it?'

'As you say, I mentioned that. But it's clear that Dostoevsky takes with one hand what he gives with the other. Throughout this passage it's the goodness of the Christian doctor he emphasizes and, though the doctor is good to Jews, they're not allowed any real agency. You can see this even more clearly when he imagines that the whole story could be encapsulated in the kind of genre painting popular at the time. The picture shows the eighty-year-old doctor tearing up his shirt to use for the newborn baby of a destitute Jewish family. Then…' he paused and brought up a document on his laptop, which he then read out. 'Then—I'm quoting—he has the doctor say, "This poor little Yiddisher will grow up, and, perhaps, he himself will take his shirt off his shoulders and, remembering the story of his birth, will give it to a Christian… Will this come to pass? Most probably not." So, what I take from this is that even the self-sacrificial example of the good Christian is not going to be enough to move the Jew to be equally charitable. Why not? Because, as I've said, Dostoevsky regards the Jew qua Jew as deeply and essentially morally corrupt and immune to compassion.'

I couldn't complain that I hadn't had a full answer. I still thought what he said was probably too one-sided but I didn't immediately have a counter-quotation at my fingertips. I'd also wanted to say something about how he read the figure of Isay Fomich, which I remembered as being far more positive. But while I was thinking, another voice joined in. This was a middle-aged woman sitting just the far side of Carl. She had short wavy brown hair and a likeable, rather humorous face. When she spoke, it was with a distinct Russian accent, though her English was very assured. She didn't wait to be asked by the chair but just spoke up.

'Of course, we know all this about Dostoevsky and anti-Semitism. Anti-Semitism is fact of Russian life. People are anti-Semitic, the Church is anti-Semitic, even Communists were anti-Semitic. But—so what? I'm Russian, I'm Jewish, I'm Orthodox. Theoretically, this shouldn't be possible, but here I am. You know what Dmitri Karamazov said about Russia and Russians: Russia is broad, it contains many contradictions. Dostoevsky contains many contradictions and the fact that he was anti-Semitic didn't stop him writing beautiful things about Christ, about love, about reconciliation. I don't see the problem. This is life, not putting people in pigeon holes. Anti-Semitic, not anti-Semitic, blah blah blah.'

Again, I caught the latecomer out of the corner of my eye and noticed that he was shifting uncomfortably.

One of the students stifled a laugh.

'Well, it's not so funny,' she continued, adjusting her scarf, patterned with brightly coloured flowers on a black background. 'Quite a lot of Jews converted to Orthodoxy in the eighties. Maybe it was the ritual. Maybe it was because it was one of the few ways of expressing spiritual life. Maybe it was a space of intellectual freedom. But it's a fact.'

'Thank you, Irina,' said the chair. I sensed that he had previous experience—at least in his mind—of Irina as a disruptive presence in the seminar. 'Peter?' he asked, turning to the speaker.

'Sure. People are not always consistent. That's obvious,' he said fairly brusquely, clearly irritated by this latest intervention, 'but it's not a question of Dostoevsky as an individual or the Russian character. For us, these are historic texts and we have to read them objectively. If you want to claim Dostoevsky as an important source for modern thought, then you have to be clear as to just what he says and just what kind of influence he had. And he may well have written beautiful things about Christ but that doesn't—that can't—justify what he says about Judaism nor the effect that his words had on those who would turn these words into action.'

'This is not what reading Dostoevsky is about,' said Irina, dismissively, 'but, whatever…'

The chair looked questioningly at her in case she wanted to turn this rather vague comment into a proper question or response, but she just smiled and raised her eyes, as if to say that it would be entirely pointless to try to say anything more.

The next question wasn't about Dostoevsky at all but about Russian Orthodoxy and Jewish–Christian relations in Russian history. The questioner was clearly wanting to see this in a more positive light, but Professor Greenhill-Jones wasn't having any of it. I wasn't so interested in this rather more theological discussion but went on trying—and failing—to identify what it was I thought the speaker was missing and trying to remember just what exactly Dostoevsky had said in the story about the doctor. I was sure that what Greenhill-Jones had read out hadn't been the last word.

After the last question, the chair announced next week's topic, thanked Professor Greenhill-Jones for a 'provocative' paper, and said that although the speaker had to leave promptly to catch a train back to London anyone who wished to join him in the pub to continue the discussion would be welcome.

There was a general shuffling about as people gathered their bags and coats. I asked Carl if he was going to the pub but he had another seminar to go to. Making my way down the stairs I found myself next to the elusively familiar late-arriving man.

'That was, as the chair said, "provocative",' I remarked.

He nodded, with a slight shrug of the shoulders. It was a gesture I'd become familiar with from our previous conversations and I recognized it immediately. It was Fyodor Mikhailovich, looking (I now realized) as he looked in the photographs taken of him while he was serving in the army, out in Siberia.

'Fyodor Mikhailovich!' I exclaimed, keeping my voice down so as not to draw attention. 'I didn't recognize you!'

'Yes,' he smiled, almost mischievously, though also rather ashamedly. 'I thought it might be best for an occasion like this to look a bit younger and less like a slightly disreputable old man.'

By now we were leaving the building and at the bottom of the steps we both stopped. The small crowd was separating out. Carl had already shot off at top speed to his next event and Fyodor Mikhailovich and I found ourselves standing alone. I hadn't noticed how it happened, but he now looked more like the Dostoevsky I knew from our previous encounters, which I found both unsettling and reassuring.

'I'm Not Going to Defend Myself'

'Are we going to talk?' I asked, not quite sure how to begin. 'I appreciate this must have been rather difficult for you.'

'Difficult—yes. And—talk? Yes. That's why I came—I've heard all the arguments before, of course. I'll walk down the road with you and we can talk as we go.'

The light was starting to fade as we turned towards the main gates of the campus in the shadow of the towering Victorian edifice of the main university building.

I soon discovered that walking with Fyodor Mikhailovich was not entirely straightforward. At moments he strode along quite quickly and the faster he went the more rapidly he spoke. Then he would slow down as he worked through a difficult idea and even stopped altogether to deliver an especially momentous conclusion. I got an early warning of this when he came to a more or less immediate halt after just a couple of steps and, looking straight ahead, put his hand on my back and made the following declaration.

'The very first thing to say is that I'm not going to defend myself. Each of us is guilty of everything, before everyone, and I most of all. Do you remember?'

I nodded. 'Naturally, that applies to me as much as to anyone else. I am guilty, most of all. Whatever else I have to say, remember that. Even if it sounds like I'm making excuses, I know that I'm guilty. This has to be where we start from, as we already discussed. Each of us. But' (and he now began walking, pulling me gently with him) 'at the same time I would ask you to remember the context. Not what the professor said about everybody being anti-Semitic, which certainly doesn't make anything better—the lecturer was right there—but the fact that the bloody pogroms had not yet started. That was only after my death. Of course, we knew such things had happened in the past but, really, whatever our arguments with Jews or theirs with us, we had no conception of the violence that was to come—in Russia or across Europe. Each of us is guilty—I'm not forgetting that and, as a writer, I more than anyone should have been alert to the power of words. We cannot just say things and imagine our words will float off into the air and evaporate. Words have effects. Perhaps in what I wrote about the Jewish question I attempted a bit of banter, as if it was a light-hearted matter that feuilleton writers and their readers could talk about in an ironic-humorous manner—but, of course, it wasn't light-hearted at all.'

'You're absolutely right there, at least,' I said, realizing that, despite Fyodor Mikhailovich's acknowledgement of guilt, I was actually quite angry with him. 'Some of your expressions were...well...horrible. I don't see how you could possibly have thought you were being light-hearted.'

'Yes, yes, yes—again, you're right. I'm saying this was my mistake—one of many. But even then I was learning.'

'How, learning?'

'As I said in my articles, I wrote what I wrote in response to those Jewish readers who upbraided me for what I'd written about their people in *The Diary* (though, I should say, none of them ever complained to me about the characters in my fiction). And what your speaker didn't say was that it was one of them, Sofia Efimovna Luria, who sent me the story about the doctor that I printed in *The Diary*, as I made clear. I didn't tell that story. She did.'

When he mentioned Sofia Luria he looked rather wistful, as if her name conjured a good memory.

'You see, she'd written to me long before that and even came to see me several times when she was still at school—a very clever, very proud, and, I think, very noble spirit. She was wanting to give up her studies and to volunteer as a nurse for the Balkans. Who wouldn't have admired her courage, her spirit, her readiness to give herself to the Russian cause? And, for me, whether a person was Jewish or Muslim, what mattered was whether were ready to stand with Russia and with the Russian people—and then that, as far as I was concerned, was that. And remember, when I edited *Time*, we took the side of the Jews against the anti-Semites. Whatever else is to be said, that cannot be denied.

'Sofia Efimovna. Hmmm. Yes, I greatly admired her spirit, as I've just said, but I was sensible. I counselled her to finish her studies. There would be other opportunities for sacrifice and, in the end, her father's wishes prevailed, which was perhaps as it should be. It was natural, then, that when she sent me this story, I had to print it. Your speaker complained of my denying the Jews any agency, as he put it, but I only printed what she sent me.'

'Still, you seemed sceptical about whether the Jewish child for whom the old doctor gave up his shirt would do the same if he ever encountered a Christian in need.'

'Yes, yes, yes, but that was nothing to do with his being Jewish. I was only saying that that's how life goes: remember the story of Christ healing the ten lepers and only one returning to give thanks. That's not the point, though. The point is that stories like the story of Dr Hindenburg create a good memory and it's those good memories that provide us with a basis for going out to do good in our own lives, especially memories from childhood and youth. After that, it's down to each individual person whether those memories bear fruit—you remember Christ's parable of the sower. Sometimes the seed falls on the bare rock, sometimes it gets trampled underfoot, and sometimes, just sometimes, it falls in the good fertile soil, where it gets broken down and yields rich fruit. Mostly, I think, few enough of us, Jews or Christians, really do yield rich fruit. But each of us can—if we're prepared for self-sacrifice. As, I think, Sofia Efimovna was. And there were not a few Jews who fell in Russia's cause.'

He fell silent and seemed thoughtful.

'Fyodor Mikhailovich,' I began, trying to sound a little light-hearted, 'I think you were rather susceptible to those ardent and beautiful young women admirers!'

He shook his head.

'Maybe that's true, but is it a bad thing? I also wrote that the future was going to be shaped by young women like her and perhaps it was right that we of the older generation should listen to them. We had the past, but they were already seeing what was to come. They saw beyond some of the lines of division that we thought were immutable. Who knows?'

We walked on for a few moments in silence.

'I thought what he said about Isay Fomitch was a bit unfair,' I said. 'I didn't remember the passages he discussed that clearly, but it seemed to me that he was in some ways a sympathetic character—even if you did make him a bit of a caricature.'

'Yes, of course he was! Sympathetic, that is. I thought I made it clear that we all loved him. As the prisoners said, he was "our Jew" and, in prison, there were only two classes of people, us and them, and if you were one of us, that was all that needed to be said. As you've probably realized by now, I can't help developing a story when I think it needs developing and, strictly speaking, he wasn't the only

Jewish prisoner, but there certainly weren't many. And maybe I did exaggerate a bit…and throw in a couple of literary allusions that could have been received badly…And, yes, when he first appeared among us there were some pretty harsh words, which, obviously, I had to tone down for publication, and it was only too understandable that he looked scared. But he stood up for himself and, after that, they respected him. And, yes, he was a money-lender—that's what he was, why hide it—and he had special privileges, especially when it came to practising his religion. You might have thought the other prisoners would resent him for that but, actually, I think they liked to see that there was a limit to the authorities' power, though no one put it quite like that. That time I wrote about, when the major came in and shouted at him while he was saying his prayers and he just carried on—it was priceless; especially because, as he told me later, he hadn't even noticed the major standing there bawling him out.'

Dostoevsky's description of Isay Fomitch at his prayers suddenly came back to me quite vividly.

'That's all true, but isn't the way you describe how he said his prayers in a wailing singsong voice a bit ridiculous? Don't you make him a figure of fun?'

'It's how it was—or how it seemed in that strange, brooding, monotonous world. And remember also how I wrote that when his wailing and sobbing was at its height he would suddenly turn it into a song of joy. This is important. He explained to me that this was a way of remembering how the Jews' exile in Babylon would be followed by the joyful return to Jerusalem and that the way to joy goes through the deepest despair. It may all have been a bit theatrical, but I learned a lot from it. In a way, it was my own experience. "If I forget you, O Jerusalem…" Some people say I made him seem insincere, but that wasn't my intention. You must know by now that I often slip in some of my most important points under the guise of absurdity. We talked a lot. As I said, we loved him. There was no hatred—even though he was very different from the others and really quite peculiar, probably more so than most Jews.'

We were getting towards the bottom of University Avenue and the large junction where this connected with Byers Road, a broad, busy shopping street with many cafes and bars favoured by students. There was nearly always, as there was now, a large crowd waiting for the lights to change.

'Look,' Fyodor Mikhailovich resumed, 'I'm not going to go through all the passages from the novels that he spoke about. I'm not trying to justify myself at all, as I said at the outset. And though I can't exactly say that the young man who said that *The Diary* was only a kind of thought experiment was right, there's something in what he said. As I said last time, whoever the narrator in any given novel is, he is, by definition, a Russian man—or woman—of the nineteenth century. Whatever we see, we see through a nineteenth-century Russian narrator's eyes, whether that is me or, as *in The Brothers Karamazov*, a person in the novel. Whatever is said about the Jews on any particular occasion is never the last word. Never.'

We had now joined the crowd waiting to cross the road and I should explain that, in Glasgow, the traffic lights at major crossroads are timed so that pedestrians can cross from all directions at once—and do. It seems like a ridiculously small thing, but it creates a sense of quite extraordinary elation when a busy road is suddenly flooded with people walking from all sides. Reclaiming the streets. Knowing the sequence of the lights, I could tell it would soon be our turn to cross.

'All the same,' I said, trying to keep close to him in the seething, impatient crowd, 'if Russia was some kind of chosen nation, as you believed, doesn't that mean God must have rejected the Jews? You can't have two chosen peoples can you? Isn't there necessarily going to be conflict between them?'

At that moment the lights changed and we all started to move, carried in a surge towards the waves of other pedestrians coming from right and left and straight ahead.

'Don't worry,' he said, as we wove an awkward path across the road. 'Vladimir Sergeyevich had some theories about how that could be resolved. I dare say he's right. He's very clever. But'—at that moment we were separated by having to manoeuvre round a very slow moving old couple—'but, you know, they probably are a chosen people. If you could understand the Jewish people, you would probably understand God. As for me, I've never been able to imagine a Jew without God, even those amongst them who call themselves atheists'.

'Ah! *God!*' I exclaimed. 'That's what we started talking about all those weeks—months—ago but then we always seemed to end up talking about something else,' I said, shifting to the right to avoid a large man in painter's overalls who was in my way.

We'd momentarily lost contact several times in the short crossing and I fully expected to see him again, but, reaching the pavement and looking around, I couldn't spot him anywhere. The lights were now changing and the crowd was thinning out. But he was nowhere to be seen. His words 'I've never been able to imagine a Jew without God' were ringing in my ears. What on earth did this mean? Was Fyodor Mikhailovich trying to put in a good word about Jews? But just what good did having some sort of connection to God mean, anyway? What was it to be 'with' God or, for that matter, 'without' God? Whether you were Jewish, Russian, Orthodox, Catholic—or just a semi-secular Anglo-Scot like me? Could we non-Jews live without God? Perhaps we'd been living without God for a long time? Perhaps we hadn't even noticed He'd gone? So what to do when we want to find him again? Where could we begin?

All in all, it was rather an unsatisfactory ending to a difficult subject, but perhaps it couldn't be otherwise. Maybe I just had to accept that, however unpleasant some of the views he'd committed to writing, he really had moved on and now, in his new state, was truly on the way to becoming his better self. I also remembered Zosima's warning that a judge is as guilty as the person he judges. I mean, most of us probably think and say things that seem quite normal at the time but turn out to have been really obnoxious and for myself I hate to think of some of the things I thought were funny when I was a teenager—and, no, I'm not going to elaborate. The point is, you have to set a person's bad opinions against their life as a whole and all the good they do, which none of us ever really knows—though I was in no doubt that Fyodor Mikhailovich had done incalculable good to who knows how many readers, helping them believe in themselves and in each other. Nor could I imagine that the person who wrote Ivan Karamazov's protest against the cruelties inflicted on children could possibly have endorsed the Nazis' murderous extermination programme. On the contrary, for people at the time, people like Albert Camus, Ivan's were the only words that did justice to the horror of what happened in the 'Final Solution'. I'm not saying that what Fyodor Mikhailovich did say was acceptable, but I like to think—no, I'm sure—that there was a point where he'd have drawn a line.

I made a point of looking up Solovyov's ideas about the Jews, which were quite interesting. He seemed to think that the different Churches—the Catholics, the Protestants, and the Orthodox—could never really be unified until the split between Christianity and Judaism was resolved. But this wouldn't be the result of Christians converting Jews, as many Christians like to imagine; instead, it would be an entirely free reunion in which each side recognized the validity of the other's witness. It didn't seem very likely, but it was a nice idea, anyway.

Seventh Conversation

We Are All Here

In the Garden of Remembrance

I crossed the Bridge of Sighs.
  And no, I wasn't in Venice.
  I was in Glasgow.
  It was Easter Saturday and I'd decided to take a walk out to the Necropolis—the Bridge of Sighs being the rather grand name for the short service road leading to the entrance gates. Laura was in town meeting friends for coffee and we'd arranged to have lunch in the Merchant City, giving me just over an hour to myself. As I didn't really have anything urgent to do, the Necropolis seemed the obvious choice, especially on a beautiful April morning like this. It has one of the best views over the city and gives you a very different perspective on the world, literally and metaphorically—and perspective was just what I needed after the last few months. Down there it was a normal Saturday morning, humming with the noise of traffic and shoppers, while up here it all just blended into a distant murmur. Even better, there was a hint of warmth in the sun when it occasionally broke through the drifting mounds of clouds to the south-west. Not bad for Scotland in early April. The trees that sheltered the winding paths that led up to the crest of the hill were freshly in leaf and there were clumps of daffodils and narcissi in full flower.
  Glasgow's Necropolis isn't just any old graveyard but a real city of the dead, an accumulation of columns, obelisks, mausoleums, chapels, crypts, rotundas, and urns clustered on the sides of a steep hill that rises above the dark bulk of the great medieval cathedral. I have to admit that it isn't the most romantic of graveyards: the respectable dead who are taking their eternal rest here were serious Protestants and there aren't too many weeping angels, tearful infants, or other concessions to emotionalism such as you're likely to see south of the border. It's all very solemn and straight-faced. From the top of a towering column blackened by a hundred years' worth of soot the grim reformer John Knox looks down on the whole assembly, as if announcing the triumph of eternity over time. Which is ironic, because if the well-heeled Victorian citizens who paid for all this marble, granite, and stone really thought that they were buying an eternal memory, they were very, very wrong. Just a mere hundred and fifty years on, many of the inscriptions have been eroded to the point of illegibility, mausoleum gates have rusted and come off their hinges, stonework has peeled and cracked, and vandalism and graffiti have mocked the devout hopes of the subterranean inhabitants.
  Nothing last for ever. That's it. What more is there to say? Well...for a start there was Dostoevsky. If nothing lasts forever, if death is just the end and nothing more, what was he doing in my life? Dostoevsky...Solovyov...who else was going to start turning up from...from—where, exactly? Weren't his visits some kind of proof of...well, something?

I wasn't surprised—it was predictable almost—that, as I thought these thoughts, I became aware that someone was standing next to me: someone—that is, Fyodor Mikhailovich. I turned towards him but he didn't respond and was seemingly absorbed in looking out over the city, holding his battered fedora hat to his chest while the light wind ruffled his straggly hair. For some minutes we both stood in silence.

Eventually I was the one to speak.

'Look…' I began.

'About last time?' he asked.

'Well, yes…but, honestly, I don't know what to say. Except that I'm not your judge. We're all guilty, in the end. As you said.'

'Yes, and, in this case, "I more than anyone". And, by the way, I'm well aware—and happy—that many of my best readers have been Jews. "Long live brotherhood"—I meant it.'

I couldn't really think of anything useful to add. It was as if we were both staring into some kind of black hole that, in the end, no one could really make sense of.

We fell silent.

We needed to move on.

'Well,' I said, 'if you weren't standing next to me, Fyodor Mikhailovich, I'd be tempted to say, "That's it". The end. I mean death. But here you are.'

He nodded his head in acknowledgement but continued silently contemplating the view.

'I mean, all these people wanting to be remembered for ever, but for the most part, no one now really knows who any of them were. I suppose their children remembered them, and maybe their grandchildren, but even their grandchildren died a century ago. Everything gets forgotten in the end. All the effort they put into these monuments…all their protestations about eternal memory…all in vain, really.'

'Memory's never in vain,' said Fyodor Mikhailovich softly, without turning towards me.

'Yes, but even memory gets forgotten in the end, doesn't it? I mean we remember people like you or Beethoven or Shakespeare or Caesar…but the vast majority of us just get forgotten. Even if our names appear on some gravestone or can be found in some archive, no one really knows anything about the life represented by that name, do they?'

'You're in a very sombre mood today—and after everything we've talked about,' Fyodor Mikhailovich remarked.

'Sorry. Don't get me wrong. I'm not depressed or anything like that. It just seems to me that this is how it is. It's simply a matter of facing facts.'

'And these facts don't depress you the way they did back in November?'

I grimaced.

'Maybe it's the spring weather makes the difference?' I said a little shamefacedly, remembering the somewhat melodramatic thoughts about death and the meaninglessness of life that were the starting point of our conversations.

'Hmm,' he said, 'if only everybody's existential despair was as easily cured as that.'

'I'm sure our conversations have helped,' I replied quickly, not wanting him to think his visits had been wasted.

He raised his eyebrows and breathed deeply.

'Well then, what do you think?' he asked. 'Is it worthwhile remembering the dead? Or should we just forget them, seeing that they'll all be forgotten in the end anyway, the sooner the better?'

'No, not at all. That's not what I'm saying. We can't help remembering them. I often find myself thinking of my parents and others I've known who've died. It's a human thing. Only I don't think it really leads anywhere. I mean, it doesn't prove anything, does it?'

'Should it have to "lead anywhere" or "prove anything"?'

'You mean, it's worth doing for its own sake?'

'As you say, it's part of being human…to remember one another, to keep each other in mind. And even if it doesn't prove anything, isn't that the very heart of love? Perhaps you've heard the saying that forgetfulness leads to exile and memory to redemption? I didn't write it, but it isn't a bad summary of some of my ideas.'

'Redemption? That's quite strong, isn't it?'

'Let's walk a bit,' said Fyodor Mikhailovich. I nodded and we turned and continued slowly along a gently curving path leading up the hill.

'Think of it like this,' he continued, putting on his hat; 'much of what goes wrong in the world goes wrong because people forget, like old man Karamazov forgot that he was meant to be a father to his children and perhaps even forgot that he had them. The truth is that his forgetfulness and neglect did as much to set the whole catastrophe in motion as his drunkenness and lechery. And that's also why Alyosha taught his young disciples to treasure the memory of the good deed they'd shared and why he insisted that such a memory can nourish us throughout our lives and go on giving us hope—not only that life is worth living but also that opening up to each other in love is worthwhile. Remembering those moments of goodness reminds us that if we can experience love once, we can experience it again.'

'Yes, yes,' I agreed, thinking back to *The Brothers Karamazov*. 'And Zosima too, doesn't he talk about the importance of memory, especially childhood memories, like his own memories of going to church or reading Bible stories?'

'Exactly. Those are the kind of memories that provide the basis for a good and wholesome life.' He sighed and then paused. For a minute or two we walked on in silence.

'The sorrow of it is,' he resumed, 'that some children have few enough such memories and many have even more powerful memories of cruelty, sickness, or loss, though perhaps—I like to think—there's no life completely devoid of some good memory, if only we know how to find it and hold on to it and treasure it. That kind of remembering may even be a more effective route to healing than reliving our traumas. In fact, if we don't have the perspective of some good memory, remembering our traumas is probably only ever going to be destructive. Fixating on evil and forgetting the good is just what the devil wants.'

I was tempted to say that 'fixating on evil' was what some of Dostoevsky's critics had complained of in his writing, but I wondered whether you could make quite such a simplistic division between good and bad memories. Some of the most vivid memories are 'beyond good and evil', to coin a phrase—like Alyosha Karamazov's memory of his hysterical mother, holding him up to the icon of the Mother of God as 'the slanting rays of the setting sun' streamed in through the windows until someone comes in and snatches him from her. It obviously plays an important part in the novel, but what does a memory like that *mean*? Even though Alyosha treasures it as a memory of his mother, it's not really a good memory. Some would say that it's more like a traumatic memory, beautiful *and* disturbing like a dissonant chord in a minor key. I put these thoughts to Fyodor Mikhailovich and asked him how a memory like that could lead to anything good.

He didn't answer immediately.

I waited.

'Yes, yes, yes. Human life is always mixed and Alyosha's memory too is mixed. The sun...the icon...birth and death...her madness...and her mother's love, even if her love was unbalanced, confused, and desperate, as human loves often are.'

'So maybe it's a good memory because of the way he remembered it...because he remembered it with love.'

Fyodor Mikhailovich punched his right fist emphatically into the palm of his left hand and shook his clenched hands energetically.

'Exactly! If we remember with love, then what we remember will be love!'

'Isn't that circular...?'

'And why not? Love begets love. How else would it work? And we mustn't stop there...with the childhood memories that is. We must do all we can to remember the good—the love—in each other throughout our lives. Even remembering the good in those we don't know.'

'How do you mean?'

'Don't you remember how Zosima told the monks that they should pray every day for all those who were dying, even if they didn't know them or know anything about them? Even if you can't name them, even if you know nothing about them, even if no one knows anything about them and they've been forgotten by the whole world, remembering them before God is a good thing.'

'All the same, I still want to know whether it achieves anything,' I couldn't help commenting—again.

'Who knows? What do any of us know about the consequences of what we do and don't do—but it's a good thing. It increases love. It binds us more closely together, even if only by the merest fraction. Remember the onion! It keeps us connected to God. And I'm not denying that living like that, keeping humanity connected in loving prayer, isn't challenging. It's hard enough remembering what we should be remembering in our own lives. Even Alyosha, so nearly a saint—and perhaps he would have grown up to become a saint if I'd managed to finish his story—even Alyosha forgot about his brother Dmitri at a crucial moment and his forgetfulness too contributed to the final denouement. As for me, if I'd really remembered what Anna Grigoryevna needed and deserved from me, then I'd never have gone to the roulette hall. I was too busy pursuing my idea of becoming fantastically wealthy or, at least, escaping my debts, that I simply forgot about this real, living person who loved me so much and to whom I owed so much. No, remembering isn't easy. Truthful remembrance is only possible if you're prepared to face up to your guilt and responsibility—as I said in our very first conversation. But when we forget, that's when things go really wrong.'

He paused and turned round again to look back towards the city. When he continued, it was almost as if he was talking to himself.

'I think that science tells us that all matter is subject to entropy, everything is gradually slowing down and will end by collapsing into an unmoving and immoveable mass. I don't believe that—science has been wrong before—but it does seem to me that it's a good image of what remembering is like, an unending struggle against entropy. In the spiritual sense, of course.

'And, naturally, it isn't easy. We all need help; trying to struggle forward on our own is never going to succeed. This is what's so difficult for you children of Western individualism to grasp—you all want to do it in your own way. You may argue about what the prayers of the Church can achieve, but one thing they do achieve is that you're not left to remember on your own—and our individual memories are not so very strong. But the Church prays for all and reminds us, each of us, to pray for all, to pray for our dead, for example, for all sufferers, for those we love, and for our enemies.'

He gestured towards a nearby gravestone that was etched with the image of a downturned torch.

'In the ancient world, as I'm sure you know, the dead had to pass through the water of forgetfulness on their way into the underworld, forgetting the world they'd left behind and being forgotten by it. But if, as Christians, our hope is that we will rise and be with Christ, sharing the light in which he lives, then we must strive to overcome forgetfulness and remember.'

'Remember what, exactly?' I interjected.

He laughed.

'Ideally, everything! All that has been, all that is, and all that will be! But seeing it all in His light. "Do this in remembrance of me," He said, meaning that we might start by remembering Him. Even when we're burning in the furnace of doubt.'

After another brief pause, he continued again.

'You see, that's what I was trying to do in my novels. Just that.'

'Sorry, I don't follow—just what?'

'Remember everything. His light in the darkness. And remember it in such a way that my readers remembered it too.'

'I still don't follow... Weren't your novels fictions—you yourself told me that they were all "made up"? I remember *that* quite clearly. I think you even said they were lies. So how can they be memories? And even if they were your memories, they're not my memories, so how could they help me remember everything in my life in "His light", as you put it?'

I'd got past worrying whether my questions were too aggressive, having learned that Fyodor Mikhailovich wanted me to be honest and say what I thought—to be less 'English', as he'd said on one occasion.

'You're right,' he said. 'This needs some explaining. If you bear with me, I'll do the best I can; though, remember, I was never a philosopher, only a novelist, a writer, as you say—*of fictions*!'

* * *

'Where to begin?' he mused. Falling silent, he seemed transfixed by a tree to our right that was just coming into leaf. 'Look at that!' he said, 'How can anyone look at that and not be filled with joy?' His voice fell to a confidential whisper. 'Perhaps all those books weren't necessary after all!' He smiled and touched me lightly on the shoulder. 'Let's carry on,' he added, and we resumed our climb.

'Well then. Raskolnikov. Sonia Marmeladova. Myshkin. Aglaya. Stavrogin. Old man Karamazov and his sons. The blessed Elder Zosima. It's true, none of them ever existed, not in the way a living flesh-and-blood human being existed—and, by the way, you won't get anywhere by trying to find the so-called real-life characters that some people think they were based on. Does that mean they're not real? Not at all! Maybe they're even more real in a certain sense. As I've said before, being true to life isn't the same as just holding up a camera to everyday reality. Genuine realism means looking beyond the external appearance and seeing what it is that makes those appearances appear as they do, seeing what makes reality tick, as I think your contemporaries might put it. It's what I called a higher realism.'

I nodded.

'So it's a bit like what you were saying when we talked about the Bible; that these characters are rather like archetypes.'

'Yes—but archetypes as they appear in life. As I wrote somewhere, it's quite likely that you've never ever met anyone who's exactly like one of my characters but, as you read, you suddenly realize that this is a true portrait of someone you really do know—and maybe you even understand them for the very first time.'

'The play's the thing...'

'Exactly. Shakespeare understood this very well. You've probably never known a would-be terrorist who's just like Raskolnikov, for example, but you've probably known many a disillusioned and angry young man who is a Raskolnikov at heart—even though he'd never hurt a fly, let alone murder two defenceless women. And, equally, you've probably never met a saint like Zosima, but through Zosima you see the saintliness in all the people you have met who are saints or, at least, on their way to saintliness.'

'The mirror of art,' I murmured. And then, more loudly, 'By the way, Fyodor Mikhailovich, it's not only characters—it's situations. When I first read your novels I found all those scandal scenes very extreme, very Russian. But more recently I've realized that they're fairly accurate descriptions of some of the rows that happened in my own family when I was a child. Of course, all the details are entirely different, but it's basically the same. Even though we're all very English. Believe me!'

He laughed.

'Yes, indeed! Even without axes or pistols, human passions can be quite destructive, just as hell doesn't need to be fitted out with hooks or pits of fire to be well and truly hellish. Just a quiet word can be enough to condemn a person to endless torment. As I say, it's not the struggle against physical entropy that matters: it's the effort to achieve and maintain spiritual remembrance. The mirror of art, as you called it, points in two directions: towards the everyday world (my nineteenth-century world, your twenty-first-century world), but also towards... well, what I'd call the true world.'

'A kind of magic mirror, then,' I said.

'How so?'

'You think you're looking at one thing—St Petersburg in 1866, for example—and you're actually looking at something different, something spiritual, metaphysical maybe?'

'Yes, yes, yes. That's very interesting. Yes, I think so.'

I thought for a moment or two. When we'd been talking with Vladimir Sergeyevich Solovyov we'd touched on Platonism and Plato's idea of reality being defined by eternal ideas or archetypes.

'You are a Platonist, then?' I asked.

'A Platonist? Would that be a bad thing?'

'I didn't say it was a bad thing, exactly, but it does seem to devalue the world, the everyday world, what most people call the real world, in favour of what you call spiritual truths—ideas—archetypes... As if our life in this world is just a kind of stepping stone to something else... But surely this life earthly matters in its own right... and surely it mattered to you, otherwise you couldn't have described it or recreated it in such detail, so, well, realistically?'

'Thank you, thank you,' Fyodor Mikhailovich replied. 'And you're right, obviously. This world—your world—matters. We've discussed this several times. It's where we begin to learn what love is and what it is to love. If we don't start there, we won't start anywhere. Remember what we said before about the earth and being true to the earth. Heaven is not some separate place but heaven and earth are inseparably and eternally bound up together. What you call Platonism isn't turning away from earth: it's seeing earth in the light of eternity.'

I wasn't too sure about this. From everything I'd read it did seem to me that Plato wanted us to forget about the material world for the sake of the eternal ideas. In fact, when I'd raised this with Vladimir Sergeyevich he'd seemed to half-concede the point—and he was, after all, a bona fide philosopher.

'I see what you're saying, Fyodor Mikhailovich,' I began, cautiously, 'but I'm not sure if that's really what Plato was saying.'

He stopped and shook his head.

'No. You're probably right—but it's what the blessed apostle John did with Plato. What matters is not just the idea (that is, the Word) but the Word incarnate. Made flesh. Not turning away from the world but showing what the world could be; that is, what we, each of us, could be—the ideas, the words, the truths we could make our own and live by. The idea becoming true by becoming life! Yes,' he paused and thought for a moment, 'you'll find this all in John's gospel: "In the beginning was the Word, and the Word became flesh, in him was Life and the Life was the Light of men."'

I was finding it easy to be carried along by Fyodor Mikhailovich's ecstatic words, but they also reminded me of one of Nietzsche's more acerbic comments about Christianity. 'Platonism for the people, then, just like Nietzsche said,' I commented, under my breath.

'A lot of people say all sort of things,' said Fyodor Mikhailovich sharply and rather dismissively. 'But John didn't forget—in fact, he insisted—that the Word must become incarnate. To put it in terms we've talked about, the Christ who passed through Russia dressed like a Russian peasant, enduring all the indignities that the Russian peasant endured is just as truly Christ as the Christ whose light lit up the heavenly banquet of Cana of Galilee, a light no human can ever directly see. Whatever people—and whatever poor dear Nietzsche said—John understood that perfectly.'

* * *

'We seem to have come a long way from your novels,' I ventured. 'Or perhaps not...'

'Certainly not! But it wasn't up to me to say again what could only be said by someone who had seen the Word made flesh with his own eyes. I was only ever a writer of novels, a teller of tales, an inventor of fictions. And yet, for my time—and maybe still for some people in your time—my words were able to remind them of his word, John's word *and His*, a word they'd mostly forgotten or were constantly on the edge of forgetting. You never knew Raskolnikov, you never knew Zosima—but they and all the rest of them, my whole human comedy, could nevertheless remind you of what was most important in your own life.'

'And yet, Fyodor Mikhailovich, till you actually appeared, I think your novels raised more questions than answers...for me, at least. When you first came, what I was reading reminded me more of my despair than of anything to do with Christ or eternal life. And not every reader is going to have the benefit of having you come and explain it all,' I added, doubtfully.

He laughed quietly, as if to himself.

'Well, perhaps it's important that, before anything else, we remember to ask the right questions! It seems to me that when it comes to faith the whole discussion gets skewed by the fact that it's usually the wrong questions people insist on—like when they want to know about the historical facts behind the gospels. That might be an interesting historical question, but it's not a question that's ever going to help anyone find faith.'

'So what sort of questions should we be asking?'

'The questions we should be asking—the questions we might just need reminding about—are questions about ourselves, about what we're looking for, and about what we really want.'

'That sounds great, Fyodor Mikhailovich—but the thing is that when I ask those sorts of questions, I don't get any answers.'

He looked quizzically at me and I realized that what I'd just said could seem rather churlish, not only in the light of his constant willingness to respond to my often rather crass and even impertinent questions and comments but also because his novels didn't just pose questions, they also provided many positive images of faith. There wasn't only Raskolnikov—there was also Sonia; there wasn't only Ivan—there was also Alyosha (and, of course, Zosima). And everyone in between.

'OK,' I conceded. 'Here's the thing. Let's say I was trying, really trying, to be true to the best and most inspiring memories from my own past, the question that we started with still remains.'

'And that was?'

'Whether...whether the universe really cares...whether the best we can do isn't, in the end, Quixotic, like your Prince Myshkin.'

Fyodor Mikhailovich bowed his head and looked thoughtful. We continued walking silently for a few paces. Then he stopped, putting his hands on his hips and seeming to breathe deeply (I don't know if he could 'breathe' but he could definitely talk, so why not?).

'Well, at least we've solved one problem,' he declared.
'Really? What's that?'
'We're not talking about Platonism any more!'
'We're not?'
'No—or not in the sense you meant. The questions we're talking about now—the kinds of questions I wanted to remind my readers of—they're not ideals that have nothing at all to do with life. They're what people in the twentieth century would call existential questions, questions about how to live, or, even better, about the sort of person you want to be.'
'Not metaphysical questions, then?'
'On the contrary, very much "metaphysical"—but only to the extent that they're first and foremost existential.'

I thought for a moment.

'Fine,' I said, hesitantly. 'But can we come back to what I just said about the universe…about the universe not caring. To put it bluntly: is there a God? Is there immortality?'

He turned to me and put one hand on my elbow. His touch was very gentle, but there was a definite pressure. What absorbed my attention, though, were his eyes. I don't really know how to describe them. The pupils had expanded and, meeting his gaze, I found myself being drawn into a vast pool of darkness, like the darkest of night skies, glistening with points of warm, radiant light. A luminous darkness you might call it. It made me feel somehow dizzy, as if I was going to pass out.

If I'd allowed myself to think that his visits were something I'd got used to—that they were *normal*—I was getting a sharp reminder as to just how great the gulf between us really was. It was unnerving, like feeling out of one's depth in the sea and, for a moment, not remembering how to swim.

'Fyodor Mikhailovich,' I blurted out, almost panicking, 'what do you see *there*? What kind of life is it? Did you see Masha again? *Did* you—*do* you? And Anna Grigoryevna? And do you, *there*, remember us, as we remember you?'

He didn't immediately withdraw his gaze but, ever so slowly, it seemed to come back into focus. He moved his hand, as if brushing something off my shoulder and turned further round, so as to look back at the city. I followed his cue.

'Now that's a lot of questions,' he said. 'Did I see Masha again? And Anna Grigoryevna?'

Masha, I should say, had been his first wife and he'd written an eloquent private note about his thoughts while standing over her dead body, asking himself whether he'd ever see her again. These notes had a special connection to the story I'd been reading when he first visited me, *A Gentle Spirit*. Although Dostoevsky's wife didn't kill herself, as the woman in *A Gentle Spirit* does, both texts reproduce the thoughts of a man standing by the body of a wife he had wronged. Anna Grigoryevna was his second wife, with whom, by all accounts, he'd finally found happiness.

I waited for him to say more.

He looked at me slyly.

'You're not trying to catch me out, are you?' he asked.

'Catch you out? How?'

'Your question reminds me of how the Sadducees tried to trick Christ.'

'Sorry...I don't follow...'

'Surely, you remember—when they asked Him the question about whose wife a woman who had been predeceased by seven husbands would be...at the resurrection?'

'In the resurrection they neither marry nor are given in marriage.' It was a text I ought to have known. Unlike the Sadducees, though, my question was serious and he hadn't really answered it—any more than Jesus really answered the Sadducees.

'You know,' he continued, in a more easy-going voice, 'I once wrote that three-quarters of the happiness to be found in life is to be found in marriage. Of course, I also knew that forgiveness is never more needed than when things go wrong between man and wife. I experienced that too. We are all guilty. And there is happiness.'

Shedding the Ego

He stopped and looked down, perhaps absorbed in his memories. I knew he'd had two very eventful marriages and there was obviously a lot to remember. Not all of it to his credit. Finally, he raised his head and looked out over the city.

'The thing is, it's almost impossible to explain. It almost goes without saying that He was right—that nothing here is quite like how we imagine it while we're on earth. Our questions are never quite right and our answers are no answers at all. As we were just saying, the questions that really matter are the questions about ourselves, about who we are, but even here we mostly start off on the wrong foot—especially if we've been reading some philosophy.'

'How do you mean?'

'It's not so difficult and I think we've touched on it before. It's the ego, the "I". The problem is that we just seem to take it for granted that this is a simple fact. As the philosopher said, "I think, therefore I am." We may not be philosophers but each of us tends to assume that that "I am" is the most basic fact there is. It's something you just can't get beyond or behind and therefore it colours everything we think, do, or feel. Which is a mistake, because if we really think about what happens in love, there has to be something more basic, more powerful than the ego. "A god greater than I", as the Italian poet wrote. That's just as true for the most ordinary everyday kind of love as it is for the love we see in the saints, though they love to a much more intense degree.'

'But, Fyodor Mikhailovich, I seem to remember that when we were talking about Christ you said that only He could love perfectly because He was the only person in history whose life wasn't based on egoism, whereas the rest of us can never free ourselves of it entirely.'

'No more we can. Even here, where I am now, we're still in the process of shedding the last illusions of what you call egoism. Nevertheless, I didn't say we couldn't love at all. What I said was that although our love was always going to be limited or distorted by our inveterate egoism, we also had the example of one who had appeared in time and shown the truth of a love utterly devoid of egoism and because of that we are able to direct our efforts towards the right goal. Even for us, egoism isn't the only factor. From the very beginning of our lives we're surrounded and fed by a love—our mother's love—that moulds our basic response to life. And when the baby smiles back at its mother, that's not egoism, it's love. Remember Raphael! Everything we've talked about in connection with brotherhood is only possible because there's more to us than egoism. To know that your life is not just about what you as a single individual want to do or feel like doing but is connected to what you owe your brothers—and sisters (you see, I'm not forgetting about the sisters)—this too is more than egoism. And, as I said before, this is something that you don't need to have explained to you, it's something you feel; it's as immediate as your feeling of your own self.'

'Yes, though you also said that those of us in the West, at least, had forgotten this—that we only had liberty and equality, but not fraternity.'

'Yes, and it's true—to a great extent. I'm not saying and never did say that everyone in the West was completely incapable of love. You wouldn't be human if you couldn't love at all—as Zosima said, you'd be in hell because it's only in hell that the possibility of love is completely annihilated. And who knows, perhaps not even there, just reduced, so to speak, to a quadrillionth of its proper power. No. No one could go on living at all if they didn't have some sense of being part of something greater than themselves. Remember Zosima again: everything flows. When we are thinking from within the boundaries of the ego we think of each other as self-contained units, like Leibniz's monads, but that's a false point of view. These boundaries are themselves part of the illusion. To be a person, a real human person, is to be much more than an ego, a self, an "I".'

'And yet, Fyodor Mikhailovich, all these characters in your novels—they're all individuals aren't they, each with a distinctive personality and none of them quite like any of the others?'

'Indeed, that's what I tried to achieve as a writer—but, at the same time, to show how none of these individuals existed alone; that they were who they were and became whoever they became only in and through how they responded to each other. Someone like Raskolnikov tried to be master of his own life and to cut all the ties that bound him to family and friends—but he couldn't do it. It was a fantasy. As for the brothers Karamazov, as you yourself pointed out, the narrator wrote a novel whose "hero", as he called him, was Alyosha, but I wrote a novel about all three—even Alyosha needed the others every bit as much as they needed him. Even though he doesn't himself know why, he's drawn to them and is eager to get to know them. Why? Because he knows that the secret of his own life is only to be found in the life he shares with his brothers. Nowhere else. If he's to grow in love, he quite simply has to let go of whatever "ego" or "self" there still is in his heart.'

'Quite simply! It sounds rather difficult to me!'

'It is difficult and—as I said—it's not something that any human being can fully achieve in earthly life.'

What Fyodor Mikhailovich was saying about letting go of the ego reminded me of various things I'd read from time to time about Buddhism. In fact, it seemed to be a commonplace of what some people call the new spirituality.

'I'm thinking, Fyodor Mikhailovich—and forgive me if I said this before—this is all sounding rather like Buddhism. Don't Buddhists teach that there's no ego, no self, that it's all an illusion?'

Fyodor Mikhailovich pressed the palms of his hands together, almost as if he was praying. He smiled.

'I didn't really know very much about them in my lifetime,' he said, 'though I was interested—and I don't think they're completely wrong. Some would say there's something Buddhist-like about our Russian Christianity. Perhaps there is. We look East as well as West, and Christ fulfils all human longings. In any case, East or West, the point is that it's not just about seeing through the illusions of the ego: it's about becoming active in love.'

'So who do we love and who does the loving if there's no ego and no self?'

A wave of warm air came up on the soft south-westerly breeze. Fyodor Mikhailovich removed his hat by the crown, shook his head, and let his hand, still holding the hat, fall to his side.

'It's such a beautiful day, isn't it?' he said.

I waited. I was getting used to the way in which he often avoided giving a direct or immediate answer to my questions.

He looked at me out of the corner of his eye, almost slyly.

'Assuming you're not just playing with words,' he said, 'I'd just point out that I never said that when you let go of the ego you're left with nothing. On the contrary, when you let go of the ego you have life, life in all its fullness, without the limits and boundaries that our rational ego places on it. When the seed bursts its shell, you could say that it dies but it doesn't just cease to be. It has to "die" in order to bring forth new life. You know that verse from John, of course, and I'm sure you know I took it as the motto for my *Brothers*.'

I grunted affirmatively.

'And remember also what He said about loving your life and losing it: the only way to find life is to lose it.'

'All the same, if everyone were all of a sudden to give up their egos, wouldn't the whole of society grind to a halt? I can see that things might be better if there were a few more ego-free saints of love to help us stay optimistic, but...could *everyone* live like that?'

'And you don't think society is grinding to a halt already? Perhaps you don't read the newspapers like I did.'

He had a point. You couldn't really hold up the kind of society we had now as any kind of model. Some kind of change was clearly needed—and if it wasn't going to be in the direction of increasing love, then the prospects really were rather grim.

In Christ's Light

I'm very aware that one of my faults is a tendency to be flippant when talking about serious things. If I had a therapist, I expect he'd say it was a strategy of avoidance. Probably it is.

'Is it a mistake, then, to give your love to just one person for the whole of your life, like in marriage? Isn't that a kind of egoism too, a kind of possessiveness? The way we say *my* wife, *my* husband...perhaps the people who call themselves polyamorous are right?'

He sighed.

'Look. In the course of a human life we all know a variety of loves. But the fullness of love isn't less than a whole human life, it's more. If you really could perfectly love just one other human being, you'd have achieved a miracle. To be sure, the way we love is sometimes very egotistical and people use what they call love to make themselves more interesting or exciting as individuals. It's a delusion, of course—though sifting the true from the false isn't always easy. Just think of some of the relationships I described in my novels. Does Myshkin love Aglaya or Anastasia Phillipovna? Does Katerina love Dmitri or Ivan? Does Stavrogin love Liza? And whatever way you decide, how real is that love? Is it love or passion? A lot of ink has been spilled over these questions. And I'm not the only novelist to have noticed it. The lie can do a very convincing imitation of the truth and true love sometimes hides itself behind the lie. And yet, if there is some seed of genuine love in any of our loves, it will abide and bring forth fruit. To get back to your question, then, yes: Masha...Anna Grigoryevna...even Suslova...not to mention my little Alyosha...and, of course, you already know about Vladimir Sergeyevich...they are all here, *we* are all here...but, how can I say, it's not our feast, we're only guests, and our joy is no longer for ourselves only, it's for the bridegroom, for the one whose feast we're celebrating. This is the joy that unites us.'

'You mean Christ?'

He nodded.

'So...how is it? I mean, is it like Dante's "mystic rose" where all the saints sit round looking up at God?'

He shook his head, incredulously.

'I've told you before, haven't I, that I may not tell you how it is here. And even if I were permitted to speak, I couldn't. It's not possible. It really is indescribable.'

Again, I had a momentary twinge of anxiety, sensing the great gulf between us and realizing that this man I was talking to had been but no longer was a man quite like me. This time, though, it was less intense. Maybe this was because I sensed a tone of sympathy, even regret, in what he said. Not quite like me—but human, all the same. As if wanting to allay my fears, he continued, slipping into what was by now a familiar schoolteacherly tone.

'What you say about Dante's heaven isn't quite accurate and, anyway, I don't think you were being entirely serious, but we'll leave that. Of course, Dante spoke and could only speak in images, figures, parables—as he himself said. He could say nothing of what he had experienced except by adjusting it to the minds of his readers, his Euclidean readers, you could say. You might object that I'm now speaking to you from the very place that he spoke about and that I should therefore know what he only imagined. But even if that's so, then—as long as I'm talking to you—I'm forced to use those same images, figures, and parables. Well, not exactly the "same" because he was a man of the Middle Ages and I was a man of the modern world, the modern city, and the modern capitalist system, living in a world of railways, steamships, newspapers, and stock markets. But I can say this much: that we're not, as you put it, sitting around looking at Him. He is everywhere, His light is everywhere, and we don't need to look at it because we see it when we look at each other. That's what I mean by seeing each other in His light.'

'Each other? Most of what I've read about heaven speaks about the saints contemplating God, not each other!'

'This is why I'm saying that it's so difficult to explain. You ask: "Is it this?" or "Is it that?" but it's not exactly either and not exactly both. We don't—as you put it—sit around looking at Him. We see Him, but we see Him in the light in which we see each other and to see each other in His light is to see Him. It's a matter of love again, you see. Even on earth, we sometimes have moments (at least, I did) when we feel that if only we could all let go of our prejudices, our suspicions, our fears, our jealousy, our pride, and all the rest of it and see each other as we are, as the best in us is always wanting to be—why, then, we might be in heaven already.'

'Markel,' I said, referring to the ecstatic visions of Zosima's younger brother that Dostoevsky described in *The Brothers Karamazov* and who said that if we saw the world as it truly is we'd be in paradise now.

'Markel, and not only Markel. You see, it's not a matter of choosing between each other and Him or between earth and heaven. We just have to learn to see things in the right way—but learning always takes time. Perhaps there are those like Markel who see it in an instant but for most of us learning to see the truth takes a lifetime—and more. You could even say that it's unending.'

'So you don't see him directly at all?'

'Please, don't try to make me say what I've just said quite clearly I cannot say. Think back to when Alyosha dreams of seeing Zosima amongst the guests at the wedding in Cana and Zosima calls to him to come and join them and to behold Him, their Sun, their light. But the light is far too bright and Alyosha cannot look, any more than you could look at the sun with your naked eyes.'

I don't for a moment believe that God—whatever God is—plays tricks with the weather, but as Fyodor Mikhailovich was speaking the sun momentarily came out from behind the clouds that had been thinning out as the morning progressed and I had to raise my hand to shade my eyes.

'Fair enough,' I was forced to admit. 'But that's a physical thing. Christ's light is spiritual, isn't it? So why can't Alyosha look at Him?'

He tutted. 'Now listen—I need you to listen very carefully,' he said. 'Alyosha couldn't look at Him because he was still limited by his earthly body and humanity, but Zosima and the other guests—they could see Him. In fact, it's in Him and through Him that God's light, the ultimate and uncreated light, becomes visible, "acquires a human face", you could say.'

I wondered whether Fyodor Mikhailovich had actually meant to quote William Blake and, if so, where he'd encountered his poetry. But I still didn't quite get it.

'Fyodor Mikhailovich,' I complained. 'This is all very confusing. Help me out a bit. I mean, if this divine light is so bright that we can't look at it, how can you see it in a human face?'

Fyodor Mikhailovich put his hands to his head in what I hoped was only mock frustration.

'Is that so incredible? Haven't you had moments in your life when you've suddenly found yourself face to face with a beautiful woman who's literally so radiant that you can hardly look at her?'

'But that's different!'

'Obviously it's not the same, but just think of the effect Beatrice had on Dante. It taught him about "the god that is greater than I" again. Isn't that a start? Everything I've been saying should be telling you that earthly love, imperfect earthly love, is the best way of learning divine love.'

Divine love. This was a long way from where our conversations had started: with a vision of a loveless world beneath a dead sun.

God

Down to the right of where we were standing loomed the great dark mass of the cathedral, the one medieval building surviving the constantly repeated demolition and rebuilding of the surrounding city, its spire steadily but wearily pointing those who might care to look upwards towards God. Or so the faithful hoped. I couldn't help thinking of Nietzsche's madman who described Christendom's empty churches as tombs of God. What such a building or its God had to do with our conversations was hard to say.

'So, Fyodor Mikhailovich. God.'

He looked surprised and watched me for several seconds as if waiting for me to say more.

'God?'

'Yes, God. We've been talking, I suppose, about immortality, but in *The Brothers Karamazov* it seems like the question about immortality is also a question about God. So, then, God. Does he exist? I suppose if there's immortality, he must—but maybe this immortality is all just part of some great cosmic process, some eternally evolving collective mind in which Christ is the most highly evolved individual, or something like that?'

I almost surprised myself by how philosophical I sounded. It's true that I'd dipped in to Solovyov's writings since that conversation in the park and I realized that what I'd just said was probably an echo of what he'd written, though (obviously) in a very simplified version.

'God? Yes. Where does the light come from if not from God? We, I'm afraid, don't generate too much light. Not left to ourselves. Reptiles devouring each other in some dark primeval swamp. But there is light. The world is flooded with light once we have eyes to see.'

'Sorry, I don't want to niggle about words, but I thought you said the light you see each other by was Christ's light. So: Christ—God. What's the difference? Is there any difference? How does that work?'

'Don't you remember—it seems you don't—the apostle's word about the light of God's glory shining in the face of Christ? Christ's light is God's light and that's the light in which we see each other for who we really are. As I've said, that doesn't mean that all human beings are ready to see that light. Perhaps none of us can see it directly while we're on earth and, even here, it takes some time to adjust to. The source, of course, is hidden and will always remain hidden, but we know it by the light it emits—and I'd add, the joy.'

'The joy?'

'The joy. It's the only real answer there is to all those interminable eternal questions. Even if you can't see the light or aren't aware that you're seeing it, the joy you feel in your life is almost a direct awareness of God. You can't see Him, but you can have joy in Him and having joy in Him is to know Him. If I may mention Zosima again, remember how he exhorted his monks to pray for joy and to be as joyful as children and as the birds from heaven. Joy, in the end, is the answer to all our prayers. Only, of course, it's not an answer that any philosopher would accept, though the best of the Church Fathers knew it.'

'But how do you mean, "joy", Fyodor Mikhailovich?' I asked. Part of me warmed to what he was saying but joy didn't really seem like an explanation and, anyway, what kind of joy was he talking about? There was the joy we experienced in physical exercise, in listening to music, in work, in being out in nature, and, well, sex. Was this what he was talking about or did he mean some special kind of religious joy? In that case, I didn't really know what he was talking about. So I put the question to him, pretty much in those terms.

Slowly, thoughtfully, he put his hat back on and pressed it down firmly. Despite the fact that we were now talking about joy he seemed to become quite sombre, almost withdrawing into himself.

'Questions, questions, questions,' he said, almost reproachfully. 'Listen. There's nothing wrong with asking questions, but you have to ask them in the right way. As I said in our very first conversation, why ask me, why not ask God? You said that he hadn't turned up and, since I was there, you had to make do with asking me.'

'Yes, yes, I remember.'

'I didn't object and, as you know, you've asked me a lot more questions since then. I've done my best to tell you what I can, but, in the end, it really isn't me you need to be asking.'

'It's God,' I said.

'Exactly.'

'But how do I ask God? Do you mean going to church and joining in the prayers?'

'That's one way,' he said, 'as long as you pray in the right way.'

'And just how do I pray in the right way? And who can tell me what the right way is? We were just talking about joy, but I don't always see the people who go to church being very joyful. In fact, I have to admit that I sometimes find their services rather dismal.'

'Let me tell you a story,' he said. 'It's a true story and I wrote about it in *The House of the Dead*. It's rather appropriate because it happened during Holy Week—and I think this is your Church's Holy Week now?'

I nodded.

'Yes, tomorrow's Easter Day.'

'Good, well you can think about this tomorrow. Now, listen. When I was in the camp, we were taken to church each year for the Holy Week services—under armed guard. And make no mistake, the rifles were loaded. Can you imagine that?' He stopped, giving me time to grasp the irony of taking people to church under armed guard. Ready to shoot them if they stepped out of line. 'When we arrived, a great crowd of us, shaven-headed, chained, many of us branded, were corralled into a place at the back of the church where we could hardly see anything, though we could hear the voice of the priest, smell the incense, and see the light pouring in through the windows in the cupola. A bright Siberian light. And I couldn't help remembering how, in my childhood, our family had always stood towards the front, if not in the very best places then in the next-to-best places, along with the other middle- and upper-class people. Like any child, my attention drifted from time to time and sometimes when I looked round I'd notice the common people massed by the door: poor, shabby, and, frankly, smelly. I was even a bit frightened of them. And now, now—I was one of them, and worse, because we were several rungs below the common people, we were convicts, men to be feared, but—the way the Russian people understood the situation—also men to be pitied. Some even offered me alms, as if I was a beggar. But I tell you, it was there, amongst those men, the lowest of the low, men who knew their own degradation and prostrated themselves before God in full knowledge of their depravity and guilt, asking for a forgiveness they knew they didn't deserve—it was there I learned what it really meant to pray. Pray like that, and your prayer will be answered.'

What could I say? We've all had moments when we felt like outsiders, but I'd never experienced anything remotely like that in my life and almost certainly never would. So where did this leave me?

On several previous occasions, I'd notice how Fyodor Mikhailovich seemed to read my thoughts and what he went on to say might have been an answer to my unspoken questions.

'Of course, you haven't experienced that, few people have. And I should say that there's nothing good about suffering that kind of degradation. Whatever people think I said, suffering itself doesn't bring you nearer God. Some of those penitents who sought out suffering by tramping all over Russia, starving themselves, and wearing chains, perhaps some of them found forgiveness, it's true. But it wasn't the hunger or the chains that saved them. It was their desire, their hope, their truth. And for those prisoners, there and then, for me too, there was honesty, there was truth. When we prayed "Save us" we meant "Save us." And, believe me, we needed saving. It wasn't just a formula spoken in a polite and well-trained voice. It was everything, the whole content of our lives gathered into that moment, that word. None of them could have put it like this—I couldn't have done so myself at the time—but when you're praying like that, even while you're still praying, you know you're being heard, and despite the fact that you have to go back to the camp and maybe serve another ten years there's a seed, a seed of joy, and you feel it, even then. That', he concluded, 'is the truth that makes you free.'

It seemed that we were back to the beginning—questions, despair, truth. But, as he spoke, I began to understand, perhaps for the first time (or perhaps I'd always known) that it wasn't an explanation I was looking for. I didn't need convincing that God existed or that the world had some sort of purpose. What I needed was joy.

Looking back on that time now, I wouldn't say the joy had gone out of my life but it's true that I'd neglected it; maybe I'd become a bit stoical, as you're inclined to be in middle age, taking the bad with the good, gritting your teeth and getting on with it; struggling on. All those clichés that somehow help you to get through the next day and deal with whatever's going on. Yet the joy wasn't really gone, just eclipsed. Waiting for me to accept it. It was such a small thing, nothing grand or heroic, nothing uncommon, nothing that only deep thinkers or mystics could find, just the joy that any child or one of Dostoevsky's peasant criminals could experience. I didn't even have to have some great conversion experience, like Paul on the Damascus road. I just had to be honest with myself about what I wanted. And ask.

I've no doubt there were many, far too many, people down there in the city who were weren't able to enjoy the spring sunshine. There were families squabbling, couples splitting up, addicts dragging themselves through the streets, and tormented souls wondering whether it was worthwhile going on living. Just beyond the cathedral was the Royal Victorian Infirmary, where who knows how many stories of sickness and grief were unfolding at this very moment. Down to the east was one of the poorest areas in the whole city and all the misery that goes with poverty. There was so much—too much—that needed to be done. There were things I needed to do. Debts I needed to pay. And I don't mean money. I mean everything I'd received from other people that made life possible, people I knew and people I didn't. And yet—it was a good day. At least, there was good in it and that was something to be glad about.

'Thank you, thank you,' I said. 'Maybe I'm starting to get it.'

He didn't respond.

In fact, he wasn't there. Gone—without saying goodbye. I was left alone, but I didn't feel alone. Something, something I couldn't quite find the words for, had come into my life and, as I write this now, seems to have stayed with me. I'm not talking about anything like those flashes of inspiration that Dostoevsky described Prince Myshkin as having in the moment before one of his epileptic fits, visions in which time seemed to stop and he felt like he was being lifted up into heaven. No. Just feeling, well, different. More rooted? Perhaps. But also lighter. Ready. Ready for what? For whatever came next.

'Thank you,' I repeated in a whisper, as if speaking to myself.

I looked at my watch. Time to go. It was a good fifteen minutes' brisk walk to the restaurant where I was meeting Laura, but I didn't need to rush. It was, as I said, a good day. Leaving the necropolis, I turned round and began to walk back towards the city.

Epilogue

The next day, Easter Day, I did go to church. I'd been planning on doing so anyway, but my last conversation with Dostoevsky gave me additional motivation. I should immediately say that I wasn't full of the ecstatic enthusiasm of a new convert. Once again, the service wasn't especially wonderful. I couldn't really follow the sermon or hear the prayers that were given rather inaudibly by a member of the congregation. I didn't have any deep religious experience. The heavens didn't open. But it made sense. 'I am the resurrection and the life.' Perhaps we spend so much time arguing about the first part of this, the resurrection, that we forget about the second, the life—'we', that is, atheists and believers alike. Find the joy in life and the resurrection will, perhaps, look after itself. Whether I was (or am) anything more than half a believer, I'm still not quite sure, but I now knew that I believed in life and, if life, then love; if love, then joy. Not, as I say, in any special 'religious' way. Just the human way of a child and a convict, the innocent and the guilty. And, if Fyodor Mikhailovich was right: if joy, then God. And though I wasn't yet fully convinced of this, I didn't dismiss it.

That was my last conversation with Dostoevsky, but I did see him one more time.

Towards the end of May, Laura and I took a Sunday afternoon walk up to the Botanical Gardens. The good weather had come quite suddenly, after the promise of early April had turned into a cold, overcast spring that seemed to go on for ever. Overnight the city put on its summer best and the crowds were out in force. It was almost a party atmosphere.

We found a bench outside the Victorian hothouses and sat there, letting the sun warm our pale winter skin and watching people having a good time: playing, laughing, talking, eating, texting, reading. The seemingly endless crowds streaming past where we were sitting provided a constantly changing spectacle for any half-curious people-watcher, a bit like the passeggiata in an Italian seaside town, only not as leisurely. Here in the north, you never knew how long summer was going to last, so you had to get your pleasure in quickly. You could almost sense the urgency.

Then, amongst a wave of people coming towards us, I saw him. He was wearing a rather crumpled old-fashioned white linen suit and a straw hat, looking like a character in one of those Russian plays where they all sit around in their dachas having affairs and intrigues. He was walking quite slowly and I saw several people loop round him, clearly finding him in the way, but he appeared to be oblivious of them. His hands were clasped behind his back and he seemed to be cheerfully talking to himself. He could almost have been trying out some dialogue for a new novel. As he approached us, he looked up, raised his hat and, without changing his pace, gave us a smile of acknowledgement.

'Fyodor Mikhailovich!' I burst out, without thinking.

I could see that Laura had already noticed him, which wasn't surprising. Although his summer outfit might not have been so unusual in the south of

England it did stick out here in Glasgow, not to mention the way he was talking to himself. He looked undeniably eccentric—at the very least. When I spoke his name Laura turned to look at me, then back at him, then me again.

He didn't pause to speak and was soon absorbed into the crowd. Gone.

'Was that...?' she asked.

I shook my head self-consciously and a little ashamedly.

'It was.'

I'd said it.

'We need to talk,' she said, looking both alarmed and curious.

Of course, I couldn't tell her everything at once. And she couldn't take it all in at once. That's why I've written it down like this, so she could read it all. She has. I think I mentioned that around Christmas time she'd started reading *The Brothers Karamazov*. We didn't discuss it much at the time, though when she finished the last page, she did turn to me and say, 'That was the most amazing novel I've ever read.' I could only agree. What she'll make of this, I don't know.

Postscript

Writing these Conversations up wasn't as straightforward as I'd imagined. I don't have a photographic memory and I'm not pretending that I remembered every last detail of what was said. On the other hand (a phrase I once hear Margaret Atwood describe as a writer's best friend), each conversation had (obviously) made a massive impression on me and I went over every word many times before putting it down on paper. These were probably the most remarkable conversations I've ever had or ever will have in my life, which made it all the more important to be as accurate as possible and to leave a complete and fair account for posterity. Or, at least, for Laura.

I'd hope to be finished by the end of the summer vacation, but summer vacations are never quite as free as one imagines they're going to be. I had two PhD theses to read and was committed to a week-long conference in Germany that had nothing to do with Dostoevsky. Not to mention a family holiday (James had even consented to come with us this year). Once university started up again it was difficult to find the right wavelength for this very non-academic kind of writing. The Christmas vacation came and went. That year we hosted Laura's parents, who were visibly ageing and needed a lot of looking after.

I did try church again (I hadn't actually been since Easter), and found that I was a bit more tuned in to what was going on. As I mentioned before, I'd always thought the idea of the world-making God becoming a helpless 'babe in the manger' was very moving in a poetic kind of way, though I still couldn't think of it as a 'fact'. But did that matter?

Then, as we all know, Covid happened and there were two years of craziness, having to invent a whole new way of teaching and having to respond to a very stressed cohort of students. I was quite stressed myself. Like everybody else. I was determined to keep at my notes, though, and by early January 2022 I'd managed to get a more or less readable text together. Laura thought I should try to get it published, but I wasn't so sure. It certainly wasn't the kind of thing that would count as research and it wasn't really a novel either. Obviously, if it ever did get published, I couldn't claim that it was all 'real'. Maybe something a bit like Plato's or Hume's philosophical dialogues or Lucian's 'Dialogues of the Dead'. Well, not exactly like these, and I'm not comparing myself with Plato (or Hume or Lucian)! Even so, some colleagues would probably think I'd gone slightly crazy and would have been better employed doing serious academic work. It all had to be thought about very carefully. Certainly, a publishable version couldn't say everything I'd put down in Laura's version, which included intimate references to our marriage—and my mistakes.

Meanwhile, the crisis in Ukraine was creeping up the news rankings. The Americans were even claiming that Putin was planning an invasion, though since the Iraq War I'd been very sceptical about anything coming out of the American and British security agencies. Then, first thing in the morning on 24 February,

I got a WhatsApp message from James: 'Fuck. Putin's done it.' It didn't take long to find out what he'd done and, as the days went on, it just got worse. Horror on horror.

You could say that, at one level, this had nothing to do with Fyodor Mikhailovich, who had, after all, been dead for nearly one hundred and fifty years and who'd insisted that he didn't want to comment on our world today—but I read of at least one university that had taken his works off their reading lists. I also found a couple of online articles that depicted Fyodor Mikhailovich as having inspired the Russian president's political philosophy. Was this fair? Well, it wasn't hard to see why some Russians today could read what he wrote about Russia's world mission and see it as justifying what they were doing in Ukraine. Especially as it seemed the patriarch of the Orthodox Church had given his blessing to the whole thing. I think he even called it a 'metaphysical war'. Wasn't this just what Fyodor Mikhailovich had wanted to see: Holy Russia rising up to restore true Christian values to the world? A Russian student I was corresponding with even informed me that Putin was a new tsar on a sacred mission to overthrow Western secularism. This was jaw-dropping stuff—but would Fyodor Mikhailovich really have agreed?

One thing I did remember from when we were talking about nationalism was that Fyodor Mikhailovich had explicitly said that a president wasn't a tsar and that after seventy years of Soviet rule you couldn't simply identify today's Russia with 'his' Russia. He'd also pointed me to the passage in his *Diary* where he said that Russia should never use its military power against fellow Slavs. But what else might he have to say?

As he'd shown in our first Conversation, Fyodor Mikhailovich had an extraordinary ability to spin multiple alternative stories out of apparently simple mundane events—so why should his mind be less productive when it was given a larger canvas to work on? 'The Grand Inquisitor' was superficially an attack on the Catholic Church, but wasn't it also an attack on any leader who tries to use the language and rituals of the Church to exercise political power—like Putin and the Patriarch were doing today? Then again, the story of the complex and secretive deals by which the Russian president and the ruling elite came to power might have reminded him of the doings of *The Possessed*'s Peter Verkhovensky, the ruthless leader of a network of covert cells dedicated to the cause of revolution. Obviously, the Russian president wasn't seeking that kind of revolution, but he too was pursuing a seizure of power involving systematic and strategic violence and deception. As he himself is reported as saying, 'There's no such thing as an ex-KGB officer'! And there could be other possibilities. Perhaps everything since 1917 was a repetition of Russia's time of troubles a few centuries ago, a time when Russia was ruled by a 'false tsar'. Fyodor Mikhailovich referred to this story in *The Possessed*, so might he not have seen Russia's president as just such 'false tsar'?

And, being Dostoevsky, he could probably have thought of many alternatives that I can't even begin to imagine.

To be fair, some of the online articles that tried to make the Dostoevsky–Putin link phrased their conclusions in terms of 'could have' or 'might have'. Well, many figures from the past 'could have' or 'might have' thought just about anything about the world today. I didn't go all the way with Carl's view that literature had to be kept separate from politics and I was fairly certain that Fyodor Mikhailovich really wanted to—and did—contribute to shaping Russian social and political attitudes in his day. And while it's easy to fixate on the nationalism or anti-Semitism, some of his interventions—in criminal justice, for example—were ahead of his time. Maybe Carl did have a point: there's never a direct line from great literature to political decisions, *whatever* we know about the writer's own attitudes and actions. Really great literature always says more than writers themselves know or intend. I mean, few of us today would probably want to live in a society ruled by Shakespeare's ideal kings, but this doesn't stop us enjoying his plays. And unscrupulous leaders and their cheerleaders will always pick and choose what they want from any writer.

I admit that this isn't very satisfactory and I've several times wished that Fyodor Mikhailovich would turn up just one more time so that I could get some kind of final answer out of him, though he'd probably refuse to comment. And perhaps no one has any final answer to this kind of question. In any case, the truth is that many of our favourite authors didn't think as we do and held views that we're likely to find offensive. It's said that the past is another country, but perhaps it's more accurate to say that it speaks another language—even when it superficially looks the same. Teaching literature for the last twenty-five years has made me realize that the language of the past—even the quite recent past—isn't a language that any of us can ever become fully fluent in, though we can reach an approximation. And yet...and yet...I read the pawnbroker's despairing monologue, I listen to Ivan's howl of protest, I hear the story of Markel, and it's almost as if Fyodor Mikhailovich was sitting here now, speaking, as heart speaks to heart, person to person. Whether or not God exists, that too is a miracle.

PART TWO
COMMENTARY

Introduction

Conversations with Dostoevsky is an exploration of Dostoevsky's Christian view of life and his self-understanding as a novelist and commentator on Russian affairs. Dostoevsky's Christianity was not the outcome of academic study but a personal and artistic demonstration of the way in which Christian experience might enter into, shape, and transform the whole of human life. This holism requires the Conversations to explore how Dostoevsky's witness to Christ combined with his literary and political ambitions, including his nationalism and anti-Semitism, painful as these topics may be for contemporary readers. As in many conversations, not all points get neatly settled and themes blend and diverge in ways that don't always fit under convenient labels.

The Dostoevsky who speaks in these Conversations both is and isn't Dostoevsky. He is Dostoevsky in the sense that the views he expresses have significant support in the historical Dostoevsky's fiction, journalism, and letters, as well as in the memoirs of his contemporaries. These include not only small details such as his admiration for Raphael's *Madonna della Seggiola* (referred to in his letters and in his wife's memoirs) but also major interpretative issues, such as whether Ivan Karamazov's 'rebellion' against God is also Dostoevsky's or whether Prince Myshkin is intended to be a kind of Christ figure. I certainly don't presume to offer conclusive solutions to such issues, but I do believe that the positions that 'Dostoevsky' sets out have significant textual and historical support.

At the same time, the Dostoevsky represented here clearly isn't Dostoevsky—or not the historical Dostoevsky. The Dostoevsky who speaks here has, of course, been dead for nearly one hundred and fifty years and although the Conversations provide few details he is assumed to be in what is sometimes referred to as 'a better place' and is therefore able to take a calmer view as to the meaning of his life's work and its reception than he did in his earthly life. This Dostoevsky is a Dostoevsky recontextualized in the twenty-first century and responding to questions that may be 'eternal', but which are phrased and developed very differently from how they were in late nineteenth-century Russia. At the same time, he cautions against simplistic applications of his writings to discussions of twentieth- and twenty-first-century Russian history.

More than many writers, Dostoevsky invites fictionalization. His personality has lent itself to fantastic exaggerations that both attract and repel. His sickness, fascination with crime, gambling addiction, and often chaotic love life, coupled with the trauma of his father's murder, the dramatic events of his arrest, mock execution, and penal servitude in Siberia all provide rich materials for imaginative invention.[1] It has several times happened that the violent events and extravagant characters of the novels became conflated with Dostoevsky himself. The most extreme and troubling instance of this conflation is the recurrent rumour that Dostoevsky was guilty of the crime of Stavrogin, that is, the rape of a twelve-year-old girl, a charge for which significant historical evidence is, I believe, lacking.

Fictionalizing Dostoevsky, then, can be a dangerous business—yet it enables controversial points to be expressed with a sharpness and sometimes a passion that are for the most part only implicit in scholarly writing (most Dostoevsky scholars I know are passionate about their subject, but the passion is, rightly, regulated by the requirements of scholarly exchange), while the conversational format allows genuinely ambiguous or unresolved questions to remain undecided.

Fictionalizations come in a variety of forms. At one end of the spectrum is the kind of narrative biography written by Henry Troyat, which tells Dostoevsky's story in a straightforward linear fashion. A librarian would probably classify this as non-fiction, but while Troyat draws extensively on Dostoevsky's letters and other historical materials he also makes use of invented conversations and narrative links when these are necessary for maintaining the narrative flow.[2] Alex Christofi's *Dostoevsky in Love* also employs a linear narrative, although he scrupulously uses italics for passages that directly quote Dostoevsky's own words and, unlike Troyat, supports the main text with relevant footnotes.[3] More fully fictionalized is Stephen Coulter's biography *The Devil Inside*, which freely uses scenes from the novels as incidents in Dostoevsky's own life. Coulter describes Dostoevsky's use of a child prostitute with some detail and without comment, suggesting to any reader who did not have access to other sources that this was a proven fact of Dostoevsky's life.[4] J. M. Coetzee's *The Master of Petersburg* takes great care to recreate the atmosphere of Dostoevsky's city, which he then uses as the stage for an entirely imaginary and extremely implausible story about the writer. Nevertheless, whilst historically fantastic, the issues Coetzee addresses are genuinely Dostoevskian, concerning the nature of political terrorism, conflict and misunderstanding between parents and children, and the possibility of redemption and forgiveness in the face of death. At the same time, Coetzee's writing allows for a range of nuances and shifts of perspective that can likewise be seen as

---

[1] Although Dostoevsky himself believed that his father had been murdered, the exact circumstances of his death remain obscure.

[2] Henry Troyat, *Firebrand: The Life of Dostoevsky*, trans. Norbert Guterman (London: Heinemann, 1946 [original version in French, 1940]).

[3] Alex Christofi, *Dostoevsky in Love: An Intimate Life* (London: Bloomsbury, 2021).

[4] Stephen Coulter, *The Devil Inside: A Novel of Dostoevsky's Life* (London: Jonathan Cape, 1960); on the supposed visit to the prostitute see pp. 88–90: this incident is also the subject of the title page illustration.

true to the spirit of his subject.[5] Leonid Tsypkin's *Summer in Baden Baden* alternates between retelling Dostoevsky's travels in Germany at the height of his gambling addiction and scenes from his (or his narrator's) own life in contemporary (1980s) Russia. Specifically, Tsypkin uses this interplay between past and present to explore the challenge that Dostoevsky's anti-Semitism poses for Jewish readers.[6] Coetzee and Tsypkin thus use the vehicle of fictionalization to focus particular issues or sets of issues that are in play in Dostoevsky's work.

A somewhat different example, discussed in Conversation Three, is the 1932 Soviet film of *The House of the Dead*. The screenplay, by the critic Viktor Shklovsky, has Dostoevsky being invited by Konstantin Pobedonostsev, the chief censor, to work as an anti-socialist propagandist for the Tsarist government. As the conversation goes on, Dostoevsky becomes increasingly distressed until, as he falls into an epileptic fit, he declares, 'You remind me of the Grand Inquisitor!' There then follows a retelling of *The House of the Dead* in flashbacks, a device that enables Shklovsky to rescue the social realist and Soviet-approved Dostoevsky from the Tsarist apologist of the writer's later years. Dostoevsky's political radicalism is also talked up in a screenplay commissioned by Michael Cimino (director of *The Deer Hunter*, 1978) from Raymond Carver and Tess Gallagher. The script picks out key moments in Dostoevsky's life and, in an invented episode, has him defying the camp commandant and receiving a hundred lashes as punishment.[7]

With regard to Dostoevsky's Christianity, a fictional approach allows us to bring themes and texts into kinds of relationships that are not immediately connected at a critical-biographical level but that, from the point of view of a contemporary reader (at least, *this* contemporary reader), bring to the fore crucial aspects of what is being discussed. Such an approach also allows us to hint at the variety of moods and voices in which his views were expressed. This is important, since although Christian believers commit to the truth of Church teachings, it is generally acknowledged that Christianity involves more than mere theoretical assent to a set of propositions: it requires commitment to a whole way of life. Once this is recognized, it is clear that *how* something is said becomes as important as *what* is said.

Dostoevsky read widely in theological and philosophical literature but there is no reason to be surprised if what he wrote about Christianity is marked by uncertainties, inconsistencies, and an occasional lack of clarity. Even those who spend entire academic careers attempting to systematize Christian teaching rarely succeed in tying up all the loose ends and, were they to do so, the outcome might not

---

[5] J. M. Coetzee, *The Master of Petersburg* (London: Secker and Wartburg, 1994).
[6] Leonid Tsypkin, *Summer in Baden Baden: From the Life of Dostoyevsky*, trans. Roger and Angela Keys (London: Quartet, 1987). For further discussion of this see the Commentary on the Fifth Conversation, 'The Jewish Question'.
[7] Raymond Carver and Tess Gallagher, *Dostoevsky: A Screen Play* (Santa Barbara, CA: Capra Press, 1985). The film was never made.

bear much relation to Christianity as it is lived. For Dostoevsky, as for others, his beliefs therefore emerge better in a conversational structure than in a systematic exposition. Again, Dostoevsky is not so unlike many other believers in giving voice to positions that were and are controversial. A notable example is the use of idealist philosophy as a means of articulating religious belief, a move that some see as an acceptable and even necessary apologetic move but which others decry as betraying the very foundations of faith. The quarrels of Athens and Jerusalem are of ancient vintage, and everyone who enters the fray each must find their own position somewhere on the spectrum between antagonism and reconciliation (on this particular point the present writer probably finds himself most at home in a winding back street of ancient Alexandria).

When it comes to the representation of Christianity in the novels, we have to understand what is said in relation to character, situation, and action in the context of the novel in question. Perhaps none of Dostoevsky's characters speaks unambiguously for their author and even a decisively Christian character such as the saintly Elder Zosima (if, pace some critics, he is a decisively Christian and saintly figure) may be expressing what, for Dostoevsky himself, was more of an aspiration than a final and confirmed life view. Everything must be sifted and weighed.

Finally, I should add—emphatically—that the narrator is not myself. In any case, the narrator is not the important person here. He 'exists' chiefly in order to bring into view a set of interrelated issues in Dostoevsky's writings that I regard as important and compelling—although he addresses these issues from a position of unbelief and I address them from a position of (albeit conflicted) faith. Yet on such points, belief and unbelief are perhaps not so far apart as popular debates suggest. The believer's 'I believe, help my unbelief' (Mark 9.24) is not entirely remote from Pasolini's prayer 'to the God in whom I do not believe'. The convergence and divergence of these confessions is the tension that drives the enquiry prosecuted in the Conversations.

When quoting Dostoevsky, I have mostly used the translation by Constance Garnett. In the main body of the Conversations, there are very few direct quotes. In the Commentaries, I have checked translations against the Russian text and, on occasion, other translations. Translation is always a controversial matter and it is clear that no English translation is ever going to be 'the same' as the original Russian text. Every translation is an interpretation. I like the nineteenth-century feel of Garnett's translation, but I am also aware of significant shortcomings. In a crucial scene between Sonia and Raskolnikov, for example, Garnett has Raskolnikov thinking that she is a 'religious maniac', which obscures the connotations of the Russian 'holy fool'. When teaching, I mostly used the commendable Richard Pevear and Larissa Volokhonsky translation, though this too has its critics. At different times I have also used other translations, largely according to availability. Having also taught Dostoevsky in Denmark, I know that similar debates arise about Danish translations, where the standard older translation is tone-deaf to many of the religious allusions in Dostoevsky's text. Doubtless this is true of translations in other languages too. To repeat, no translation is 'the same' as the Russian original, not only in the narrow sense of the text as text but also because Dostoevsky never has had and never can have the same cultural resonance outside Russia as he has had within it. For us he will always belong to a different, though related, history. The story of the relatedness of these two histories, Russia and the West, remains tragically contested but it is also a story that has been extraordinarily generative across the spectrum of cultural production—and translation and retranslation remain urgent moral and political as well as literary imperatives.[8]

Abbreviations to Works by Dostoevsky

Works in Russian

PSS = *Polnoe Sobranie Sochinenii v tridtsati tomakh* [Complete Collected Works in thirty volumes] (Leningrad: Nauka, 1972–88).

Works in English

BK = *The Brothers Karamazov*, trans. Constance Garnett (London: Heinemann, 1912).
CP = *Crime and Punishment*, trans. Constance Garnett (London: Heinemann, 1914).
DW = *The Diary of a Writer*, trans. Boris Brasol (Haslemere: Ianmead, 1984).
HD = *The House of the Dead*, trans. Constance Garnett (London: Heinemann, 1915).
HT = *An Honest Thief and Other Stories*, trans. Constance Garnett (London: Heinemann, 1919).
I = *The Idiot*, trans. Constance Garnett (New York: Macmillan, 1951).
P = *The Possessed*, trans. Constance Garnett (London: Heinemann, 1914).
RY = *A Raw Youth*, trans. Constance Garnett (London: Heinemann, 1916).
WN = *White Nights and Other Stories*, trans. Constance Garnett (London: Heinemann, 1918).
WNSI = *Winter Notes on Summer Impressions*, trans. Kiril Fitzlyon (London: Alma 2021).

---

[8] A defence of Garnett is given in Christofi, *Dostoevsky in Love*, 224–6; a scholarly appraisal that is both appreciative and critical is A. N. Nikoliukin, 'Dostoevskii in Constance Garnett's Translation', in W. J. Leatherbarrow, *Dostoevskii and Britain* (Oxford: Berg, 1995), 207–27.

Commentary on the First Conversation, Part One

Introduction

The starting point for the first Conversation is the conclusion of Dostoevsky's story *A Gentle Spirit* (also translated as *The Meek One* and *A Gentle Creature*). As the narrator says, it is a passage that could be compared with the more harrowing and better-known 'Rebellion' (from *The Brothers Karamazov*) that is widely regarded as having anticipated the protest atheism of the twentieth century. However, where 'Rebellion' catalogues an almost unbearable litany of cruelties inflicted on children, *A Gentle Spirit* focusses on just one case, a young woman driven to suicide by the mental cruelty of her abusive husband. Yet the conclusion is equally devastating in its presentation of a world without metaphysical consolation, reminding the narrator of his own youthful experience of what the existential theologian Paul Tillich called 'the despair of meaninglessness' and which now resurfaces to challenge the apparent equilibrium he has found in marriage and work. The Conversations that follow lead us through the various dimensions of Dostoevsky's religious rejoinder to such despair, including the Bible, Christ, the Church, and his vision of eternal life and God.[1]

The story of *A Gentle Spirit* is summarized in the main text. It is widely regarded as one of Dostoevsky's most successful stories. One contemporary, M. E. Saltykov-Schedrin, called it one of 'the pearls of European literature', whilst another, N. K. Mikhailovsky, despite calling Dostoevsky 'a cruel talent', praised its artistic perfection. Knud Hamsun and André Gide were amongst later admirers.[2] It was adapted for film by Robert Bresson, who updated it to 1960s Paris (see Conversation Three). Robert E. Belknap has called the conclusion 'the most personal, most emotional, most religious and intertextually most moving passage [Dostoevsky] ever wrote'.[3] Similar praise comes from Dostoevsky's biographer Joseph Frank, who also connects it to the figure of the 'underground man', another significant anticipation of protest atheism.[4] Katherine Jane Briggs says that

---

[1] See Paul Tillich, *The Courage to Be* (London: Fontana, 1962), 137–51. On Dostoevsky and existentialism see the second section of the Commentary on the third Conversation.

[2] PSS24, 390.

[3] Robert E. Belknap, *The Genesis of the Brothers Karamazov: The Aesthetics, Ideology, and Psychology of Making a Text* (Evanston, IL: Northwestern University Press, 1990), 35.

[4] Joseph Frank, *Dostoevsky: The Mantle of the Prophet, 1871–1881* (Princeton, NJ: Princeton University Press, 2002), 350.

'it contains a richness of interpretation in the fields of religious symbolism and human relationships which is out of proportion to its length'.[5]

A Gentle Spirit broaches two themes that are central to Dostoevsky's response to existential despair: suicide and the possibility of life beyond death. A third theme emerges from the way in which the story, narrated by the husband as he stands watch over his wife's body, reveals a very different truth from what he consciously intends. In face of life's most fundamental challenges, what counts as truth, what as falsehood?

1. The Metaphysics of Suicide

Suicide is a recurrent theme of Dostoevsky's fiction and all of the major novels include actual or attempted suicides. The best-known of Dostoevsky's fictional suicides or would-be suicides (Svidrigailov in *Crime and Punishment*, Ippolit in *The Idiot*, Kirillov and Stavrogin in *The Possessed*, Smerdyakov in *The Brothers Karamazov*) establish a connection between suicide and nihilism, for which Kirillov is the most explicit spokesman. Kirillov's big idea is that by killing himself he will become God. This clearly needs some unpacking.

Kirillov believes that the highest human achievement is to live and act according to the dictates of one's own will, anticipating Nietzsche's *Übermensch* and Sartre's existentialist view of human freedom. However, human beings as we know them encounter multiple limitations to the exercise of freedom. For a start, we are animals with an inbuilt propensity towards somatic decay and, ultimately, death. Death and, more importantly, the fear of death thus constitute a limit against which we appear powerless. Kirillov disagrees. He argues that by committing suicide and doing so entirely freely he will show the fear of death to be illusory. It is crucial, of course, that such a suicide be a free act. It is not a response to terminal illness, to unendurable physical suffering, to a broken heart, or to any mental distress. It must be for no reason at all other than to demonstrate the sovereignty of the will in the face of death. Such a suicide can therefore liberate humanity from its age-old bondage to death and usher in a utopian age of fully autonomous life.

As Kirillov frames the issue, it is also theological. He sees 'God' as the quintessential symbol of ultimate limitation, a givenness against which we are powerless. As Kirillov puts it: 'If God exists, all is His will and from His will I cannot escape. If not, it's all my will and I am bound to show self-will... Man has done nothing but invent God so as to go on living, and not kill himself; that's the whole of universal history up till now. I am the first one in the whole history of mankind who

---

[5] Katherine Jane Briggs, *How Dostoevsky Portrays Women in His Novels* (Lampeter: Edwin Mellen Press, 2009), 171.

would not invent God.'[6] In other words, the balance of power between God and human beings is a zero-sum game: all power is on one side or the other. There can be no middle ground.[7]

Given the profound connection between modernity and the pursuit of autonomy, Dostoevsky might seem to be arguing that suicide reveals modernity to be what Pope John Paul II called a civilization of death. This is the view of John F. Desmond, who argues that Dostoevsky's analysis shows the nihilistic outcome of unlimited personal autonomy (freedom), an outcome to which (he argues) Dostoevsky's own religious outlook provides the only adequate response.[8]

This, however, is only to see one side of Dostoevsky's position. In *The Diary of a Writer*, a self-published journal that ran from 1876 to 1877 and from 1880 to 1881, he returned repeatedly to the subject of suicide, mostly with reference to cases from contemporary newspapers. *A Gentle Spirit* was itself published in the *Diary* and offers a fictionalized variation on the case of Maria Borisova, a young woman who, like the eponymous 'gentle spirit', killed herself by jumping out of an apartment window and, also like her, was found to have been clutching an icon of the Mother of God as she fell to her death. It is striking that whereas the prominent suicides in the novels are all male, a majority of the cases discussed in the *Diary* are female and several prove to have been very differently motivated from what we see in Kirillov and the other fictional male suicides.[9] In one article, Dostoevsky described the case of a peasant woman who had been subjected to protracted and horrific abuse by her husband, sometimes being hung upside down and whipped by him. Her eventual suicide is clearly something very different from Kirillov's metaphysical fantasies, and Dostoevsky's condemnation is reserved for the court's leniency in sentencing her abuser to a mere eight months.[10]

Dostoevsky contrasts Borisova's case with that of another recent female suicide, Liza Herzen, daughter of the radical exile Alexander Herzen. Herzen left a suicide note in which she invited her friends to celebrate with champagne if she failed and came back to life, but, if she succeeded, to make sure she was really dead before burying her, because 'it is very disagreeable to awake in a coffin in the earth, It is not *chic*!'[11] This time Dostoevsky's tentative conclusion is that her attitude to death was connected to the atheistic philosophy in which she had been brought up and that 'she simply died of "cold, darkness and tedium" with,

---

[6] P, 561–2/PSS10, 470–1.
[7] Most of Dostoevsky's fictional suicides offer variations on this theme, although the differences can be important, as when Ippolit (in *The Idiot*), a teenage boy dying of consumption, explains that suicide is the one free act that he is still able to do.
[8] See John F. Desmond, *Fyodor Dostoevsky, Walker Percy, and the Age of Suicide* (Washington, DC: Catholic University of America Press, 2019).
[9] See Nina Pelikan Straus, *Dostoevsky and the Woman Question: Rereadings at the End of the Century* (New York, NY: St Martin's Press, 1994), 97–117.
[10] DW, 20/PSS21, 22.   [11] DW, 469/PSS23, 145.

so to speak, animal and unaccountable suffering; she began to suffocate as if there were not enough air'.[12] Though lacking the theoretical articulation of Kirillov, Dostoevsky seems to see the same nexus of nihilistic ideas at work in this case too. Borisova's death, however, elicits a very different judgement: 'This holy image in the hands is a strange, as yet unheard-of, trait in a suicide! This was a timid and humble suicide. Here apparently, there was no grumbling or reproach: simply it became impossible to live, "God does not wish it"—and she died, having said her prayers'.[13]

Ideological suicide is not absent from the *Diary* and the discussion of Mlle Herzen and Mlle Borisova is immediately followed by a speech of self-justification put in the mouth of an imaginary ideologue, 'a suicide *out of tedium*—of course, a materialist'.[14] His speech concludes as follows: 'I sentence this nature, which has so unceremoniously and impudently brought me into existence for suffering, to annihilation, together with myself... And because I am unable to destroy nature, I am destroying only myself...'.[15]

In Dostoevsky's time the Church condemned suicide as the ultimate sin and those who took their own lives were refused burial in consecrated ground. In *A Raw Youth*, however, the wandering holy man Makar Ivanovitch tells a heart-rending story of a man whose cruelty towards his wife's twelve-year-old son resulted in the boy drowning himself. Later, in an attempt to make amends, the man asks a painter to paint a picture of the scene and to show the angels flying to meet the boy. The painter objects that because the boy committed suicide he must face divine judgement, but, he adds, 'We won't open the heaven, and there's no need to paint the angels, but I'll let a beam of light, one bright ray of light, come down from heaven as though to meet him. It's all the same as long as there's something.'[16] In *The Brothers Karamazov*, the Elder Zosima, ever the spokesman for the most compassionate and inclusive of Dostoevsky's religious insights, makes the point directly: 'They tell us that it is a sin to pray for [suicides] and outwardly the Church, as it were, renounces them, but in my secret heart I believe that we may pray even for them. Love can never be an offence to Christ.'[17]

In such ways, Dostoevsky's interpretation of suicide is many-faceted, emphasizing the circumstances and motive of each case. As he wrote in *The Idiot*, 'the causes of human actions are usually immeasurably more complex and varied than our subsequent explanations of them'.[18] At the same time, suicide provides an eminently dramatic and poignant focus for the conflicting ideologies of

---

[12] DW, 470/PSS23, 146. Responding to a reader's letter, Dostoevsky makes clear that he is not judging Herzen: 'One has to take a more humane attitude toward such a spiritual condition,' he writes, 'Here, suffering was obvious and certainly she died of spiritual anguish, having greatly suffered'; again, though, he underlines the role of ideology: 'involving an erroneous conception of the sublime significance and aims of life, a deliberate extermination in her soul of all faith in its immortality'—DW, 547/PSS24, 54.

[13] DW, 470/PSS23, 146.   [14] DW, 470–3/PSS23, 146–8.   [15] DW, 473/PSS23, 148.
[16] RY, 392/PSS13, 319–20.   [17] BK, 337/PSS14, 293.   [18] I, 473/PSS8, 402.

materialistic nihilism and Christianity—although (as so often in Dostoevsky) the picture is complicated by internal tensions on either side. The nihilist too may be a victim who deserves sympathy and the Church may or may not be the authentic voice of Christian love. Yet the conflict, a fundamental and defining one in Dostoevsky's work, remains. By virtue of the way in which it condenses this issue in the cry of despair presented in its final paragraph, *A Gentle Spirit* therefore establishes an appropriate point from which to begin an investigation of what might be called Dostoevsky's Christian world view.

2. Life beyond Death?

As many commentators have noticed, *A Gentle Spirit* evokes an important passage from Dostoevsky's personal notebooks that offers his most extensive account of his views on immortality, Christ, and God. Dated 16 April 1864, the passage begins with the words 'Masha is lying on the table. Will I ever see Masha again?' and records his thoughts while watching over the body of his first wife, Maria Dmitrievna.[19] Although her death was due to natural causes, there is a clear resonance with the overall situation of a husband reckoning with the failure of love in his married life (during Maria Dmitrievna's last illness Dostoevsky had spent much of his time criss-crossing Europe in pursuit of the much younger Apollinaria Suslova).

The conclusion of Dostoevsky's monologue is as positive as the pawnbroker's is negative.[20] Although the notes continue with the declaration that 'To love a person *as oneself*, according to Christ's commandment, is impossible' (because the 'I' is both a necessary element in being human and an insurmountable obstacle to such love), Dostoevsky gradually moves towards a positive answer to his opening question.[21] How?

Christ, he argued, achieved a sacrifice of the 'I' for the other and therefore presents 'the *ideal of man in the flesh*'. Though we cannot attain this, it provides an ideal we can strive to realize. However, it is also unattainable in this life and so, Dostoevsky concludes, unless there is the possibility of perfection beyond death, life itself becomes 'completely senseless' and 'consequently there is a future heavenly life'. However, the kind of beings we will be in this future heavenly life will be very different from how we are now and we are unable to know much about the future state, except that it will involve leaving behind the most valued human

---

[19] An English translation of this text and accompanying critical discussion is provided in Steven Cassedy, *Dostoevsky's Religion* (Stanford, CA: Stanford University Press, 2005), 116–19. See PSS20, 172–5. See also Joseph Frank, *Dostoevsky: The Stir of Liberation* (Princeton, NJ: Princeton University Press, 1986), 296–309.

[20] James Scanlan sees arguments for the immortality of the soul as 'particularly prominent in Dostoevsky's writings'; see James Scanlan, *Dostoevsky the Thinker* (Ithaca, NY: Cornell University Press, 2002), 19–40.

[21] Cassedy, *Dostoevsky's Religion*, 116/PSS20, 172.

relationships that we know in marriage and family life, at least in their present form. It will, he suggests, be a state in which our being 'is full synthetically, eternally taking delight and eternally filled, being for which, as a result, "there will no longer be time".'[22] This eternal being, fulfilled, joyful, and timeless, is the synthesis of all that is: it is God. Christ, understood as God appearing the flesh, provides a synthetic link by which human beings can be joined to this infinite life beyond worldly life: 'We shall then be persons who never cease to fuse with the "all", persons who neither are given in marriage nor marry...Everything at that time will feel and know itself forever. But how this will occur, in what form, in what nature— this is hard for humanity to imagine in any definite way.'[23] In the meantime, failure to sacrifice oneself for the other (that is, failure to love) is sin—as in his and Masha's relationship. The Conversations will reflect the idea that the next life is itself progressive, as this passage suggests, and that the process of shedding the ego and becoming ever more united to the dynamic life of the universal synthesis continues beyond death, a point also hinted at in Kant's comments on immortality.[24] Of course, these notes are not a dispassionate piece of philosophical reasoning but are Dostoevsky's attempt to use what he has learned from philosophy to illuminate his own anguished existential situation.

'Will I ever see Masha again?' is a primary source for the view of immortality presented by Dostoevsky in the Conversations. It anticipates key passages from the novels, such as the chapter 'Cana of Galilee' and the teachings of the Elder Zosima, both from *The Brothers Karamazov*. And because it shows what Dostoevsky owed to German Idealism, it shows how his thinking dovetailed into the kind of development seen in his friend Vladimir Solovyov, arguably the most influential figure of non-Marxist Russian philosophy.[25] Again, the link between these notes and *A Gentle Spirit* confirms the appropriateness of this latter text as a starting point for the exploration of Dostoevsky's Christian view of life. Further aspects of Dostoevsky's treatment of immortality will be considered in the commentary on the final Conversation, 'We Are All Here'.

3. Lies, Literature, and Sin

A major theme of the first Conversation concerns what might count as truthful testimony concerning ultimate metaphysical and religious truths. The issue is

---

[22] Cassedy, *Dostoevsky's Religion*, 117/PSS20, 173–4.
[23] Cassedy, *Dostoevsky's Religion*, 118/PSS20, 174–5.
[24] See I. Kant, *Critique of Practical Reason*, in *Practical Philosophy*, ed. and trans. Mary J. Gregor (Cambridge: Cambridge University Press, 1996), 238–9. A good discussion of Kantian themes in Dostoevsky, though not referencing the question of immortality, is Evgenia Cherkasova, *Dostoevsky and Kant: Dialogues on Ethics* (Amsterdam: Rodopi, 2009).
[25] On Solovyov, see Commentary on the fifth Conversation. The connections to German Idealism are primary factors in leading Steven Cassedy to conclude that Dostoevsky's religion was *not* Christianity. See Cassedy, *Dostoevsky's Religion*.

compounded by Dostoevsky's views regarding the ubiquity of lying in human and, particularly, in Russian culture. The problem is not just individual mendacity but concerns a basic tendency in human beings' relation to the world and, especially, the mediation of the world by language.

Considering the seriousness with which Dostoevsky took his vocation as a writer, it might seem strange to have him putting himself on the same level as Fyodor Karamazov, the self-styled 'father of lies', a title that John's gospel applies to the devil.[26] The comment comes in the opening scene of *The Brothers Karamazov*, which takes place in the presence of the respected and saintly Elder Zosima. Fyodor Karamazov behaves inappropriately from the start, inventing stories, asking absurd questions, and deliberately insulting other attendees. But it is not only Fyodor Karamazov's malevolent buffoonery that is at issue.

In Dostoevsky's view, lying is endemic in fallen humanity and is maybe even the cause of humanity's fall from paradise. In the short story *The Dream of a Ridiculous Man* (published, like *A Gentle Spirit*, in *Diary of a Writer*) the narrator dreams that he travels to another planet inhabited by human creatures who are still living in a time of innocence.[27] However, the narrator himself inadvertently corrupts them and observes them learning to lie, to enjoy lying, and to see a beauty in lying.[28] As he comments, it might have started innocently, with a joke or a flirtatious exchange, but 'this atom of deceit' sets in train a whole string of consequences, including voluptuousness, jealousy, cruelty, mutual alienation, shame, criminality, and the guillotine. Ultimately, they believe that even stories of their own previous happiness are a myth and are left to erect temples to their own ideas and desires, like the self-deifiers of the nineteenth century.

In view of the connection he sees between lying and sin, it is unsurprising that Dostoevsky's novels are overflowing with habitual liars. Fyodor Karamazov is an especially egregious case. But lying not only reveals the character of the individual liar. The connection between lying and shame that we see in Fyodor Karamazov is also a social nexus in Dostoevsky's Russia.[29] In an article entitled 'Something about Lying', Dostoevsky argues that Peter the Great's policy of ruthless Westernization resulted in Russians becoming ashamed of who they are and that they therefore resort to lying in order to present a more acceptable social persona. In Dostoevsky's view, this had, by the mid-nineteenth century, pervaded every aspect of Russian life.[30]

The frequency and variety of liars in Dostoevsky's novels is striking. A close second to Fyodor Karamazov in brazen mendacity is *The Idiot*'s Lebedev, a man

---

[26] BK, 39/PSS14, 41. See John 8.44. Karamazov immediately qualifies this remark in his typically blustering way by saying that he is not the father but the son of lies: if not the devil, then the devil's son.
[27] HT, 307–25/PSS25, 104–19. [28] HT, 321/PSS25, 116.
[29] See Deborah A. Martinsen, *Surprised by Shame: Dostoevsky's Liars and Narrative Exposure* (Columbus, OH: Ohio University Press, 2003). For discussion of the social nexus that connects lying and shame see Chapter 2 'Something about Lying', 18–51. I am indebted to Martinsen's book throughout the following discussion.
[30] See F. M. Dostoevsky, 'Something about Lying' in DW, 133–42/PSS21, 117–25. This is a dynamic to which post-colonialist literature has more recently made us attentive.

who claims that his leg was blown off by a cannonball during the Napoleonic invasion (which happened before he was born), that he buried the leg with due ceremony, and that his wife never even noticed that it had been replaced with a wooden leg.[31] Yet Lebedev is also an interpreter of the Book of Revelation and several of his interpretations accord with Dostoevsky's own views, as when he says that the present age is one in which people care only about their own rights, are indifferent to their neighbours,[32] and that the railways and the system of financing the railways reveal the tribulations of the last days.[33] As so often in Dostoevsky, Lebedev is a character capable of speaking both truth and falsehood—again, everything is to be sifted and weighed!

A similar ambivalence can be seen in Stepan Trofimovich Verkhovensky (*The Possessed*), who has created the self-aggrandizing myth that he had once been at the centre of the progressive movement and remained a person of concern to the authorities. This, he suggests, is why he abandoned a stellar academic career to become a house tutor in the provinces. Only at the end of the novel does he confess that he has lied all his life. And yet it is he who applies the story of the Gadarene swine to Russia, identifying the demons that are exorcised from the possessed man with the nihilists led by his own son Peter. In this moment, at least, he seems to be speaking for his author.[34]

As Dostoevsky says in the Conversations, love provides manifold opportunities for deceit and self-deceit, as in the case of Katerina Ivanovna, who has deceived herself into believing that she is in love with Dmitri Karamazov and he with her. Towards the end of the novel, she visits Dmitri in the cell where he is being held after being falsely convicted of murdering his father and in the anguished conversation that follows they declare their love. As the narrator comments, 'they murmured to one another frantic words, almost meaningless, perhaps not even true, but at that moment it was all true, and perhaps both believed what they said implicitly.'[35] As the chapter title puts it, 'For a Moment the Lie Becomes Truth'.

At various points the Conversations indicate that a general context for Dostoevsky's life and work was the capitalist revolution of the nineteenth century. A characteristic feature of this was the repeated and multifaceted dissolution and realignment of the social status of individuals and groups as a result of massive and often sudden changes in wealth, positive and negative. This provides a context in which individual mendacity can reveal larger societal changes and tensions (a major theme in Martinsen's study), but it also points to another way in which human relationships are systematically falsified, namely, through the emergence

---

[31] I, 484–5/PSS8, 410–11. The 1812 campaign is also the background for the tragi-comic tall story in which General Ivolgin, another habitual liar in *The Idiot*, claims to have been appointed page-in-waiting to Napoleon during the occupation of Moscow.
[32] I, 195/PSS8, 167–8. See Rev. 6.6.   [33] I, 364–8/PSS8, 309–12. See Rev. 8.11.
[34] P, 595–6/PSS10, 498–9. The text cites Luke 26–39; this is also used as the novel's motto.
[35] BK, 810/PSS15, 188.

of a money economy and, particularly, the availability of credit. The references in the conversation to Goethe and Shakespeare refer, respectively, to *Faust* Part 2, when Faust and Mephistopheles introduce paper money into the Holy Roman Empire, bringing about a fantastic but illusory economic miracle, and to Shakespeare's eloquent commentary on money's alchemical properties, found in *Timon of Athens* Act IV, scene 3, where Timon observes that 'much of this will make black white, foul fair, | Wrong right, base noble, old young, coward valiant... Will knit and break religions, bless the accursed, |Make the hoar leprosy adored, place thieves | And give them title, knee and approbation | With senators on the bench...'.

Karl Marx, referencing both Timon and Goethe, says of money that 'It is the visible divinity, the transformation of all human and natural qualities into their opposites, the universal confusion and inversion of things; it brings together impossibilities'; and, secondly, 'It is the universal whore, the universal pimp of men and peoples.'[36] Likewise, Arkady Dolgoruky, the eponymous hero and narrator of *A Raw Youth*, believes that fulfilling his ambition to become a Rothschild will enable him to overcome the social shame of his illegitimacy, and he imagines how money will not only help him be loved by women, but that, despite his lack of education, the Galileos, Copernicuses, Charlemagnes, Napoleons, Pushkins, and Shakespeares will all bow down to his money.[37] In such ways, a money economy is institutionalized mendacity, a world of semblance and deceit.[38]

In light of all this, it might seem odd to make Dostoevsky a spokesman for the view that literature itself is a species of lying. This is a charge that goes all the way back to Plato and has been repeated by both religious and secular critics, ancient, medieval, and modern. Amongst Dostoevsky's Russian contemporaries, the left-wing radicals tolerated literature only to the extent that it served a modernizing social agenda. For them, petroleum was more important than Shakespeare or Raphael—a view that Dostoevsky vigorously disputed in the voice of Stepan Trofimovich Verkhovensky, who, again, speaks here for his author.[39]

Dostoevsky did think that beauty and the artistic creation of beauty had intrinsic value, but he was also aware that, when it comes to the most profound human feelings and the articulation of essential religious truths, language is only ever approximate. Bakhtin spoke of the Dostoevskian novel as unfinalizable. There is always something more to be said. Truth cannot be pinned down and stated as a

---

[36] Karl Marx, 'Economic and Philosophic Manuscripts', in *Early Writings*, trans. Rodney Livingstone and Gregor Benton (Harmondsworth: Penguin, 1975), 377.

[37] RY, 87/PSS13, 76–7.

[38] Dostoevsky's more or less constant financial embarrassment was further aggravated by periods of compulsive gambling that usually ended in massive losses. At one point, a four years' sojourn in Europe was his only recourse to avoiding the debtors' prison. Money (or the lack of it) is a major theme of *Crime and Punishment*, *The Idiot*, *A Raw Youth*, and *The Brothers Karamazov*. On the role of money in Dostoevsky's fiction see Jacques Catteau, *Dostoevsky and the Process of Literary Creation*, trans. Audrey Littlewood (Cambridge: Cambridge University Press, 1989), 135–68.

[39] P, 439/PSS10, 372–3.

simple fact. Even when characters are speaking the truth, there is always something missing and there is no 'last word'. It is especially striking that at the end of *The Brothers Karamazov* we really have little or no idea as to how things will go in future for any of the main characters.

This is also the case when it is religious or metaphysical beliefs that are at issue. In *The Idiot*, the eponymous idiot, Prince Myshkin, experiences something like a classical mystical experience in the split second before the onset of an epileptic attack. 'His mind and his heart were flooded with extraordinary light; all his uneasiness, all his doubts, all his anxieties were relieved at once; they were all merged in a lofty calm, full of serene, harmonious joy and hope.'[40] Yet when he tries to describes this in the language of metaphysics and religion as 'ecstatic devotional merging in the highest synthesis of life' he has to admit that these are just 'vague expressions', even though they are 'very comprehensible' to him.[41]

This sense of the impossibility of direct speech about God and the future life has sometimes been linked to the apophatic mysticism of the Eastern Churches, that is, the acknowledgement that whatever is said of God is said only indirectly or 'as if', since the divine being is in itself ultimately mysterious. This is further connected to Eastern practices of hesychasm or silent prayer.[42] These themes perhaps hover below the surface in the Elder Zosima's comment that 'many of the strongest feelings and movements of our nature we cannot comprehend on earth'.[43] True knowledge, as Zosima says, is 'hereafter' while, for now, it is only 'the precious image of Christ' that provides true assurance.[44]

Of course, to acknowledge that everything we know about the world, about the future life, and about God is edged about with uncertainty and imprecision is not the same as to say that everything we claim to know is simply a lie. It is, however, to admit that our knowledge falls short of the fulness of truth and may therefore be hard to distinguish from falsehood. Conversely, something that may be virtually indistinguishable from a lie may prove to be the best pointer we have to truth. And this, I suggest, provides a significant clue to reading Dostoevsky as a Christian novelist, namely, as a writer of fictions that, as he says in the conversation, nevertheless direct us towards a point from which we may be able to see the truth.

---

[40] I, 219/PSS8, 188.

[41] I, 220/PSS8, 188. Note again the idea of 'the highest synthesis of life', found also in 'Will I ever see Masha again'. There, too, Dostoevsky says that the future state is 'impossible to understand on earth', though we can have a 'presentiment' of it.

[42] See, e.g., Malcolm Jones, *Dostoevsky and the Dynamics of Religious Experience* (London: Anthem Press, 2005), 139-46; Olga Stuchebrukhov, 'Hesychastic Ideas and the Concept of Integral Knowledge in Crime and Punishment', *Dostoevsky Studies*, New Series, Vol. 13 (2009), 77-91; Paul Evdokimov, *Der Abstieg in der Hölle: Gogol und Dostojewskij* (Salzburg: Otto Müller Verlag, 1965), 273.

[43] BK, 333/PSS14, 290.   [44] BK, 334/PSS14, 290.

Additional Points

Reading Dostoevsky while on her honeymoon in 1912, Virginia Woolf wrote, 'It is directly obvious that he is the greatest writer ever born.'[45]

The expression 'the truth once uttered is a lie' is from the poem 'Silentium' by Dostoevsky's contemporary Fyodor Tiutchev.

George Brandes was one of the most important literary critics of the late nineteenth century and played a key role in promoting both Kierkegaard and Nietzsche, as well as Dostoevsky. He spent a year in Russia and, on his return, gave an influential account of contemporary Russian literature, identifying Dostoevsky as the writer who best epitomized the spiritual mood of Russia. His lurid description of Dostoevsky typifies the 'orientalist' approach to Russia and to Dostoevsky in particular during the late nineteenth and early twentieth centuries.[46]

The story told by Dostoevsky about a young man walking with his child on a Sunday afternoon is an abbreviated version of a passage in his *Diary of a Writer*.[47]

---

[45] Roberta Rubenstein, *Virginia Woolf and the Russian Point of View* (Basingstoke: Palgrave Macmillan, 2009), 20.
[46] See Georg Brandes, *Indtryk fra Rusland* (Copenhagen: Gyldendal, 1888), 407–8.
[47] DW, 124–6/PSS21, 111.

Commentary on the First Conversation, Part Two

1. Guilt

The formula 'Each of us is guilty in everything before everyone, and I most of all' is introduced in the story of the death of the Elder Zosima's brother Markel in *The Brothers Karamazov*. Markel, dying of consumption, tells his mother that 'every one of us is guilty in everything before everyone, and I more than all'.[1] She immediately upbraids him since, she says, he has done nothing to compare with the sins of murderers and robbers. He responds by reiterating his statement in a slightly altered form: 'each of us is guilty before everyone, for everyone and everything'.[2] Variants of the saying or allusions to it subsequently occur about a dozen times in the novel, sometimes with direct reference to Markel, sometimes not. These variants do not mark any essential change in the content of the saying, however, but show Dostoevsky's skill in tracking the way in which aphoristic sayings of this kind are subject to inevitable transformations in the process of oral transmission.

As the narrator says, many contemporary readers are likely to react negatively to making guilt a privileged moment in self-development since popular forms of psychotherapy see guilt as likely to obstruct our freedom to act and to love. Rowan Williams speaks for many when he comments that 'being guilty for all' is 'not the most helpful of translations' and prefers to think of what is being said in terms of responsibility.[3]

Certainly, Dostoevskian guilt implies responsibility and as such serves as a kind of counterpoint to the motif of 'Am I my brother's keeper?' that recurs throughout *The Brothers Karamazov*. Nevertheless, guilt cannot be entirely dissolved into responsibility. Cain's resentful question 'Am I my brother's keeper?' is asked in the aftermath of the first murder, suggesting that in life as we know it the summons to responsibility occurs in a context that has already fallen away from an original amity. In becoming responsible, we are becoming responsible for all the ill that has occurred and that torments our world and its human and animal inhabitants. Becoming responsible therefore also involves acknowledging our

---

[1] BK, 297 (translation amended)/PSS14, 262.
[2] BK, 297 (translation amended)/PSS14, 262. Note that in the first quotation Garnett has 'has sinned' rather than 'guilty' and in the second 'responsible' rather than 'guilty', though the Russian text has the same word (*vinovat*) in each case.
[3] Rowan Williams, *Dostoevsky: Language, Faith and Fiction* (London: Continuum, 2008), 168.

guilt for things being as they are, a point forcefully made in section (h) of Zosima's 'Talks and Homilies', where judges are urged to know that they too are criminals, exactly like those who stand before them, and a judge is perhaps 'more than all men, to blame for that crime'.[4] In the same spirit we are also guilty for what we have each of us failed to do, for the light we have not shone into the dark places of the world. In loving the sinner in his sin we are not condescending to someone who is 'lower' than ourselves, but recognizing that we stand on the same level. As long as the world continues to fall short of its best possibilities, we are co-responsible for this shortfall and, in this sense, guilty.

Paul J. Contino has noted that although 'responsible' is to be found in some English translations, 'guilt' is the more accurate translation of Dostoevsky's Russian. Following Martin Buber, Contino helpfully distinguishes between existential and neurotic guilt feelings.[5] As Buber says, there is a 'real guilt' that is 'fundamentally different from all the anxiety-induced bugbears that are generated in the cavern of the unconscious'. This 'real' or 'existential' guilt relates to features of the human condition that are built in to being human. Existential guilt, Buber writes, 'occurs when someone injures an order of the human world whose foundations he knows and recognizes as those of his own existence and of all common human existence'.[6] By not being all that I could be, I damage not just myself but the common fabric of human life. To this, Buber adds insight into 'the impossibility of recovering the original point of departure and the irreparability of what has been done', which he also connects to 'the irreversibility of lived time'.[7]

A further gloss on the use of 'guilt' rather than 'responsibility' can be found in the thought of Emmanuel Levinas, who took Markel's words as a leitmotif for his own ethics of unremittable obligation.[8] Levinas made the biblical commandment to care for the widow, the orphan, and the stranger the basis of his own existential philosophy, arguing that we can never slip the demand established by the commandment. Therefore, as he puts it, we exist under accusation. In French (in which he mostly wrote) this suggests taking the standpoint of the 'me', the self in the accusative case, rather than the 'I', the Cartesian ego that was the then standard starting point of most philosophical approaches to human existence. As a Russian speaker from childhood, he might also have recalled that the accusative case in Russian is called the *vinitel'nye padezh*, sharing a root with *vina*, guilt—the 'guilty case', we could say. In this sense, guilt, what I owe the commandment, is prior to responsibility, which would be the action of the 'I' or subject, supervening

---

[4] BK, 334 (translation amended)/PSS14, 291.

[5] Paul J. Contino, *Dostoevsky's Incarnational Realism* (Eugene, OR: Cascade Books, 2020), 64.

[6] Martin Buber and Maurice S. Friedman, 'Guilt and Guilt Feeling', *CrossCurrents*, Vol. 8, No. 3 (1958), 197.

[7] Buber and Friedman, 'Guilt and Guilt Feeling', 196.

[8] See A. Toumayan, '"I more than the others": Dostoevsky and Levinas', *Yale French Studies*, 104, *Encounters with Levinas* (2004), 55–66.

upon the situation of being-guilty. In this context, guilt also resonates with Dostoevsky's polemic against the overemphasis on the 'I', the subject, that he saw as typical of Western views of human being.

However, it is not difficult to understand why Williams might have found 'guilt' unhelpful. Religious authorities have long used guilt to exert an improper control over their flocks, especially in relation to sexuality. Augustinian theology taught that original sin has incapacitated human beings to such a degree that not only are we incapable of doing good but we are not even capable of knowing or willing what is good. Indeed, our very being is perverted from the ground up, since each of us was conceived and born in sin. The Augsburg Confession (1530) taught that each of us, simply by virtue of birth, is rightly damnable. The joke that life is a sexually transmitted disease is not a bad summary of what some versions of Augustinianism have taught, and in German and Scandinavian languages the term for 'original sin' is, literally, 'inherited sin'.

None of this should be read into Dostoevsky, however, since (like Orthodoxy more generally) he does not share the Augustinian view of original sin. As Ivan Karamazov puts it, children have not eaten the apple. Dostoevsky was clearly aware that even quite young children are capable of doing very bad things and children may be corrupted at an early age, perhaps, as Zosima speculates, by seeing the anger or hearing the foul language of a passing adult; but they are not born guilty.[9] Human beings are originally innocent, not sinful. Yet guilt is not solely a matter of individual fault but a recognition of our entanglement in the situation in which we and our fellow human beings find ourselves today. As long as there is something wrong in the world we are guilty. But—versus Augustinianism— we can only be guilty because we are free and therefore also free to change.

Although it is in *The Brothers Karamazov* that we find the clearest and most thorough account of guilt and its role in personal religious development, it is a theme that can be found throughout the post-Siberian novels. *Uncle's Dream* (1859) centres on the attempt by the ambitious Marya Alexandrovna to get her daughter Zina married against her will to the rich but aging and befuddled 'uncle'. In a climactic scene, Zina steps forward and acknowledges her guilt: 'I take it all upon myself for I am more guilty than any one. I, I by consenting, set this vile ... intrigue ... going!'[10] Yet she is objectively the least guilty and had long resisted her mother's plans, remaining true to a former love—just as Markel is not guilty in any moral or forensic sense. Zina's guilt is precisely an acknowledgement of her implication in a situation of deceit and greed—but by declaring it she regains agency and freedom.

Markel's original statement of universal and unremittable guilt follows closely on his declaration that 'life is paradise, and we are all in paradise, but we won't see

[9] BK, 332–3/PSS14, 289–90.   [10] HT, 127/PSS2, 385.

it, if we would we would have heaven on earth the next day.'[11] Later, Zosima recalls Markel's words as saying 'Mother, my little heart, in truth we are each guilty before all for all, it's only that men don't know this. If they knew it, the world would be a paradise at once.'[12] Becoming guilty is not to embark upon a guilt trip but is a way to open the gates of paradise. But how?

We are already familiar with the first and most important part of Dostoevsky's answer, namely, that acceptance of guilt is the rediscovery of human solidarity and deliverance from the isolation that Zosima sees as the 'spiritual suicide' pursued by the wealthy and progressive part of the modern world in its pursuit of endlessly multiplying needs and the consequent competitiveness of all social relations.[13] Likewise, the possibility of freely choosing to make ourselves guilty means that we are liberated from the despondency generated by the idea that we are merely products of our environment. 'Fly from that dejection, children!' exhorts Zosima. 'There is only one means of salvation, then take yourself and make yourself guilty of all men's sins, that is the truth…it really is so, and you are guilty for everyone and for all things.'[14] Knowing the pain of others and our responsibility in relation to that pain means we are no longer alone but, in the most emphatic sense, *with* one another. We will never be able to exhaust the demand, but life under the demand is itself a life lived in solidarity with others, a purposeful life, a life in which there is always something more to be done.

One of the primary objections of the post-Christian world to Christian guilt culture is that guilt is essentially isolating, locking us up with the punitive memories of all we believe ourselves to be guilty for. Dostoevsky's vision is the opposite. Accepting our guilt reveals what the Anglican writer Charles Williams called our coinherence and, thus understood, opens us up to new levels of relatedness that help restore a paradise that, Dostoevsky believes, will always remain lost to those who define themselves solely with the interests, aims, and objectives of the rational autonomous ego.

2. *Pro et Contra*

The continuation of the first Conversation turns at one point to Hegel, the German philosopher famous for producing a system of idealist philosophy that offered a synthetic account of nature, history, culture, and even, in his *Logic*, an analysis of the mind of God. Though often lampooned for his abstruse style and apparently extravagant claims, Hegel's system was hugely influential across Europe and, later in the nineteenth century, globally.

---

[11] BK, 296/PSS14, 262. [12] BK, 309–10 (translation amended)/PSS14, 270.
[13] BK, 325–6/PSS14, 284. [14] BK, 333 (translation amended)/PSS14, 290.

Hegel's thought was strongly influenced by Christian doctrine, as in the view—versus Platonism—that ideas only become meaningful through being incarnated in concrete historical life. Many Christian theologians accepted Hegel as a Christian philosopher, though others, amongst them the Dane Søren Kierkegaard, saw his thought as hollowing out traditional Christian claims. Kierkegaard objected: (1) that Hegel reduced God to a function of human consciousness; (2) that his philosophy was so abstract that it ultimately subordinated life to logic; (3) that he explains historical change as occurring through necessity and does not give due scope to the role of human freedom.[15] This could also serve as a summary of the negative side of Dostoevsky's reception of German Idealism, although it is very unlikely that he knew of Kierkegaard's writings.[16] It is striking that at the end of *Crime and Punishment* he describes the first moments of Raskolnikov's regeneration with the words 'instead of dialectics there was life'.[17]

Did Dostoevsky himself read Hegel? On leaving prison in 1854, he wrote to his brother Mikhail for money and books, including Hegel's *History of Philosophy*.[18] A year later, his friend Baron Wrangel writes that he and Dostoevsky are translating works by Hegel and C. G. Carus, but does not say which.[19] In the brilliant essay *Dostoevsky Reads Hegel in Siberia and Bursts into Tears*, László F. Földényi suggests it might have been *The Philosophy of History*.[20] Földényi argues that Hegel's comment that Siberia 'does not concern us, since the northern regions...lie outside of history' is likely to have especially caught Dostoevsky's eye and to have provoked the reaction I follow Földényi in ascribing to him.[21]

At the time of Dostoevsky's literary debut, several leading Russian intellectuals had been influenced by Hegel, amongst them T. N. Granovsky (sometimes seen as a model for Stepan Trofimovich Verkhovensky) and V. G. Belinsky, the leading literary critic whose good opinion was especially valued by Dostoevsky.[22] While attending meetings of the Petrashevsky circle (1847–9), Dostoevsky also borrowed books from Petrashevsky's library, including the *Life of Jesus* by the Left-Hegelian

---

[15] On Kierkegaard and Hegelianism see my *Kierkegaard and the Theology of the Nineteenth Century* (Cambridge: Cambridge University Press, 2012), 30–79.

[16] In 2019 a monument to Dostoevsky was placed in the churchyard where Kierkegaard is buried with the intention of honouring what was seen as their spiritual kinship.

[17] CP, 492/PSS6, 422. Garnett has 'theory' but the Russian has 'dialectic'.

[18] PSS, 173 (Letter 89).

[19] See Joseph Frank, *Dostoevsky: The Years of Ordeal, 1850–1859* (Princeton, NJ: Princeton University Press, 1983), 189.

[20] Lázló F. Földényi, trans. Ottilie Mulzet, *Dostoevsky Reads Hegel in Siberia and Bursts into Tears* (Newhaven, CT: Yale University Press, 2020).

[21] G. W. F. Hegel, *Vorlesungen über die Philosophie der Geschichte*. Werke, Vol. 12 (Frankfurt: Suhrkamp, 1970), 130.

[22] See Andrzej Walicki, *A History of Russian Thought from the Enlightenment to Marxism* (Oxford: Clarendon Press), 988, 115–34; Robert Harris, 'Granovsky, Herzen and Chicherin: Hegel and the Battle for Russia's Soul', in Lisa Herzog (ed.), *Hegel's Thought in Europe: Currents, Crosscurrents and Undercurrents* (Basingstoke: Palgrave Macmillan, 2013), 35–48.

theologian D. F. Strauss.²³ The Hegelianism that Dostoevsky encountered in this period epitomized the kind of Westernized liberalism that he would persistently criticize in his later post-Siberia writings.

One aspect of Hegelianism is especially likely to have aroused Dostoevsky's antipathy, namely the view that historical change occurs by necessity. In later Marxist versions of this idea, it would be claimed that the laws of historical development are as necessary as the laws of physics. The empirical science of the day similarly tended towards a deterministic view of the world as a machine, incapable of generating freedom and autonomous vitality.²⁴ Although Hegelianism and materialist natural science are philosophically incompatible, they could often be conflated at a popular level, especially as regards their critical potential vis-à-vis religion and metaphysics. Both fed into what become known in the 1860s as nihilism.

The 'blind force' with which the closing howl of despair in *A Gentle Spirit* opens is Garnett's translation of a Russian term also translatable as 'inertia', indicating the background view of the world that the narrator accepts and Dostoevsky challenges.²⁵ The idea makes its presence felt also in the notes 'Will I see Masha again?' where Dostoevsky writes that 'The teaching of the materialists is universal inertia and the mechanization of matter, it amounts to death. The teaching of true philosophy is the annihilation of inertia, it is the thought, it is the center and Synthesis of the universe and external form, matter, it is God, it is eternal life.'²⁶

Dostoevsky's best-known assault on determinism is in *Notes from Underground*. The 'underground man' attacks the view that the world is entirely subject to immutable natural laws and rails against those whose behaviour doesn't rise above the level of instinctual animal life, the kind of person he calls *l'homme de la nature et de verité*.²⁷ Acceptance of naturalism, he says, will lead to people believing that happiness can be determined by mathematical laws—logarithms²⁸— reducing the human being to 'a piano-key' to be played upon by forces over which it has not control.²⁹ His protest is summed up in his refusal to accept the universal validity of twice two is four. 'Twice two makes four seems to me simply a piece

---

²³ On the intellectual atmosphere of the Petrashevsky circle see Walicki, *History*, 152–61; also Joseph Frank, *Dostoevsky: The Seeds of Revolt, 1821–1849* (Princeton, NJ: Princeton University Press, 1976), 239–91; and, in a lively narrative account, Kevin Birmingham, *The Sinner and the Saint: Dostoevsky, a Crime and Its Punishment* (London: Allen Lane, 2021), 68–86. Strauss was a leading Left Hegelian and his *Life of Jesus* dismissed most of the gospel account of Jesus as myth. It was a massive succès de scandale and was translated into English by George Eliot (Marian Evans).

²⁴ This is the theme of Liza Knapp's *The Annihilation of Inertia: Dostoevsky and Metaphysics* (Evanston, IL: Northwestern University Press, 1996).

²⁵ Knapp, *Inertia*, 4.   ²⁶ See Knapp, *Inertia*, 2/PSS20, 175.

²⁷ That he speaks of *l'homme de la nature et de verité* in French insinuates that this is part of an alien world view that is not natural to the Russian reader.

²⁸ WN, 68–9/PSS5, 113.

²⁹ WN, 73/PSS5, 117. As Knapp explores at length, the polemic against determinism continues through all of Dostoevsky's major novels.

of insolence... Twice two makes four is an excellent thing but if we are to give everything its due, twice two makes five is sometimes a very charming thing too.'[30]

None of this excludes Dostoevsky having taken some inspiration from Hegel's idea that history involves the ongoing conflict between dialectically opposed polarities: '*pro et contra*', as he says in the conversation (alluding to the title of Book V of *The Brothers Karamazov* in which Ivan's rebellion against God is opposed by Zosima's defence of Christianity). Hegel's was, of course, only one form of dialectics, though probably the best known and most influential in Dostoevsky's own time. Ksana Blank finds antecedents and parallels not only in ancient philosophy and Christianity but also in East Asian thought. As she writes, 'In [Dostoevsky's] universe, opposites form a single unity and cannot exist or be cognized without each other. The pros and contras involved in this eternal dialogue form a single, *antinomic* whole.'[31] She sees this outlook reflected in Nicholas Berdyaev's influential reading of Dostoevsky, which begins by declaring Dostoevsky to be 'a dialectician of genius' and states that 'this dialectic is of the very essence of his art.'[32] A salient feature of this reading is Berdyaev's emphasis on freedom. 'Freedom,' he writes, 'is the centre of [Dostoevsky's] conception of the world... [and] his hidden pathos is a pathos of freedom.'[33] Since 'Christianity is the religion of freedom' this is also key to Dostoevsky's Christianity.[34] It may be unfair to Hegel to read him as a thoroughgoing determinist but this is how he is likely to have been seen by Dostoevsky, which makes Dostoevsky's insistence on the freedom to persist in despair or to allow oneself to be transformed by faith anti-Hegelian. Dostoevsky's dialectic is transcended only through the dynamic and antinomic freedom of life, which (unlike Hegel's) therefore remains open and unfinished.[35]

---

[30] WN, 75/PSS5, 119.

[31] Ksana Blank, *Dostoevsky's Dialectics and the Problem of Sin* (Evanston, IL: Northwestern University Press, 2010), 7. James Scanlan also speaks of 'the dialectical method of [Dostoevsky's] philosophizing'—see Scanlan, *Dostoevsky the Thinker*, 231.

[32] Nicholas Berdyaev, *Dostoevsky*, trans. Donald Attwater (New York, NY: Meridian, 1957), 11.

[33] Berdyaev, *Dostoevsky*, 67.   [34] Berdyaev, *Dostoevsky*, 71.

[35] In his study *Pro et Contra* the Soviet critic Viktor Shklovsky concludes that Dostoevsky's dialectic had to remain open because the real dialectic of social development had not reached a point in his time when an authentic synthesis could be achieved, as it would do under communism. See Viktor Shklovsky, *Za i Protiv: Zametki o Dostoevskom* (Moscow: Sovetskii Pisatel', 1957).

Commentary on the Second Conversation

1. The Bible

All the texts referred to in this conversation are known to have been read and valued by Dostoevsky. He read the Gothic novels of Mrs Radcliffe as a child, and the Dostoevsky brothers' enthusiasm for Walter Scott is well documented. Dostoevsky's first publication was a translation of Balzac's *Eugénie Grandet* (1843) and he read *Jane Eyre* while remanded in the St Peter and St Paul fortress prior to the mock execution of 1849. In the prison camp his reading was officially limited to the New Testament, a copy of which had been given to him by members of a group of women who did charitable works for convicts en route to the camps. However, thanks to a well-disposed doctor in the infirmary, he was able to get the Dickens novels mentioned in the conversation.[1] Later, as a literary editor, he commissioned a translation of Mrs Gaskell's *Mary Barton*. His admiration for George Sand, Victor Hugo, Schiller, Goethe, Shakespeare, and Cervantes is well known and much commented on in the secondary literature. Perhaps there is scarcely a page of Dostoevsky's novels without some discussion, quotation, or allusion to other writers, many of them non-Russian. He himself said that, as a writer, he had two patrimonies, Russia *and* Europe.

It almost goes without saying that Russian literature from Pushkin onwards was also a constant point of reference in his work, not least with regard to the hope that Russia was destined to express a 'new word' in world history. This hope found expression in the Pushkin Memorial speech that Dostoevsky gave in 1880 and which honours Pushkin for having pioneered a new dramatis personae of literary types that reveal distinctively Russian characteristics for the very first time, thus providing a point of departure for subsequent Russian writers. In a preface to the speech, Dostoevsky also claimed that Pushkin showed a no less distinctively Russian trait, namely, the ability to enter into the spirit of other nations and to identify with and express their distinctive truth. This 'all-unifying' spirit, he insists, is not claimed in denigration of Europe. Nor does Russia need to complete a 'European' process of modernization in order to achieve it and speak

---

[1] The conversation focusses on the echo of Dickens's Little Nell in the character of Nelly in *The Insulted and the Injured*. *The Old Curiosity Shop* is also discussed in *A Raw Youth* (see Commentary on the seventh Conversation).

its word. Russia may be a 'destitute and confused land' but the promise of a new word is vouched for by the vitality of the Russian people.[2]

Dostoevsky's sources are not only literary and, while in prison, he wrote down and compiled popular sayings and expressions that he heard amongst the peasant convicts.[3] This interest in popular speech is connected to Dostoevsky's idea of his own writing as a kind of higher realism, as can be seen from two late notes. In one much-quoted remark he says of himself that 'they call me a psychologist. It is not true. I am simply a realist in a higher sense, that is, I portray all the depths of the human spirit.'[4] The immediately preceding note connects this both to Dostoevsky's self-understanding as a Christian author and to the place of the Russian people in his authorship: 'For a thorough-going realism [the task is] to find the man in man. This is a Russian trait par excellence, and in this sense I am ultimately of the people (since my approach flows from out of the depths of the Christian spirit of the people)—although this is not known to the Russian people now but will become known in the future.'[5] At the deepest level this connection had to do with what he saw as the people's spontaneous affinity with Christ, signalled in Tiutchev's lines, quoted at the end of Dostoevsky's Pushkin speech, 'Christ, in a serf's garb, has traversed [this destitute land] to and fro, with a blessing.'[6]

The Bible, and especially the New Testament, becomes a crucial intertext in all Dostoevsky's major fiction after the four years in prison camp. He had known the Bible since childhood, from its use in Church services and from Johan Hübner's *One Hundred and Four Bible Stories for Children* (still in print today), from which he, like the Elder Zosima, learned to read. But Dostoevsky not only drew on the Bible as an exceptionally rich source of quotation and inspiration. He also aimed to make the biblical word be heard anew in the essentially secular milieu of contemporary Russian society, where it had become peripheral to cultural formation.[7]

There are, however, major challenges involved in introducing the Bible into modern realistic prose fiction. Christianity regards the Bible as having divine and therefore unconditional authority, but literary realism is limited to the complex relativity of human life and its characters cannot therefore be authoritative mediators of the biblical word—quite apart from the fact that they are fictional. The biblical narrative also involves events or actions of a miraculous nature that have no place in a novel that represents the world in which readers live their average everyday lives.[8]

---

[2] DW, 959–67/PSS26, 129–36.
[3] See Linda Ivanits, *Dostoevsky and the Russian People* (Cambridge: Cambridge University Press, 2008).
[4] PSS27, 65.   [5] PSS27, 65.
[6] DW, 980/PSS26, 148. The reference is to Tiutchev's poem, 'From these poor villages'.
[7] See, for example, Simonetta Salvestroni, *Dostoïevski et la Bible*, trans. Pierre Laroche (Paris: Lethielleux, 2004).
[8] For further discussion see Diane O. Thompson, 'Problems of the Biblical Word in Dostoevsky's Poetics', in George Pattison and Diane O. Thompson (eds.), *Dostoevsky and the Christian Tradition: Reading Dostoevsky Religiously* (Cambridge: Cambridge University Press, 2001), 69–99.

Dostoevsky's response to these challenges involves a variety of literary tactics. One is the direct quotation of the biblical text in the novel. Such quotations take many forms and reveal a range of attitudes to the words being quoted. When Ivan Karamazov asks, 'Am I my brother's keeper?' he is citing the words of Cain, murderer of his brother Abel, thereby indicating his own moral peril. When Fyodor Karamazov induces his servant Smerdyakov to entertain his other sons with his simplistic and rationalistic objections to the creation narrative of Genesis, he clearly intends to ridicule the Bible and Smerdyakov believes he is successfully refuting it. In *The Idiot*, as mentioned in Commentary 1.2, Lebedev has a reputation as an interpreter of the Book of Revelation but is mocked by other characters for claiming that 'the star wormwood' of Revelation 8.10–11 signifies the coming of the railways and the whole capitalist and industrial system that they represent.

There are three occasions in the major fiction when Dostoevsky has a character read aloud an extended passage of Scripture in such a way as to offer a potential key to the novel as a whole.[9] The best-known is the passage in *Crime and Punishment* in which Sonia reads the story of the raising of Lazarus to Raskolnikov. It is a scene of intense melodrama in which both characters seem to be teetering on the edge of insanity and even perdition and the text pointedly raises the question as to whether either of them can be resurrected from their wretched predicaments.[10]

In *The Possessed*, Stepan Trofimovich Verkhovensky falls into the company of a travelling Bible seller who reads to him from the Bible, culminating in the story of the man possessed by many demons that Jesus exorcises and sends into a herd of swine who thereupon plunge into a nearby lake and are drowned (Luke 8.32–6). Stepan Trofimovich applies this to the 'demons' of nihilism that have possessed Russia and for which, as he now acknowledges, he too shares responsibility.[11] But the passage also points towards Russia being healed, once the demons have been cast out. Despite Stepan Trofimovich's chronic mendacity, this application seems to be close to Dostoevsky's own and is used as one of the novel's mottos.

The third example is from *The Brothers Karamazov*, where the story of the miracle that took place at a marriage in Cana in Galilee, when Christ turned water into wine, is read aloud during the vigil over the dead body of the Elder Zosima. Zosima's disciple Alyosha falls asleep during the reading and dreams that he is transported to the marriage feast where he sees Zosima who invites him to join him and the other guests, including Christ himself, their 'Sun' (as Zosima calls him), whose radiance is, however, too bright for Alyosha to look at directly. Waking up, he rushes out into the garden and has an ecstatic experience in which the deep night sky seems to fuse with the earth that he kisses and waters with his

---

[9] According to Eric Ziolkowski, the act of reading aloud enacts the incarnational movement of the Word that 'became flesh and dwelt among us'. See Eric Ziolkowksi, 'Reading and Incarnation in Dostoevsky', in Pattison and Thompson, *Dostoevsky and Christian Tradition*, 156–70.
[10] CP, 295-9/PSS6, 248–51.   [11] P, 595-6/PSS9, 498–9.

tears, while longing 'to forgive everyone and for everything, and to beg forgiveness. Oh, not for himself but for all men, for all and for everything'—words that echo Markel's threefold summons to become guilty. This too is a transformational moment, of which the narrator says that 'something firm and unshakable as that vault of heaven had entered into his soul'.[12]

Like the raising of Lazarus, the miracle of Cana is found in St John's gospel, which seems to have been the gospel of greatest significance to Dostoevsky, as evidenced both by the markings in his personal copy of the New Testament and its use in his novels.[13] This is unsurprising, given its general prominence in the Eastern Church, sometimes referred to as the Johannine Church, in contradistinction to the 'Petrine' (Catholic) Church and the 'Pauline' (Protestant) churches. It is also the source for the motto to *The Brothers Karamazov*, 'Very truly, I tell you, unless a grain of wheat falls into the earth and dies, it remains just a single grain; but if it dies, it bears much fruit' (John 12.24). Again, the passage points to regeneration but also, implicitly, to self-sacrifice as the means of regeneration.[14]

In such ways, the Bible not only enriches the palette of Dostoevsky's intertextual references but also provides a framework for his Christian world view. In the conversation I have introduced Northrop Frye's idea of the Bible as 'the great code', meaning that it provides an overarching mythical structure through which to explicate and interpret human beings' meaning-creating acts of imagination.[15] I am not wanting to make Dostoevsky subscribe to this theory in its specifics but he does seem to share Frye's view that through stories and images the Bible speaks to the existential situation of the living human being and that attempts to read the Bible as history are essentially irrelevant to its human importance.[16]

---

[12] BK, 379/PSS 14, 328. As Thompson sums up, 'Dostoevsky aimed to reanimate the authoritative word of conventional Christianity, grown calcified through formulaic repetition, by making it internally persuasive, and thus authoritative at a deeper level of psychological and spiritual complexity' and in this way to set in motion a new encounter with Christ. See Thompson, 'The Biblical Word', 94.

[13] On Dostoevsky's New Testament see Geir Kjetsaa, *Dostoevsky and His New Testament* (Atlantic Highlands, NJ: Humanities Press, 1984); also Irina Kirillova, 'Dostoevsky's Markings in the Gospel According to St John', in Pattison and Thompson, *Dostoevsky*, 41–50.

[14] This motto has had a mixed history in English translations. It is missing from the Garnett translation, while in the 1992 Pevear and Volokhonsky translation published by Vintage it is effectively hidden amongst the bibliographical data. It was dutifully included in the Soviet Academy edition, being placed prominently at the top of the first page of the narrative.

[15] See Northrop Frye, *The Great Code: The Bible and Literature* (London: Routledge and Kegan Paul, 1982). In the symbolist Vyacheslav Ivanov's interpretation, the mythical world informing what he calls Dostoevsky's 'novel-tragedies' reveals universal mythical structures that are not specifically biblical. See Vyacheslav Ivanov, *Freedom and the Tragic Life: A Study in Dostoevsky*, trans. Norman Cameron (New York: Noonday, 1960).

[16] It was noted in the last commentary that Dostoevsky had read David Friedrich Strauss's *Life of Jesus*, perhaps the most influential and devastating attack on the idea that we can find the historical facts behind the gospel narrative.

2. Suffering

The conversation raises the question of suffering in a number of contexts, including the deaths of children, sexual exploitation, the suffering of the peasants, and the suffering Christ. Some critics have indeed complained that there is simply too much suffering in Dostoevsky's novels. The conversations allude to Mikhailovsky's jibe that his was a 'cruel talent' and that he took a kind of active, even sadistic pleasure in subjecting his characters to the most extreme sufferings, a charge taken up by Maxim Gorky, who used the word 'Karamazovism' for what he saw as a pathological focus on suffering.[17] But is this fair?

Like many of his contemporaries, Dostoevsky saw and was appalled by the miseries consequent upon the rapid industrialization and urbanization of the nineteenth century. It is no surprise that novels set in the world in which he and his readers were living should depict the multiple sufferings of poverty and social displacement, inclusive of disease (notably tuberculosis), mental illness, alcoholism, crime, and, not least, the violence relentlessly perpetrated against women. In Dostoevsky's case, the field of observation was considerably widened by his firsthand experiences of the brutality of prison life. Nor is it surprising that a writer of Dostoevsky's psychological acuity should also explore in depth the moral and personal torments of his characters. Perhaps only the horrors of war are missing from the litany of sufferings that seems to resound throughout Dostoevsky's major fiction (although Ivan Karamazov does allude to atrocities reportedly committed by Ottoman forces against the Bulgarians).

Against this background, it can be argued that Dostoevsky's treatment of suffering is more a matter of unflinching witness than pathology. In support of this view, I shall adduce four aspects of his approach, though sceptics will probably remain unpersuaded.

The first is the simple observation that, as noted above, any novelist situating their work in the urban environment of mid-nineteenth-century Europe and making any claim to realism had to face up to the sufferings that were everywhere to be seen by those who had eyes to see. To the extent that these sufferings were not inevitable aspects of the human condition but were the result of human actions such as the drive to maximize profit or judicial incompetence, it is also clear that Dostoevsky did not merely counsel acceptance but argued for specific ameliorative actions, as in his support for the emancipation of the serfs, his denunciation of

---

[17] See Robert L. Jackson, *Dialogues with Dostoevsky: The Overwhelming Questions* (Stanford, CA: Stanford University Press, 1993), 121–33. Gorky linked this to Dostoevsky's social conservatism, reflecting a widespread perception that conservative social and political thought typically rejects progressive ideals on the grounds that human beings are incapable of moral improvement (Christian thinkers putting this down to sin) and therefore need the kind of discipline that only political and/or religious authority can provide. Russian also produced a noun, 'Dostoevschina', referring to this aspect of the writer's work.

child prostitution, and his writings about the justice system, including his intervention in the case of Ekaterina Kornilova, when he argued for an acquittal on the grounds that she was suffering from what we would call postnatal depression (mentioned in the first Conversation), as well as offering support to an experimental rehabilitation project for young offenders.[18]

The second point is to underline that Dostoevsky did not see suffering as having intrinsic value. Suffering does not necessarily ennoble the sufferer and abuse can generate its own cycle of self-hatred and resentment, as he showed in the character of Nellie (*The Insulted and the Injured*), the resentful tirades of *Notes from Underground*, Anastasia Phillipovna (*The Idiot*), Stavrogin (*The Possessed*), and, I suggest, Ivan Karamazov. Rage against life and what Kierkegaard called 'the despair of defiance' make for an only too understandable response on the part of those whose own life opportunities have been taken away or corrupted.

That suffering is not itself a solution is also illustrated by Dostoevsky's comments on religious asceticism. Nikolai Nekrasov's poem 'Vlas' tells the story of a Russian peasant who, after killing his wife, embarks on a life of perpetual wandering, living as a barefoot mendicant, wearing iron chains round his body to make movement more arduous (a well-known ascetical practice in Russia at the time). Writing about this poem, Dostoevsky expresses a certain awe in face of the Russian capacity for extreme suffering and he writes of the fundamental spiritual character of the Russian people as shaped by the desire for suffering.[19] Nevertheless, he elsewhere expresses or implies considerable reservations regarding such extreme ascetic practices. The rootless aristocrat Valkovsky (*The Insulted and the Injured*) is also rumoured to have wandered 'with chains', but it is clear that this has not brought relief to his soul. In *The Brothers Karamazov*, the hermit Ferapont is described as living a life of exceptional asceticism—but he is also seen to be full of hate and is envious of the reputation of the more gentle Zosima, not to mention being subject to hallucinatory experiences of diabolic presences. The point seems clear: mortifying the flesh is of no value if it does not come from or lead to love. Indeed, Dostoevsky's apparent rejection of asceticism was one of the points used by Konstantin Leontiev to argue that Dostoevsky's religion was not authentically Orthodox.[20] We may compare this with Zosima's own teaching, mentioned in the fourth Conversation, that the suffering of hell is, quite simply (but terrifyingly) the suffering of not being able to love.

Thirdly, however, Dostoevsky does seem to accept the view that suffering can be beneficial. This view is deeply engrained in the founding traditions of both Judaism and Christianity. Israel's slavery in Egypt and later exile in Babylon are

---

[18] On Kornilova see DW, 459–65/PSS23, 136–41, DW, 527–35/PSS24, 36–43, DW, 690–1/PSS25, 119–21, DW, 913–35/PSS26, 92–110. On rehabilitation see DW, 172–82/PSS22, 17–26.

[19] DW, 31–43/PSS21, 31–41. On Dostoevsky's view of suffering in the lives of the peasants, see Ivanits, *Dostoevsky and the Russian People*.

[20] For more on Leontiev see the next section of this commentary.

interpreted as necessary moments in God's providential plan for the people's ultimate salvation, a pattern internalized into the personal piety of many psalms and moral and religious instructions. Christianity sees Christ's suffering and death (echoed in the suffering and death of his martyrs) as a precondition of his final exaltation. This, for example, is the argument of Philippians 2.5–11, which (discussed further in the commentary on the fourth Conversation) speaks of Christ's self-emptying, taking the form of a servant and suffering death on the cross—but, as the passage concludes, 'Therefore God also highly exalted him and gave him the name that is above every name' (Phil. 2.9). Hebrews 12 speaks of how, 'for the sake of the joy that was set before him', Jesus 'endured the cross, disregarding its shame' and has now 'taken his seat at the right hand of the throne of God' (Heb. 12.2). Hebrews goes on to frame this in terms of God disciplining his people as a father disciplines his children, describing suffering of this kind as a means of bringing about a greater holiness, also a motif frequently deployed in the Hebrew Scriptures (Heb. 12.5–11).

Modern literature and culture has found this kind of argument largely unconvincing and has repeatedly drawn attention to its utilization in enforcing submission to authority, often backed up by sadistic systems of punishment, from the schoolroom to the factory to the slave plantation. Why, then, should we give any credence to it when we find it in Dostoevsky? Isn't this the 'cruel talent' in action?

Bearing this objection in mind, Dostoevsky's counterargument would seem to be that, nevertheless, suffering can be used to break down the egoism that, as he sees it, is the major obstacle to human happiness. However, it is immediately important to emphasize that although it *can* function in this way it does not do so necessarily. Examples such as Nellie, the underground man, and Nastasia Phillipovna show that suffering can also entrench the sufferer in their misery. For suffering to be educative it must be freely chosen and guided by love. When Dostoevsky praises the Russian peasant's capacity for suffering, this is because he sees this as inseparable from their mutual compassion, illustrated by their perception of the convicts as 'unfortunates' rather than malefactors.[21] It is the ethics of 'we're all in it together'.

A striking example of how suffering might engender compassion and in this way serve personal redemption is Dmitri Karamazov and, in the opening scene of the novel, it is said to be a vision of Dmitri's future suffering that causes the Elder Zosima to bow down before him.[22] As the critic Ivanov pointed out, his name already signals an affinity to ancient myths of death and resurrection and his character also reflects Dostoevsky's longstanding interest in the legend of 'the great sinner', that is, a man who, having committed a horrific crime and

---

[21] HD, 19/PSS4, 18–19.   [22] BK, 71/PSS14, 69.

renouncing belief in God eventually returns to faith after many years of self-abnegation. The pattern of such a life is well established in Christian literature: Paul, the persecutor of the Church who became apostle to the gentiles, is an early paradigm. The theme has attracted other important modern writers: Flaubert used the story of St Julian the Hospitaller, who unwittingly killed both his parents, as the basis for one of his *Three Tales*, while Thomas Mann's *The Holy Sinner* adapts an apocryphal legend of Pope Gregory in which Gregory is the child of an incestuous brother–sister union who later marries his mother. Both stories (like *The Brothers Karamazov*) have echoes of the Oedipus story and in each case the sinner expiates his sin through heroic works of poverty and service to others, finally achieving sanctity.

If some of Dostoevsky's ideas for the continuation of the novel had come to fruition, Alyosha too might have become another example, losing his faith, becoming a terrorist, and finally returning to the monastery. In the case of Dmitri, we are from the beginning alerted through his 'confession in verse' to his essential duality: on the one hand his earthly sensuousness ('Sodom') and on the other his longing for a higher ideal ('the Madonna'). But before he can attain his ideal he is subject to the torment of arrest, prosecution, and the prospect of many years servitude in Siberia. A crucial turning point takes place in the night of his arrest, when he has a dream of a ravaged landscape and mothers mutely holding their starving babies. The dream awakens an immense compassion in Dmitri and he gradually becomes capable of accepting punishment for the crime of parricide (of which he is innocent) as penance for his previous life. We do not see Dmitri achieve a resolution of his situation and although we anticipate that he may never be saintly in any narrow sense, we are persuaded that, aided by the love of Grushenka, he is on the way to redeeming the feckless self-centredness of his young life. As with the peasants, the experience of suffering and the capacity for compassion are importantly interlinked.

An important background motif in Dostoevsky's treatment of suffering is the Book of Job. Job himself epitomizes a righteous man rewarded with material prosperity and social respect. His righteousness provokes Satan to wager that even Job is corruptible, and God gives permission for him to test Job as he will. First of all, he has Job's children killed and herds stolen, then Job is afflicted with painful and unsightly sores—his wife counselling him to 'curse God, and die' (Job 2.9). Initially, Job humbles himself under his suffering, saying the words often quoted in Christian funeral services: 'The Lord gave, and the Lord has taken away; blessed be the name of the Lord' (Job 1.21). The Elder Zosima reports that this passage had made a particular impression on him as a child, suggesting that Dostoevsky might be straightforwardly endorsing the message of patient acceptance of suffering, with which, in Christian tradition, Job became synonymous (as in the saying 'the patience of Job'). However, in the Bible itself, Job's attitude seems to change from Chapter 3 onwards and we hear Job powerfully complaining to God, accusing Him of injustice and, even worse, vindictiveness. He prays to God to leave him alone and let him die. A group of friends tries to make him change his mind, using arguments familiar from the subsequent history of religious teaching. Either you are being punished for some secret sin, they say, or else God has some purpose in what is happening to you, and, in any case, mortals have no right to question God. Job rejects all their arguments and, eventually, God himself speaks, declaring that it is in fact Job who has spoken rightly while stressing that He, God, is indeed beyond all comprehension. Job finally repents 'in dust and ashes', whereupon God restores his fortunes and blesses him with new children, a turn that astounds Zosima, who asks, 'But how could he love those new ones when those first children are no more, when he has lost them? Remembering them, how could he be fully happy with those new ones, however dear the new ones might be? But he could, he could.'[23]

Yet, on this occasion, it would be wrong to straightforwardly equate Dostoevsky's own position with Zosima's counsel of acceptance. For it is not only the Job who eventually submitted to God who is present in the novel. Ivan's protest against the unjustifiable suffering of children echoes the powerful chapters in which Job himself rebels against the apparent injustice of divine rule. In a further echo of Job, the inconsolable misery of Captain Snegiryov, the father of the child Ilyusha whose death and funeral conclude the novel, represents a level of suffering that, like Job, wants only to die: 'Why is light given to one in misery, and life to the bitter in soul,' Job asks (Job 3.20). Patient acceptance may come in the end, but, as in the Book of Job itself, the way to such acceptance is long, winding, and, at many points, barred by seemingly impassable obstacles.[24]

Suffering is, fourthly and finally, not only a means of breaking through egoism to a larger, more compassionate view of life, it is also a way of entering into and participating in the sufferings of Christ. Here the Orthodox Church's category of 'passion-bearers', as distinct from 'martyrs', seems relevant. Whereas the martyr is killed because of his or her witness to Christ, the passion-bearer is one whose suffering may not have directly resulted from their witness but, nevertheless, reveals something of Christ's suffering in the world. Here, the identification of Christ with the Russian peasant in the Tiutchev poem cited in Dostoevsky's Pushkin speech seems apt.[25] The sufferings of the peasant are not those of the martyrs, but, through a kind of reciprocal affinity, they connect them to Christ.

However, while Dostoevsky certainly alludes to the humility of Christ, his image of Christ has an essentially luminous quality, as in Alyosha's vision of Cana

---

[23] BK, 301/PSS14, 264–5.
[24] On the threefold use of Job in *The Brothers Karamazov*, see my article 'Hiob als Intertext: Dostojewskis "Die Bruder Karamasow"', in L. Ratschow and H. von Sass (eds.), *Die Anfechtung Gottes* (Leipzig: Evangelische Verlagsanstalt, 2016), 263–76.
[25] For further discussion see the second section of the Commentary on Conversation Four: 'Self-Deification and Divine Self-Emptying'.

of Galilee, where, to adapt the words of a well-known hymn, Christ is hidden by the glory of his own light. Describing the human Christ of the legend of the Grand Inquisitor, Ivan says that 'The sun of love burns in His heart, light and power shine from His eyes, and their radiance, shed on the people, stirs their hearts with responsive love.'[26] Dostoevsky nowhere dwells on the physical sufferings of Christ, as we find in many Protestant and Catholic spiritual writers and in much sacred art.

Again we may think of Philippians 2 and the kenotic understanding of the Incarnation, according to which Christ's physical suffering and death are only the ultimate term of a movement that is not directed to suffering as such (as in those theories of the atonement that require suffering as the ransom price or satisfaction needed to bring about forgiveness), but is to be understood from the point of view of the self-emptying, humble movement of love, for the sake of the other. It is becoming nothing that others may be. This resonates, for example, with the view expressed in Dostoevsky's notes following the death of his first wife that Christ brings about reconciliation through the attractiveness of a love that is without egoism. 'Beautiful' is a characteristic adjective, as in the letter to Mme Fonvizina, who had given him the New Testament that he took with him to Siberia: 'nothing is more beautiful, profound, sympathetic, reasonable, manly, and more perfect than Christ'.[27] It is the beauty manifest in Christ's humility, not the horror of his sufferings, that creates sympathy and in this way enables human beings to rise above their own conflicting egoisms towards salvation. If, for example, Alyosha does indeed have Christlike traits, it is then likely that these are to be found in the quality that attracts other sufferers to him and moves them to entrust themselves to him.[28]

These comments broach the larger question as to Dostoevsky's vision of Christ and whether and how it does justice to the Christ of Christian doctrine: God incarnate and Saviour of humankind. It is therefore to this question that we must now turn.

3. Dostoevsky's Christ

In the classic Christian view, the Bible is from start to finish directed towards and focussed on the figure of Christ. It is therefore unsurprising that the discussion of the Bible should lead to a discussion of Christ.

---

[26] BK, 255/PSS14, 226–7.
[27] PSS28.1, 176. For discussion of the letter to Mme Fonvizina see Joseph Frank, *Dostoevsky: The Years of Ordeal, 1850–1859* (Princeton, NJ: Princeton University Press, 1983), 159–62.
[28] On 'active compassion' as a Christlike attribute, see Alina Wyman, *The Gift of Active Empathy: Scheler, Bakhtin, and Dostoevsky* (Evanston, IL: Northwestern University Press, 2016), 6–7 and, in specific relation to Alyosha, 225–9.

The importance of Christ for Dostoevsky is rarely doubted. In the letter to Mme Fonvizina, mentioned in the last commentary, he famously declared that even if it could be proved that Christ was 'outside the truth' he would choose Christ over truth. In the same letter he also states that, as a child of the nineteenth century, his faith was forged in a crucible of doubt, a statement repeated in one of his last notes.[29] Both of these statements indicate that while Christ was of supreme importance for Dostoevsky, he was also a figure whose meaning for contemporary humanity was contested in a variety of ways. Many still regarded him as an ideal and even exemplary human being, a great moral teacher and even a social visionary (perhaps even a *socialist*), as Dostoevsky himself may have done prior to his Siberian experience. Others, including both the Left Hegelians and the advocates of scientific positivism, not only rejected Christ's divinity but, in many cases, brushed him aside as being without contemporary human significance. At the same time, the nineteenth century was prolific in attempts to recreate the image of Christ on the basis of a historical study of the gospels, stripped of the interpretations provided by Church teaching. Amongst the most successful of these was the *Life of Jesus* by Ernest Renan, whose Jesus is a beautiful soul, possessed of an intuitive empathy for women and children, but eventually crushed by the harshness of Roman realpolitik.[30]

Christ is present in Dostoevsky's novels in a variety of ways. One is through scriptural verses quoting his words or actions. These may provide possible points of reference for interpreting the novel in question as a whole or, more modestly, the moral and spiritual character of the person who speaks them or to whom they are applied. As the conversation indicates, Christ Himself makes an appearance in Ivan Karamazov's 'Legend of the Grand Inquisitor' and there are also figures, such as Prince Myshkin, eponymous hero of *The Idiot*, who might seem to be Christ figures in a special sense.

As described in the conversation, Ivan's story seems to refer to the Christ of the gospels, returning to earth at the time of the Spanish Inquisition. He is imprisoned by the Grand Inquisitor, who upbraids Him for having demanded too much of people. The Inquisitor focusses on the three temptations in the wilderness: to turn stones into bread, to leap down from the Temple in the assurance that angels would rescue him, and, finally, to worship Satan and be rewarded with rule over all earthly kingdoms. In Ivan's view these questions constitute 'the most stupendous miracle' in all of history.[31] They represent the 'absolute and eternal' truth of the human condition. For human beings need bread and will ultimately follow those who give it them ('It's the economy, stupid'), someone to rule over them,

---

[29] See note 27 above. On the 'crucible of doubt' see also PSS27, 86.
[30] I am referring here throughout to 'Christ', as Dostoevsky himself usually does. The historical approach focussed instead on 'Jesus', as in the title of Renan's book, that is, Jesus without the overlay of ecclesiastical doctrine, including the identification of him as 'Christ'.
[31] BK, 258/PSS14, 229.

and a uniform and universal social order. Instead, Christ offered only a freely given love. The Church, the Inquisitor says, has corrected His teaching and given them 'miracle, mystery, and authority', sparing them the trials of freedom. All this time, Christ says nothing and, at the end, His only answer is to kiss the Inquisitor on his 'bloodless' lips, whereupon the Inquisitor releases Him. Nothing more is said.

The legend is widely regarded as one of Dostoevsky's most brilliant achievements and is often seen as presaging the totalitarianisms of the twentieth century. For Berdyaev, it is 'the high point of Dostoevsky's work and the crown of his dialectic' and presents readers with the choice confronting every one of us: 'the Grand Inquisitor or Jesus Christ'.[32] Acknowledging that the Christ of the legend 'is a shadowy figure who says nothing', Berdyaev states that 'efficacious religion does not explain itself, the principle of freedom cannot be expressed in words'.[33] This is, of course, to assume that Ivan is merely a vehicle used by Dostoevsky to teach his own views.

Others have not been so sure. P. Travis Kroeker and Bruce K. Ward note that Ivan's Christ is rather similar to a Renan-style 'idealist', and even though the introduction to the story speaks of miracles, they suggest that this could be read simply as part of Ivan's introductory mise en scène, without significance for the substance of the story.[34] Nevertheless, they defend Christ's silence and suggest that His parting kiss 'is exactly faithful to the revelation of Christ: it is an invitation to intimacy with God and neighbor... The identity and authority of the Godman cannot be seen or spoken about directly, and one therefore cannot control its meaning or its reception by others in the world. It can only be encountered through the sacrificial self-giving of intimate love...'.[35]

In his lucid and thoughtful account of 'the religion of Dostoevsky', A. Boyce Gibson sees the Christ of the legend as an 'anarchist' Christ, whose values are incompatible with what he calls a 'solidarist church' based on the principle of *sobornost'*, a Russian term indicating a kind of community gathered into a transindividual unity on the basis of common feeling rather than intellectual, doctrinal, or ecclesiastical authority. This, Gibson contends, is what Dostoevsky saw and valued in Russian Orthodoxy. Ivan's anarchist Christ cannot, then, be Dostoevsky's.[36] As Rowan Williams points out, such a Christ would indeed be 'outside truth' and, consequently, a Christ who was powerless in the world. However, Williams goes on to argue that when Alyosha repeats Christ's gesture by kissing Ivan this

---

[32] Nicholas Berdyaev, *Dostoevsky*, trans. Donald Attwater (New York: Meridian, 1957), 188.
[33] Berdyaev, *Dostoevsky*, 189.
[34] P. Travis Kroeker and Bruce K. Ward, *Remembering the End: Dostoevsky as Prophet to Modernity* (Boulder, CO: Westview Press, 2001), 242–6.
[35] Berdyaev, *Dostoevsky*, 260.
[36] A. Boyce Gibson, *The Religion of Dostoevsky* (London: SCM Press, 1973), 187–8.

actually counts as a refutation of 'The Grand Inquisitor' since it shows that Christ's love *can* become real in the actual world of the characters.[37]

There are many issues in play in the flux and reflux of critical opinion, not least commentators' varied relations to Christianity and their confessional perspectives (Orthodox, Catholic, liberal Protestant, etc.). Where Boyce Gibson sees Dostoevsky as steering a path towards Orthodoxy, the Lutheran theologian Konrad Onasch (working in the communist German Democratic Republic) presents Dostoevsky as commending a 'nonconformist Christ', an 'alternative Orthodoxy' that he describes as a 'deconfessionalized and ecumenical community'. Such a community promotes the spirit of neighbour love to the point of being ready to fall silent regarding Christ's divinity.[38] Yet it is the deconfessionalized character of Dostoevsky's Christianity that leads Steven Cassedy to conclude that Dostoevsky's religion isn't really Christianity at all.[39]

A similar criticism was already made by Dostoevsky's contemporary, Konstantin Leontiev. As has been mentioned, Leontiev argued that the kind of religion represented in Dostoevsky's novels and in the Pushkin speech was far closer to a sentimental and Western kind of liberalism than to Orthodoxy. Dostoevsky's prioritization of love overlooks the authentically Christian conviction that Christian life begins with the 'fear of the Lord' and that this is the only basis on which truly Christian love can be established. Generally, he argues, Dostoevsky neglects the essential role of the Church. Sonia Marmeladova may read the Bible but she reads it, Leontiev says, like an English Protestant, alone, relying on her own judgement, and not guided by the teaching of the Church. Even when Dostoevsky leads us to a monastic milieu, as in *The Brothers Karamazov*, the monks speak more like Western liberals than like the heirs of Athonite spirituality. Certainly, there is a discernible progression, 'step by step', in the novels towards Orthodoxy but little or no trace of it in the Pushkin speech, Dostoevsky's clearest statement of his own world view, delivered in his own voice.[40]

---

[37] Rowan Williams, *Dostoevsky: Language, Faith and Fiction* (London: Continuum, 2008), 28–33.

[38] Konrad Onasch, *Der verschwiegene Christus: Versuch über die Poetisierung des Christentums in der Dichtung F. M. Dostojewskis* (Berlin: Union Verlag, 1976), 203-4. Onasch emphasizes that Dostoevsky's attempts to create an image of Christ for his time was essentially poetic and cannot be abstracted from how he fulfilled his task *as a writer*—an insight that remains crucial for our continuing discussions of Dostoevsky's Christology.

[39] See Steven Cassedy, *Dostoevsky's Religion* (Stanford, CA: Stanford University Press, 2005). Both Onasch and Cassedy connect the discussion to the philosopher Vladimir Solovyov, but whereas Onasch sees Solovyov as helping us to draw out Dostoevsky's own view, Cassedy sees him as misrepresenting Dostoevsky and offering an essentially non-Christian version of idealist philosophy. See also Steven Cassedy, 'Who Says Miracles Can't Be the Basis for Faith? More Reasons Why Dostoevsky's Religion Isn't Christianity', *Dostoevsky Studies*, New Series, Vol. 13 (2009), 37–45.

[40] See K. N. Leontiev, *O Vsemirnoĭ Lyubvi: Rech F. M. Dostoevskogo na Pushkinskom Prazdnike* (On universal love: Dostoevsky's speech at the celebrations in honour of Pushkin), http://www.odinblago.ru/filosofiya/leontev_kn_o_vsemirno/ (accessed 5 June 2023).

In the case of *The Idiot* it is not a question of a putatively direct representation of Christ (as in 'The Legend of the Grand Inquisitor') but of a character, Prince Myshkin, who has several markedly Christlike features. Dostoevsky said that in this novel he was attempting to portray 'a perfectly beautiful human being' and, as in Renan, the idea of Christ as a 'beautiful' personality seemed to many in the mid-nineteenth century to best describe his 'divine' effect on the world.[41] Furthermore, the notebooks speak of a 'Prince-Christ', seemingly implying that the prince is to be identified with Christ.[42] Then come the apparent clues in the novel itself, listed in the conversation: what some commentators see as Myshkin's physical similarity to the icon of Christ,[43] his arrival from a mysterious 'other' place, his clairvoyant gifts, sermon-like speeches, ecstatic visions, and his acceptance of fallen women (Nastasia, Marie). Perhaps even his name 'Lev', meaning lion, may allude to the messianic title Lion of Judah, albeit qualified by his surname, 'Myshkin', meaning 'mousekin'.

Yet the critical consensus is that if this was Dostoevsky's idea, it failed. As Gibson writes: 'Myshkin, then, fails in his task as a redeemer, because he is not sufficiently incarnate.'[44] Williams likewise argues that Myshkin displays a kind of timelessness that keeps him aloof from 'the labor of choice and self-definition' that belong to authentic life in the world.[45] Because he is an innocent who lives outside of history, he is abstracted from 'the mundane truth of the world' and therefore cannot help those trapped within its deadly abysses.[46] To the extent that he does interact with them, he is likely to cause harm and is 'unwittingly a force of destruction'[47]—as is evident in the fact that the story ends badly for all the key protagonists: he himself relapses into idiocy, Nastasia Phillipovna is murdered by Rogozhin (who is sent to Siberia for fifteen years), and Aglaia marries a fraudulent Polish count with non-existent estates and is alienated from her family. Myshkin's 'coming', it seems, has only made things worse. No one is saved. Several have also noted his affinity to the 'idiot' Christ declared by Nietzsche to be the true figure

---

[41] Dostoevsky's notes show Renan to have been very much on his mind in the period of composition of *The Idiot*. 'Beautiful' is also the first descriptor applied to Christ in Dostoevsky's letter to Mme Fonvizina.

[42] See Dostoevsky, *Notebooks*, 198, 201/PSS9, 246, 249.

[43] This claim is made by Irina Kirillova, *Obraz Khrista v tvorchestve Dostoevskogo: Razmyshlenia* (Moscow: Tsentr knigi VGBIL im. M. N. Rudomino, 2010), 82–102.

[44] Gibson, *Religion*, 109.

[45] Williams, *Dostoevsky*, 47–57. However, he rejects Michael Holquist's influential argument that Myshkin's timelessness reflects Christ's own timelessness, which, in Holquist's view, makes the figure of Christ unreproducible in a novel that depends on the unfolding of events in time. See Michael Holquist, *Dostoevsky and the Novel* (Princeton, NJ: Princeton University Press, 1977), 102–23. As Williams points out, this overlooks how Christianity sees Christ as fully incarnate in historical time.

[46] Williams makes this point with reference to Salvestroni, *Dostoïevski et la Bible*, 107–24.

[47] Williams, *Dostoevsky*, 54. See also Thompson, 'Problems', 73–6.

behind the gospels, a 'decadent' whose only achievement was to die on the cross.[48] Others have gone further. Murray Krieger, for example, states that 'Myshkin does not bring light but darkness, not help but destruction; he does not still the outrages of the world, but generates them; he is not a bright angel, but a dark emissary.'[49]

Myshkin himself seems to have found a near impassable obstacle in Hans Holbein's remorselessly brutal depiction of the dead Christ, of which he says that a man could lose his faith looking at such a picture.[50] As the young nihilist Ippolit says, this is a Christ so dead that if the disciples had seen him like that, they could no longer have believed in him as Son of God. The painting, he says, shows nature 'in the form of a huge machine of the most modern construction which, dull and insensible, has aimlessly clutched, crushed and swallowed up a great priceless Being, a Being worth all nature and its laws, worth the whole earth, which was created solely for the sake of the advent of that Being.'[51] To the extent that this picture not only haunts but even defines the novel, we may even see it as a novel of the death of God rather than a portrayal of a beautiful Christlike man.[52]

A different view is provided by Romano Guardini, one of the most influential Catholic theologians of the first half of the twentieth century. Guardini declares that 'Every consideration of the spiritual world of Dostoyevsky must take up the question: what is the meaning of his deepest religious work, his novel *The Idiot*?'[53] His own answer is that Myshkin is indeed to be read as a symbol of Christ. However, this does not mean one-on-one identification. As Guardini puts it, 'The image of the existence of Christ is translated into the image of this man, which surely is possible only if—from a purely human point of view—the image remains that of a perfect "impossibility."' In other words, 'what is incomprehensible in

---

[48] On Dostoevsky's role in the formation of Nietzsche's image of Jesus see Paolo Stellino, *Nietzsche and Dostoevsky: On the verge of Nihilism* (Bern: Peter Lang, 2015), 107–17. Stellino notes Nietzsche's regret that there wasn't a Dostoevsky present to record the world of Jesus's first followers; cf. Brandes's view that Dostoevsky's novels were replete with the kinds of characters encountered in the New Testament: 'all of them are the same poor and pitiable types—kind-hearted ignoramuses, sensitive simpletons, noble prostitutes, nervous wrecks, habitual hallucinators, gifted epileptics, and enthusiastic seekers after martyrdom'. See George Brandes, *Indtryk fra Rusland* (Copenhagen: Gyldendal, 1888), 409.

[49] According to Edward Wasiolek in his introduction to the Notebooks for *The Idiot*. See Fyodor Dostoevsky, *The Notebooks for The Idiot*, ed. Edward Wasiolek and trans. Katharine Strelsky (Chicago, IL: University of Chicago Press, 1967), 15.

[50] I, 212/PSS8, 182. However, Myshkin immediately adds that when he said this he was almost joking, a point that could be connected to John Given's 'comedic' interpretation discussed below.

[51] I, 400/PSS8, 339.

[52] The issue is complicated by the gospels' own emphasis on Christ's abandonment by God in the moment of death. Nariman Skakov connects this to *The Idiot* in his article 'Dostoevsky's Christ and Silence at the Margins of The Idiot', *Dostoevsky Studies: The Journal of the International Dostoevsky Society*, New Series, Vol. 13 (2009), 121–40.

[53] Romano Guardini, 'Dostoyevsky's Idiot, a Symbol of Christ', trans. Francis X. Quinn, *Cross Currents*, Vol. 6, No. 4 (Fall 1956), 359. See also *Versuche über die religiose Existenz in Dostojewskijs großen Romanen* (Leipzig: Hegner, 1933), reissued as *Religiöse Gestalten in Dostojewskijs Werk* (Munich: Kösel Verlag, 1977). Guardini's argument is repeated in L. A. Zander, *Dostoevsky*, trans. Natalie Duddington (London: SCM Press, 1948).

Christ' (and Christ must be incomprehensible to human beings, he believes) 'is here translated into human impossibility'.[54] The novel does not mimic Christ's redemptive work but points us to the fact that what is here laid bare as humanly impossible is possible only for God. Only God can save, not a character in a novel.[55] That there is no redemption within the action of the novel is therefore entirely appropriate.

In another positive reading of Myshkin's Christlikeness, John Givens draws attention to the comedic elements of the novel and shows how these extend from near-slapstick elements to a comic world view that subsumes the death-oriented narrative arc into a final harmony. For Givens, Myshkin's final collapse is not a failure but a voluntary act of love towards Rogozhin that echoes Christ's own self-emptying, non-egoistic love for other. He emphasizes that the death scene, as Myshkin and Rogozhin keep vigil by Nastasia's body, is not the end of the novel, which is the short chapter emphatically entitled 'Conclusion' and which includes several pointers to a new and better society emerging amongst those who had been influenced by Myshkin's coming.[56]

In John's gospel it is said that the Word made flesh 'came to his own and his own received him not'. But, as we know, Peter, Andrew, and others, and then, later, those from beyond Israel, did receive him and believed in him. But what if there really had been no one who received him? Perhaps the thought experiment that Dostoevsky carries out in *The Idiot* addresses just such a question. Is Dostoevsky perhaps playing with what he might well have thought a very real possibility, that if Christ were indeed to return to Russia today (as, in 'The Grand Inquisitor', He returned to sixteenth-century Seville), there might be none amongst 'his own' to receive him?[57] In the gospel, those who are about to stone the woman taken in adultery drop their stones and walk away when Christ challenges them to reflect on their own guilt. However, apart from Myshkin himself, no one else acknowledges their guilt vis-à-vis Nastasia Philippovna. Myshkin's failed messianic career does not give us a precise or allegorical image of Christ, but it does remind us of what it is to live in a world that has lost or is losing its capacity to see beyond the horizons of its everyday experience and could not know a call to mutual love, acceptance, and forgiveness were such a call to be issued.

Additional Points

The rumour that Dostoevsky met Dickens when he was in London has been exposed in Eric Naiman, 'When Dickens Met Dostoevsky: How the Report of an

---

[54] Guardini, 'Dostoyevsky's Idiot', 380.   [55] Guardini, 'Dostoyevsky's Idiot', 382.
[56] See John Givens, 'A Narrow Escape into Faith? Dostoevsky's "Idiot" and the Christology of Comedy', *The Russian Review*, Vol. 70, No. 1 (January 2011), 95–117.
[57] Such a question would have had a special poignancy for Dostoevsky, writing *The Idiot* in exile, having fled Russia to avoid a debtor's prison.

Unlikely Meeting Revealed a Sprawling Literary Mystery' (*The Times Literary Supplement*, 11 April 2013).

The philosopher who said that today God could be represented as appearing in the world only in the form of Shakespeare's Poor Tom or Dostoevsky's Prince Myshkin was Paul Ricoeur, answering a question from the present author at a seminar in the Faculty of Theology in Copenhagen University on 2 May 2003.

Examples of the twentieth-century literary 'weak Christs' referred to include Nikos Kazantzakis's *The Last Temptation of Christ*, Graham Greene's *The Power and the Glory*, and Mikhail Bulgakov's *The Master and Margarita*.

Commentary on the Third Conversation

1. Dostoevsky in Film

Film adaptations of Dostoevsky's novels go back to the early days of Russian cinema and, by the time of the Revolution, all the major novels had been filmed. As Dostoevsky became known in the West, film adaptations soon followed. According to one website, there have been 124 film adaptations in total.[1] The largest number is from Russia, with the USA and France close behind, and there are significant contributions from Germany, Italy, India, and Japan. The list of major directors who have directed Dostoevsky films includes Robert Bresson, Robert Wiene[2] (*Crime and Punishment*, 1923), Akira Kurosawa (*The Idiot*, 1951), Andrzej Wajda (*The Possessed*, 1988 and *The Idiot*, 1994[3]), Luigi Visconti (*White Nights*, 1957), Karel Reisz (*The Gambler*, 1974), as well as several leading Russian directors. It is known that Andrei Tarkovsky wanted to film *The Idiot* but was unable to get official permission to do so.[4] Other directors have taken central themes of Dostoevsky's novels and stories and used them as the basis for original works. Martin Scorsese's *Taxi Driver* is one well-known example, while Woody Allen's *Match Point* (2005), discussed in the conversation, is half-way between an adaptation and a variation on a theme.

Even films that keep relatively close to the original novel's narrative structure often make significant changes to the plots and personalities. In the case of *The Brothers Karamazov* this has several times involved highlighting the role of Dmitri, whose larger than life persona has a clear dramatic appeal—although the 1931 *Der Mörder Dmitri Karamasoff* is an extreme, eliminating Alyosha and Zosima entirely. The 2009 Russian television adaptation uses direct visual borrowings from the 'Russian Christ' episode of Andrei Tarkovksy's 1966 film *Andrei Rublev* to represent Dmitri himself as a Russian Christ, which has some basis in the text but is nevertheless a bold interpretative move. Similarly, adaptations of *The Possessed* have several times (in 1917 and in the 1992 version by Vladimir

---

[1] See http://dostoevsky-bts.com/blog/124-dostoyevsky-film-adaptations/#others (accessed 8 February 2021).

[2] Best known for *The Cabinet of Dr Caligari*, a classic of silent cinema.

[3] Entitled *Nastasia* and with a renowned kabuki theatre actor playing the roles of both Myshkin and Anastasia Phillipovna.

[4] See Tamara Djermanovic, 'Estética de Dostoyevski y Tarkovski: la creatividad como visión del hombre, del apocalipsis y de la posibilidad de salvación', *Mundo Eslavo* 16 (2017), 64–72.

Khotinenko) focussed on the character of Stavrogin, the novel's arch-demon and a kind of Byronic anti-hero, even cutting out the figure of Stepan Trofimovich Verkhovensky who, for all his faults, begins and ends the novel and provides its biblical key.[5] Dramatically, this is understandable, though it sells Dostoevsky short.

Film versions produced in the Soviet Union had to steer cautious paths through complex censorship situations, not least with regard to the religious aspect of Dostoevsky's work and his anti-revolutionary views.[6] The 1932 *House of the Dead*, discussed in the conversation, exemplifies one way of dealing with this. The 1968 Russian *Brothers Karamazov* is at ease with the monastic scenes but while showing Alyosha's (temporary) loss of faith in one of the most filmicly intense moments of the entire production, it doesn't show the renewal of that faith shortly afterwards.

For different reasons, Western adaptations too are often hesitant about the religious aspect. As Tamsin says, the 2005 BBC adaptation of *Crime and Punishment* eliminated the speech by Marmeladov, a pathetic figure whose alcoholism has led to his daughter being prostituted. Despite his complete lack of moral credibility, Marmeladov delivers an astonishing speech that ends with the claim that even those, like himself, who are 'swine' and made 'in the image of the beast' will on the Last Day be called by Christ to come into his kingdom. It is a dramatic tour de force that has been a highpoint of several stage and screen productions.

As a medium, film is inevitably challenged when it is a matter of expressing interior religious experience and many 'religious' films reduce religious passion to a mawkish, bombastic, or otherwise inappropriate sentimentality. Bresson provides one solution to this, since his actors (who are rarely screen professionals) do not indulge in overt emotional expression. Their delivery is often flat, their bodies strangely static, and each seems enveloped in a kind of silence. There is only a sparse use of background music to give emotional clues as to how we are to interpret what we are seeing. Yet although Dostoevsky's characters frown, gesticulate, grind their teeth, jump up and down, and often seem to be in states of near-hysterical emotional excitement, Bresson's approach paradoxically allows us to experience a similar emotional effect, indicating his grasp of the difference between narrative prose and film. Melissa Frazier has identified the counter-intuitive kinship of the two artists when she speaks of how they each give a 'large interpretive space' to the viewer/reader by the way in which they each shift between different points of view.[7]

---

[5] On the importance of Stepan Trofimovich for understanding *The Possessed* as a whole, see R. M. Davison, 'Dostoevsky's *Devils*: The Role of Stepan Trofimovich Verkhovensky', in W. J. Leatherbarrow (ed.), *Dostoevsky's Devils: A Critical Companion* (Evanston, IL: Northwestern University Press, 1999), 119–34.

[6] See N. M. Lary, *Dostoevsky and Soviet Film: Visions of Demonic Realism* (Ithaca, NY: Cornell University Press, 1986).

[7] See Melissa Frazier, 'Sun-Bathed Steppes in French Prisons: Bresson Reading Dostoevsky', *Ulbandus Review*, Vol. 15, Seeing Texts (2013), 133–52. Frazier's article is specifically focussed on the relationship between *Crime and Punishment* and *Pickpocket*. Frazier also sees similarities in their respective treatment of materiality, which is simultaneously both intensely material but also spiritual.

2. Dostoevsky and Existentialism

Existentialism became a global phenomenon in the wake of Jean-Paul Sartre's popularizing lecture 'Existentialism and Humanism', in which he ascribed to Dostoevsky the fundamental existentialist tenet that 'If God does not exist, then everything is permitted.'[8] However, Sartre does not remind his listeners that this quotation is spoken by a character, Ivan Karamazov, who cannot be taken as a simple mouthpiece for Dostoevsky's own views. The lecture was not, of course, about Dostoevsky, but it fed into an image of Dostoevsky as representing the kind of protest atheism that was very much a part of the existentialist image.

Dostoevsky's key works had been translated into French in the nineteenth century (it was in French that, for example, Nietzsche and Henry James first read Dostoevsky) and he was cited as a major inspiration by several major twentieth-century French writers, including Proust, Claudel, Malraux, and Gide, the last of whom gave a series of lectures on Dostoevsky in 1922, subsequently published in multiple editions.[9] Of the defining figures of the so-called 'existentialist café' (Sartre, de Beauvoir, Camus, and Merleau-Ponty), it was Camus who was most deeply influenced by the Russian writer. He himself acted the part of Ivan Karamazov in a theatrical adaptation in 1937 and later wrote his own stage adaptation of *The Possessed* (1958), a novel that he ranked amongst the greatest works of world literature, alongside the *Odyssey*, *War and Peace*, *Don Quixote*, and Shakespeare.[10] In his theoretical works, it is chiefly the figures of revolt, Ivan Karamazov and Kirillov, whom he discusses. Ivan is presented as a figure of 'metaphysical revolt' and Kirillov, the theorist of self-deification through suicide (see Commentary 1.1), as a representative of the absurd. At the same time, Camus was well aware that Dostoevsky offered a Christian response to both these figures and provided a frame of reference that mitigates the scandal of absurdity or what Sartre called the 'abandonment' of the human situation, which, in Camus's terminology, made Dostoevsky an 'existentialist' rather than an 'absurd' novelist.[11] As he writes of *The Brothers Karamazov*, 'It is not an absurd work that is involved here but a work that propounds the absurd problem.'[12] Even though Camus thus distances himself from Dostoevsky, Dostoevsky's figures of revolt, self-assertion, and atheism are paradigmatic for his own philosophy of the absurd.

This is true also of the existentialist reception of Dostoevsky more generally, in which Ivan, Kirillov, and the Underground Man feature most regularly. Walter Kaufmann's widely used 1956 anthology, *Existentialism from Dostoevsky to Sartre*,

---

[8] Jean-Paul Sartre, *Existentialisme est un humanisme* (Paris: Nagel, 1970), 36.
[9] André Gide, *Dostoevsky* (Norfolk, CT: New Directions, 1961).
[10] Quoted in Michel Niqueux, *Dictionnaire Dostoïevski* (Paris: Institut des Études Slaves, 2021), 54.
[11] Albert Camus, *The Myth of Sisyphus*, trans. Justin O'Brien (Harmondsworth: Penguin, 1975), 101.
[12] Camus, *The Myth of Sisyphus*, 101.

opens with an extended passage from *Notes from Underground*, although he notes that 'we must not ascribe to [Dostoevsky], who after all believed in God, the outlook and ideas of his underground man', going on to add, 'I can see no reason for calling Dostoevsky an existentialist, but I do think that Part One of *Notes from Underground* is the best overture to existentialism ever written.'[13]

Sartre's brand of left-bank existentialism was preceded by 'the philosophy of existence' of Karl Jaspers and Martin Heidegger. Although Dostoevsky is not an obvious presence in either of their philosophical works (*Being and Time* cites Tolstoy, but not Dostoevsky), Heidegger mentions Dostoevsky along with Nietzsche, Kierkegaard, Rilke, and Trakl as amongst the influential figures of the 'stirring' years 1910–14.[14] From the late nineteenth century onwards, Dostoevsky had already been linked with both Kierkegaard and Nietzsche, each regularly cited as a precursor of existentialism. Already in 1903, Lev Shestov published his study *The Philosophy of Tragedy: Dostoevsky and Nietzsche* (French translation, 1926). Although at this point the word 'existential' (still less 'existentialist') had not acquired the sense it would have thirty years later, many of the commonalities that Shestov sees in his two subjects fit the existentialist profile. Nietzsche, he thinks, is Dostoevsky's 'brother' and 'continuator' and both oppose the attempt to reconcile the agony of human existence with the world as it is. Neither nature nor moral ideals such as 'the good and the just' offer either explanation or consolation for the great cry of abandonment that, according to Shestov, is Nietzsche's sole question: 'My God, why have you forsaken me?'[15] 'Those who know tragedy, the "abandoned ones", are obliged to fight a twofold struggle: against the "necessity" and against their neighbours who are still able to adapt and who, therefore, without even knowing it, are in league with the cruellest enemy of the human race.'[16]

By the time of Shestov's *Kierkegaard and Existential Philosophy* (1936), the term 'existential' had decisively entered the philosophical vocabulary and this book can itself be seen as a response to Heidegger.[17] Although Kierkegaard is its main subject, an introductory chapter compares Kierkegaard and Dostoevsky, both of whom Shestov describes as 'voices crying in the desert'. They are so similar in their essential ideas, he says, that 'Dostoevsky might be called Kierkegaard's double'.[18] He claims that both opposed Hegelian rationalism and advocated a

---

[13] Walter Kaufmann, *Existentialism from Dostoevsky to Sartre* (Cleveland, OH: Meridian Books, 1956), 14.
[14] Martin Heidegger, *Frühe Schriften* (Frankfurt am Main: Vittorio Klostermann, 1972), x.
[15] Léon Chestov, *La Philosophie de la Tragédie: Dostoïevski et Nietzsche*, trans. Boris de Schloezer (Paris: Le Bruit du Temps, 2012), 225. The allusion is to Christ's cry of dereliction from the cross: 'My God, my God, why have you forsaken me?' (Matt. 27.46). The French 'abandoné' also points forward to the 'abandonment' that, according to Sartre, is one of existentialism's fundamental premises.
[16] Chestov, *La Philosophie de la Tragédie*, 266.
[17] See Benjamin Guérin, 'Chestov—Kierkegaard: Faux ami, étranger fraternité', in Ramona Fotiade and Françoise Schwab (eds.), *Léon Chestov—Vladimir Jankélévitch: Du tragique à l'ineffable* (Saarbrücken: Éditions universitaires européennes, 2011), 113–32.
[18] Léon Chestov, *Kierkegaard et la philosophie existentielle* (Paris: Vrin, 1936), 28.

thoroughly irrational view of freedom to which the Bible provided better testimony than the systems of the philosophers. The extent to which Kierkegaard and Dostoevsky were really saying 'the same' is debatable, although both offered extensive criticisms of nineteenth-century Idealism and doctrines of progress while pointing to dimensions of human existence that resisted incorporation into philosophical or scientific frames of reference. Nevertheless, Shestov's book presents an image of Dostoevsky as an irrationalist that would be influential on, amongst others, Camus. Camus's discussion of Kierkegaard in *The Myth of Sisyphus* is expressly indebted to Shestov and we may suppose that he would have approved of Shestov's identification of Kierkegaard with Dostoevsky.

Clearly, if existentialism is identified with radical and self-deifying subjectivism, Dostoevsky was not an existentialist. Nevertheless, versus Sartrean subjectivism and Camus's focus on Dostoevsky's figures of revolt, Simone de Beauvoir cites Zosima's teaching that 'Each is responsible for all, before all.'[19] Both in her *Ethics of Ambiguity* and in *Pyrrhus and Cinéas*, she argues against Sartre's view that each individual is essentially free to choose his or her own way of being in the world since, as she says, 'human beings are not alone in the world'.[20] Consequently, she offers a view of human beings as essentially co-present to each other in such a way that our individual formation emerges in and through our interactions with others rather than through violent opposition—an approach more compatible with Dostoevsky's.

Berdyaev, often counted as a Christian existentialist, emphasized freedom as energetically as did Sartre but contextualized the freedom of the individual in the context of relations to others.[21] On this point, he draws on the long-standing Russian tradition of distinguishing between the 'I' and the 'person' to which Dostoevsky also alludes.[22] Berdyaev explains that the Cartesian 'I' leads to an empty and abstract account of what it is to be human since it is defined more by its self-relation rather than by its relation to others. By way of contrast, the person is said to be a concrete individual, embedded in the matrix of its primary social relations and inherently other-oriented and other-influenced. On this account, the reality of other minds is not a philosophical problem to be solved but an integral element in the person's own self-constitution. A philosophy that starts from

---

[19] Simone de Beauvoir, *Pyrrhus et Cinéas* (Paris: Gallimard, 1971), 90. I note that de Beauvoir uses 'responsible' rather than 'guilty'. On the significance of this point see Commentary 2.1. I have noted the importance of this saying for Emmanuel Levinas. The convergence of de Beauvoir and Levinas is discussed in Jennifer McWeeny, 'Origins of Otherness: Non-Conceptual Ethical Encounters in Beauvoir and Levinas', *Simone de Beauvoir Studies*, Vol 26. (2009–10), 5–17.
[20] de Beauvoir, *Pyrrhus*, 65.
[21] On Berdyaev as Christian existentialist, see my article 'Berdyaev and Christian Existentialism', in Caryl Emerson, George Pattison, and Randall Poole (eds.), *The Oxford Handbook of Russian Religious Thought* (Oxford: Oxford University Press, 2020), 450–63.
[22] WNSI, 68–70/PSS5, 79–80. See Nikolaj Plotnikov, 'The Person Is a Monad with Windows': Sketch of a Conceptual History of "Person" in Russia', *Studies in East European Thought* Vol. 64, No. 3/4 (November 2012), 269–99.

the 'I' is always going to have difficulty in giving an account of love, whereas a philosophy of personhood readily finds a place for love at the ground of being. Berdyaev applies Martin Buber's notion of I-and-thou as the foundation of human being, a notion also embraced by his friend Gabriel Marcel.[23] Here, then, we have a better framework for interpreting Dostoevsky philosophically than the extreme individualism and subjectivism of the 'existentialist café', though, at the same time, resonating with existentialism's critique of objectivizing and abstract approaches to human existence.

On this point, I would argue that the philosophers of relationship—Buber, Marcel, and Berdyaev, amongst others—are no less 'existential' than the philosophy of extreme subjectivity found in *Being and Nothingness*. All three acknowledged a debt to Dostoevsky. Berdyaev was an important mediator of Dostoevsky's ideas in the West, while Buber credited Dostoevsky and Kierkegaard for his philosophical awakening. Unsurprisingly, Marcel spoke of being affected more by Alyosha Karamazov than Ivan, although he approves of the fact that Dostoevsky's novels are not 'edifying' and that part of their strength is that a character such as Ivan remains essentially conflicted and the issues that he puts forward are unresolved.[24]

The narrator's hesitations about identifying Dostoevsky with existentialism seem justified, although it is also clear that the situations, conflicts, and self-understanding of many of Dostoevsky's characters played an important role in feeding and to some extent forming the existential imaginary. Perhaps what we make of this relationship comes down to how we answer the two questions: 'Which Dostoevsky?' and 'Which existentialism?'

3. The 'Woman Question'

Berdyaev stated that 'Woman never appears as an independent being for Dostoievsky... Dostoievsky was interested in her solely as a milestone on the road to man's destiny',[25] while Barbara Heldt describes him simply as a 'misogynist'.[26] Nina Pelikan Straus comments that 'A late twentieth century woman reader, finding few statements of his commitment to ending women's social oppression, might feel justified in supporting [this] evaluation of the writer as a perpetrator of

---

[23] See especially Nicholas Berdyaev, *Solitude and Society*, trans. George Reavey (London: Geoffrey Bles, 1947 [1938]).

[24] 'Interview', in Jacques Catteau (ed.), *Dostoïevski* (Paris: Herne [Série Slave], 1973), 148. In the same interview, Marcel expressed admiration for Camus's adaptation of *The Possessed*, although his interviewer is more critical.

[25] Nicholas Berdyaev, *Dostoevsky*, trans. Donald Attwater (New York: Meridian, 1957), 112.

[26] Quoted in Katherine Jane Briggs, *How Dostoevsky Portrays Women in His Novels* (Lampeter: Edwin Mellen Press, 2009), 3.

male chauvinist attitudes and female stereotyping.'[27] Klaus Trost's study of Dostoevsky and love is subtitled 'between dominance and humility', subjecting Dostoevsky's relationships with women to merciless scrutiny.[28] He argues that the young Dostoevsky made regular use of prostitutes, possibly also hypocritically dressing such visits up as attempts to save the young women concerned—although he concedes that the evidence for this is very uncertain.[29] He also considers the rumours that Dostoevsky either raped or purchased sex from a young girl—the crime of Stavrogin in *The Possessed*. Again, though, he acknowledges that the evidence for this is susceptible of alternative explanations.[30] Laura's view that 'for Dostoevsky, the only good woman is a dead woman' seems not unprecedented.

Certainly, Dostoevsky seems to have embraced then current ideas of woman as defined by devotion and the service of pure and noble ideals, but also by motherhood and domesticity. Yet, paradoxically, he had several strong, albeit sometimes tempestuous, relationships with women who were active in promoting greater freedom for women. Even though his second wife, Anna Grigorievna Snitkina, can seem to fit the role of a woman who devotes her life entirely to her husband's genius, her professional training as a stenographer and collaboration in his work (including, crucially, its business side) made her far more than a merely passive support, and she saw herself as belonging to the new wave of professional women who appeared in the 1860s.

Katherine Jane Briggs rejects charges of misogyny, concluding that Dostoevsky showed 'sympathy with the sufferings of women' and 'empathy with their efforts to survive in a hostile environment'. 'He portrays the efforts of his female characters to find work in order to support themselves and their families, and the agonizing decisions they have to make when faced with family pressure to marry a man who may not be their choice. Dostoevsky's women are shown in situations where they have to fight against evil, and "live the Gospel" through active love in their daily lives and relationships.'[31] Straus finds his contribution to be focussed on the interactions between men and women, specifically his 'multiple exposures of the way men's liberties conflict with women's liberations'[32] and the ways in which he unmasks 'the masculinist will-to-power complex'.[33] Both Briggs and Straus give a chapter to *A Gentle Spirit* alongside the major novels.

---

[27] Nina Pelikan Straus, *Dostoevsky and the Woman Question: Rereadings at the End of the Century* (New York, NY: St Martin's Press, 1994), 2.

[28] Klaus Trost, *Dostojewski und die Liebe. Zwischen Dominanz und Demut* (Hamburg: Tredition, 2020).

[29] Trost, *Dostojewski*, 50–7.

[30] Trost, *Dostojewski*, 317–25. This 'event' is vividly described in Stephen Coulter's fictionalized biography, *The Devil Inside. The Tragic Life of Dostoevsky* (London: Jonathan Cape, 1960), 84–90.

[31] Briggs, *How Dostoevsky Portrays Women*, 288.

[32] Straus, *Dostoevsky and the Woman Question*, 1.

[33] Straus, *Dostoevsky and the Woman Question*, 154.

Dostoevsky went unusually far for a male novelist of his time in attempting to give women an autonomous voice. *Poor Folk*, his debut novel, is an exchange of letters of which one half are by the female correspondent. Several novels explore intense same-sex relationships between women, including the unfinished novel *Netochka Nyezvanova*, which also had a female first-person narrator.[34] The relationship between Lizaveta Prokofoyevna Epanchina and her daughters is an important theme in *The Idiot* and, although she displays a Mrs Bennett-like concern for their marriage prospects, she is a complex three-dimensional personality. Indeed, despite her comical aspects (frequently mocked by her daughters), she is widely regarded as one of Dostoevsky's most striking and successful female characters and it is to her that the last word of the novel is, literally, given. A darker mother–daughter relationship is explored in *The Brothers Karamazov* (Mme Khokhlova and Lisa).

In *The Diary of a Writer* (where female suicide is a significant theme), Dostoevsky explains how the many letters he received from women readers strengthened his view as to the role of women in the current development of Russia. He also notes his own 'incompetence' in answering their questions as to what they should do. But although his comments often illustrate his negative view of aspects of women's emancipation, he did call for the immediate opening up of higher education to women and putting Russia, in this regard, in the vanguard of European development.[35] Writing to his niece Sonya, he urges her against being pressured into marrying against her will and recommends the example of Nadezhda Suslova who had just graduated in medicine from Zürich University.[36] In a further letter, he suggests that she study stenography so as to have an independent income.[37] His response to the letters of a young Jewish woman, Sofia Luria, again emphasizes his belief in the importance of women's education and, later, he is influenced by Luria in his approach to the Jewish question (see Conversation Six). He wrote a fulsome eulogy over George Sand, a figure who scandalized many opposed to women's emancipation, though he refrained from commenting on her more radical works.[38]

Many of the female figures in the major novels are at first glance portrayed in terms of their relations to men. However, to see them as mere agents of the men's

---

[34] The three novels are *Netochka Nyezvanova*, *The Idiot* (see Nastasia's letters to Aglaia), and *The Brothers Karamazov* (Grushenka and Katerina Ivanovna). However, as in many of the heterosexual relationships explored in the novels, sexuality in the narrow sense is only one element in the passion that fatefully draws two people together.

[35] DW, 340–1/PSS23, 36–7. Women had started taking university courses in Russia in 1859 before being excluded by an act of 1863. Thereafter a number of 'higher courses for women' were established outside the university system, a situation that continued until 1917. See Ruth A. Dudgeon, 'The Forgotten Minority: Women Students in Imperial Russia, 1872–1917', *Russian History*, Vol. 9, No. 1 (1982), 1–26.

[36] PSS28/2, 252.   [37] PSS28/2, 293.

[38] DW, 344–50/PSS23, 32–7.

development would be to belittle both them and their author. Sonia may, as Laura complains, seem to efface herself to the point of vanishing, but this can be seen from another angle. Heitor O'Dwyer de Macedo too speaks of Sonia as one who has become nothing and as such 'pure space: a space of shelter, a place of transit—it depends'. To do this, he adds, 'requires the suspension of all self-esteem', but this is not only the attitude 'of a good primary maternal figure' who can give total acceptance (and thus far a feminist critic will certainly not be impressed), it is also the attitude required of a good analyst who must be able to listen to everything that is said so as also to hear more than the speaker is aware of saying. This is because, despite appearances, the analyst (Sonia) is *not* completely passive but comes to the encounter with her own theoretical framework for understanding what is said.[39]

Much will depend here on the reader's own attitudes to humility and self-assertion. Christianity has consistently regarded humility as the basic virtue and self-assertion as implying rebellion against God. We shall consider these themes further in relation to Dostoevsky's kenotic view of Christ and his critique of masculine self-deification (see Commentary on the fourth Conversation). There is no doubt that this has and does often lead to women internalizing negative self-images that are socially and psychologically damaging. But is it nevertheless possible to value humility as a primary Christian virtue while also understanding it as affirming personal dignity and worth?

Sonia may seem to recycle standard sentimental tropes of the good-hearted prostitute that stretch back to Rahab the harlot (Joshua 2) and to the New Testament figure of Mary Magdalene, conflated in Christian tradition within several other sinful women forgiven by Jesus. Literary sources are also in play, but Dostoevsky never hesitated in transforming the types and situations he took from literature, scripture, and art. Whereas his friend N. A. Nekrasov wrote a predictably sentimental story of how a prostitute is saved by what Joseph Frank calls the 'ardent and unprejudiced love' of her benefactor, *Notes from Underground* reveals the would-be benefactor as incapable of the great gesture he plans, relapsing into cynicism, bullying and humiliating the prostitute Liza and thus subverting the sentimentality of Nekrasov's story.[40] Sonia, even more surprisingly, becomes the primary agent of Raskolnikov's redemption, tweaking the trope still further. Of course, to refer to her as a prostitute rather than a girl who has been prostituted is already prejudicial and through her story Dostoevsky shows that 'prostitute' is not a natural category of womanhood but the outcome of a choice that, for Sonia as for many others, is forced by poverty and family breakdown. Dostoevsky's

---

[39] O'Dwyer de Macedo, *Clinical Lessons on Life and Madness: Dostoevsky's Characters*, trans. Agnès Jacob (London: Routledge, 2019), 81–2.
[40] WN, 150–5/PSS5, 175–9. See J. Frank, *Dostoevsky. The Stir of Liberation 1860–1865* (Princeton, NJ: Princeton University Press, 1986), 332.

analysis is not only moral (a prostitute may be a good person beneath the rouge and satin) but also social, revealing the effects of social displacement brought about by the destabilizing acceleration of emergent capitalism. Yet Sonia is not simply a victim: she is proactively doing what she can to support her family and protect her sister from having to make the same choice in the near future. We also learn that she has been studying books of world history and the psychology of G. H. Lewes. She is not merely a creature of emotions. And, as Macedo points out, she is someone who commands both fear and respect amongst nearly all who meet her, even the arch roué Svidrigailov.

Sonia's character is certainly more complex than Laura allows and (versus Berdyaev) she is no mere foil for the male hero's development. The same is true in the case of Nastasia Phillipovna in *The Idiot*. Groomed by her guardian from childhood and kept as his mistress until her twenty-sixth birthday, we know that she is more sinned against than sinning—a Magdalene to Myshkin's Christ, perhaps (and there are clear references in the text to the scene between Jesus and the woman taken in adultery and threatened with stoning). L. A. Levina qualifies this view by calling her an 'unrepentant Magdalene'. Whereas the biblical woman taken in adultery obeys Jesus's command to 'Go and sin no more', Nastasia Phillipovna rejects Myshkin's offer of marriage and runs off with the fiery and violent Rogozhin, leaving her quiet and secluded life for a world of rumoured orgies and public scandals. Myshkin himself worries that she is becoming mad. Perhaps, Levina suggests, Myshkin's affirmation of her goodness had shut down the opportunity for her to make a full reckoning with her situation, including her own complicity in it, enjoying the luxuries and ease that being Totsky's mistress had brought her. She explicitly rejects earning a living by working.[41] This is not to blame the victim that she clearly is: the point is that she is a complex personality whose life and motivations cannot be neatly fitted into any one formula. In the same scene in which Myshkin offers her his hand, she demonstrates extraordinary resourcefulness in exposing to public gaze the machinations of the men who have been planning to marry her off. If her subsequent career is driven by the internalized shame of the victim of abuse, she is nevertheless agent as well as victim. In short, she is a three-dimensional character who cannot be reduced to a cipher for mythological or theological ideas and, in the end, everything depends on the persuasiveness with which Dostoevsky presents her and his other characters as plausible actors in a contemporary world that was fully recognizable to his readers. Most are flawed, some are good, none, or virtually none, conforms straightforwardly to literary stereotypes and only a detailed

---

[41] L. A. Levina, 'Nekaiushaiasia Magdalena ili Pochemu knaz' Myshkin ne mog spasti Nastasiu Phillipovnu' ['The unrepentant Magdalene or why Prince Myshkin cannot save Nastasia Phillipovna'], in *Dostoievski i mirovaia kul'tura*. Almanakh No. 2 of the *Obshestvo Dostoievskogo* (St Petersburg: Dostoevsky Museum Publications, 1994), 97–118.

case-by-case reading can ultimately decide the issue of Dostoevsky-as-misogynist versus Dostoevsky-as-proto-feminist.

The character who says that women need a despot to rule over them is Arkady Dolgoruky, the eponymous hero of *A Raw Youth*,[42] although he himself admits that he knows nothing about women and doesn't want to.[43] His passage from resentful ignorance to adult relationships with women as real people is a significant sub-theme of the novel.[44] He also narrates the 'prank' of going up to a young woman and talking loudly and indecently over her.[45] Elsewhere, Dostoevsky has the nihilists of *The Possessed* create a scandal by placing pornographic photographs in the bag of a travelling female Bible-seller.[46]

Additional Points

Colours play a significant part in Dostoevsky's mise-en-scène. In *Crime and Punishment*, as discussed in the conversation, green links together diverse objects that have special spiritual significance.[47] I was alerted to the potential of colour in teaching Dostoevsky by a student, Tansy Troy, who, instead of reading a paper, arrived with a set of paints and paintbrushes and distributed them round the class, asking us to paint the colours that came to mind in the passage set for discussion. This initiated one of the more productive discussions of the whole term.

Carl's views regarding the need to keep literature separate from political life is loosely based on the social philosopher Jürgen Habermas's development of Marx's idea of art (in the broadest sense) as a mere reflection of the underlying techno-economic relations of production while giving art a more fully independent role than Marx allows.

The radical psychiatrist R. D. Laing used Raskolnikov's mother's letter to her son in teaching students the emotional power of the 'double bind'.[48]

---

[42] RY, 443/PSS13, 360.   [43] RY, 7/PSS13, 10.
[44] Dostoevsky's comments about the effect on him of his women readers' letters suggests he knew himself to be in a similar process of learning.
[45] RY, 89–90/PSS13, 78–9.   [46] P, 291/PSS10, 51.
[47] See Jacques Catteau, *Dostoevsky and the Process of Literary Creation*, trans. Audrey Littlewood (Cambridge: Cambridge University Press, 1989), 399–411; Antony Johae, 'Towards an Iconography of *Crime and Punishment*', in George Pattison and Diane O. Thompson (eds.), *Dostoevsky and the Christian Tradition: Reading Dostoevsky Religiously* (Cambridge: Cambridge University Press, 2001), 177–80.
[48] See R. D. Laing, *Self and Others* (Harmondsworth: Penguin, 1969), 165–73.

Commentary on the Fourth Conversation

1. The Madonna

Dostoevsky's admiration for Raphael's *Madonna della Segiola* is recorded in letters and in his wife's memoirs. He was even more forcibly struck by the same artist's *Sistine Madonna* that he later saw in Dresden, which he saw as the ideal of human beauty. Some years later he was given a large-scale photographic reproduction of the latter work by the Countess Sofia Tolstoya in cahoots with Anna Grigorievna. This was hung in his study, supplementing the Marian icon 'The Joy of All Who Sorrow'. Dmitri Karamazov describes the human drama as being acted out on a scale stretching from Sodom to the Madonna, and, as he adds, there may be many in Sodom who nevertheless yearn for the Madonna.[1]

Clearly, there are many issues in play here: the nineteenth century's sentimental idealization of womanhood, to be sure, but also the Christian devotion to Mary as Mother of God and, as such, the protector of all sufferers; some also discern archetypal images of the Great Mother, earth, against which many of Dostoevsky's characters rebel, only to discover their need to return and be reconciled with this same earth, 'to water it with their tears' (as Zosima instructed).[2] This last is especially likely in the case of Dmitri Karamazov, since his name links him to Demeter, a primordial earth goddess, referenced also in the Schiller poem that he recites when explaining himself to Alyosha.[3]

In Orthodox Christianity, Mary is certainly more than a Christmas card ideal of female beauty. As Mother of God, she participates in the saving work of Christ her son and the faithful seek her intercession with God. In some stories she acts independently on behalf of sufferers, as in the legend of 'The Journey of the Mother of God through Hell', referenced by Ivan Karamazov when introducing the story of the Grand Inquisitor. In the legend, Mary descends so deep into hell that she reaches a place of torment forgotten by God himself. Returning to heaven, she pleads to God for those imprisoned there, and He grants an annual amnesty from Good Friday to Pentecost. In some versions of the legend, these are, specifically, Jews, although Ivan does not mention this.[4]

---

[1] BK, 106/PSS14, 100.
[2] This last is a central feature of Ivanov's symbolist interpretation of Dostoevsky.
[3] He quotes from both the 'Ode to Joy' and, more extensively, from 'The Elysian Mysteries'.
[4] BK, 253/PSS14, 225.

As Lisa Knapp has shown, themes of motherly care play an important part in *The House of the Dead*. Although such care is conspicuously absent in the prison camp, it remains a powerful memory for many of the prisoners and, in one case, a distant mother successfully intercedes for her son's release. Such memories, she suggests, also have a Mariological reference.[5] Sonia Marmeladova's relation to Raskolnikov too has a motherly dimension and, in Siberia, the other prisoners look on her as a 'little Mother', an appellation that has clear Marian overtones.[6] These are reinforced by the note that at Christmas she gave the prisoners a kind of pastry called kalaches, the distribution of which in *The House of the Dead* prompts what Knapp calls 'an improvised, carnivalized and ecumenical maternal eucharist.'[7] The convict Fedka explains that even in the moment in which he stole pearls from an icon of the Mother of God, he had a dim faith that the tears she wept for him would perhaps save him.[8]

2. Self-Deification and Divine Self-Emptying

Yuval Harari's 2015 bestseller *Homo Deus* prompts discussion of self-deification, but the idea that human beings can now take over the role previously identified with God was already widespread in nineteenth-century thinking about religion.[9] German Idealism interpreted the Christian idea of Christ as both divine and human as symbolic of humanity's own divinity. David Friedrich Strauss concluded his *Life of Jesus* by observing that 'In an individual, a God-man, the properties and functions which the church ascribes to Christ contradict themselves' (i.e. an individual human being cannot *be* God); 'in the idea of the race, they perfectly agree. Humanity is the union of the two natures—God become man, the infinite manifesting itself in the finite and the finite spirit remembering its infinitude...it [humanity] is the worker of miracles, in so far as in the course of human history the spirit more and more completely subjugates nature, both within and around man, until it lies before him as the inert matter on which he exercises his active power...'[10]

---

[5] See Lisa Knapp, 'Dostoevsky's "Journey through the Torments": Maternal Protest in *Notes from the Dead House*', in Stefano Aloe (ed.), *Su Fëdor Dostovskij: Visione filosofica e sguardo di scrittore* (Naples: La scuola di Pitagor, 2012), 413–30.

[6] On Sonia's 'motherly' relation to Raskolnikov, see O'Dwyer de Machedo, *Clinical Lessons on Life and Madness: Dostoevsky's Characters*, trans. Agnès Jacob (London: Routledge, 2019), 77–93. See CP, 489/PSS6, 419.

[7] Knapp, 'Dostoevsky's "Journey through the Torments"', 420.

[8] P, 509/PSS10, 428.

[9] See George Pattison, 'Man-God and "Godmanhood"', in John Arblaster and Rob Faesen (eds.), *Theosis/Deification: Christian Doctrines of Divinization East and West* (Leuven: Peeters, 2018), 171–90.

[10] David Friedrich Strauss, *The Life of Jesus Critically Examined*, trans. M. Evans, ed. P. Hodgson (London: SCM Press, 1973), 780.

Feuerbach and other Left Hegelians gave Strauss's position a materialist twist such that material advancement of the human species replaced the hope of heaven. This was the kind of position that Dostoevsky encountered in the radical discussion group known after its leader Mikhail Petrashevsky as the Petrashevsky Circle.[11] Yet already in 1835, Heinrich Heine had referred to Feuerbach, his old friend Marx, and other exponents of this position as 'godless self-deifiers' and urged them to seek edification in the story of Nebuchadnezzar, the king who mistook himself for God and ended up crawling on the ground and eating grass like a beast of the field.[12]

In picking out self-deification as a sign of the times, Dostoevsky was thus intervening in a well-defined debate about the nature of modern humanity. Kirillov's desire to become God by voluntary suicide is perhaps the most startling example of self-deification, but he is neither the first nor last Dostoevskian anti-hero to attempt such a thing. Raskolnikov's crime is motivated by the desire to prove to himself that he is an 'extraordinary man' who 'has the right...that is, not an official right, but an inner right, to decide in his own conscience to...overstep certain obstacles, and only in case it is essential for the practical fulfilment of his idea (sometimes, perhaps, of benefit to the whole of humanity)'.[13] As he further glosses this suggestion, he adds that, as a matter of fact,

> all...the legislators and leaders of men, such as Lycurgus, Solon, Mahomet, Napoleon and so on, were all without exception criminals, from the very fact that, making a new law, they transgressed the ancient one, handed down from their ancestors and held sacred by the people, and they did not stop short at bloodshed either, if that bloodshed—often of innocent persons fighting bravely in defence of ancient law—were of use to their cause.[14]

Raskolnikov's self-elevation to the status of a Mohammed or Napoleon may not be complete self-deification, but its logic is Kirillov's: that there is no God to set limits to human beings who have the freedom to set their own limits—if they are ready to use it.

Ivan Karamazov has perhaps the most fully worked out version of this theory. Early on in the novel we are introduced to his idea that 'if God does not exist, then everything is permitted', and in a hallucinatory interview with the Devil Ivan is reminded of a youthful essay he wrote called 'The Geological Cataclysm' that

---

[11] It was Dostoevsky's participation in this group that led to his mock execution and imprisonment in 1849.
[12] Heinrich Heine, 'Zur Geschichte der Religion und Philosophie in Deutschland', in *Werke in Fünf Bänden*, Vol. 5 (Weimar: Volksverlag, 1962), 10. August Comte's 'religion of humanity' is another nineteenth-century variant on this theme.
[13] CP, 237/PSS6, 199.   [14] CP, 237/PSS6, 199–200.

fills out this rather abstract statement. The story envisages a future in which human beings will have finally destroyed the idea of God. At that point,

> Men will unite to take from life all that it can give, but only for joy and happiness in the present world. Man will be lifted up with a spirit of divine Titanic pride and the man-god will appear. From hour to hour extending his conquest of nature infinitely by his will and his science, man will feel such lofty joy... that it will make up for all his old dreams of the joys of heaven. Everyone will know that he is mortal and will accept death proudly and serenely like a god. His pride will teach him that it's useless for him to repine at life's being a moment, and he will love his brother without need of reward. Love will be sufficient only for a moment of life, but the very consciousness of its momentariness will intensify its fire, which now is dissipated in dreams of eternal love beyond the grave.[15]

Even if such a state never comes to pass (and, the Devil surmises, it is unlikely to do so for a thousand years), the 'new man', who knows the truth that there is no God and no immortality, 'may well become the man-god, even if he is the only one in the whole world, and promoted to his new position, he may light-heartedly overstep all the barriers of the old morality of the old slave-man if necessary. There is no law for God. Where God stands, the place is holy. Where I stand will be at once the foremost place... "all things are lawful" and that's the end of it.'[16] The utopian vision of universal harmony in a world emancipated from belief in God is a deception. Instead, the idea of the man-god is the ideology of individual or collective agents who give themselves the right to do as they will and impose that will on others. It is the same logic as the Grand Inquisitor's 'correction' of Christianity.

We find a 'softer' version of this logic in *The Possessed*, where we are told about an early allegorical poem by Stepan Trofimovich Verkhovensky. Somewhat in the manner of Schiller's *Ode to Joy*, the poem evokes the universal development of life through its manifold forms and culminating in a new Tower of Babel that 'certain athletes at last finish building... with a song of new hope, and when at length they complete the topmost pinnacle, the Lord (of Olympia, let us say) takes flight in a comic fashion, and man, grasping the situation and seizing his place, at once begins a new life with new insight into things'.[17] The narrator clearly finds it all very amusing, yet the poem's logic is not dissimilar to that of the violent man-god of Raskolnikov's and Ivan's fantasies (and we remember that Stepan Trofimovich is the father of Peter, ringleader of the nihilistic revolutionary cell, and was tutor to the arch-demon Stavrogin).

---

[15] BK, 688/PSS15, 83.   [16] BK, 688–9/PSS15, 84.   [17] P, 4/PSS10, 9–10.

Against this ideology of the man-god, the conversation's Dostoevsky pits Paul's letter to the Philippians 2.5–11:

> Let the same mind be in you that was in Christ Jesus, who, though he was in the form of God, did not regard equality with God as something to be exploited, but emptied himself, taking the form of a slave, being born in human likeness. And being found in human form, he humbled himself and became obedient to the point of death—even death on a cross. Therefore God also highly exalted him and gave him the name that is above every name, so that at the name of Jesus every knee should bow, in heaven and on earth and under the earth, and every tongue should confess that Jesus Christ is Lord, to the glory of God the Father.

From the Greek verb for 'emptying', this passage has been taken as the basis for what is called a 'kenotic' view of Christ. On this view, Christ did not retain any divine powers or attributes (such as omniscience) in becoming incarnate. The kenotic Christ is a thoroughly humble and even humiliated Christ, like the Russian Christ 'in peasant garb' in Tiutchev's poem.[18] Such a Christ also requires a parallel self-humbling on the part of his followers.

Kenoticism of this kind is often seen as a distinctive feature of Russian spirituality and therefore part of the background against which Dostoevsky's own 'kenotic' spirituality, exemplified in the Elder Zosima, was developed.[19] Cassedy casts doubt on the representation of Russian Christianity as distinctively kenotic, though he affirms the centrality of suffering and humility in Dostoevsky's Christianity.[20] In fact, he argues that it was through Dostoevsky, interpreted by the Orthodox theologian Mikhail Mikhailovich Tareev, that the word kenosis was first introduced to Russian theology in 1892![21] On a broader view, it seems to be the case that, as Paul L. Gavrilyuk has pointed out, the representation of God as self-emptying and suffering has, from the nineteenth century onwards, had an unprecedented role in modern Christian theology.[22] This has, moreover, been true across Christian denominations.[23] In this perspective, Dostoevsky's kenoticism is not uniquely Russian or even uniquely Orthodox (as he may have thought) but represents a larger ecumenical tendency of the time.

---

[18] See Nadejda Gorodetzky, *The Humiliated Christ in Modern Russian Thought* (London: SPCK, 1938).

[19] See, e.g., Margaret Ziolkowski, 'Dostoevsky and the Kenotic Tradition', in George Pattison and Diane O. Thompson (eds.), *Dostoevsky and the Christian Tradition: Reading Dostoevsky Religiously* (Cambridge: Cambridge University Press, 2001), 31–40.

[20] See Steven Cassedy, *Dostoevsky's Religion* (Stanford, CA: Stanford University Press, 2005), 149–55.

[21] Cassedy, *Dostoevsky's Religion*, 11–13.

[22] See Paul L. Gavrilyuk, *The Suffering of the Impassible God: The Dialectics of Patristic Thought* (Oxford: Oxford University Press, 2004), 1–5.

[23] On British kenotic theologians see David Brown, *Divine Humanity: Kenosis Explored and Defended* (London: SCM Press, 2011).

Kenoticism by no means denies Christ's divinity. On the contrary, it is a particular interpretation of the 'how' of that divinity: he is divine in self-humbling. It is also intimately paired with ideas regarding the deification of human beings in Christian theology. This is again often seen as a distinctively 'Eastern' Christian idea, though it is found also in the West. The key idea here is that, as Athanasius, the most orthodox of all Church Fathers put it, 'He became human that we might become divine', epitomizing what Ruth Coates calls a 'kenosis–theosis axis' in Patristic thought (theosis being the Greek term for deification).[24] In the writings of Dostoevsky's friend Vladimir Solvovyov this becomes the argument that 'the kenosis of the Logos makes possible in principle the theosis of humanity' and, indeed, the natural universe.[25] In this way the deification of the human being becomes 'an expression of the Orthodox conception of synergy, or cooperation with God in the work of salvation'.[26] This not only provides a very different theoretical basis for deification from that of Left Hegelianism, it also points to very different implications for human behaviour, responding to self-deification and self-assertion with the kind of humility promoted by Zosima and exemplified (however problematically) by Sonia Marmeladova, Prince Myshkin, and Alyosha Karamazov.

The view that Christ is unique in being from eternity without ego is found in 'Will I ever see Masha again?'[27] Dostoevsky seems to have had little interest in theories of the atonement, a major and hotly debated focus of Western and especially Protestant Christian theology (as indicated in the comments about the evangelical 'Alpha course', where a specific view of the atonement is regarded as a sine qua non of true belief). Christ, it seems, saves by virtue of an incarnational movement that unites human nature to the divine nature and enables us to begin the process of shedding the ego and participating ever more fully in the universal synthesis.

The critical comments about the French ideals of *liberté*, *égalité*, and *fraternité* are based on *Winter Notes on Summer Impressions*.[28]

3. Christ's Christmas Tree

Dostoevsky adapted the story 'The Little Boy at Christ's Christmas Tree' from Friedrich Rückert's 'Des fremden Kindes heiliger Christ' ('The holy Christ of the

---

[24] Ruth Coates, *Deification in Russian Religious Thought between the Revolutions, 1905–1917* (Oxford: Oxford University Press, 2019), 36.
[25] For a fuller discussion of Solovyov, see the fifth Conversation and accompanying commentary.
[26] Coates, *Deification in Russian Religious Thought*, 75. See also Brown, *Divine Humanity* and Rowan Williams, *Looking East in Winter. Contemporary Thought and the Eastern Christian Tradition* (London: Bloomsbury Continuum, 2021).
[27] PSS20, 172, 174.   [28] WNSI, 59–73/PSS5, 74–82.

stranger child') and the story superbly illustrates his self-consciousness regarding the limits of writing. In the opening line Dostoevsky states that 'I am a novelist, and I suppose I have made up this story'[29] and, at the end, he asks himself, 'Why have I made up such a story?'[30] To which he says that 'I keep fancying that all this may have happened really—that is, what took place in the cellar and on the woodstack; but as for Christ's Christmas tree, I cannot tell you whether that could have happened or not.'[31] However, Dostoevsky changed Rückert's story at one crucial point: where the original ends with the edifying assurance that the child is now in heaven, he sets a question mark against whether the vision of heaven is real. This, I suggest, is to be understood as an acknowledgement that the novelist's art shares the limits of human language and cannot directly express such a reality. Fiction can point, but it cannot demonstrate or prove such things.

T. A. Kasatkina has interpreted the story as a kind of obverse of the icon of the Nativity, with the boy's mother lying dying in the cellar paralleling Mary lying in the cave, the boy's ejection from the bourgeois households inversely reflecting those who come to the Christ child with their gifts, and his death as a counterpoint to the Christ child's life.[32] As Dostoevsky says in the conversation, this exemplifies the kind of reversal that Christ speaks of in the parable of the sheep and the goats, where his presence in the world is identified with the hungry, the homeless, and the prisoners. Again, the message seems to endorse the kenosis–theosis axis of which Coates speaks.

The tsarevna's response to hearing Dostoevsky read the story is historically attested.[33] A shortened version of the story was read in *Carols from King's* broadcast on BBC television on 24 December 1991.

Additional Points

When talking about how we are saved by Christ's death on the cross the narrator confuses two influential theories. The first is the satisfaction theory set out by Anselm of Canterbury in his *Cur Deus Homo* (Why God became human). This argues that sin had offended God and that therefore, in the manner of a feudal king, God's honour had to be satisfied before the sin could be forgiven. The other is the ransom theory developed round the idea that humanity has become captive to the devil and that we can only be released if he is paid a ransom: the death of an innocent person. The trick, of course, is that Christ is raised from the dead and so humanity is saved and the devil doesn't get to keep his ransom. It should be said

---

[29] HT, 248/PSS22, 14.   [30] HT, 251/PSS22, 17.   [31] HT, 251/PSS22, 17.
[32] T. A. Kasatkina, *Dostoievski kak Filosof i Bogoslov: Khudozhestvenny Sposob Vyskazyvania* (Moscow: Volodei, 2019), 255–76.
[33] See Joseph Frank, *Dostoevsky: The Mantle of the Prophet, 1871–1881* (Princeton, NJ: Princeton University Press, 2002), 496.

that in popular Christianity these theories are often held side by side, so our narrator can be forgiven his confusion. These theories are absent from Dostoevsky's oeuvre and, as Susan McReynolds has put it, he 'suffered from profound discomfort with the Crucifixion as a vehicle of redemption'.[34] The Eastern Churches more generally have typically been less preoccupied with the exact mechanism involved in how the crucifixion secured human redemption, placing a greater emphasis on the salvific nature of the Incarnation itself and, not least, the resurrection. Stressing that this is a matter more of emphasis than strict delineation, Dostoevsky is in this regard typically 'Eastern' in his approach.

Fyodor Mikhailovich's statement that a king is never without his army is from John of Damascus, an author he is known to have read.

The claim that Dostoevsky saw some similarity between Italian and Russian peasants is noted in Anna Grigorievna's memoirs.[35] Frank notes that the Italians are the only foreigners about whom Dostoevsky never expressed negative opinions.[36]

---

[34] Susan Mc Reynolds, *Redemption and the Merchant God: Dostoevsky's Economy of Salvation and Antisemitism* (Evanston, IL: Northwestern University Press, 2008), 9.

[35] Anna Dostoevsky, *Dostoevsky: Reminiscences*, trans. Beatrice Stillman (London: Wildwood, 1976), 156.

[36] Joseph Frank, *Dostoevsky: The Miraculous Years, 1865–1871* (Princeton, NJ: Princeton University Press, 1995), 348.

Commentary on the Fifth Conversation

1. Dostoevsky's Politics (I)

Dostoevsky's political views are a defining feature of the *Diary of a Writer*. As he says in this conversation, these have mostly not been well received in the anglophone world and many critics make a sharp distinction between these 'publicist' writings and the novels.[1] However, this distinction is precarious, as I hope to indicate. I shall discuss these views in three stages. I shall here present an outline of Dostoevsky's politics in the context of his own time. In the commentary to the next conversation ('The Jewish Question') I shall more briefly consider aspects of his influence in the twentieth century, and in the commentary on the Postscript, I shall discuss his relation to contemporary Russian nationalism.

Dostoevsky's participation in the Petrashevsky circle, the mock execution that followed, and his imprisonment and exile in Siberia won him lifelong respect amongst Russian radicals, further enhanced by his chronicle of prison life in *The House of the Dead*. His ideological position during the Petrashevsky period is hard to define exactly (and perhaps he had no exactly defined position) but was probably a kind of non-supernatural Christian utopianism that was far from Marxist communism (at that point not yet an active element in Russian political life). However, during his time in prison, Dostoevsky underwent a radical change of views and emerged as a fervent supporter of the tsar, as testified by three poems written in 1854 and 1855. These declare that Russia's cause in the Crimean War is Christ's, while Britain and France are portrayed as the new crucifiers of Christ, in league with the Muslim Turk.[2] The third of the poems is dedicated to the new tsar, Alexander II, widely expected to inaugurate an era of reform, including the abolition of serfdom.

The exact timing and nature of Dostoevsky's 'conversion' have been much debated. On the basis of *The House of the Dead*, it seems to have been linked to the experience of Easter in prison and to new insights, reinforced by childhood memories, of the deep kindness and Christian charity found beneath an often

---

[1] A full English translation was not published until 1984, long after the major novels had each gone through several translations.

[2] See Joseph Frank, *Dostoevsky: The Years of Ordeal, 1850–1859* (Princeton, NJ: Princeton University Press, 1983), 181–3, 198–9. The poems are to be found in PSS2, 403–10.

brutal exterior in the hearts of the peasants.[3] Whatever the precise details, it is clear that by the time of his release from prison and the start of his military service, Dostoevsky's thinking about Russia's political and social order and its place in world history was guided by three defining elements: a belief in the benign and paternal sovereignty of the Russian tsar, the spirit of Orthodox faith, and the Christlikeness of the peasant, i.e. 'Russian', heart.[4] However, while the last two elements appear in a number of the novels, the role of the tsar is limited to the *Diary of a Writer*.

Dostoevsky saw the principal threat to the Russian world of tsar, Church, and people as being from the kind of Western, liberal values that he associated with Britain, France, and German Idealism. These alien influences became manifest in the nihilism of the 1860s, and while each of the major novels thematizes the issues revealed in nihilism to some degree, it is *The Possessed* that develops these in an unambiguously political manner.[5] The novel draws on the recent and notorious Nechaev case, named after one of the most extreme political nihilists of the time, whose *Catechism of a Revolutionary* created the image of the ruthlessly single-minded revolutionary activist that would be emulated by many later Bolsheviks. Like Nechaev, the novel's Peter Verkhovensky orders his revolutionary cell to murder one of their own members in order to cement their loyalty. Stavrogin, whom Verkhovensky plans to install as the charismatic figurehead of the revolutionary movement, has similarly been compared to Mikhail Bakunin, an important nineteenth-century theorist of anarchism.[6]

Dostoevsky's analysis of revolutionary terrorism has been seen as 'prophesying' the coming Russian Revolution, and while the Soviet authorities accepted his social realism and his critical portrayal of capitalism, *The Possessed* was, for a long time, kept out of print.[7] More recently, André Glucksmann has applied Dostoevsky's analysis to contemporary Islamic terrorism, arguing that despite its religious rhetoric, it is an essentially nihilistic movement. As Glucksmann sums up: 'The inner nature of this nihilistic terrorism is that everything is permissible,

---

[3] The episode of 'the peasant Marei', a peasant who comforted Dostoevsky as a child when he was frightened by reports of a wolf in the vicinity, is often cited; see DW, 205–10/PSS22, 46–50.

[4] The final conversation, 'We Are All Here', will offer a variant on these speculations.

[5] Despite a vague claim that he will redistribute the proceeds amongst poor students, Raskolnikov's crime is not political in the same sense as the conspiracy at the heart of *The Possessed*.

[6] Nechaev is introduced as personally known to Dostoevsky in J. M. Coetzee's *The Master of St Petersburg* (London: Secker and Warburg, 1994), although this has negligible historical basis. The identification of Stavrogin with Bakunin was originally made by the Soviet critic Leonid Grossmann and is discussed in James Goodwin, *Confronting Dostoevsky's Demons: Anarchism and the Specter of Bakunin in Twentieth-Century Russia* (New York: Peter Lang, 2010).

[7] James Goodwin shows how this suppression is connected to shifting views regarding Bakunin's place in the genealogy of the Revolution. See Goodwin, *Confronting Dostoevsky's Demons*, 101–82.

whether because God exists and I am his representative, or because God *does not* exist and I take his place.'[8]

It is important to note that the cowardly and self-aggrandizing liberal Stepan Trofimovich Verkhovenksy is not only the biological father of Peter but had also been Stavrogin's house tutor, implying that the relatively mild Hegelianism of the 1840s has spawned the brutal and violent nihilism of the next generation. At the end of the novel Stepan Trofimovich discovers that it is from amongst the peasants and not the intellectuals or middle classes that Russia will be renewed. In this regard, although Dostoevsky's opposition to nihilism alienated many of his younger readers, he did applaud the populism of the 1870s, especially the young people who consciously sought to reconnect with the people and, often at great personal cost, went out to teach or engage in social work in remote and impoverished regions. In the case of Stepan Verkhovensky, the return to the people also involves the rediscovery of the Bible, a theme that is also found in the teachings of Zosima, for whom the Russian peasant has a natural affinity with the teaching of the Bible.[9]

A variant on nihilism is the idea that Russia itself has the potential to achieve divine status, powerfully expressed by Shatov, who is sometimes seen as ventriloquizing Dostoevsky's own views. In the course of a nighttime conversation with Stavrogin, Shatov declares that Russia is a 'god-bearing' people…destined to regenerate and save the world in the name of a new God' and it is to this people that 'the keys of life and of the new world' are to be given.[10] He rejects Stavrogin's objection that this reduces God to an attribute of nationality. 'On the contrary,' he says, 'I raise the people to God.'[11] He claims that every great nation, starting with the Jews, has been defined by faith in its own divine calling. But, he continues, 'there is only one truth, and therefore only a single one out of the nations can have the true God, even though other nations have great gods of their own. Only one nation is "god-bearing", that's the Russian people…'[12]

A further dimension of what is involved in the 'god-bearing' potential of the people is the set of ideas developed by Dostoevsky in the 1860s known as *pochvennichestvo*, a word derived from *pochva* or 'soil'. Crudely, we might render it as faithfulness to the Russian earth and those who worked it. Practically, it meant

---

[8] Quoted from André Glucksmann, 'Bin Laden, Dostoevsky and The Reality Principle: An Interview with André Glucksmann', https://www.opendemocracy.net/en/article_1111jsp/ (accessed 14 October 2022). See Glucksmann, *Dostoïevski à Manhattan* (Paris: Robert Laffon, 2002); also John P. Moran, *The Solution of the Fist: Dostoevsky and the Roots of Modern Terrorism* (Lanham, MD: Lexington Books, 2009). A critical view of Glucksmann's argument is offered in Christoph Garstka, 'Osama bin Stavrogin: Die Dämonen des islamistischen Terrors. Eine Auseinandersetzung mit André Glucksmann's *Dostoïevski à Manhattan*', *Dostoevsky Studies*, New Series, Vol. 22 (2018), 45–57.
[9] BK, 298–304/PSS14, 263–8.   [10] P, 223/PSS10, 196.   [11] P, 227/PSS10, 199.
[12] P, 228/PSS10, 200.

encouraging the Russia intelligentsia to reconnect to the life of the people.[13] As previously noted, 'earth' is a theme that recurs in several novels, from the arguably insane earth-fetishization of Maria Lebyatkina through to Zosima's injunction to stay true to the earth.[14]

Some have taken Shatov at face value as expressing Dostoevsky's own beliefs. In an influential article from 1947, Hans Kohn sums up what he sees as the author's and character's shared view as 'The exclusive fanaticism of a racial God', which, he states, 'is proclaimed here, as in most primitive antiquity, without any trace of the ethical sublimation into the God of universal justice demanded by the Hebrew prophets.'[15] More recently, a 2014 television adaptation validates Shatov's speech by changing the setting from night to day and having him speak against a background dominated by the golden domes of a Russian church, reflecting the sun that often has associations of divinity in Dostoevsky's writing, thus visually linking the speaker's 'Russian God' to Orthodoxy.[16] However, at least until recently, Shatov's ideas would be unrecognizable to any 'orthodox' Orthodox theology, the starting point of which is the Trinitarian revelation of God in Christ.[17]

But are Shatov's and Dostoevsky's convictions the same? In the conversation itself we learn that Shatov had originally learned this idea from Stavrogin, who has since disowned it. Stavrogin also makes the perhaps obvious objection that Shatov is reducing God to an attribute of nationality and it is not clear that, despite his fervour, Shatov's response succesfully deflects the charge. Challenged by Stavrogin as to whether he actually believes in God, Shatov stutters, 'I will... I will believe in God.'[18] Starting with its nocturnal setting and the atmosphere of near-hysteria that Dostoevsky creates, the text thus gives reasons to doubt Shatov's visionary but uncertain messianism. Interestingly, the conversation takes place immediately after another of the nihilists, Kirillov, has explained his ambition to become God by committing suicide (see Commentary 1.1), thus freeing humanity from religion. Perhaps, then, Dostoevsky is taking us on a short tour of the varieties of self-deification to be found amongst those who

---

[13] For a helpful account of Dostoevsky's *Pochvennichestvo* and related ideas see Sarah Hudspith, *Dostoevsky and the Idea of Russianness: A New Perspective on Unity and Brotherhood* (London: Routledge, 2004), 38–63.

[14] BK, 336/PSS14, 292.

[15] Hans Kohn, 'Dostoevsky's Nationalism', *Journal of the History of Ideas*, Vol. 6, No. 4 (October 1945), 403.

[16] See Irina Kuznetsova, 'Demons on the Screen', *Mundo Eslavo*, Vol. 16 (2017), 154–62. We shall return to the contemporary political implications of this adaptation in the commentary to the Postscript.

[17] The 'Declaration on Russian World Teaching' (13 March 2022), signed by over 1500 Orthodox theologians, condemns what it calls the heresy of 'ethno-phyletism', that is, the Russian Patriarch Kirill's view that God's cause in the world can be identified with a particular nation (Russia). The declaration notes that this was already condemned at the Council of Constantinople in 1872. For further discussion see the commentary to the Postscript.

[18] P, 229/PSS10, 201.

have left Orthodoxy behind, from Kirillov's individual self-deification to Shatov's collective self-deification?

If this is the case, then it is surprising to find the same expression in the mouth of the Elder Zosima.[19] He too is insistent on the intimate bond between God and the Russian people. However, versus Shatov, he assumes that God does indeed exist: it is God who will answer the monk's prayer and who will save Russia. The truth that the monks preserve is the truth kept 'from the times of the Fathers of old, the Apostles and the martyrs'[20] and their task requires 'obedience, fasting, and prayer'.[21] Russia will reveal this truth to the world—as Zosima puts it, 'That star will arise from the East'[22]—but it did not invent that truth. There is an important difference here: a people who is the vehicle of God's coming into existence is very different from a people called to serve God in humility. But can there be a 'politics of humility'?[23] And just how might we distinguish between narratives of national humility and the narratives of national humiliation that have often fed the ressentiment that drives states to vengeful self-assertion?

When we turn from the novels to the *Diary of a Writer*, Dostoevsky's view of Russia's role in the international order is easily portrayed as a case of nineteenth-century imperial nationalism—as it seems to the narrator of the Conversations. Dostoevsky applauds the young Russians who volunteered to defend Bulgaria against Ottoman repression and wholeheartedly supports the open declaration of war in 1877. As he argues in the conversation, he suggests that war can have a cleansing effect on a nation.[24] Russia, he believes, has been ordained by divine providence to take Constantinople and re-establish it as the capital of Orthodoxy.[25] At some points, Dostoevsky's Russian exceptionalism seems to imply that Russia can only be judged by the standards that it itself deems appropriate. For example, he states that while a policy of 'peace, and not blood' is generally true and even holy, it cannot, in the particular situation of the time, be applied to Russia: 'But in this case, somehow, they are inapplicable to Russia...Russia at this particular historical moment constitutes, so to speak, an exception.'[26]

---

[19] BK, 327/PSS14, 285. Garnett's translation obscures this point, saying only that 'he [the peasant] has God in his heart'.
[20] BK, 325/PSS14, 284.   [21] BK, 327 PSS14, 285.   [22] BK, 325/PSS14, 284.
[23] John P. Moran suggests that Zosima's 'politics of humility' is 'compelling': John P. Moran, 'This Star Will Shine Forth from the East: Dostoevsky and the Politics of Humility', in Richard Avramenko and Lee Trepanier (eds.), *Dostoevsky's Political Thought* (Lanham, MD: Lexington Books, 2013), 69. In the same collection, Ron Srigley argues contrariwise that Zosima's humility is a case of 'humble love employed for the purpose of conquest'; Ron Srigley, 'The End of the Ancient World: Dostoevsky's Confidence Game', in Avramenko and Trepanier (eds.), *Dostoevsky's Political Thought*, 217–18; cf. Kohn: 'In his glorification of Russia there was no trace of humility' (Kohn, 'Dostoevsky's Nationalism', 399).
[24] DW, 297–301, 665–71/PSS22, 122–6, PSS25, 98–103.
[25] DW, 360–5, 626–8, 902–8/PSS23, 46–50, PSS25, 65–7, PSS26, 82–7.
[26] DW, 666/PSS25, 99.

Nevertheless, it is important to note nuances that may not assuage the doubts of a twenty-first-century Western reader but that are important to understand Dostoevsky's position, which, even in the *Diary*, is not entirely monological.

His argument hinges on the specifically Christian character of the tsar's rule.[27] Russian action, he claims, is not directed at territorial conquest but at liberation of the Balkan Slavs. In these terms, his claim in the conversation that what he was seeking is a humanitarian intervention has some prima facie justification. Likewise, although he insists that Russia should maintain its power in Constantinople and not make it into an open international city, he also argues that this is the only way of securing its role for all Orthodoxy.[28] Tellingly, he defines his own views as 'utopian', indicating his awareness that others will dismiss them as incompatible with the realities of international affairs. So too in his defence of war, he first assigns the argument that war can be good for a nation to an anonymous 'dreamer' whom he calls a 'paradoxicalist', although he later makes the same argument in his own voice.[29]

Again, he insists that Russia's aim vis-à-vis Western Europe is not to subordinate the West. On the contrary, he writes that 'we seek to achieve our own welfare not through the suppression of national individualities alien to us, but, on the contrary, that we perceive our welfare in the freest and most independent development of all other nations and in brotherly communion with them'—although he anticipates being laughed at for these views whilst simultaneously preaching the justice of Russia's cause versus Turkey and the European powers.[30]

The Slavophilism of figures such as Alexei Khomiakov and Ivan Kireevsky viewed Russia's medieval past as a time when the Russian peoples lived in an organic and almost prehistoric harmony in the context of a unified Church order.[31] Against this kind of medievalism (for which there are many parallels in Western romanticism), Dostoevsky's Panslavism was essentially historical. It was not the past he wished to recreate and, indeed, there are elements in the novels that point to a particularly dark and violent streak in archaic Russian society.[32] Instead, he looks to a new movement now coming to birth in the spirit of the

---

[27] From 1876 onwards, the Procurator of the Holy Synod, Konstantin P. Pobedonostsev, one of the most powerful figures in the Russian establishment, sent copies of Dostoevsky's writings to the tsarevich, Alexander. In 1877 he was introduced to court circles and acted as a kind of informal adviser to some of the younger members of the royal family. See Joseph Frank, *Dostoevsky: The Mantle of the Prophet, 1871–1881* (Princeton, NJ: Princeton University Press, 2002), 380–2, 413, 489, 496.

[28] DW, 902–8/PSS26, 82–7.   [29] DW, 297–301, 665–71/PSS22, 122–6, PSS25, 98–103.

[30] DW, 667/PSS25, 100. However, similar things have been said by Vladimir Putin: see Commentary on the Epilogue and Postscript.

[31] A useful introduction to Slavophile thinking is the anthology translated and edited by Boris Jakim and Robert Bird, *On Spiritual Unity: A Slavophile Reader. Aleksei Khomiakov. Ivan Kireevsky* (Hudson, NY: Lindisfarne Books, 1998).

[32] This seems to be associated with the Old Believers. Examples include the characters Murin in *The Landlady* and, most notably, Rogozhin in *The Idiot*.

Russian people.[33] This may resonate with Shatov's idea of Russia as a god-bearing people but it can also be correlated with Dostoevsky's advocacy of moral and social reform within Russian society itself. It is less a matter of regaining what has been lost but of looking at what Russians need to be doing now to bring about a more just and harmonious social order worthy of being called 'Christian', a society in which education, cultural formation, the enhancement of the place of women, and the development of a robust legal framework are especially emphasized.[34]

Although Dostoevsky's universalism is questionable as a political proposal, it is arguably more plausible in his view of the relationship between Russian and European literature. This is prominent in the speech he gave at the celebrations accompanying the unveiling of the statue to the poet Alexander Pushkin in Moscow in 1880. The speech was received with extraordinary enthusiasm and was the climax of his life as a public personality in Russian society. In the speech, Dostoevsky insists on Pushkin's specific genius and, by extension, the genius of Russian literature as a whole as consisting in a capacity 'for universal susceptibility and all-reconciliation'.[35] Rephrasing this claim, we may say that, according to Dostoevsky, the Russian writer is able to enter into and to reveal a vision of spiritual life that is truer to Europe's own unrealized aspirations than is European literature itself. In other words, Russia's contribution to Europe will essentially be a vision of human life that provides a significant and specifically Christian alternative to the political economy that now dominates European life. In this sense, it is not entirely delusional to say that history has partially vindicated his prognostications. Russian literature and a certain vision of 'the Orthodox heart' (historically accurate or not) became important, even crucial, elements in Western European cultural and religious development in the twentieth century.[36] Dostoevsky himself, of course, but also Tolstoy, Chekhov, and others, were received as a new revelation of what literature could be or do. For all his Russianness, Dostoevsky became a universal voice.[37]

---

[33] As Sarah Hudspith writes, for Dostoevsky 'the Russians are a people of potential, of becoming', making his works 'living, organic, forward looking': Hudspith, *Dostoevsky and the Idea of Russianness*, 175–6.

[34] Nevertheless, all such progress was, for Dostoevsky, to be entrusted to the tsar and his government.

[35] DW, 961/PSS26, 131.

[36] With specific regard to the religious influence of 'the Russian idea' one need only point to the ubiquity of Andrei Rublev's Holy Trinity icon now to be seen in innumerable Catholic, Anglican, and Protestant churches and to the influence of Orthodox thought on a series of major Western religious thinkers and personalities, from Paul Tillich to Rowan Williams. In addition to Williams's study of Dostoevsky, see his collection *Looking East in Winter: Contemporary Thought and the Eastern Christian Tradition* (London: Bloomsbury, 2021).

[37] On the cultural impact of Russia on Western modernity see Caroline Maclean, *The Vogue for Russia: Modernism and the Unseen in Britain, 1900–1930* (Edinburgh: Edinburgh University Press, 2015).

Whether it is easy or ultimately possible to separate out Dostoevsky's literary-spiritual vision from his politics remains questionable. We could, like Berdyaev, simply disregard the theocratic speculations.[38] However, I note, firstly, that we do not have to take the views found in the *Diary* as his final or definitive word, not even on politics; and, secondly, that there is some element, however subordinate, of internal uncertainty and debate, even in his most thoroughgoing nationalist declarations. These views are, then, Dostoevsky's, but they are not the whole Dostoevsky and whether he achieved a final, stable political philosophy is itself debatable.

In conclusion it is worth noting that the one instance when he does start to give flesh to his idea of a new kind of community is the story of how Alyosha Karamazov reconciles a group of quarrelling boys and, at the very end of the novel, gathers them together before sending them out into the world in a deliberate analogy to Christ and his disciples. Although Alyosha is known to be a Christian, he has at this point left the monastery and is living as a secular man in the world. The actual content of his dealings with the boys is not overtly 'religious', other than that it is a story of forgiveness, community-formation, and ends by invoking the possibility of an 'eternal memory' for their dead friend, Ilyusha. Strikingly, the boys who are gathered into this community are not peasants but middle-class schoolboys. Once more we must acknowledge that Alyosha's story was not finished, but on the basis of what we have and to the extent that it is his 'work' that provides the template for the renewal of Russia, Dostoevsky's vision would seem to be more of a bottom-up democracy of practical Christian love rather than the reinforcement of state-legislated Orthodoxy.

2. Vladimir Solovyov

Vladimir Sergeyevich Solovyov (1853–1900) was a key figure in the history of Russian philosophy.[39] His work provided a point of reference for nearly all of the major Russian religious thinkers of the twentieth century, as well as secular thinkers such as Alexandre Kojève.[40] Solovyov rose to prominence when, between 1878 and 1881, he gave a series of lectures that were published under a title variously rendered in English as 'Lectures on Godmanhood' and 'Lectures on Divine

---

[38] Nicholas Berdyaev, *Dostoevsky*, trans. Donald Attwater (New York: Meridian, 1957), 210.
[39] His name appears variously in English as Solovyov, Soloviev, and Solov'ev: I use 'Solovyov' as this is the closest English form to the Russian pronunciation. He is not to be confused with the leading pro-Putin TV journalist of the same name!
[40] Kojève wrote his PhD thesis on Solovyov under the direction of Karl Jaspers. See Alexandre Kojève, *The Religious Metaphysics of Vladimir Solovyov*, trans. Ilya Merlin and Mikhail Pozdniakov (London: Palgrave Macmillan, 2018). His lectures on Hegel were a foundational moment in modern French philosophy.

Humanity'.[41] The lectures were an extraordinary success and were attended by both Tolstoy and Dostoevsky, amongst many others. Subsequently, Dostoevsky and the much younger philosopher became close friends and Solvoyov accompanied the writer to the Optina Pustina monastery in June 1879, where Dostoevsky sought counsel from the Elder Amvrosy (a likely inspiration for the Elder Zosima) after the death of his son Alexei. Solovyov has been seen as a model for both Ivan and Alyosha Karamazov, reflecting perhaps the duality of his own intellectual and mystical-humanitarian impulses.[42]

As mentioned in the conversation, Solovyov wrote to Tsar Alexander III seeking clemency for the assassin of his predecessor (killed in March 1881, a couple of months after Dostoevsky's death), an intervention that led to his removal from the university. Thereafter, he led a peripatetic existence while continuing to work on important theological and philosophical contributions, notably *Russia and the Universal Church* (published in French in 1885), the short but influential work *The Meaning of Love* (1892–4), and the larger systematic treatise *The Justification of the Good* (1897). Unlike Dostoevsky, he believed strongly in the reunification of the Eastern and Western Churches, and there have been consistent rumours that he received communion from a Catholic priest shortly before his death. His ecumenism also extended to Judaism, and he was a prominent campaigner for civil rights for Jews in Russia. His *Short Story of the Anti-Christ* proposes not only the reunification of the three main branches of Christendom, Catholic, Orthodox, and Protestant (which he identifies as the Petrine, Johannine, and Pauline Churches respectively) but also reunification between Christians and Jews as a precondition of the defeat of the Anti-Christ.[43]

Influenced by German Idealism, Solovyov does not see God as ontologically separate from the world. Instead, both God and world participate in a shared, albeit agonal, history, in and through which each comes to their respective perfection. Within this process, Solovyov saw the irreducible interconnectedness of opposite principles (divine/human, nature/spirit, etc.) as a basic feature of reality, meaning that no individual is purely individual but is participant in manifold yet unified dimensions of life. This process is already manifest in the evolution of nature and in pre-Christian history, but is supremely exemplified in Christ, fully divine and fully human—thus the title 'Godmanhood' or 'divine humanity'. In this regard, Christ is not, as it were, a one-off but is the prototype of our common

---

[41] Vladimir Solovyev, *Lectures on Godmanhood*, trans. Peter Zouboff (London: Dobsom, 1948) and, in a revision of Zouboff's translation by Boris Jakim, as Vladimir Solovyov, *Lectures on Divine Humanity* (Hudson, NY: Lindisfarne, 1995).

[42] For a full discussion of the Solovyov–Dostoevsky relationship see Marina Kostalevsky, *Dostoevsky and Soloviev: The Art of Integral Vision* (New Haven, CT: Yale University Press, 1997).

[43] The 'short story' is in Vladimir Solovyev, *War, Progress and the End of History*, trans. A. Bakshy (London: Hodder and Stoughton, 1915).

human destiny. Solovyov extends divinization (or theosis) to humanity as a whole, although it is something to be achieved freely by each individual.

There are also distinctively Russian features in Solovyov's argument. The most striking is his development of the idea of the divine Wisdom or Sophia. Solovyov himself seems to have had visionary experiences of the divine Wisdom, one of which occurred in the Reading Room of the British Museum library. But the idea also had roots in what he believed was an authentic ancient Russian tradition, attested by the icon of the divine Sophia in Novgorod, and his development of it was influenced by elements of Neoplatonism and possibly by the theosophical writings of the Protestant mystic Jacob Boehme, as well as the Swedish visionary Emmanuel Swedenborg.[44] According to Solovyov, the divine Wisdom is a quasi-independent principle, intimately related to but not identifiable with the Godhead, akin to Neoplatonic ideas of a world soul. Wisdom is the principle of divine order manifest in and unifying all of creation, a kind of middle ground between God and the world and therefore also the matrix in and through which humanity is able to realize its own divine possibilities. Importantly, Solovyov figured this Sophia as essentially feminine, the maternal principle, as it were, of divinity—in this respect following biblical precedents that likewise figured the divine wisdom as female.[45] For Solovyov's ecclesiastical critics, this teaching (which became known as sophiology) confused the proper distinction between creator and creation and introduced a fourth principle into the trinitarian Godhead. The debate about sophiology flared up again in the 1930s, when it was vigorously developed by the exiled theologian Sergius Bulgakov, drawing sharp criticism and condemnation from some other Orthodox theologians, a debate that partially reflected the split between democratic and restorationist elements amongst the Orthodox in exile.[46]

There is no explicit sophiological teaching in Dostoevsky, although ideas of the earth as a cosmic maternal principle can be glimpsed in some passages. We have seen his veneration for Mary, understood as Mother of God and perpetual intercessor for sinners and sufferers. Yet Dostoevsky scarcely demonstrates his friend's speculative interest in the female aspect of divinity.

Solovyov also struck a Russian note in his view of the historical development of the Church, arguing in the *Lectures* that Russia had preserved the integrity of the

---

[44] For the Russian reception of Boehme, see Oliver Smith, 'Boehme in Russia', in Ariel Hessayon and Sarah Apetrei (eds.), *An Introduction to Jacob Boehme: Four Centuries of Thought and Reception* (New York, NY: Routledge, 2014), 196–223; Solovyov is discussed on pp. 211–12.

[45] At Proverbs 8.22, Wisdom speaks of herself as 'the first of [God's] works' and the apocryphal Book of Wisdom is also an important source for Wisdom speculation, especially 7.22–30 (accepted as canonical in the Orthodox and Catholic Churches, though not by Protestant Churches).

[46] See the *Transactions of the Association of Russian-American Scholars in the U.S.A.*, Vol. 39 (New York, 2014–16) (in Russian). For a good introduction to Bulgakov's thought see Paul Valliere, *Modern Russian Theology: Bukharev, Soloviev, Bulgakov. Orthodox Theology in a New Key* (Edinburgh: T. & T. Clark, 2000), esp. 287–309.

divine idea, whilst the West had developed and overdeveloped the human and rational side of Christianity. Nevertheless, this does not lead to a simple repudiation of the West, since each needs the other to achieve the fullness of divine humanity. In *Russia and the Universal Church*, the same argument is couched in terms more favourable to the West. The Western Church has indeed got dirty hands as a result of its engagement in worldly affairs but, as in the parable of St Nicholas and St Cassian, this is a sine qua non for accomplishing the Church's divine mission.[47] As noted above, there have been persistent rumours that Solovyov's enthusiasm for ecclesiastical reunification extended to receiving communion from a Catholic priest and possibly reception into the Catholic Church. Even if unfounded, these rumours indicate the strength of his ecumenical orientation.

On the anniversary of Dostoevsky's death, Solovyov published the first of three speeches that emphasized the universally human aspect of Dostoevsky's legacy.[48] At the same time, he defended Dostoevsky against Leontiev's charge that his religion was not that of authentic Russian Orthodoxy.[49] For Solovyov, the national character of Dostoevsky's writings and their universal significance were not in contradiction. In this respect, the case of Dostoevsky mirrors what Solovyov had said in the *Lectures* about the Hebrew prophets: 'if true patriotism is necessarily free from national exclusiveness and egoism, then, at the same time and thereby, the true universally human point of view, true universalism, in order to possess actual force and positive content, must necessarily be an expansion or universalization of a positive national idea, not an empty and indifferent cosmopolitanism'.[50]

Solovyov's thought was not simply a philosophical transcription of ideas found in Dostoevsky, nor was *The Brothers Karamazov* (the only novel completed after the writer and philosopher became acquainted) a literary expression of Solovyovian philosophy. There are significant convergences but there are also equally significant divergences. In any case, the fact that Solovyov's thought is presented in a systematic philosophical form means that we are obliged to interpret and evaluate it otherwise than how we approach a Dostoevskian novel.[51] The difference of genre cannot be overlooked, and while it is plausible to extrapolate a body of more or less coherent ideas from Dostoevsky's novels and work them into the form of a Dostoevskian world view, this will always mean smoothing over many of the internal tensions, fractions, and hesitations of the novels and

---

[47] See Vladimir Soloviev, *La Russie et L'Église universelle* (Paris: Stock, 1922 [1885]), 1–7.
[48] I do not know of an English translation of these. See V. Solov'ev, *Sochenenia v dvukh tomakh*, Vol. 2 (Moscow: Mysl', 1990), 289–318.
[49] Solov'ev, *Sochenenia v dvukh tomakh*, 319–23. On Leontiev, see the third section of the Commentary on the Second Conversation: 'Dostoevsky's Christ'.
[50] Solovyov, *Lectures on Divine Humanity*, 74.
[51] Solovyov was himself a poet and several of his works, including the *Short Story of the Antichrist*, are written in a more literary than philosophical style.

harmonizing the multiple and often contradictory voices that are heard in them.[52] Such a systematization might yield a world view very close to Solovyov's, but its author would not be the Dostoevsky we know from his literary work—nor for that matter the conflicted and rhetorically extravagant publicist we know from the *Diary*. Equally, the philosophical system of Solovyov has its own status as a contribution to human self-understanding and its own distinctive history of reception. Each is independent of the other and yet the dialogue between them constitutes a fateful and paradigmatic moment in the history of modern thought that illustrates the mutual proximity of literature and philosophy. For in the modern era both literature and philosophy have had to respond to how questions of religion, national identity, politics, and the meaning of love have been impacted by the advent of modern industrial modernity and the scientific world view. We see similar conjunctions of literature and philosophy in the proto-existentialism of early twentieth-century Vienna as well as in the existential philosophy of France in the 1930s and 1940s—and in both cases it is striking that Dostoevsky is a significant presence.[53] Applying a distinction found in existential philosophy, we may say that what is at issue in the Dostoevskian novel is human being itself—that is, who we essentially *are*—, thus inviting philosophical interpretation and challenge. At the same time, modern philosophy, notably but not solely existential philosophy, has been compelled to support its theoretical deliverances on the meaning of being human with reference to thick descriptions of the lived quality of life, i.e. the kind of existential exemplification that we find in the Dostoevskian novel. For both novelist and philosopher our being and our existence are bound together in a constantly refigured sequence of manifestations, and both philosophy and literature offer equally essential and equally demanding means of achieving an interpretation of our lived reality that is true to its most decisive expressions.

3. Living Life

Georg Brandes's description of the writer's sickly, unwholesome, half-criminal physiognomy provided a paradigm for the early reception of Dostoevsky in the West, extending also to Dostoevsky's dramatis personae of simpletons, neurotics, and would-be martyrs. In the twentieth century, readers like E. H. Carr

---

[52] Perhaps the most thorough attempt to 'systematize' Dostoevsky is Reinhard Lauth, *'Ich habe die Wahrheit gesehen': Die Philosophie Dostojewskis in systematischer Darstellung* (Munich: Piper, 1950). A more modest attempt that eschews a 'systematic' approach and acknowledges the polyphony of the novels is James P. Scanlan, *Dostoevsky the Thinker* (Ithaca, NY: Cornell University Press, 2002).

[53] Amongst those representing the proto-existentialism of Vienna are Franz Kafka, Martin Buber, and Georg Lukács, all of whom were well read in Dostoevsky (for France see the second part of the Commentary on the third Conversation).

experienced Dostoevsky's world as 'a small clearing in a forest of dark forces which man can neither control nor understand'.[54] On this account, Dostoevsky's gift to posterity was nothing to do with the promotion of Christian love but a clearer insight into the violent unconscious forces that drive us to torture each other and ourselves.

Dostoevsky's novels do indeed show us a manifold of characters whose lives are a torment to themselves and to others and they portray extremes of violence, cruelty, and unhappiness. Yet that is only half of the story and it is equally possible to argue that what really drives Dostoevsky is the desire to affirm and communicate life, 'living life' to use a phrase he employs on a number of occasions.[55] When Raskolnikov finally begins to recover from the ideological delirium that has led him to murder and self-contempt, Dostoevsky tells us that 'life had replaced dialectics'.[56] More emphatically, the homilies of the Elder Zosima, echoing the deathbed ecstasies of his brother Markel, call us to a celebration of life in its manifold forms. 'Love all God's creation,' Zosima urges his listeners, 'the whole and every grain of sand in it. Love every leaf, every ray of God's light. Love the animals, love the plants, love everything. If you love everything, you will perceive the divine mystery in things.'[57] More than this, we have 'a precious mystic sense of our living bond with the other world, with the higher heavenly world, and the roots of our thoughts and feelings are not here but in other worlds'.[58] But this is not to be taken in the sense of turning away from the earth since earth and heaven are not ultimately divided: 'all is like an ocean, all is flowing and blending; a touch in one place sets up movement at the other end of the earth'—and this, I suggest applies also to the relation of heaven and earth.[59] 'Kiss the earth and love it with an unceasing, consuming love. Love all men, love everything,' he exhorts the monks, for loving the earth is the key to loving heaven.[60]

Carr, then, was surely wrong to define Dostoevsky exclusively as an analyst of dark, pathological forces. It is only slightly less misleading when he also comments that Dostoevsky was 'supremely careless of the details of existence in the visible world in which we move. He has no interest at all in the meticulous observation and objective recording of material surroundings.'[61] It may be true that Dostoevsky was not a *paysagiste*, but he was certainly interested in the material

---

[54] E. H. Carr, *Dostoevsky 1821–1881* (London: Unwin Books, 1962), 246.

[55] In his entry on 'vie vivante', Michel Niqueux compares this with the *vita vitalis* of Augustine, albeit without suggesting that Dostoevsky knew this expression from the Latin Father; see Michel Niqueux, *Dictionnaire Dostoïevski* (Paris: Institut des Études Slaves, 2021), 291. The affirmation of life is the major theme of Predrag Cicovacki, *Dostoevsky and the Affirmation of Life* (New Brunswick, NJ: Transaction, 2012).

[56] CP, 492/PSS6, 422.

[57] BK, 332/PSS14, 289. The word *zhivotnikh*, which Garnett translates as 'animals' could more literally be translated as 'living beings', emphasizing all the more the theme of life.

[58] BK, 334/PSS14, 290.   [59] BK, 333/PSS14, 290.   [60] BK, 336/PSS14, 292.

[61] Carr, *Dostoevsky*, 247.

and visible environment in which his dramas are played out. This applies not only to descriptions of squalid St Petersburg apartments or to the ravages wrought by suffering on his characters' appearance, but also extends to the world of nature. Raskolnikov's 'conversion' is prefaced by a scene in which he looks out over the river towards the landscape beyond, bathed in sunlight. Hearing the singing of the nomads beyond the river and seeing their distant tents, he is taken out of his own time and place—'as though the age of Abraham had not passed'.[62] Describing his walks in the romantic landscapes of the Alps, Prince Myshkin comments that 'I kept fancying that if I walked straight on, far, far away and reached that line where sky and earth meet, there I should find the key to the mystery, there I should see a new life a thousand times richer and more turbulent than ours.'[63] Similarly, Alyosha's ecstasy in the garden takes place on a late summer night, with the Milky Way arching above the sleeping flowers', as 'the silence of earth seemed to melt into the silence of the heavens. The mystery of earth was one with the mystery of the stars…'[64]

What the experiences of Raskolnikov, Myshkin, and Alyosha suggest and the teachings of Zosima proclaim is that our lives are embedded in a cosmic whole that far exceeds our powers of reckoning. Not only are our lives rooted and grounded in the natural environment, but the life we feel within ourselves is a life that is everywhere in nature, in the plants, the birds, the animals. We are part of a great and dynamic continuum of life. The question is: what attitude are we going to take to it? Ivan confesses his love for the sticky buds that presage the coming of spring and yet he is almost embarrassed to say so. He worries that his lust for life is essentially no different from that of an insect, lowering his estimation of human beings to the level of nature conceived as an ensemble of the blind, impersonal, and unalterable laws of nature against which the underground man rails. Markel, Zosima, and Alyosha, by way of contrast, are able to affirm and celebrate the continuity of life and to rejoice that the life they feel in themselves is manifest throughout creation.

Somewhat different from each of these is Dmitri, whose name evokes Demeter, goddess of the earth, a connection reinforced by his garbled quotations from Schiller in the chapter 'Confessions of an Ardent Spirit in Verse' in which he is fully introduced to the reader. 'Glory to God in the world, Glory to God in me…' we hear him repeating.[65] Dmitri proves to be the manifestation of the vitalistic forces presaged in these poetic effusions, a military man with a firm, strong stride, brimming with energy, sexually potent, hard-drinking, brawling, impetuous, but also generous and, at a turning point in his development, discovering a great compassion within himself. In a dream vision of starving mothers and babies in a desolate, scarred landscape he realizes that his own suffering is part of a more

---

[62] CP, 491/PSS6, 421. [63] I, 55/PSS8, 51. [64] BK, 378/PSS14, 328.
[65] BK, 101/PSS14, 96.

universal struggle for life. In this regard, the 'broad' Grushenka, sensuous yet sensitive to Alyosha's grief, practical in worldly affairs yet ready for love, is his perfect female foil. Neither have the overt religiousness of Markel, Zosima, or Alyosha, yet in Dmitri's journey of self-discovery there are possibilities of redemptive suffering that hint at the Christian mystery of regeneration through cross-bearing.

The discussion of life in this conversation is seen as common ground between Dostoevsky and Solovyov. Certainly, Dostoevsky did not need Solovyov to develop ideas of a cosmic life force in which human beings too participated. For his part, Solovyov here follows the lead of German Idealism. Integral to the original impulse of Hegel's phenomenology of spirit was the desire to make philosophy capable of showing the movement of life, rather than developing a set of abstract ideas that were only problematically connected to living experience. His critics typically regarded this as a failed project, and Hegel himself was often accused of having ended up by producing an abstract and lifeless system. Somewhere along the line the lived quality of life had gone missing. Nevertheless, Hegel can be seen as giving a significant inspiration to later philosophies of life. The same can be said, perhaps even more emphatically, of Schelling, whose philosophy was especially focussed on the manifestation of spirit in nature, making him congenial to those for whom nature provided a privileged manifestation of the divine.

Less optimistically, Schopenhauer saw nothing divine in the ultimate source of life, only a blind and purposeless will, endlessly pouring itself out into the manifold of appearances. This too implies that all things living do indeed participate in one single flow of life: the same life lives in both predator and prey as well as in every human being, but under the conditions of individuation life becomes turned against itself and the self-fulfilment of one individual means the suppression and even death of the other. Consequently, the will-to-live leads inevitably to conflict and suffering and the only solution is to surrender this will, as we see in ascetic systems. This is paralleled in Dostoevsky's view that as long as we are individual 'I's we must always find ourselves in conflict with each other.[66] For Solovyov, as also for Dostoevsky, however, love is ultimately stronger than the power of egoism, and he can see history in an essentially positive and Hegelian light as the story of a cosmic and human progression towards all-embracing divinization. What conjoins the multiplicity of life forms is not their origin in blind will but their participation in the divine wisdom. At the same time, there was always the possibility of tragic wrong turns. The final outcome was not preordained as a matter of necessity but required the co-operation of human freedom.

---

[66] As in 'Masha is lying on the table'.

This reminds us again that Dostoevsky's Slavophilism was not a matter of trying to re-evoke the days of Kievan Rus' or some imaginary pre-industrial world. It was very much based on what—rightly or wrongly—he saw stirring in the people of his own time. Here it is important to remember that for many in the nineteenth century, Russians and non-Russians, Russia, like America and in contrast to 'old Europe', was a young country, brimming with new life.

The conversations and commentaries indicate that Dostoevsky's views here are not unproblematic, but we are a long way from the 'pale criminal' who exemplified the decadence of a sickly masochist.[67] Dostoevsky was not the underground man but, to use the title of René Girard's study, an expositor of resurrection from the underground: 'instead of dialectics, there was life'.

Additional Points

The narrator's views on the conflict in the Donbas and the Russian annexation of Crimea in 2014 are not intended as an objective judgement on these events but as reflecting what I take to be the average response of even a relatively well-informed member of the public in the West at the time (2019, before the full-scale invasion of 2022).

The Crystal Palace was a vast glass and steel structure built to house London's 1851 Great Exhibition, later moved to a site at Sydenham Hill in south London. The Russian socialist Nikolai Chernyshevsky envisaged future societies living communally in buildings of this kind and for Dostoevsky it therefore became a symbol of scientific utopianism. It is unclear whether he saw the original Crystal Palace on his 1862 visit to London or the 'Palace of Art and Industry' in the International Exhibition at Kensington in that year.

---

[67] 'The pale criminal' refers to Nietzsche's *Thus Spoke Zarathustra*. Although this is probably not directed specifically at Dostoevsky, Nietzsche (Zarathustra) here castigates those who—like Dostoevsky—thought that their 'I' was something that had to be overcome and who disown their own transgressions of existing laws. Raskolnikov perhaps? See Friedrich Nietzsche, *Also Sprach Zarathustra I–IV*, ed. Giorgio Colli and Mazzino Montinari (Berlin: de Gruyter, 1988), 45–7.

Commentary on the Sixth Conversation

1. The Jewish Question

As stated in the conversation, Dostoevsky devoted much of the March 1877 *Diary of a Writer* to 'the Jewish question'.[1] Dostoevsky's earlier correspondence with Sophia Luria is also mentioned in the *Diary*, though her Jewish identity is not mentioned.[2] In a striking case of heteroglossia (that is, the introduction into the text of a distinct voice, different from the author's), it was her account of the German doctor whose funeral united Jewish and Christian communities that Dostoevsky published in the *Diary*. Elsewhere in the *Diary* we encounter repeated remarks about Disraeli, linked to the idea that Jews were involved in an international anti-Russian conspiracy.[3] A particular focus of the *Diary* (not emphasized in the conversation) is Dostoevsky's anxiety about Jews forming a 'state within the state'.

There are few references to Jews or Judaism in the pre-Siberian writings, although Dostoevsky planned but never completed a story called 'The Jew Yankel'. One reason for this dearth may be that Jews were not allowed to live outside the Pale, a strictly delimited area in the west of the Russian Empire, including much of the present-day Baltic states, eastern Poland, and Ukraine. This restriction was only rescinded in 1861 and Dostoevsky would therefore have had little or no interaction with actual Jews prior to his imprisonment. The 1861 decree itself became the occasion for what David L. Goldstein has called 'Dostoyevsky's vigorous defense of the Jews' as editor of the journal *Time*.[4] Responding to fury and alarm from the conservative and Slavophile press, *Time* defended opening up Russian society to Jewish participation in articles certainly approved and possibly written by Dostoevsky—as Fyodor Mikhailovich mentions in his own 'defence'.

The figure of Isay Fomich Bumstein from *The House of the Dead* is based on a prisoner known to Dostoevsky and is given extended treatment. Certainly, negative stereotypes are in play here, though, as Fyodor Mikhailovich claims, it is also possible to see positive features and the narrator indicates a certain respect for Bumstein's religious practices, despite their weirdness (as he experiences them), and he alludes to their having discussed them together. Otherwise, there

---

[1] See DW, 637–60/PSS25, 74–96.   [2] In June 1876. See DW, 366–9/PSS23, 51–3.
[3] See, e.g., DW, 430–1/PSS23, 108; DW, 640–1/PSS25, 77.
[4] David L. Goldstein, *Dostoyevsky and the Jews* (Austin, TX: University of Texas Press, 1981), 41.

are mostly only passing references to Jews in the fiction. As Fyodor Mikhailovich claims, these references, which are mostly unsympathetic, can in several cases be seen as reflecting the prejudices of the characters as much as the author's own views. If we also accept that Dostoevsky's narrators are rarely directly identifiable with their author, this may be taken as providing a further buffer zone between Dostoevsky himself and anti-Semitic elements in the novels—but opinions will vary on this. In *Crime and Punishment*, the despairing roué Svidrigailov encounters a Jewish fireman whose face 'wore that perpetual look of peevish dejection, which is so sourly printed on all faces of Jewish race without exception'.[5] The eponymous raw youth's fantasy of becoming a Rothschild plays on the association of Jews with exploitative finance and capital, although he distinguishes how he will use his wealth from the selfish money-grabbing of the Jewish financier. Goldstein sees this as played out in the antithesis between Jewish finance and Arkady's (the raw youth's) Christian socialism.[6] The most developed Jewish character in the post-Siberian fiction is Lyamshin, one of the conspirators in *The Possessed*. Although the conspirators are all fairly repulsive, Lyamshin has the distinction of breaking down in terror at the murder of Shatov—not through pity for the victim but simply because of fear—and it is Lyamshin who betrays the conspirators to the police.[7]

Most troubling for some commentators is Alyosha Karamazov's failure to challenge Lisa Khokhlakova's regurgitation of the long-standing anti-Semitic trope of Jews crucifying Christian children, the so-called 'blood libel'. In response to her question as to whether it is true or not, he simply says that he does not know. In this case, however, it could be worth considering the nature of the conversation more broadly. Important as it is, the blood libel is only one element in an extraordinary tirade, in which Lisa confesses to wanting to participate in just such a ritual torture and killing. It is clear from start to finish that Alyosha is deeply shocked by what she is saying and is deeply pained to see in her words the influence of his brother Ivan's nihilism. There is nothing in what Lisa says that Alyosha affirms. Yet he refrains from challenging Lisa's hateful outburst. Why? Does his silence mean consent or could it be seen as analogous to the silence of therapist, whose role is not to cross-examine or debate but to allow the hidden nexus of Lisa's own anger and unhappiness to come to expression.[8] This is the attitude that Macedo ascribed to Sonia Marmeladov (see the Commentary on the third Conversation), namely, 'to be a place' that allows the other to give full expression

---

[5] CP, 460/PSS6, 394.   [6] Goldstein, *Dostoyevsky and the Jews*, 61–7.
[7] For discussion see Goldstein, *Dostoyevsky and the Jews*, 67–87.
[8] Macedo includes an extended passage of this conversation, concluding from it that the sources of murderous violence are shown by Dostoevsky to be not merely contempt of others but 'the sadness of never having been loved': O'Dwyer de Macedo, *Clinical Lessons on Life and Madness: Dostoyevsky's Characters*, trans. Agnès Jacob (London: Routledge, 2019), 188.

to their desire, a therapeutic attitude that requires 'the suspension of all self-esteem' and therefore refraining from intruding personal opinions.[9]

Nevertheless, it is troubling that Dostoevsky rejected the acquittal in March 1879 of nine Georgian Jews accused of kidnapping and murdering a Christian girl on the eve of Passover in what was a clear case of the blood libel. However, as Frank notes, Dostoevsky had previous history with the defence attorney, who had defended a woman perceived by Dostoevsky as clearly guilty of the attempted murder of her lover's wife. Nor does Dostoevsky explicitly mention any of the elements of the blood libel in his comments.[10]

In an extended examination of what she calls 'the economy of salvation', Susan McReynolds suggests that Dostoevsky's belief in the blood libel can be connected to his discomfort in the kind of Christian theology that makes the death of Christ (the Son) a necessary condition for propitiating the wrath of the divine Father. This, she argues, involves 'the never explicitly stated belief that the God of the crucifixion is a bad Jewish utilitarian whose presence within Christianity is intolerable'.[11] At the same time, it is also connected to supposed historical and contemporary crimes against children perpetrated by Jews. Yet, as she concludes, 'Dostoevsky was still seeking answers when he died. This search seems to have led him to find some certainty in the construction of a clear opposition between the "Russian" and "Jewish" ideas of his mature imagination; the ultimate direction his thinking might have taken will never be known.'[12]

The idea of a conflict between Jewish and Christian messianism is found in Shatov's 'god-bearing nation' oration (*The Possessed*), when he declares that a people's faith in its own god must be exclusive: only one nation can bear this torch.[13] Yet, as discussed in the commentary to the previous conversation, this speech is clearly presented as problematic in the novel and there are several reasons to doubt the extent to which it reflects the author's own views.[14]

With reference to McReynold's concluding hesitancy as to Dostoevsky's future development, she hints that perhaps he could have become open to a more conciliatory view under the influence of Solovyov. Solovyov's view is developed in a

---

[9] Macedo, *Clinical Lessons*, 81–2.

[10] Joseph Frank, *Dostoevsky: The Mantle of the Prophet, 1871–1881* (Princeton, NJ: Princeton University Press, 2002), 423.

[11] Susan McReynolds. *Redemption and the Merchant God: Dostoevsky's Economy of Salvation and Antisemitism* (Evanston, IL: Northwestern University Press, 2008), 9–10.

[12] McReynolds, *Redemption and the Merchant God*, 198. Modern liberal theology has also turned away from ideas that God demanded the death of his Son as the price for being reconciled with sinful humanity and instead, like Dostoevsky, has emphasized a doctrine of atonement through love, rather than substitutionary punishment. See also the discussion in Conversation Two.

[13] The conversation takes place in Part 2, Chapter 1.VII. P, 223–32/PSS10, 196–203. See Goldstein, *Dostoyevsky and the Jews*, 55. See also Commentary on the first section of Conversation Four.

[14] As we saw in the first section of the Commentary on the fifth Conversation, Shatov is forced to acknowledge that his own faith in God is dubious. 'I...I will believe in God,' he says, adding that 'I haven't told you that I don't believe...I will only have you know that I am a luckless, tedious book, and nothing more so far, so far...' (P, 229/PSS10, 201).

number of places, most vividly in his 'A Short Story of the Antichrist', in which the Christian Churches are reunited in opposition to the Antichrist, but a condition of their success is the further reunification with Judaism. As Dominic Rubin has put it, 'Soloviev rephrased the anti-Semites' "Jewish question" as a "Christian question": how can Christians rediscover the Judaic concrete "sacred materialism" inherent in Christianity and behave with true Christian love to the Jews, who would then see the truth of Christ and without losing their national identity, take their place in the truly ecumenical church?'[15]

While the balance of evidence cannot exculpate Dostoevsky from charges of anti-Semitism, it is also clear that his view was, at least to some extent, conflicted and it may be worth adding that it is more historical rather than racial. In the context of his writings on the Balkan wars against Turkey he writes that if Muslim citizens of the Russian Empire support Russia's cause then they effectively count as 'Russian' and the correspondence with Sofia Luria implies that the same logic might seem to apply to Russian Jews: if they embrace Russia's cause as their own, then there is nothing further to be held against them.

Felix Phillip Ingold discerns both the importance of 'the Jewish question' to Dostoevsky and its undecidability in the very style of the argument presented in the *Diary*, marked by shifting voices that present 'criticism and self-criticism, direct and indirect speech, polyphony and autoreferential rhetoric, questions and answers, for and against forced together'.[16] Again, while the balance of evidence clearly tilts one way, there may be sufficient ambiguity to find some basis for a more positive development.

Given all of the above, it is perhaps surprising that Dostoevsky's writings have consistently appealed to Jewish readers and (not least in the Soviet Union) many of his most insightful commentators have been Jewish. This paradox is a major theme of Leonid Tsypkin's novel *Summer in Baden-Baden*, where he writes that 'it struck me as being strange to the point of implausibility that a man so sensitive in his novels to the suffering of others, this jealous defender of the insulted and injured who fervently and even frenetically preached the right to exist of every earthly creature and sang a passionate hymn to each little leaf and every blade of grass—that this man should not have come up with even a single word in the defence or justification of a people persecuted over several thousands of years— could he have been so blind?—or was he perhaps blinded by hatred?'[17] Offering a roll call of distinguished Russian Jewish Dostoevsky scholars, Tsypkin wonders

---

[15] Dominic Rubin, 'Judaism and Russian Religious Thought', in Caryl Emerson, George Pattison, and Randall Poole (eds.), *The Oxford Handbook of Russian Religious Thought* (Oxford: Oxford University Press, 2020), 346. See also Vladimir Solovyov, *The Burning Bush: Writings on Jews and Judaism*, ed. Gregory Yuri Glazov (Notre Dame, IN: University of Notre Dame Press, 2016).

[16] Felix Phillip Ingold, *Dostojewskij und das Judentum* (Frankfurt am Main: Insel Verlag, 1981), 164.

[17] Leonid Tsypkin, *Summer in Baden-Baden: From the Life of Dostoyevsky*, trans. Roger and Angela Keys (London: Quartet Books, 1987), 115–16.

whether Dostoevsky perhaps provides them with bona fide credentials for their Russianness—or perhaps just reflects the enthusiasm they bring to involvement in any aspect of Russian culture.[18] But it is not only Russian Jews who have been inspired by Dostoevsky—Martin Buber, one of the leading Jewish thinkers of the twentieth century, identified Dostoevsky (with Kierkegaard) as having awoken him to the possibility of philosophy. The importance of Dostoevsky for Emmanuel Levinas, another major modern Jewish philosopher, has also been mentioned several times already. Even Goldstein's depressingly well-evidenced account of Dostoevsky's anti-Semitism concludes with a hint that, despite everything, Dostoevsky himself could still hope for a future reconciliation of Christians and Jews.[19]

Unfortunately, the twentieth century showed that the issue was far darker than Dostoevsky himself ever realized and that his own words would not only find many brilliant Jewish readers but would also speak to those in Germany, Russia, and elsewhere whose minds were set on the historical destruction of Judaism and the Jewish people. In face of those crimes, it is, again, words from Dostoevsky (that became something of a leitmotif in the work of Emmanuel Levinas) that seem most apt: that we are all guilty, of everything, before everyone, and I most of all.[20]

2. Dostoevsky's Politics (II)

The seminar paper summarized in this chapter is fictional, as are the views put forward by the seminar participants, and no allusion is intended to any actual persons, living or dead. That being said, the argument put forward by 'Professor Greenhill-Jones' is not implausible.

As the 'paper' points out, the reception of Dostoevsky's political writings was very different in the Germanophone and anglophone worlds. *The Diary of a Writer* was first translated into English in 1984 but was included in the German translations published between 1906 and 1922. The volume of *Politische Schriften* (Political Writings) was first published in 1917 and republished in 1922 with two introductions, one by Arthur Moeller van den Bruck (1876–1925), the general editor of the series, the other by the Russian émigré writer Dmitri Merezhkovsky (1866–1941). Van den Bruck is indeed credited with popularizing the expression 'the Third Reich', the title of his 1923 book, and his political philosophy strongly influenced the 'conservative revolution' of the interwar years, although he had a

---

[18] Tsypkin, *Summer in Baden-Baden*, 116. [19] Goldstein, *Dostoyevsky and the Jews*, 163.
[20] See the first section of the Commentary on Conversation One, Part Two. These words should clearly not be applied to victims of the Holocaust and related crimes against humanity: it is rather a word to the perpetrators, the bystanders, and their historical heirs.

personal antipathy to Hitler. Merezhkovsky was a writer and critic of brilliant complexity whose works, like Dostoevsky's, reveal significant shifts of opinion and the co-presence of often conflicting voices. He had met Dostoevsky in his youth and had written an important work comparing Dostoevsky and Tolstoy that was a milestone in Dostoevsky criticism.[21] Like van den Bruck, he too became associated with the conservative revolution. There are multiple attestations to the influence of their presentation of Dostoevsky as a political writer. In 1920, Martin Heidegger, the most eminent philosopher to support Hitler in 1933, wrote to his wife encouraging her to read the *Political Writings*, assuring her that they would make a great impression.[22]

Van den Bruck's introduction, 'The Political Presuppositions of Dostoevsky's Ideas', traces Dostoevsky's political thought back to Russia's essentially Byzantine political order, combining this with Panslavic, conservative, and mystical tendencies. Van den Bruck argues that Russian history has followed the lines laid down by Dostoevsky, only without the religion. The prophecies of the collapse of the West have likewise been vindicated.[23] Merezhkovsky's essay on 'The Religious Revolution' is characteristically complex (or perhaps just muddled) and he manages to say both that Dostoevsky's political philosophy was completely wrong and also that his real message is being borne out by events. Dostoevsky's explicit political thought, focussed as it was on autocracy, Orthodoxy, and nationalism, has proved mistaken. Tsarist autocracy was not the benign and gentle monarchy of Dostoevsky's imagination but, via Byzantium, a continuation of pagan Caesarism. Behind the Christian mask, the true face of autocracy is that of the Beast—as early Christians knew only too well.[24] Orthodoxy itself was far from the ideal image portrayed in Zosima, since it too was prepared to use coercive force and never even attempted, as the Catholic Church attempted, to bring about a universal brotherhood.[25] Like Stavrogin, Merezhkovsky argues that the claim that Russia is a god-bearing people is to make the people absolute and God relative. True Christian faith is not faith in a collective but in the revelation of God in a single and personal human being.

At the same time, Merezhkovsky claims that this threefold faith (autocracy, Orthodoxy, nationalism) is essentially at odds with Dostoevsky's own more profound thought, which he depicts as a kind of apocalyptic spiritual anarchism pointing to a 'third testament', a new religion of the earth, since 'only in the religion of holy earth is the universal unification and evolution of human beings

---

[21] Dmitri Merezhkovsky, *Tolstoy as Man and Artist: With an Essay on Dostoievski* (London: Constable, 1902).
[22] G. Heidegger (ed.), *'Mein liebes Seelchen!' Briefe Martin Heideggers an seine Frau Elfride 1915-1970* (Munich: Deutsche-Verlags-Anstalt, 2005),107.
[23] Arthur Moeller van den Bruck, 'Die politische Voraussetzungen der Dostojewskischen Ideen', in F. M. Dostojewski, *Politische Schriften*, trans. E. K. Rahsin (Munich: Piper, 1922), ix–xiv.
[24] Dmitri Mereschkowski, 'Die Religiöse Revolution', in Dostojewski, *Politische Schriften*, xxxix.
[25] Mereschkowski, 'Die Religiöse Revolution', xxxii.

naturally comprised in both Church and State'.[26] In Merezhkovsky's own political thinking, the coming state of apocalyptic anarchy, revealed in Bolshevism, means that the true religion will require a leader capable of confronting and defeating these dark forces. In the first instance he seems to have seen Mussolini as just such a leader, later transferring his hopes to Hitler.

The idea of Dostoevsky as prophet of the Russian Revolution and the downfall of the West became virtually ubiquitous in the German reception of Dostoevsky in the 1920s, along with the related 'prophecy' of the advent of the 'new man'.[27] One important channel linking Dostoevsky to extreme right-wing thought in Germany was the White émigré community. Michael Kellogg singles out Alfred Rosenberg, whose *The Myth of the Twentieth Century* became one of the key works of popular Nazi philosophy, as especially significant. He argues that Dostoevsky was an important influence on Rosenberg, particularly with regard to anti-Semitism.[28] Rosenberg held prominent government positions and was directly involved in the implementation of the Holocaust. He was executed by order of the Nuremberg judges. Rosenberg is in this sense a living link between Dostoevsky and National Socialism, which might seem to vindicate the case made by 'Greenhill-Jones'.

However, the 1920s was a high point of Dostoevsky reception in the German-speaking world and virtually all of the major figures influencing the development of German culture and society mentioned him, those on the left as much as those on the right, often in support of their own positions. Amongst the leading religious figures who acknowledged a significant influence were the Protestant theologians Karl Barth and Paul Tillich, both of whom were committed anti-Nazis.[29] Romano Guardini, a leading Catholic apologist and author of an influential monograph on Dostoevsky, was stripped of his entitlement to teach by the

[26] Mereschkowski, 'Die Religiöse Revolution', xlv.
[27] Note the title of Herman Hesse's essay 'The Brothers Karamazov—the Downfall of Europe', published in his essay collection *Blick ins Chaos* (Bern: Seldwyla, 1922). In his 1921 introduction to the novels of Dostoevsky, Stefan Zweig wrote that 'The novel of Dostoevsky is the myth of the new Man and his birth from the womb of the Russian soul.' See W. J. Dodd, 'Ein Gottträgervolk, ein geistiger Führer: Die Dostojewskij-Rezeption von der Jahrhundertwende bis zu den zwanziger Jahren als Paradigma des deutschen Rußlandbilds', in L. Kopelew (ed.), *West-östliche Spiegelungen, Reihe A: Russen und Rußland aus deutscher Sicht*, Vol. 4: *Das zwanzigste Jahrhundert* (Munich: Wilhelm Fink, 2000), 864.
[28] Michael Kellogg, *The Russian Roots of Nazism: White Émigrés and the Making of National Socialism, 1917–1945* (Cambridge: Cambridge University Press, 2005), 220–3. Kellogg points out that over and above Dostoevsky's explicitly anti-Semitic statements in the *Diary*, his German interpreters did not hesitate to 'doctor' their quotations to serve their argument. Kellogg, *Russian Roots*, 221. However, Kellogg mistakenly refers to Solovyov as anti-Semitic (see the reference to Dominic Rubin above (section 1).
[29] Karl Barth, *The Epistle to the Romans*, trans. Edwyn C. Hoskyns (Oxford: Oxford University Press, 1933), 4. See also Edurd Thurneysen, *Dostoevsky*, trans. Keith Crim (Louisville, KY: John Knox Press, 1964 [in German, 1921]). Paul Tillich, 'On the Boundary', trans. N. A. Rasetzki, in *The Interpretation of History* (New York: Charles Scribner's Sons, 1936).

National Socialist government and lived largely on the hospitality of friends and supporters until 1945.[30]

The Whites were, of course, not the only Russian voices in exile. Berdyaev, one of the best-known interpreters of Dostoevsky in the period, argued vociferously against the kind of violent restorationist ideology promoted by 'White' thinkers such as Ivan Ilyin.[31] In fact, virtually every major religious and philosophical figure of the emigration wrote important and appreciative work on Dostoevsky, the majority being deeply opposed to the 'conservative revolution'.[32]

We cannot exculpate Dostoevsky entirely from some of the worse fruits of his literary inheritance. Nevertheless, 'Professor Allan' is correct in saying that many Nazi readers often took whatever they wanted and ignored the inner tensions, fractures, dissonances, and ongoing revisions of Dostoevsky's thought, both in the novels and, albeit to a lesser extent, in the *Diary*. The 'conservative revolutionary' reading of Dostoevsky is a historical fact, but it falls far short of offering a persuasive reading of Dostoevsky as a whole and we are under no obligation to give it more credence than it merits.

Additional Points

The extract from *Diary of a Writer* quoted by the narrator is from DW, 644–5/PSS25, 80. The extract read out by 'Greenhill-Jones' is from DW, 658/PSS25, 91.

---

[30] Romano Guardini, *Der Mensch und der Glaube: Versuche über die religiose Existenz in Dostojewskijs großen Romanen* (Leipzig: Hegner, 1933).

[31] On the debate between Berdyaev and Ilyin (often quoted by Vladimir Putin), see Antoine Arjakovsky, 'The Way, the Journal of the Russian Emigration (1925–40)', in Emerson et al. (eds.), *The Oxford Handbook of Russian Religious Thought*, 441–4.

[32] Examples include L. Shestov, S. L. Frank, S. Bulgakov, A. Steinberg (Shestov, Frank, and Steinberg were also Jewish). Berdyaev's work was translated into German in the 1920s.

Commentary on the Seventh Conversation

1. The Poetics of Memory

The Brothers Karamazov is both an eminent and a representative example of Dostoevsky's treatment of memory and of the co-presence of a variety of temporal sequences in the narrative frame of the novel. Writing about what she calls the poetics of memory in this novel, Diane Thompson has referred to it as 'a poetic system of cultural and individual memory'.[1] The narrator himself reminds us that the action of the novel took place thirteen years ago and that he has carefully reconstructed it from his own and others' memories. Dovetailed into these events are memories from even more distant times. There are local memories of Fyodor Karamazov's early life of dissipation and we learn about Alyosha's childhood memory of being held up by his mother to the icon of the Virgin, while the slanting rays of the setting sun streamed in through the window.

Alyosha himself is an important mediator of others' memories, since it is he who has written up Zosima's recollections and farewell teachings—although it is made clear that these are not a precise transcript but more of a collage of teachings and sayings probably given over a period of time and shaped by the way in which they have been filtered through Alyosha's own memory. Even Alyosha's convulsive experience in the garden, which seems to involve direct experience of some supra-human power, is shot through with memories of Zosima's words, words that provide a compelling interpretation of what he is experiencing. What looks at first like an immediate contact with the divine is clearly mediated by what Alyosha has internalized from his beloved teacher.

All of this underlines Zosima's explicit teaching that there is nothing that provides a better basis for spiritual life than nurturing good and beautiful memories from childhood. He himself recalls childhood memories of going to church and hearing the Bible being read. We find a clear application of this teaching in the story of Alyosha and the boys. When Alyosha gathers his schoolboy followers after the funeral of their friend Ilyusha, he tells them to cherish the memory of being reconciled with a boy they had once ostracized throughout their lives. Invoking the funeral liturgy, he urges them to let this be an 'eternal memory',

---

[1] Diane O. Thompson, *Dostoevsky and the Poetics of Memory* (Cambridge: Cambridge University Press, 1991), 2.

implying that it is a direct link between their lives and the eternal world of divine reality.[2]

The same point is illustrated from the opposite side when we are told that Fyodor Karamazov seemed to have forgotten about his children, while, at a crucial point in the action, Alyosha forgets to visit Dmitri, making him a contributor to the impending catastrophe. In the conversation Dostoevsky cites the saying of the Baal Shem Tov, a charismatic leader of Hasidic Judaism in the eighteenth century, 'Forgetfulness leads to exile but remembrance is the secret of redemption.' This was not likely to have been known to the historical Dostoevsky but it seems to epitomize his own view.

The phenomenon of memory provides Dostoevsky with an easy and natural segue to major themes of Christian teaching and practice. The Eucharist, the defining sacrament of believers' continuing union with Christ, is a ritual repetition of Christ's last supper with the disciples and invokes his own words to 'do this in remembrance of me', placing memory at the very heart of believers' fellowship with Christ.[3] However, this is more than a simple act of historical memory, paralleling how nations remember their war dead (for example). It also contains a subtle future element. This too is hinted at in the Scriptural record of the last supper, when Christ says that he will not drink of the fruit of the vine again until he drinks it anew with them in God's future kingdom (Matt. 26.29). Union with Christ is in this way understood as not only related to the past but also extending in hope and anticipation into the future and even beyond time.[4] Some liturgies speak explicitly of 'remembering' both the events of Christ's life on earth and the future coming of his kingdom. In the same way, it seems, Alyosha's hope is that the boys will not only carry this particular memory forward into their future lives but that it is also a pledge of a still greater fellowship—a reading supported by Alyosha's affirmation that 'we will meet again' in the very last lines of the novel. In a felicitous phrase, Kroker and Ward title their study of Dostoevsky's religion 'remembering the end' and this seems accurately to epitomize a central feature of Dostoevsky's own faith and of Christianity itself.[5] Faith remembers not just what we have been and are but what we shall be: and it is precisely this that holds open the twin possibilities of forgiveness and personal respect in even the most ruined lives.

The theme of remembrance relates directly to ideas of eternal life, which underwent a major revision in the nineteenth century. For much of Christian history 'eternal life' had meant a post-mortem life involving a future judgement on

---

[2] BK, 820/PSS15, 196.
[3] Thompson also makes this connection to Christian liturgy: Thompson, *Dostoevsky*, 1–2.
[4] P. Travis Kroeker and Bruce K. Ward, *Remembering the End: Dostoevsky as Prophet to Modernity* (Boulder, CO: Westview Press, 2001).
[5] A classic study of this futural dimension of liturgy remains Geoffrey Wainwright, *Eucharist and Eschatology* (London: Epworth Press, 1971).

each individual's final state. With antecedents in the Platonic tradition and in some mystical writings, the nineteenth century saw a greater emphasis on eternity as a quality of present time. Rejecting narratives of survival, Friedrich Schleiermacher, a defining figure of modern Protestant theology, wrote that 'To be one with the infinite in the midst of the finite and to be eternal in a moment, that is the immortality of religion.'[6]

At the same time, the nineteenth century was also the century of spiritualism, perhaps the most materialist version of 'survival' ever developed. Dostoevsky took a critical interest in the 'spiritism' becoming popular in some Russian circles in his time, though the major expansion of occultism in Russia came after his death.[7] We have already seen that Kant could be read as allowing for some idea of the soul's progress towards perfection after death and that, at least at the time of his first wife's death, Dostoevsky seems to have entertained similar ideas.[8] Nevertheless, Dostoevsky eschews any physical conception of the afterlife, and even the Devil concedes that hell no longer produces the 'ancient fire', while Zosima defines the suffering of hell as being unable to love.[9] When, via Ivan, Dostoevsky retells the folk legend of the Virgin Mary's visit to hell, he is clearly not inviting us to a literal faith in the geography of hell but indicating an existential possibility of extreme abandonment—and it is significant that the lowest depths of hell are figured precisely in terms of being 'forgotten by God.'[10]

Lev Shestov spoke of Dostoevsky as one of those to whom the angel of death had granted an additional eye, enabling him to see human life in a perspective closed to the majority of humankind, absorbed as they are in the busy affairs of life.[11] In fact, his retelling of the moments before the scaffold does not suggest that he was expecting his individual self-consciousness to survive the firing squad's bullets, but texts such as 'Will I see Masha again?' and the testimony of the novels indicate that immortality became a defining part of his faith. When old man Karamazov asks his sons Ivan and Alyosha whether they believed in God, he makes the question one of God *and* immortality. These, it seems, are indivisible and for many readers the religious climax of the novel is Alyosha's luminous dream vison of Zosima sharing the eternal banquet of Christ's presence, figured in the biblical image of the wedding feast at Cana of Galilee.[12]

---

[6] Friedrich Schleiermacher, *On Religion: Speeches to its Cultured Despisers*, trans. and ed. Richard Crouter (Cambridge: Cambridge University Press, 1988), 140.

[7] DW, 192–6/PSS22, 32–7. On Russian occultism see Bernice Glatzer Rosenthal (ed.), *The Occult in Russian and Soviet Culture* (Ithaca, NY: Cornell University Press, 1997).

[8] See Commentary 1.2.

[9] On the 'ancient fires' see BK, 683/PSS15, 78; for hell as the impossibility of loving see BK, 336/PSS14, 292.

[10] BK, 253/PSS14, 225.

[11] See Marina C. Ogden, *Lev Shestov's Angel of Death: Memory, Trauma and Rebirth* (Oxford: Peter Land, 2021), 26–37.

[12] The Book of Revelation also uses 'the marriage feast of the lamb' (i.e. Christ) as a symbol of the Christian heaven (Rev. 19.9).

Over and above figures of luminosity, divine presence, and joy, Dostoevsky does not offer much detail regarding what a life after death might be like, although this is equally true of much religious teaching. Indeed, many would say that too much detail is inappropriate since a significant level of mystery is inherent in the subject itself. Dante gave a famously detailed account of the successive levels of hell, purgatory, and heaven, but he also insists that the visible forms of the afterlife are determined more by the space-and-time-bound character of our imaginations than the reality that is being represented.[13]

Perhaps more interesting than trying to reconstruct a systematic account of Dostoevsky's belief in immortality is to observe how he represents immortality in his novels. To borrow a distinction favoured by Kierkegaard, it is less a matter of *what* he says and more a matter of *how* he says it.

There are two elements here.

The first has to do with the representative character of fiction. When Dostoevsky published *Poor Folk*, his first novel, many felt that he had given cultural acknowledgement to those 'poor folk' who had, until then, had no place in literature. From then on, such people are no longer forgotten but are 'remembered' through their literary representatives. It is true that these are not actual individuals, but it is possible for actual individuals who see themselves in them to know that through such literary representation their lives are recognized and validated—perhaps, in a religious context, to know that they are remembered before God. In this perspective, it was Dostoevsky's service to remember precisely those marginal characters that so offended Brandes—the drunkards, prostitutes, simpletons, and all-round failures who peopled his fictional world. Dostoevsky's human comedy serves as a testimony or memorial to just these people, an invitation to expand our memory beyond the heroes and cultural icons to the whole company of suffering humanity.

Another level of novelistic memory has to do with the way in which the novelist not only records what happened to his characters, he also shares their memories and in doing so creates new memories for his readers. These are not just memories of events, but also of those events becoming part of the characters' inner lives. A striking example of how this works is the motif of 'the slanting rays of the setting sun'. These are part of Alyosha's childhood memory of his mother, but, as noted in the Commentary on the second Conversation, the image is also found in Dickens's *The Old Curiosity Shop*, when Little Nell stands in the porch of an old church looking out at the last rays of the sun. This passage is specifically referred to in *A Raw Youth*, in which it is cited by Trishatov, a minor character, who adds that what we see in Nell is 'a soul full of wonder, as though before some mystery, for both alike are mysteries, the sun, the thought of God, and the church,

---

[13] See *Paradiso*, Canto IV, 40–57.

the thought of man…'. He goes on to tell Arkady (the 'raw youth') that this stirs a memory of reading the novel with his sister on the terrace of their country house, also when the sun was setting, 'and suddenly we left off reading, and said to one another that we would be kind too, that we would be good…'.[14]

Although this passage is marginal to the overall narrative of *A Raw Youth*, it offers a very concise illustration of how a memory created by fiction becomes woven into our actual memories and shapes our interpretation of them. At the same time, the case of Trishatov complexifies the matter further, since all we know of him is that he has fallen into bad company, was arrested for some misdemeanour, and has been disowned by his family. His promise to be kind and good seems not to have come to fruition. This contradiction is perhaps implicit in the image of the setting sun, that is, a sun that gives light but not the warmth necessary for life. It is the symbol of an aspiration to goodness that lacks the moral energy necessary for its realization. Something similar seems to be in play in other passages where the setting sun is significantly emphasized by Dostoevsky: Claude Lorraine's landscape paintings of the golden age, Nastasia Phillipovna's imaginative picture of a sentimentalized Christ figure sitting and dreamily contemplating the setting sun, and, albeit in a very different key, Alyosha's hysterical mother, who believes but is powerless to escape the horrific marriage trap into which she has fallen. In each of these examples, the mysterious fourfold of God, the sun, the church, and the meaning of human existence is in play, pointing to possibilities of existence alien to the materialism and self-interest of the nineteenth century, yet, purely as memories, they lack the power to move reality in the direction to which they point. As Trishatov says regretfully at the end of his brief oration, 'Ach…every man has his memories!'

In the beginning of Western philosophy, Plato used the sun, the ultimate source of light, as a defining metaphor for the supreme idea. John's gospel identified Christ as the divine light, the light that enlightens every human being and that darkness cannot overcome (John 1.4–5). As such it is the light in which we not only see but also understand our world, the light that helps make final sense of things. All these connotations are present in the light in which Alyosha glimpses his departed Elder amongst the guests at the heavenly wedding feast. 'Do you not see our Sun,' Zosima asks him, meaning Christ—but that light is too bright for Alyosha to look at directly. The point here is that this is not just the narrator's retelling of what Alyosha saw, it is the novelist's invention of a vision of eternal life that, like the scene of Little Nell at the church, has the potential to be taken up into readers' own memories, informing and interpreting what those memories ultimately mean. However, the light of Christ is not a light that will

---

[14] RW, 435/PSS13, 353.

fade with the passing of time: it is the light into which we are moving throughout our lives.

I have several times drawn attention to the role of Hegelianism in Dostoevsky's world and Hegel's philosophy also helps show the philosophical importance of memory. In one of his more famous sayings, Hegel commented that it is only at dusk that the Owl of Minerva, the goddess of wisdom, takes flight, meaning that it is only when an epoch of history has come to an end that we can truly understand it. At the same time, Hegel plays on the distinction between the simple memory of facts (which he calls *Gedächtnis*) and recollection (*Erinnerung*), which carries the connotation of internalization, indicating that what is important is not just to remember the facts but to understand their inner meaning and to grasp their significance for our own spiritual education.[15] Dostoevsky's art too offers more than a chronicle of fictional facts; it attempts to penetrate into what these facts reveal about that characters' *and our own* inner beliefs, hopes, fears, demons, and desires—including, of course, the desire for God and immortality. But Dostoevsky is not simply performing a literary variation on a Hegelian theme. For many of Hegel's critics, the philosopher had collapsed expectation of a life to come into the timeless contemplation of the inner truth of history, but this was not the same as Christian hope of 'the life of the world to come' to which the future-directed power of Dostoevskian memory gestures.

This difference can also be illustrated by contrasting the role of memory in Dostoevsky and Proust. For the motto of *The Brothers Karamazov*, Dostoevsky chose words from John's gospel: 'Very truly, I tell you, unless a grain of wheat falls into the earth and dies, it remains just a single grain; but if it dies, it bears much fruit' (John 12.24). The same words are used by Proust when, approaching the end of his monumental 'search for lost time', the narrator realizes that the materials of literature are simply the materials of his own life, materials that, through writing, he has been able to liberate from bondage to time, effecting a kind of rebirth and even resurrection. For those who can thus penetrate into the 'essence' of their lives 'the word death has no meaning...being situated beyond time, how might such a one fear the future'.[16] This, we may say, also exemplifies the nineteenth-century idea of eternal life as timelessness.

Dostoevsky too sees literature's highest task as effecting a kind of resurrection. Yet, where Proust's vision is achieved, in an almost Hegelian sense, through the remembrance of things past (a kind of phenomenology of the narrator's life and times), the world depicted in Dostoevsky's novels seems at first glance not to offer much hope for any kind of resurrection. In the world inhabited by Prince

---

[15] See G. W. F. Hegel, *The Philosophy of Right*, trans. T. M. Knox (Oxford: Oxford University Press, 1967), 13. This can be read as a historicized version of Plato's notion that all knowledge is recollection of the eternal ideas that we beheld prior to our birth but which are eclipsed by the materiality of earthly existence.

[16] Marcel Proust, *Le temps retrouvé* (Paris: Gallimard, 1990), 179.

Myshkin, the 'possessed', and the Karamazovian 'reptiles devouring each other', we cannot find more than ambiguous and faltering grounds for hope—no matter how scrupulously we recollect each detail of what has been lived through. Like the distraught narrator of *A Gentle Spirit*, there are too many for whom the sun is dead and the call to love an empty and alien demand. Just remembering the past will not provide grounds for hope—but Dostoevskian memory can do more.

Even with regard to this-worldly memories, Dostoevsky acknowledged that he would add to and correct the spontaneous memories that came to him in long hours of enforced idleness in prison, thus drawing out and developing a meaning that was more than the memory of a simple fact. In this way, as he put it, he lived his life again as if new.[17] In Alyosha's dream vision, he goes further and creates a memory for his readers that is not just a memory of the past—although, in the narrative frame of the novel, this is clearly something that happened to Alyosha on such-and-such a late summer evening in the late 1860s. Following Dostoevsky's Eucharistic model, the memory that is being recalled is also a memory of what we shall or—given the requirement of freely choosing—*might* be, a memory of the end. Such a memory certainly doesn't prove anything about eternal life but it does serve as an image of what eternal life is or could or might *mean*, pointing us towards the ultimate transfiguration of human possibilities in the resurrection life. This is—obviously—not an argument, but it is a counter-image to those other images of human destiny that were increasingly dominant in Dostoevsky's time. For readers, it cannot be one of those childhood memories so valued by Zosima and perhaps Dostoevsky realized that his contemporaries and following generations would have fewer memories of childhood Bible stories and awe-inspiring rituals like those cherished by his fictional Elder. In face of this cultural memory loss, 'Cana of Galilee' is offered as a memory capable of nourishing in readers the new life into which those who freely turn to Christ are to live. Without such memories, Dostoevsky's logic implies, we have nothing to build on in the face of nihilism. Neither an argument for immortality nor the mere restatement of ecclesiastical dogma would at this point be enough. If we cannot imagine eternal life in a way that moves us, then neither philosophy nor dogma will persuade us. Whether or not this particular image 'works' for readers, it shows something of what is needed if we are to imagine ourselves and our place in the world otherwise than the nihilistic combination of scientific reductionism, economic self-interest, and the politics of the anthill suggest. The slanting rays of the setting sun offer consolation to those battered by the storms of earthly existence and are certainly not despised by Dostoevsky. But that consolation is ultimately sentimental, at best the consolation of a gentle melancholy. The light that bathes the guests who drink the new wine of Christ's heavenly banquet, by way of contrast, is the light of

---

[17] DW, 207/PSS22, 47.

a new and rising sun that promises more than consolation, since it promises—and gives—the joy that Zosima teaches is the foundation of spiritual life.

Additional Points

The view of Dostoevsky as a kind of Platonist is put forward in A. Steinberg, *Dostoievsky* (London: Bowes and Bowes, 1966), 85–93. Steinberg relates this directly to the question of immortality, speaking of Dostoevsky's 'panpsychism' and 'panpersonalism'.

Zosima's teaching that joy is the foundational impulse of the Christian life has a likely source in Isaac of Syria's homily 'On the Harm of Foolish Zeal That Has the Guise of Being Divine, and on the Help That Comes of Clemency and on Other Subjects' in Isaac of Syria, *Ascetical Homilies*, trans. anon. (Boston, MA: Holy Transfiguration Monastery, 2011), 243–8.

Commentary on the Epilogue and Postscript

Dostoevsky's Politics (III)

In previous commentaries, I have sketched the outlines of Dostoevsky's politics in the context of his own life and times and in relation to the conservative revolution of the interwar years. The postscript invites us to reflect on his influence in the present time, especially with regard to the 'Russian world' ideology associated with the philosopher Alexander Dugin and the political rhetoric developed by the Russian leadership to justify the invasion of Ukraine.

Several internet pundits draw attention to links between Dostoevsky and Putinism, as in an article posted after the invasion of Ukraine that 'Dostoevsky's endorsement of the Tsar's autocratic regime and orthodoxy of the Church would lead one safely to assume that he could have supported Putin's initiatives in the renewal of Russia's place in the world as a model for mankind.'[1]

Putin for his part has certainly appealed to Dostoevsky. In his speech to the Valdai conference on 27 October 2022 (nine months after the invasion of Ukraine) he argues that despite its rhetoric of promoting freedom, Western liberalism was now engaged in the complete suppression of anything that contradicted its view of what was socially and culturally desirable. And, he told his audience, 'Fyodor Dostoyevsky prophetically foretold all this back in the nineteenth century.' Specifically, Putin cites Shigalev, one of the nihilistic conspirators in the *The Possessed*. Shigalev is a gloomy theorist who realizes that his plans for unlimited freedom will result in unlimited despotism.[2] 'This', says Putin, 'is what our Western opponents have come to.' Specifically, he applies Shigalev's remark to cancel culture, comparing it to Nazi book-burning and contrasting it with the fact that, even during the Cold War, American and Soviet leaders maintained a respect for each other's cultural achievements. Now, however, even a Dostoevsky is

---

[1] 'Dostoevsky and Nationalism', posted without authorial credit on the University of British Columbia's site UBC Wiki on 26 March 2022: https://wiki.ubc.ca/Dostoevsky_and_Nationalism. The article references Tim Brinkhof, 'What classic Russian literature can tell us about Putin's war on Ukraine', *The Past* (March 2022): https://bigthink.com/the-past/russia-literature-ukraine-putin/ (accessed 19 October 2022), which relies significantly on Kohn's article 'Dostoevsky's Nationalism', discussed in section one of the Commentary on the Fifth Conversation.

[2] See P, 365/PSS10, 331.

cancelled.[3] But this is only one example from a much larger pattern: 'the erasure of all differences is what underlies the Western model of globalization', he said. By way of contrast, where the West suppresses all differences, the Russian world allows for a genuine plurality of world views and religions to happily co-exist, each following their own path. Although he does not directly cite Dostoevsky this time, this is a thought found in, for example, Dostoevsky's Pushkin speech.[4]

The identification of contemporary Russia's Western enemies with 'the possessed' is not unprecedented. A 2014 exhibition by the artist Yurij Danich featured a work entitled *Demons*, portraying a selection of President Putin's liberal opponents as the eponymous 'demons' from the novel *The Possessed*. Indicative of the stakes in such interpretations is the fact that one of these, Boris Nemtsov, was murdered the following year in what is widely regarded as a politically motivated assassination.[5] The TV version of the novel, including an emphatic presentation of Shatov's speech on Russia's 'god-bearing' mission, was broadcast on the same day as the May 2014 presidential elections in Ukraine, with clear political implications.[6]

There is no doubt, then, that Dostoevsky has been enlisted in the Putinist cause and it must be conceded that there are many elements in his own writings, especially about Russia and the West, that resonate with what Putin's supporters are saying. I have previously noted the exceptionalist rhetoric he himself used in relation to foreign policy, claiming that even if peace is in general preferable to war, this does not apply to Russia, a comment that resonates with many of the counter-intuitive declarations made by the Russian government in the course of the war in Ukraine.[7] We must honestly, if regretfully, acknowledge that the elements to which Putinists appeal are actually there in the texts. These readings do not come from nowhere. On the other hand, even in the midst of his most bellicose writings, Dostoevsky insisted that Russia should never use force or expand its territory at the expense of other Slavic nations—such as, perhaps, Ukraine.[8]

At the same time, we can and must repeat the caution regarding Dostoevsky's conservative revolutionary readers, namely, that even the seemingly monological

---

[3] A course on Dostoevsky at the University of Milano-Bicocca was cancelled following the invasion of Ukraine but was reinstated within days following public outcry. This is very far from the picture of total suppression depicted by Putin.

[4] References are to President Vladimir Putin's address to the final plenary session of the Valdai International Discussion Club, held in Moscow on 27 October 2022 and quoted from http://en.kremlin.ru/events/president/news/69695 (accessed 15 November 2022). On the Pushkin speech see the first part of the Commentary on the fifth Conversation.

[5] See Irina Kuznetsova, 'Demons on the Screen', *Mundo Eslavo*, Vol. 16 (2017), 154–62. See also the first section of the Commentary on the Fifth Conversation.

[6] This further information is from the unpublished version of Kuznetsova's paper 'Demons on the Screen' presented at the International Dostoevsky Society conference in Granada in 2016. See the first section of the Commentary on the Third Conversation.

[7] See Commentary on the first section of the Fifth Conversation; on Dostoevsky's claim see DW, 666/PSS25, 99.

[8] DW, 900/PSS26, 80.

Diary has significant internal tensions and is at the same time very context-specific. As the narrator points out, it is not self-evident that the contemporary Russian state is the inheritor of the tsarist state that Dostoevsky admired, a point that, as Dostoevsky mentions in the fifth Conversation, is also a question of language. President Putin's political genius is perhaps letting himself be seen both as the continuator of the Soviet Union and as a new tsar, sanctified by the blessing of the Russian Orthodox Church. This may work politically, but it is theoretically incoherent, unless one resorts to Merezhkovsky's argument that it doesn't really matter whether autocracy wears a pagan, Christian, or Soviet mask—it is the same beast underneath. The narrator's view that Dostoevsky's analysis of nihilism might be applied to the Russian president seems not implausible—indeed, a similar application was already made by André Glucksmann long before the invasion of Ukraine, emphasizing Putin's ability to project multiple identities while pursuing policies of ruthless internal and external repression.[9]

Dostoevsky's political statements in the *Diary* are directly political. Yet his idealized image of Russia has perhaps a certain poetic and imaginative power that is not reducible to the political. As in many other cases, an idealized national image of one's country is Janus-faced. Seen from one angle, it presents a hostile face towards the rest of the world. Seen from another, it can be a call and a challenge to the nation concerned to live up to its own best possibilities. William Blake's 'Jerusalem' is a striking example: conceived as a quasi-revolutionary challenge to England's powers-that-be, it is today sung in national contexts in a way that seems more to affirm what 'England' is rather than what it ought to be. Dostoevsky himself was aware of the possibilities of ambiguity here, as illustrated in Prince Myshkin's hyperbolic speech about the virtues of the Russian aristocracy to an audience of aristocrats who are, in fact, infinitely far from embodying the virtues he is praising. Myshkin is naïve, but his author makes it clear that his 'praise' of the aristocracy is in fact an indictment of them—as long as they fail to be what they could be and do what they could do for Russia.[10] It is not difficult to extend the example to Russia as a whole. The vision of a nation brought together through prayerful and hard-earned solidarity with every member of society, inclusive of all its insulted and injured 'unfortunates', each of whose stories deserves remembering as part of the national story; a nation whose members are committed to mutual forgiveness and forbearance, who celebrate their distinctive cultural life, and, not least, value their natural environment, is not an ignoble vision. If this is Dostoevsky's democracy, it is not so hard to see why it may continue, rightly, to inspire those suffering the continuing tragedy of Russian history and, equally, those in many other nations where people remain condemned to subcultures of poverty, family breakdown, violence, alcohol and drug addiction

---

[9] André Glucksmann, *Dostoïevski à Manhattan* (Paris: Robert Laffon, 2002).
[10] I, 540–3/PSS8, 456–9.

and whose situation is compounded by the exclusiveness of educational, legal, and religious systems—all of which is plentifully and unrelentingly displayed in Dostoevsky's novels.[11]

This is perhaps a disappointing point at which to leave Dostoevsky, but it would be unrealistic to imagine him spared the ambiguities and tragic conflicts that mark the course of a common human history in which, as Zosima insisted, each of us is guilty. Understanding is available to any of us only as engaged participants in the ongoing self-discovery of what it is to be human effected in the work of philosophy, within and beyond the academy.[12] There is no view *sub specie aeternitatis* ('in the light of eternity'), as Kierkegaard complained about the Hegelians' claim to see history as a whole. Every new insight is provisional, partial, and requires interpretation. We must therefore resist the specious argument that the Russian world ideology's Dostoevsky is the 'true' Dostoevsky. Like other great authors, Dostoevsky continues to be generative of multiple readings and fresh insights into the human condition. For good and ill—and if for ill, then also for good.

The main focus of these Conversations has been Dostoevsky's Christian thought and how he deployed a manifold of Christian themes, images, and stories to offer a way through the 'despair of meaninglessness'. This has also led us to his politics and anti-Semitism. This was unavoidable and any account of his religious views that does not mention these is always going to fall short of entire credibility. Yet neither the religion nor the politics (nor for that matter the gambling, the women, the literary polemics, and the many other facets of his life and work) is the whole Dostoevsky. Bakhtin argued that the Dostoevskian novel was essentially polyphonic and had the quality that he called 'unfinalizability'. Whether and to what extent these claims are true of individual novels and how far they can be applied to the *Diary* are properly debatable and require attention to the specific detail of the texts in question, but to the extent that it is even possible to speak of the 'whole' Dostoevsky they certainly apply to the author of the novels and the *Diary*. Dostoevsky is not yet finished with us, nor we with him. This is not the end.

---

[11] For insights on Dostoevsky's 'ground-up' democracy, see Nancy Ruttenberg, *Dostoevsky's Democracy* (Princeton, NJ: Princeton University Press, 2008).

[12] I take 'philosophy' in this sense to be what happens whenever human beings talk seriously together and with a sustained interest in the truth of what they are saying with regard to the fundamental questions of existence, a rephrasing perhaps of Dostoevsky's own 'eternal questions'.

Bibliography

Works by Dostoevsky

The Brothers Karamazov, trans. Constance Garnett (London: Heinemann, 1912).
Crime and Punishment, trans. Constance Garnett (London: Heinemann, 1914).
The Diary of a Writer, trans. Boris Brasol (Haslemere: Ianmead, 1984).
An Honest Thief and Other Stories, trans. Constance Garnett (London: Heinemann, 1919).
The House of the Dead, trans. Constance Garnett (London: Heinemann, 1915).
The Idiot, trans. Constance Garnett (New York, NY: Macmillan, 1951).
The Notebooks for The Idiot, ed. Edward Wasiolek and trans. Katharine Strelsky (Chicago, IL: University of Chicago Press, 1967).
Polnoe Sobranie Sochinenii v tridtsati tomakh [Complete Collected Works in thirty volumes] (Leningrad: Nauka, 1972–88).
The Possessed, trans. Constance Garnett (London: Heinemann, 1914).
A Raw Youth, trans. Constance Garnett (London: Heinemann, 1916).
White Nights and Other Stories, trans. Constance Garnett (London: Heinemann, 1918).
Winter Notes on Summer Impressions, trans. Kiril Fitzlyon (London: Alma 2021).

Works on Dostoevsky

Belknap, Robert E., *The Genesis of the Brothers Karamazov: The Aesthetics, Ideology, and Psychology of Making a Text* (Evanston, IL: Northwestern University Press, 1990).
Berdyaev, Nicholas, *Dostoevsky*, trans. Donald Attwater (New York, NY: Meridian, 1957).
Birmingham, Kevin, *The Sinner and the Saint: Dostoevsky, a Crime and Its Punishment* (London: Allen Lane, 2021).
Blank, Ksana, *Dostoevsky's Dialectics and the Problem of Sin* (Evanston, IL: Northwestern University Press, 2010).
Briggs, Katherine Jane, *How Dostoevsky Portrays Women in His Novels* (Lampeter: Edwin Mellen Press, 2009).
Bruck, Arthur Moeller van den, 'Die politische Voraussetzungen der Dostojewkischen Ideen', in Dostojewiski, F. M., *Politische Schriften*, trans. E. K. Rahsin (Munich: Piper, 1922), ix–xiv.
Carr, E. H., *Dostoevsky 1821–1881* (London: Unwin Books, 1962).
Carver, Raymond and Gallagher, Tess, *Dostoevsky: A Screen Play* (Santa Barbara, CA: Capra Press, 1985).
Cassedy, Steven, *Dostoevsky's Religion* (Stanford, CA: Stanford University Press, 2005).
Cassedy, Steven, 'Who Says Miracles Can't Be the Basis for Faith? More Reasons Why Dostoevsky's Religion Isn't Christianity', *Dostoevsky Studies*, New Series, Vol. 13 (2009), 37–45.
Catteau, Jacques, *Dostoevsky and the Process of Literary Creation*, trans. Audrey Littlewood (Cambridge: Cambridge University Press, 1989).
Cherkasova, Evgenia, *Dostoevsky and Kant: Dialogues on Ethics* (Amsterdam: Rodopi, 2009).

Chestov, Léon, *La Philosophie de la Tragédie: Dostoïevski et Nietzsche*, trans. Boris de Schloezer (Paris: Le Bruit du Temps, 2012).
Christofi, Alex, *Dostoevsky in Love: An Intimate Life* (London: Bloomsbury, 2021).
Cicovacki, Predrag, *Dostoevsky and the Affirmation of Life* (New Brunswick, NJ: Transaction, 2012).
Coetzee, J. M., *The Master of Petersburg* (London: Secker and Wartburg, 1994).
Contino, Paul J., *Dostoevsky's Incarnational Realism* (Eugene, OR: Cascade Books, 2020).
Coulter, Stephen, *The Devil Inside: A Novel of Dostoevsky's Life* (London: Jonathan Cape, 1960).
Davison, R. M., 'Dostoevsky's *Devils*: The Role of Stepan Trofimovich Verkhovensky', in Leatherbarrow, W. J. (ed.), *Dostoevsky's Devils: A Critical Companion* (Evanston, IL: Northwestern University Press, 1999).
Desmond, John F., *Fyodor Dostoevsky, Walker Percy, and the Age of Suicide* (Washington, DC: Catholic University of America Press, 2019).
Djermanovic, Tamara, 'Estética de Dostoyevski y Tarkovski: la creatividad como visión del hombre, del apocalipsis y de la possibilidad de salvación', *Mundo Eslavo*, Vol. 16 (2017), 64–72.
Dodd, W. J., 'Ein Gottträgervolk, ein geistiger Führer: Die Dostojewskij-Rezeption von der Jahrhundertwende bis zu den zwanziger Jahren als Paradigma des deutschen Rußlandbilds', in Kopelew, L. (ed.), *West-östliche Spiegelungen, Reihe A: Russen und Rußland aus deutscher Sicht, Bd. 4, Das zwanzigste Jahrhundert* (Munich: Wilhelm Fink, 2000).
Dostoevsky, Anna, *Dostoevsky: Reminiscences*, trans. Beatrice Stillman (London: Wildwood, 1976).
Evdokimov, Paul, *Der Abstieg in der Hölle: Gogol und Dostojewskij* (Salzburg: Otto Müller Verlag, 1965).
Földényi, Lázló F., *Dostoevsky Reads Hegel in Siberia and Bursts into Tears*, trans. Ottilie Mulzet (Newhaven, CT: Yale University Press, 2020).
Frank, Joseph, *Dostoevsky: The Seeds of Revolt, 1821–1849* (Princeton, NJ: Princeton University Press, 1976).
Frank, Joseph, *Dostoevsky: The Years of Ordeal, 1850–1859* (Princeton, NJ: Princeton University Press, 1983).
Frank, Joseph, *Dostoevsky: The Stir of Liberation, 1860–1865* (Princeton, NJ: Princeton University Press, 1986).
Frank, Joseph, *Dostoevsky: The Miraculous Years, 1865–1871* (Princeton, NJ: Princeton University Press, 1995).
Frank, Joseph, *Dostoevsky: The Mantle of the Prophet, 1871–1881* (Princeton, NJ: Princeton University Press, 2002).
Frazier, Melissa, 'Sun-Bathed Steppes in French Prisons: Bresson Reading Dostoevsky', *Ulbandus Review*, Vol. 15, *Seeing Texts* (2013), 133–52.
Garstka, Christoph, 'Osama bin Stavrogin: Die Dämonen des islamitischen Terrors. Eine Auseinandersetzung mit André Glucksmanns *Dostoïevski à Manhattan*', *Dostoevsky Studies*, New Series, Vol. 22 (2018), 45–57.
Gibson, A. Boyce, *The Religion of Dostoevsky* (London: SCM Press, 1973).
Gide, André, *Dostoevsky* (Norfolk, CT: New Directions, 1961).
Givens, John, 'A Narrow Escape into Faith? Dostoevsky's "Idiot" and the Christology of Comedy', *The Russian Review*, Vol. 70, No. 1 (January 2011), 95–117.
Glucksmann, André, 'Bin Laden, Dostoevsky and the reality principle: an interview with André Glucksmann', https://www.opendemocracy.net/en/article_1111jsp/ (accessed 14 October 2022).

Glucksmann, André, *Dostoïevski à Manhattan* (Paris: Robert Laffon, 2002).
Goldstein, David L., *Dostoyevsky and the Jews* (Austin, TX: University of Texas Press, 1981).
Goodwin, James, *Confronting Dostoevsky's Demons: Anarchism and the Specter of Bakunin in Twentieth-Century Russia* (New York, NY: Peter Lang, 2010).
Guardini, Romano, 'Dostoyevsky's Idiot, a Symbol of Christ', trans. Francis X. Quinn, *Cross Currents*, Vol. 6, No. 4 (Fall 1956), 359.
Guardini, Romano, *Der Mensch und der Glaube: Versuche über die religiose Existenz in Dostojewskijs großen Romanen* (Leipzig: Hegner, 1933).
Guardini, Romano, *Religiöse Gestalten in Dostojewskijs Werk* (Munich: Kösel Verlag, 1977).
Holquist, Michael, *Dostoevsky and the Novel* (Princeton, NJ: Princeton University Press, 1977).
Hudspith, Sarah, *Dostoevsky and the Idea of Russianness: A New Perspective on Unity and Brotherhood* (London: Routledge, 2004).
Ingold, Felix Phillip, *Dostojewskij und das Judentum* (Frankfurt am Main: Insel Verlag, 1981).
Ivanits, Linda, *Dostoevsky and the Russian People* (Cambridge: Cambridge University Press, 2008).
Ivanov, Vyacheslav, *Freedom and the Tragic Life: A Study in Dostoevsky*, trans. Norman Cameron (New York, NY: Noonday, 1960).
Jackson, Robert L., *Dialogues with Dostoevsky: The Overwhelming Questions* (Stanford, CA: Stanford University Press, 1993).
Johae, Antony, 'Towards an Iconography of *Crime and Punishment*', in Pattison, George, and Thompson, Diane O. (eds.), *Dostoevsky and the Christian Tradition: Reading Dostoevsky Religiously* (Cambridge: Cambridge University Press, 2002), 177–80.
Jones, Malcolm, *Dostoevsky and the Dynamics of Religious Experience* (London: Anthem Press, 2005).
Kasatkina, A., *Dostoievski kak Filosof i Bogoslov: Khudozhestvenny Sposob Vyskazyvania* (Moscow: Volodei, 2019).
Kirillova, Irina, 'Dostoevsky's Markings in the Gospel According to St John', in Pattison, George, and Thompson, Diane O. (eds.), *Dostoevsky and the Christian Tradition: Reading Dostoevsky Religiously* (Cambridge: Cambridge University Press, 2002), 41–50.
Kirillova, Irina, *Obraz Khrista v tvorchestve Dostoevskogo: Razmyshlenia* (Moscow: Tsentr knigi VGBIL im. M. N. Rudomino, 2010), 82–102.
Kjetsaa, Geir, *Dostoevsky and His New Testament* (Atlantic Highlands, NJ: Humanities Press, 1984).
Knapp, Liza, *The Annihilation of Inertia: Dostoevsky and Metaphysics* (Evanston, IL: Northwestern University Press, 1996).
Knapp, Liza, 'Dostoevsky's "Journey through the Torments": Maternal Protest in *Notes from the Dead House*', in Aloe, Stefano (ed.), *Su Fëdor Dostovskij: Visione filosofica e sguardo di scrittore* (Naples: La scuola di Pitagor, 2012), 413–30.
Kohn, Hans, 'Dostoevsky's Nationalism', *Journal of the History of Ideas*, Vol. 6, No. 4 (October 1945), 385–414.
Kostalevsky, Marina, *Dostoevsky and Soloviev: The Art of Integral Vision* (Newhaven, CT: Yale University Press, 1997).
Kroeker, P. Travis and Ward, Bruce K., *Remembering the End: Dostoevsky as Prophet to Modernity* (Boulder, CO: Westview Press, 2001).
Kuznetsova, Irina, 'Demons on the Screen', *Mundo Eslavo*, Vol. 16 (2017), 154–62.
Lary, N. M., *Dostoevsky and Soviet Film: Visions of Demonic Realism* (Ithaca, NY: Cornell University Press, 1986).

Lauth, Reinhard, 'Ich habe die Wahrheit gesehen': Die Philosophie Dostojewskis in systematischer Darstellung (Munich: Piper, 1950).
Leontiev, K. N., O Vsemirnoï Lyubvi: Rech F. M. Dostoevskogo na Pushkinskom Prazdnike (On universal love: Dostoevsky's speech at the celebrations in honour of Pushkin), http://www.odinblago.ru/filosofiya/leontev_kn_o_vsemirno/.
Levina, A., 'Nekaiushaiasia Magdalena ili Pochemu knaz' Myshkin ne mog spasti Nastasiu Phillipovnu', in Dostoievski i mirovaia kul'tura, Almanakh No. 2 of the Obshestvo Dostoievskogo (St Petersburg: Dostoevsky Museum Publications, 1994), 97–118.
Macedo, O'Dwyer de, Clinical Lessons on Life and Madness: Dostoevsky's Characters, trans. Agnès Jacob (London: Routledge, 2019).
Marcel, Gabriel, 'Interview', in Catteau, Jacques (ed.), Dostoïevski (Paris: Herne [Série Slave], 1973).
Martinsen, Deborah A., Surprised by Shame: Dostoevsky's Liars and Narrative Exposure (Columbus, OH: Ohio University Press, 2003).
McReynolds, Susan, Redemption and the Merchant God: Dostoevsky's Economy of Salvation and Antisemitism (Evanston, IL: Northwestern University Press, 2008).
Merezhkovsky, Dmitri, Tolstoy as Man and Artist: With an Essay on Dostoievski (London: Constable, 1902).
Merezhkovsky, Dmitri, 'Die Religiöse Revolution', in Dostojewiski, F. M., Politische Schriften, trans. E. K. Rahsin (Munich: Piper, 1922), xxv–xlvi.
Moran, John P., The Solution of the Fist: Dostoevsky and the Roots of Modern Terrorism (Lanham, MD: Lexington Books, 2009).
Moran, John P., 'This Star Will Shine Forth from the East: Dostoevsky and the Politics of Humility', in Avramenko, Richard, and Trepanier, Lee (eds.), Dostoevsky's Political Thought (Lanham, MD: Lexington Books, 2013), 51–72.
Nikoliukin, A. N., 'Dostoevskii in Constance Garnett's Translation', in Leatherbarrow, W. J., Dostoevskii and Britain (Oxford: Berg, 1995), 207–27.
Niqueux, Michel, Dictionnaire Dostoïevski (Paris: Institut des Études Slaves, 2021).
Onasch, Konrad, Der verschweigene Christus: Versuch über die Poetisierung des Christentums in der Dichtung F. M. Dostojewskis (Berlin: Union Verlag, 1976).
Pattison, George, 'Hiob als Intertext: Dostojewskis "Die Bruder Karamasow"', in Ratschow, L., and von Sass, H. (eds.), Die Anfechtung Gottes (Leipzig, 2016), 263–76.
Pattison, George and Thompson, Diane O., Dostoevsky and the Christian Tradition: Reading Dostoevsky Religiously (Cambridge: Cambridge University Press, 2002).
Ruttenberg, Nancy, Dostoevsky's Democracy (Princeton, NJ: Princeton University Press, 2008).
Salvestroni, Simonetta, Dostoïevski et la Bible, trans. Pierre Laroche (Paris: Lethielleux, 2004).
Scanlan, James, Dostoevsky the Thinker (Ithaca, NY: Cornell University Press, 2002).
Shklovsky, Viktor, Za i Protiv: Zametki o Dostoevskom (Moscow: Sovetskii Pisatel', 1957).
Skakov Nariman, 'Dostoevsky's Christ and Silence at the Margins of The Idiot', Dostoevsky Studies: The Journal of the International Dostoevsky Society, New Series, Vol. 13 (2009), 121–40.
Srigley, Ron, 'The End of the Ancient World: Dostoevsky's Confidence Game', in Avramenko, Richard, and Trepanier, Lee (eds.), Dostoevsky's Political Thought (Lanham, MD: Lexington Books, 2013), 201–22.
Straus, Nina Pelikan, Dostoevsky and the Woman Question: Rereadings at the End of the Century (New York, NY: St Martin's Press, 1994).
Stuchebrukhov, Olga, 'Hesychastic Ideas and the Concept of Integral Knowledge in Crime and Punishment', Dostoevsky Studies, New Series, Vol. 13 (2009), 77–91.

Thompson, Diane O., *Dostoevsky and the Poetics of Memory* (Cambridge: Cambridge University Press, 1991).
Thompson, Diane O., 'Problems of the Biblical Word in Dostoevsky's Poetics', in Pattison, George, and Thompson, Diane O. (eds.), *Dostoevsky and the Christian Tradition: Reading Dostoevsky Religiously* (Cambridge: Cambridge University Press, 2002), 69–99.
Thurneysen, Eduard, *Dostoevsky*, trans. Keith Crim (Louisville, KT: John Knox Press, 1964 [in German, 1921]).
Toumayan, S., '"I more than the others": Dostoevsky and Levinas', *Yale French Studies*, Vol. 104, *Encounters with Levinas* (2004), 55–66.
Trost, Klaus, *Dostojewski und die Liebe: Zwischen Dominanz und Demut* (Hamburg: Tredition, 2020).
Troyat, Henry, *Firebrand: The Life of Dostoevsky*, trans. Norbert Guterman (London: Heinemann, 1946 [original version in French, 1940]).
Tsypkin, Leonid, *Summer in Baden Baden: From the Life of Dostoyevsky*, trans. Roger and Angela Keys (London: Quartet, 1987).
Williams, Rowan, *Dostoevsky: Language, Faith and Fiction* (London: Continuum, 2008).
Wyman, Alina, *The Gift of Active Empathy: Scheler, Bakhtin, and Dostoevsky* (Evanston, IL: Northwestern University Press, 2016).
Ziolkowksi, Eric, 'Reading and Incarnation in Dostoevsky', in Pattison, George, and Thompson, Diane O. (eds.), *Dostoevsky and the Christian Tradition: Reading Dostoevsky Religiously* (Cambridge: Cambridge University Press, 2002), 156–70.
Ziolkowski, Margaret, 'Dostoevsky and the kenotic tradition', in Pattison, George, and Thompson, Diane O. (eds.), *Dostoevsky and the Christian Tradition: Reading Dostoevsky Religiously* (Cambridge: Cambridge University Press, 2002), 31–40.

Other Works Cited

Arjakovsky, Antoine, 'The Way, The Journal of the Russian Emigration (1925–40)', in Emerson, Caryl, Pattison, George, and Poole, Randall (eds.), *The Oxford Handbook of Russian Religious Thought* (Oxford: Oxford University Press, 2020), 441–4.
Barth, Karl, *The Epistle to the Romans*, trans. Edwyn C. Hoskyns (Oxford: Oxford University Press, 1933).
Beauvoir, Simone de, *Pyrrhus et Cinéas* (Paris: Gallimard, 1971).
Berdyaev, Nicholas, *Solitude and Society*, trans. George Reavey (London: Geoffrey Bles, 1947 [1938]).
Brandes, Georg, *Indtryk fra Rusland* (Copenhagen: Gyldendal, 1888).
Brinkhof, Tim, 'What classic Russian literature can tell us about Putin's war on Ukraine', *The Past* (March 2022), https://bigthink.com/the-past/russia-literature-ukraine-putin/ (accessed 19 October 2022).
Brown, David, *Divine Humanity: Kenosis Explored and Defended* (London: SCM Press, 2011).
Buber, Martin and Friedman, Maurice S., 'Guilt and Guilt Feeling', *CrossCurrents*, Vol. 8, No. 3 (1958), 63–92.
Camus, Albert, *The Myth of Sisyphus*, trans. Justin O'Brien (Harmondsworth: Penguin, 1975).
Chestov, Léon, *Kierkegaard et la philosophie existentielle* (Paris: Vrin, 1936).
Coates, Ruth, *Deification in Russian Religious Thought between the Revolutions, 1905–1917* (Oxford: Oxford University Press, 2019).

Davison, R. M., 'Dostoevsky's *Devils*: The Role of Stepan Trofimovich Verkhovensky', in Leatherbarrow, W. J. (ed.), *Dostoevsky's Devils: A Critical Companion* (Evanston, IL: Northwestern University Press, 1999), 119–34.

Dudgeon, Ruth A., 'The Forgotten Minority: Women Students in Imperial Russia, 1872–1917', *Russian History*, Vol. 9, No. 1 (1982), 1–26.

Frye, Northrop, *The Great Code: The Bible and Literature* (London: Routledge and Kegan Paul, 1982).

Gavrilyuk, Paul L., *The Suffering of the Impassible God: The Dialectics of Patristic Thought* (Oxford: Oxford University Press, 2004).

Gorodetzky, Nadejda, *The Humiliated Christ in Modern Russian Thought* (London: SPCK, 1938).

Guérin Benjamin, 'Chestov—Kierkegaard: Faux ami, étranger fraternité', in Fotiade, Ramona, and Schwab, Françoise (eds.), *Léon Chestov—Vladimir Jankélévitch: Du tragique à l'ineffable* (Saarbrücken: Éditions universitaires européennes, 2011), 113–32.

Harris, Robert, 'Granovsky, Herzen and Chicherin: Hegel and the Battle for Russia's Soul', in Herzog, Lisa (ed.), *Hegel's Thought in Europe: Currents, Crosscurrents and Undercurrents* (Basingstoke: Palgrave Macmillan, 2013), 35–48.

Hegel, G. W. F., *The Philosophy of Right*, trans. T. M. Knox (Oxford: Oxford University Press, 1967).

Hegel, G. W. F., *Vorlesungen über die Philosophie der Geschichte* in *Werke*, Vol. 12 (Frankfurt: Suhrkamp, 1970).

Heidegger, G. (ed.), *'Mein liebes Seelchen!' Briefe Martin Heideggers an seine Frau Elfride 1915–1970* (Munich: Deutsche-Verlags-Anstalt, 2005).

Heidegger, Martin, *Frühe Schriften* (Frankfurt am Main: Vittorio Klostermann, 1972).

Hesse, Herman, *Blick ins Chaos* (Bern: Seldwyla, 1922).

Kaufmann, Walter, *Existentialism from Dostoevsky to Sartre* (Cleveland, OH: Meridian Books, 1956).

Kellogg, Michael, *The Russian Roots of Nazism: White Émigrés and the Making of National Socialism, 1917–1945* (Cambridge: Cambridge University Press, 2005).

Jakim, Boris and Bird, Robert, *On Spiritual Unity: A Slavophile Reader. Aleksei Khomiakov. Ivan Kireevsky* (Hudson, NY: Lindisfarne Books, 1998).

Kant, Immanuel, *Critique of Practical Reason*, in *Practical Philosophy*, ed. and trans. Gregor, Mary J. A. (Cambridge: Cambridge University Press, 1996).

Klimoff, Alexis (ed.), *Materialy k 'Sporu o Sofii': Transactions of the Association of Russian-American Scholars in the U.S.A.*, Vol. 39, New York, 2014–16.

Kojève, Alexandre, *The Religious Metaphysics of Vladimir Solovyov*, trans. Ilya Merlin and Mikhail Pozdniakov (London: Palgrave Macmillan, 2018).

Marx, Karl, *Early Writings*, trans. Rodney Livingstone and Gregor Benton (Harmondsworth: Penguin, 1975).

Maclean, Caroline, *The Vogue for Russia: Modernism and the Unseen in Britain, 1900–1930* (Edinburgh: Edinburgh University Press, 2015).

McWeeny, Jennifer, 'Origins of Otherness: Non-Conceptual Ethical Encounters in Beauvoir and Levinas', *Simone de Beauvoir Studies*, Vol. 26 (2009–10), 5–17.

Nietzsche, Friedrich, *Also Sprach Zarathustra I–IV*, ed. Giorgio Colli and Mazzino Montinari (Berlin: de Gruyter, 1988).

Ogden, Marina C., *Lev Shestov's Angel of Death: Memory, Trauma and Rebirth* (Oxford: Peter Land, 2021).

Pattison, George, *Kierkegaard and the Theology of the Nineteenth Century* (Cambridge: Cambridge University Press, 2012).

Pattison, George, 'Man-God and "Godmanhood"', in Arblaster, John, and Faesen, Rob (eds.), *Theosis/Deification: Christian Doctrines of Divinization East and West* (Leuven: Peeters, 2018), 171–90.
Pattison, George, 'Berdyaev and Christian Existentialism', in Emerson, Caryl, Pattison, George, and Poole, Randall (eds.), *The Oxford Handbook of Russian Religious Thought* (Oxford: Oxford University Press, 2020), 450–63.
Plotnikov, Nikolaj, 'The Person Is a Monad with Windows': Sketch of a Conceptual History of "Person" in Russia', *Studies in East European Thought*, Vol. 64, No. 3/4 (November 2012), 269–99.
Proust, Marcel, *Le temps retrouvé* (Paris: Gallimard, 1990).
Rosenthal, Bernice Glatzer (ed.), *The Occult in Russian and Soviet Culture* (Ithaca, NY: Cornell University Press, 1997).
Rubenstein, Roberta, *Virginia Woolf and the Russian Point of View* (Basingstoke: Palgrave Macmillan, 2009).
Rubin, Dominic, 'Judaism and Russian Religious Thought', in Emerson, Caryl, Pattison, George, and Poole, Randall (eds.), *The Oxford Handbook of Russian Religious Thought* (Oxford: Oxford University Press, 2020).
Sartre, Jean-Paul, *Existentialisme est un humanisme* (Paris: Nagel, 1970).
Schleiermacher, Friedrich, *On Religion: Speeches to its Cultured Despisers*, trans. and ed. Richard Crouter (Cambridge: Cambridge University Press, 1988).
Smith, Oliver, 'Boehme in Russia', in Hessayon, Ariel, and Apetrei, Sarah (eds.), *An Introduction to Jacob Boehme: Four Centuries of Thought and Reception* (New York, NY: Routledge, 2014), 196–223.
Solovyev, Vladimir, *War, Progress and the End of History*, trans. A. Bakshy (London: Hodder and Stoughton, 1915).
Solovyev, Vladimir, *La Russie et L'Église universelle* (Paris: Stock, 1922 [1885]).
Solovyev, Vladimir, *Lectures on Godmanhood*, trans. Peter Zouboff (London: Dobsom, 1948).
Solovyev, Vladimir, 'Tri Rechi v Pamniat' Dostoevskogo', in *Sochenenia v dvukh tomakh*, Vol. 2 (Moscow: Mysl', 1990), 289–323.
Solovyev, Vladimir, *Lectures on Divine Humanity* (Hudson, NY: Lindisfarne, 1995).
Solovyev, Vladimir, *The Burning Bush: Writings on Jews and Judaism*, ed. Gregory Yuri Glazov (Notre Dame, IN: University of Notre Dame Press, 2016).
Tillich, Paul, *The Interpretation of History* (New York, NY: Charles Scribner's Sons, 1936).
Tillich, Paul, *The Courage to Be* (London: Fontana, 1962).
Valliere, Paul, *Modern Russian Theology: Bukharev, Soloviev, Bulgakov. Orthodox Theology in a New Key* (Edinburgh: T. & T. Clark, 2000).
Wainwright, Geoffrey, *Eucharist and Eschatology* (London: Epworth Press, 1971).
Walicki, Andrzej, *A History of Russian Thought from the Enlightenment to Marxism* (Oxford: Clarendon Press).
Williams, Rowan, *Looking East in Winter. Contemporary Thought and the Eastern Christian Tradition* (London: Bloomsbury Continuum, 2021).

Index

For the benefit of digital users, indexed terms that span two pages (e.g., 52–53) may, on occasion, appear on only one of those pages.

apophaticism 212
Arjakovsky, Antoine 284 n.31

Bakhtin, M. M. 211–12, 296
Bakunin, M. 262
Barth, Karl 283
Belinsky, Vissarion 219
Beauvoir, Simone de 245
Belknap, Robert E. 203
Berdyaev, Nikolai 234, 245–7, 268, 284
Bible, the 51–60, 223–7, 232, 235, 285–6, 291–2
Birmingham, Kevin 220 n.23
Blank, Ksana 221
Brandes, Georg 7, 237 n.48, 288
Bresson, Robert 64–7, 203, 242
Briggs, Katharine Jane 203–4, 247
brotherhood 100, 120–1, 123–8, 176, 282
Brown, David 257 n.23
Bruck, Arthur Moeller van den 281–2
Buber, Martin 216
Bulgakov, Mikhail 112
Bulgakov, Sergei 270

Camus, Albert 243–5
Carr, E. H. 272–4
Carver, Raymond 199
Cassedy, Steven 207 n.19, 208 n.25, 235, 257
Catteau, Jacques 211 n.38
Chernyshevsky, Nikolai 100, 276
Chestov, L. *see* Shestov, L.
Christ (Jesus), Christology *see also* Incarnation, kenoticism 57–60, 97, 104, 106–14, 139, 172, 176–81, 207–8, 231–8, 254–60, 269–70, 279, 286, 289–92
Christofi, Alex 198, 201 n.8
Cicovacki, Predrag 273 n.55
Coates, Ruth 258
Coetzee, J. M. 198–9
Contino, Paul J. 216
Coulter, Stephen 198

Davison, R. M. 242 n.5
death *see also* suicide 204, 287
death of children 47–9

Devil, the 103–4, 209, 255–6, 259–60, 287
Dickens, Charles 44, 46–8, 94–5, 223, 238–9, 288–9
Dostoevsky, Anna Grigorievna 247, 253, 260
Dostoevsky, Fyodor Mikhailovich
  Works discussed:
  The Brothers Karamazov 12–14, 27, 40–2, 48, 54, 59–60, 65–6, 85–6, 95–6, 98–9, 129, 134, 138–40, 150–2, 167–9, 176, 179–81, 203, 206, 209–10, 215–18, 225–6, 229–35, 241–3, 248, 253, 255–6, 268, 273–5, 278–9, 285–7, 289–91
  Crime and Punishment 51–2, 55, 66, 73–7, 150, 200, 225, 242, 248–51, 255, 278
  Demons see *The Possessed*
  Diary of a Writer 15–16, 23–5, 106–7, 118–19, 122–4, 146–8, 150–1, 154, 158–59, 192, 205–7, 213, 248, 261, 265–8, 277, 284, 294–6
  The Dream of a Ridiculous Man 14, 209,
  A Gentle Spirit 8–10, 21–3, 25–6, 34–5, 65, 112, 174, 203–5, 207, 220, 247
  The House of the Dead 69–70, 85, 151, 159–60, 182–3, 199, 254, 261–2, 277–8
  The Idiot 57–8, 64–5, 79–80, 112, 205 n.7, 209–10, 212, 225, 236–8, 248, 250–1
  The Insulted and the Injured 48–9, 228
  Notes from Underground 101, 203, 220–1, 243–4, 249, 274
  The Possessed 14, 26–7, 78, 84, 192, 204–5, 210, 219, 225, 241–2, 251, 256, 262–5, 279, 293–4
  A Raw Youth 84, 206, 211, 251, 277–8, 288–9
  Uncle's Dream 217
  Winter Notes on Summer Impressions 258
Dostoevsky, Mikhail Mikhailovich 44, 219

existentialism 67–8, 71–2, 243–6, 271–2

faith 5, 12, 21, 35, 66–7, 91, 95–6, 109, 134, 173, 221, 233, 237, 282, 286–7
fiction, nature of 5–6, 15–18, 170, 173
fictionalization 197–9

film versions of Dostoevsky's novels 64–7, 199, 241–3
Földényi, László F. 219
Frank, Joseph 203, 249, 260, 266 n.27, 279
Frazier, Melissa 242
freedom 32, 59–60, 128–30, 204–5, 220–1, 234, 244–6, 255, 275, 293–4
Frye, Northrop 226

Gallagher, Tess 199
Garnett, Constance 200–1, 215 n.2, 219 n.17, 226 n.14, 273 n.55
Garstka, Christoph 263 n.8
Gavrilyuk, Paul J. 257
Gibson, A. Boyce 234–5
Gide, André 203, 243
Givens, John 238
Glucksmann, André 262–3, 294–5
Goldstein, David L. 277–8, 280–1
God 9, 12, 21, 24, 29, 40, 49, 57–8, 65, 93, 97, 103–4, 112, 129, 140, 161, 179–84, 204–5, 207–8, 212, 219–20, 228–31, 237–9, 237 n.52, 254–7, 263–5, 269–70, 288–90
Goodwin, James 262 nn.6, 7
Gorky, M. 227
Granovsky, T. 219
Greene, Graham 112
Guardini, Romano 237–8, 283–4
Guérin, Benjamin 244 n.17
Guilt 23–30, 33, 40–1, 104, 215–18

Hamsun, K. 203
Hegel, G. W. F. 31–2, 218–21, 275, 290
Heidegger, Martin 149, 244, 282
Heine, Heinrich 255
Hesse, Hermann 283 n.27
Holquist, Michael 236 n.45
Hudspith, Sarah 264 n.13, 267 n.33

Ilyin, I. 284
Immortality, *see also* memory 12–13, 178–81, 207–8, 286–8, 290–2
imperialism 118–19, 122–3
Incarnation, *see also* Christ, kenoticism 102–3, 139, 232–8, 259–60
Ingold, Felix Phillip 280
Ivanov, V. 226 n.15, 229–30

Jackson, Robert L. 227
Jews, Dostoevsky's attitude towards 143–62, 198–9, 248, 277–81
Job 52–3, 230–1
Johae, Antony 251 n.47

Kant, Immanuel 208, 287
Kasatkina, T. A. 259
Kaufmann, Walter 243–4
Kazantzakis, Nikos 112
Kellogg, Michael 283
Kenoticism, *see also* Christ, Incarnation 232, 257–8
Kierkegaard, S. 213, 219, 228, 244–5, 296
Kirillova, Irina 236
Kjetsaa, Geir 226 n.13
Knapp, Liza 220 n.24, 254
Kohn, Hans 264, 265 n.23
Kojève, Alexandre 268 n.40
Kostalevsky, Marina 269 n.42
Kroeker, P. Travis 234
Kuznetsova-Simpson, Irina 294

Lauth, Reinhard 272 n.52
Leontiev, Konstantin 224, 228
Levina, L. A. 250–1
Levinas, Emmanuel 216–17, 245 n.19, 281
Love 13–14, 22, 26–7, 33, 53–6, 59–60, 87, 93, 104–5, 107–10, 112, 127–9, 138–40, 168–9, 172, 175–6, 178, 180, 187, 207–8, 210, 231–2, 238, 273, 275, 279 n.12
Lies, lying 5–6, 12–15, 100, 208–13

Macedo, O'Dwyer de 248–50, 278–9
Madonna, the, *see* Mary, Mother of God
Martinsen, Deborah A. 209 n.29
Marx, Karl 211, 251, 255
Mary, Mother of God 91–7, 102–3, 253–4, 270
McReynolds, Susan 259–60, 279
Memory, *see also* Immortality 33, 134, 159, 166–8, 254, 268, 285–92
Mereschkowski, D. *see* Merezhkovsky, Dmitri
Merezhkovsky, Dmitri 281–3, 295
Mikhailovsky, N. K. 203
money 14, 85, 100, 151–2, 210–11
Moran, John P. 265 n.23

Naiman, Eric 238–9
nationalism, *see also* brotherhood, imperialism 118–19, 261–8, 282–3, 293–6
Nazism 146, 148–52, 283–4
Nekrasov, Nikolai 249
Nechaev, S. 262
Nietzsche, Friedrich 236–7, 244
Niqueux, Michel 273 n.55
Nihilism 204–7, 220, 225, 262–3

Onasch, Konrad 235
Orthodoxy (Russian Orthodox Church) 122, 128, 132–3, 212, 228, 231, 253, 257–60, 264, 267 n.36, 269–70

Pattison, George 245 n.21
peasants, Dostoevsky's view of 87, 95, 97, 100, 105, 128, 132–3, 135–6, 147, 149, 224, 230, 260–3
Petrashevsky, M. (Petrashevsky Circle, the) 219–20, 255, 261
Pobedonostsev, K. P. 199, 266 n.27
Politics 261–8, 281–4, 293–6
Proust, Marcel 290
Putin, Vladimir V. 189

Raphael 92–7, 211
Renan, Ernest 60, 233, 236
Ricoeur, Paul 239
Rubin, Dominic 280
Russia 50–1, 118, 122–4, 192–3, 209, 213, 223–5, 228, 263–7, 270–1, 276, 294–6
Ruttenberg, Nancy 296 n.11

Saint Petersburg 7–8
Saltykov-Schedrin, M. E. 203
Sartre, Jean-Paul 243
Scanlan, James 207 n.20, 221 n.31
Schleiermacher, F. D. E. 287
Schopenhauer, A. 138–9
self-deification 243, 249, 254–8
Shakespeare, William 14, 94, 211
Shestov, L. 244–5, 287
Shklovsky, Viktor 199, 221 n.35

Skakov, Nariman 237 n.52
Slavophilism 266–7
Socialism 92, 99–100
Solovyov, Vladimir Sergeyevich 126–42, 235 n.39, 268–72, 279–80, 283 n.28,
Srigley, Ron 265 n.23
Steinberg, A. 292
Strauss, David Friedrich 219–20, 254
Suffering 49–51, 53, 66–7, 102–4, 106–7, 133, 135, 183, 227–32, 257, 274–5
Suicide 8–9, 34–5, 203–7, 255

Tarkovsky, Andrei 241
Thompson, Diane O. 226 n.12, 285, 286 n.3
Tillich, Paul 203, 283
Tiutchev, Fyodor 213, 224, 231, 257
Trost, Klaus 247
Troyat, Henry 198
Tsypkin, Leonid 199, 280–1

Ukraine, Russian invasion of 118, 293–6

Wainwright, Geoffrey 286 n.5
war 265–6, 294
Ward, Bruce K. 234
Wasiolek, Edward 237 n.49
Williams, Rowan 215, 217, 234–7
woman 75–88, 246–51
Woolf, Virginia 213
Wrangel, Baron 219
Wyman, Alina 232 n.28

Ziolkowski, Eric 225 n.9